THE ORIGINS OF CAPITALISM AND
THE "RISE OF THE WEST"

The Origins *of* Capitalism
and the
"Rise of the West"

ERIC H. MIELANTS

TEMPLE UNIVERSITY PRESS
Philadelphia

TEMPLE UNIVERSITY PRESS
1601 North Broad Street
Philadelphia PA 19122
www.temple.edu/tempress

∞ The paper used in this publication meets the requirements
of the American National Standard for Information Sciences—
Permanence of Paper for Printed Library
Materials, ANSI Z39.48-1992

Library of Congress Cataloging-in-Publication Data

Mielants, Eric.
The origins of capitalism and the "rise of the West" / Eric H. Mielants.
p. cm.

Includes bibliographical references and index.
ISBN 13 978-1-59213-575-2   ISBN 10 1-59213-575-7 (cloth alk. paper)

1. Capitalism.   2. Civilization, Western.   I. Title.
HB501.M635 2007
330.94′01–dc22
2006037484

CONTENTS

Acknowledgments   *vii*

Introduction   *ix*

CHAPTER ONE: **Perspectives on the Origins of Merchant
    Capitalism in Europe**   1

    Orthodox Marxism   1
    Brennerism (or the Brenner Approach)   2
    The Modernization Theory   7
    World-Systems Analysis   11
        Temporal Predisposition   12
        Spatial Predisposition   30
    The Inter-City-State System of the Middle Ages   31
    Tentative Conclusions   42

CHAPTER TWO: **The Political Economies of China and
    Europe Compared**   47

    The Chinese Socioeconomic Revolution during
        the Sung Dynasty (circa 900–1280)   48
    China and the Mongols   55
    Ming China and Europe: Divergent Paths   60
    Conclusions vis-á-vis European Capitalism   77

CHAPTER THREE: The Political Economies of South Asia and
   Europe Compared   86

      Trade and Commodity Flows in the South Asian Region   86
      States and State Structures in South Asia   93
      The Strategies of Elites in South Asia and Europe   102
      The Impact of the Perilous Frontier   112
      Conclusions   121

CHAPTER FOUR: The Political Economies of Western Europe
   and Northern Africa Compared   125

      Northern Africa and the Sudanic States (circa 1200–1500)   125
      North African Cities, States, and the Balance of Power
         in the Mediterranean   136
      Conclusions   143

CHAPTER FIVE: Conclusion: Was the Western-European
   City-State in the Middle Ages a European Miracle?   154

      Bibliography   163
      Index   237

ACKNOWLEDGMENTS

THIS COMPARATIVE STUDY in historical sociology is, as the reader will surely notice, a hazardous endeavor.[1] It is more than the result of many years of work conducted by a single individual—I am very much indebted to many scholars upon whose writings I have had the opportunity to reflect, and at times, have had the audacity to criticize.

I must therefore express my sincere gratitude to all those who, at various points in time, bothered to read a chapter or a draft of this book manuscript as it progressed, so I could take into account their critical and perceptive comments.

Like so many scholars who engage in comparative as well as historical sociology, I am deeply indebted to the influential work of Immanuel Wallerstein (Yale University). Without his intellectual support and continuing encouragement, and this despite my criticisms of world-systems analysis, this book would never have seen the light of day. His integrity and humility continue to be an inspiration to me in the face of mainstream academia and the cynicism it occasionally generates.

I would like to thank Ramón Grosfoguel (UC Berkeley) for all of his feedback, intellectual support, and collegiality. I am similarly grateful to Mark

---

1. "The comparativist must get it right ... which demands immense vigilance on the part of the comparativist. It also requires certain qualities. The comparativist, having displayed, perhaps, the necessary 'foolhardiness' in confronting large themes, and having chosen to do so via a case-oriented approach, requires an enormous appetite for reading and a notable capacity for synthesis. The comparativist, then, may be foolhardy: in not only addressing large themes, but in risking judgment according to such standards. Yet the potential analytical rewards are great" (Byres 1995:575).

Selden, William Martin, John Chaffee, Dale Tomich, Ravi Palat, and Ricardo Laremont, all from the State University of New York at Binghamton, for their comments on a long work in progress. I'd also like to express my appreciation to Christian Lamouroux (EHESS), Norihisa Yamashita (Hokkaido University) and Om Prakash (Delhi School of Economics) for their candid comments and constructive criticism at various points in time. Thanks also to Eric Vanhaute, Erik Thoen, Marc Boone, Luc François and Piet Saey, all from the University of Ghent, Belgium, for their early encouragement of my academic project when it was in its embryonic phase. Likewise, I am grateful for the support of Maurice Aymard, the former Director of the Maison des Sciences de l'Homme, as well as its current Director, Alain d'Iribarne, which enabled me to complete my research in Paris during the summers of 2005 and 2006. It is therefore the appropriate moment to absolve all those who assisted with this book of any intellectual responsibility for any mistake I may have made; I take full responsibility for any errors or omissions in the text.

In addition, the author and publisher gratefully acknowledge permission from the original publishers of some of the material contained in this book to reproduce parts of various chapters previously printed in the *Review of the Fernand Braudel Center*, Vol. 23(2), Fall 2000, the *Review of the Fernand Braudel Center*, Vol. 25(4), Fall 2002, and in C. Chase-Dunn and E. N. Anderson (eds.), *The Historical Evolution of World-Systems*, Palgrave/Macmillan, NY, 2005.

Last but not least, I'd like to thank Moritz and Ruth Velleman for their hospitality and friendship over so many decades; my uncle Dr. Wim Mielants and his wife, Fanny Jordens, for their hospitality and support when doing research in Antwerpen, as well as other family members for their emotional support, most notably my uncle Dr. Peter Mielants; and especially, my beloved wife Meaghan, because without her continuing encouragement this study would never have appeared in print. Finally, I would like to dedicate this book to my father Dr. Marc Mielants and my grandmother Denise Pittoors, who have given me more love than I could ever give back in return.

INTRODUCTION

"Wealth is a social category inseparable from power."

HEILBRONER, *The Nature and Logic of Capitalism*

WHY, HOW, AND WHEN did capitalism as a system first come into existence? At first glance, these questions may only seem relevant to an audience engrossed in academic (and, by definition, highly theoretical) debates. They are questions that certainly preoccupied the founding fathers of the academic disciplines that emerged in tandem with modernity itself: economics (e.g., Smith), sociology (e.g., Marx, Durkheim, and Weber), and history (e.g., Pirenne). A study of the origins of capitalism and the "Rise of the West" also tends to be polemical. Indeed, over the last two centuries, various university faculties have found themselves embroiled in debate over whether capitalism can only be understood by studying the market (as economists advocate), or whether one must also look at its links with sociology, political science, and history. As David Landes recently reminded us, the answers to these questions can also have profound contemporary implications, namely, why it is that only a few in the modern world are incredibly wealthy while most are utterly impoverished?

Modern-day policies advocated by the World Bank and the IMF cannot be understood without putting the origins of capitalism into their proper context. Only by understanding why and how a certain area of the world became capitalist—while other highly successful civilizations in South Asia, China, or Northern Africa did not—can one understand the present situation. And only by understanding how, many centuries ago, a certain area of the world grew wealthier, can one begin to grasp how systematic policies of capital accumulation were derived from core countries' continuous processes of colonization, exploitation, and domination of the periphery.

It is my contention that modern forms of capital accumulation based on military and technological power, degrees of illegal and legal monopolization, neo-colonization, and the abuse of workers in dispersed geographical regions of the world are rooted in capitalist processes first generated in Western Europe. While many contemporary historiographies engage in a "systematic rejection of all theoretical approaches" (Bois 1998:316), I attempt to deconstruct the traditional historiography of Orthodox Marxism, the Smithian Modernization Theory, and part of World-System Theory, and in the process, try to present a coherent argument as to why, since the 13th century, a minority in a small area of the world has been able to enjoy the fruits of others' labor and natural resources. By engaging in a systematic interdisciplinary and comparative analysis of the developments and social structures in Europe, China, South Asia, and Northwestern Africa when normally "only the narrowest of all historical approaches are routinely rewarded and recognized" (Di Cosmo 1999b:250), it is hoped that this study will contribute to a small but growing field in world history while revalorizing economic history, which has been in crisis for some time now (Genet 1997:17). In doing so, I invite my readers to critically rethink historical processes and particularly their relevance to the modern world. After all, how we envision and interpret the past has tremendous ramifications for how we imagine the future.

THE ORIGINS OF CAPITALISM AND
THE "RISE OF THE WEST"

CHAPTER ONE

Perspectives on the Origins of
Merchant Capitalism in Europe

T HERE ARE essentially four major theoretical perspectives on the origins of capitalism in medieval Western Europe. This chapter critically examines the main arguments elaborated in those perspectives and attempts to rethink the history of socioeconomic and political processes. The four major theoretical perspectives dealt with in this chapter are, respectively: orthodox Marxism, a form of neo-Marxism that I call "Brennerism," the modernization theory, and last, world-systems analysis. Each of these perspectives, widely used in every social science discipline in order to explain modernity, has its own specific problems in dealing with the emergence of merchant capitalism.

Orthodox Marxism

Orthodox Marxism has often been used as a theoretical perspective to analyze the emergence of capitalism, yet this approach entails several problems. First, it imposes a deterministic, "stagist" evolution on historical processes (e.g., after a bourgeois revolution, an era of capitalism dawns, only to end in an Aufhebung). Second, it uses a socioeconomic infrastructure, which then determines a superstructure. Third is its usage of Eurocentric terminology (e.g., "Asian Mode of Production") that leads to frozen histories (Coquery-Vidrovitch 1981). Fourth is its framing of exploitation as a rigid, dichotomous class struggle between proletarians and capitalists within a particular unit of analysis—in most instances, the nation-state (Takahashi 1976:74).[1] And last but not least is orthodox Marxism's relegation of the market to a secondary position outside the sphere of production, while assigning "analytical priority" to the means of production (Tomich 1993:223; Rigby 2004:499).

The orthodox Marxist tradition of constructing an economic view of modernity usually dates capitalism and modern society to the 18th century, with the Industrial Revolution as its forerunner (Baradat 1988:137–161). It is only at this time that Marxists consider a *real* transition as having taken place (cf. Banaji 2007). Although Marx once acknowledged that "we come across the first sporadic traces of capitalist production as early as the fourteenth or fifteenth centuries in certain towns of the Mediterranean" (1977:876), most Marxists have dismissed the 16th century as well as the Middle Ages, with the latter considered as "une économie foncièrement naturelle" (Mandel 1962:124).[2] At most then, Marxists trace the early roots of capitalism to England in the 1640s (Cantor 1973:294), using the concept of *class* to analyze struggles that revolve around socioeconomic disparities prior to the industrial era (Godelier 1993).

Brennerism (or the Brenner Approach)

In the 1970s, a Neo-Marxian variant—"Brennerism"—came onto the scene. Unlike traditional orthodox Marxism, Brennerism is strongly preoccupied with the Middle Ages. But like its predecessor, Brennerism has its problems. Encapsulated in the Marxist tradition, it tends to focus predominantly on the mode of production and the class struggle between the *exploited* (the peasants) and

---

1. "Freeman and slave, patrician and plebeian, lord and serf, guild-master and journeyman, in a word; oppressor and oppressed, stood in constant opposition to one another" ("The Communist Manifesto" in Edwards et al. 1972:67), as if there were only two "fundamental" classes in history at any one time. It is also assumed that small family production in the countryside was identical to autosubsistence (Bois 1985:190) and could not lead to the development of capitalism. For an in-depth study of the complex transition from feudalism to capitalism in Catalonia, see Astarita (1992).

2. Given his focus on the impact of industrial production and the modern factory system, Marx concluded that the "international division of labor, a division suited to the requirements of the chief center of modern industry" occurred as recently as the modern factory (Harvey 1985:47). The international division of labor is, however, older than the 19th century. It is clear from his lack of interest in the Middle Ages or the early modern period that Marx was not really preoccupied with explaining the *origins* of capitalism; all of his statements about them were nothing more than "contextual observations dependent on his analysis of the capitalist production" during the industrial era (Guérreau 1980:57; see also Bois 1985:189; Dahl 1998:61; Kuchenbuch 1997:48). It was therefore left to 20th-century Marxists to resolve the "transition" issue from a precapitalist to a capitalist mode of production, often depicting the Middle Ages in this process as nothing more than "an archaic ruin of abandoned precapitalist collectivities" (Holsinger and Knapp 2004:469). As Duchesne (2000:168) points out, this was a major theoretical conundrum for the Marxist perspective: "If modes of production continually reproduce their own conditions of existence, how is any sort of transition ever conceivable?"

the *exploiters* (the nobility) within a given territorial unit (the nation-state) (Brenner 1977).[3] This focus on class struggle and mode of production minimizes the impact of the circulation of trade. It also overemphasizes production, specifically agrarian, at the expense of urban-centered production. Another problem with this approach is its consideration of the nobility as nothing more than a class oriented to "surplus extraction by extra-economic compulsion," indulging in so-called "non-productive consumption" (Brenner 1985:232).[4] Brenner explains the economic success of the English nobility, in comparison with the French nobility, as the major difference between a class *in* itself (France) and a class *for* itself (England) (Byres 1996:67); the latter is described as having had "extraordinary intra-class cohesiveness" (Brenner 1985:258).[5]

Brenner also follows the Marxist path by juxtaposing "absolutism in France" with "the development of classical capitalist relations on the land in England" (Brenner 1985:275, 284–299). He then constructs his narrative in such a way that it either becomes:

a) a prelude to orthodox Marxism's stagist historical evolution,[6] ending with the "rise of a capitalist aristocracy presiding over an agricultural revolution" (Brenner 1985:299), which in turn brought about "an upward spiral that extended into the industrial revolution" (Brenner 1985:327); or

b) a particular variant of the modernization theory (see infra), explaining why one territorial unit (England), unlike another (France), managed to achieve an economic "take-off."[7]

---

3. Brenner's thesis is essentially "a base consisting of unfree peasants, the direct producers, and an aristocratic superstructure supported by rents which were extracted from the former. This critical process of extraction was possible because the lords owned the land" (Harvey 1991:16–17). Cf. Lis and Soly (1993:196), who also follow Brenner's framework.

4. Does this statement mean to imply that no investments (through spending) took place within certain urban industries (van Uytven 1996b:438)? Does it also imply that no investments occurred in the countryside either (Lewis 1984:X:513)? The nobility were very active in trade, becoming the direct competitors of the peasants and merchants selling goods on the market (Pal Pách 1994:III). According to Miller: "Desired goods included luxuries as well as basic commodities. Kings and princes, noblemen, town patricians and clergymen were the consumers par excellence of goods . . . their consumption preferences played a basic part in shaping many of the commercial policies of the Middle Ages" (1976:353). See also Abraham-Thisse (1993:27–70).

5. In this respect, Brenner's focus resembles that of Barrington Moore's (1966). On the problematic issue of the extent to which one can already perceive class formations in the Middle Ages, see the arguments of Brenner (1985) and Fossier (1991:415–436) on the one hand, and Murray (1978:14–17) and Raftis (1996:128) on the other. Constable (1996:301–323) takes a careful intermediary position.

6. In a typical Marxist framework, Brenner juxtaposes the general crisis "on most of the continent" with the "critical breakthrough to self-sustaining growth in England" (Brenner 1985:275).

7. "It was the growth of agricultural productivity, rooted in the transformation of agrarian class or property relations, which allowed the English economy to embark upon a path of development

In both cases, capitalism becomes a characteristic of one nation at a specific moment in time.

Another problem with Brennerism is the extent to which Brenner relegates peasants (in his view, the "productive base" of a society) to a servile status.[8] He constructs an ideal type feudal peasant, one who avoids "specialization and dependence on exchange simply to avoid becoming subject to the dictates of the market," engaging in a permanent class struggle with the ideal type noble who simply wants to squeeze more out of the peasant in order to engage in more frivolous "unproductive consumption" (Brenner 1986:31). A consequence of this focus on class struggle is a minimization of the importance of the market.

Certainly, one can claim that some peasants only sold products on the market in order to cover their monetary requirements, which were partially generated by the coercive demands of their lords and/or state officials. In this way, some agricultural producers were "driven to the market" in order to obtain, via the sale of a part of their production, the cash needed to meet their obligations generated by the "extra-economic compulsion" of others (Aymard 1993:292–293; Gutnova 1990:111).[9] But why would feudal structures have inhibited the emergence of markets? According to Bruce Campbell (1995:133), peasant producers generally "intensify production, specialize, and participate in the market exchange when they have to, and feudalism—through the extraction of their surpluses in various forms of feudal rent—obliged them to do precisely this." Peasants actually produced abundant goods both in regional (Derville 1996:123–136) and international markets (Thoen 1988b:277–279). One should also not deny or minimize the significance of peasant agency or resistance in the face of coerced extractions (Hanawalt 1986:23–47; Hilton 1987; Imsen and Vogler 1997). But, as Guérreau noted, to consider the "power relations between lords and peasants as the primum movens of the Middle Ages would be absurd" (1980:108).[10] According to Epstein:

---

already closed to its Continental neighbors" (Brenner 1985:323). It was this English "development" that distinguished it from the continent that was suffering from sclerosis (Brenner 1985:275, 299); Brenner describes it as "capitalism", "development" and a "breakthrough in economic growth" in England, versus "crisis, stagnation, absolute monarchy" in France. This is a very unilinear way of thinking about historical evolution (Holton 1985:89). See Torras (1980:262), who also criticizes "the unilinear and strictly endogenous causality" of Brenner's approach.

8. According to Kosminsky, even in late 13th-century "feudal" England, 40 percent of the land occupied by peasants was free land and approximately the same percentage of peasant households were free (Kosminsky in Harvey 1991:18). See also Heers (1992:163–164). The peasantry simply cannot be portrayed as a homogeneous class (Whittle 2000:25).

9. Or as Hilton (1974:218) puts it: "The important thing about the development of money rent was that as soon as the peasant was told to produce his rent in money, he had to produce goods on the market in order to get the money."

10. Ellen Meiskins Wood is nevertheless also convinced this is the case since in her opinion, merchants and manufacturers were not driving the process that propelled the early development

Primarily market structures determine the character and rate of economic development in a society. By contrast, since property relations are only one (albeit crucial) determinant of market structures, one may not deduce the course of economic development from a (reified) structure of property relations alone ... one cannot infer a peasant smallholder's economic strategies from his ability to subsist on his own land (and his duty to pay rent to a feudal or other landlord); rather, his economic strategies will depend on how his access to markets is structured. (1992:22)

Along with the actual role of peasants, one also must not minimize the importance of demographic changes in Western Europe (Seccombe 1992:136–139) or the powerful dynamic impulses generated by the existence and increasing significance of the market itself. Indeed, between the 11th and late 13th centuries, England's employment in market-dependent occupations grew more rapidly than did the number of self-sufficient farmers. Specialization also occurred within the rural economy.[11] After investigating data available in the Domesday book, the economic historian Snooks estimates that 40 percent of the economy in 11th century England was involved in market activities (the *market* being the sector where "all the major economic decisions in England were made"), and 60 percent in subsistence.[12] These results challenge the

---

of capitalism (1999:94). As a "Brenner Marxist," she essentially considers most of the 17th-century world economy as nothing more than commercial networks where "the dominant principle of trade was buying cheap and selling dear" and moreover, the trade "tended to be in luxury goods." Like Brenner, she juxtaposes France with England. According to her, the latter is the most unique site of historical development in the entire world: "There was one major exception England, by the 16th century, was developing in wholly new directions." Because of its unique agricultural conditions, its "internal market" and its "capitalism in one country," this exceptional island was capable of becoming on its own the first capitalist nation-state (1999:72–130). A similar exposé can be found in Comninel (2000), Hilton (1990:203–204), and even earlier in Dobb (1947:18) who—although he admits that some capitalist features were appearing "in the Netherlands and in certain Italian cities" (1947:151) during the Middle Ages—dismisses most pre–17th-century trade in England as "primitive accumulation" (1947:88). Within this framework, a real proletariat with revolutionary potential could not have existed in the preindustrial period because a true revolutionary "consciousness" and "genuine program to overthrow the existing political order" are considered anachronistic for this particular era (Dumolyn and Haemers 2005:387–388).

11. The intensification, specialization and commercialization of the countryside also occurred in Flanders (Thoen 1993) as well as in the Netherlands (Blockmans 1993:49–50). At the same time, "commercialization changed the character of taxation. Geld, the principal tax of the 11th century, had been levied on land. By 1300 the main tax on the laity was assessed on the value of personal movable property, and this ensured that townspeople should be brought within its scope. Not only that, but townspeople usually paid tax at a higher rate than country people" (Britnell 1995:14). For the increase in taxes on personal movable property as the number of knights declined in the early 13th century, see Lachaud (2002).

12. Snooks estimates that in 1086, 32.3 percent of the English market sector was rural and 7.8 percent was urban, thus arriving at a total of 40.1 percent (1995:40). By 1300, the urban population

conventional wisdom that insists on the very limited role of market forces at
that time (Snooks 1995:39). After all, Edward I had enhanced the value of
customs duties in 1275 "when he initiated the levying of a tax on wool exports.
This levy on trade instantly became a principal support of royal finances, more
regular than any other source of income; it was the foundation upon which
the king established his credit when he wished to borrow money from Italian
merchants" (Britnell 1995:14). According to Cazel (1966:104), during the reign
of Edward I, the royal revenue from dues of foreign merchants (paid in return
for a license to trade with England) grew to nearly equal the entire domanial
revenue (Mann 1980:179). Thus, assertions like those that Brenner makes—
that individual feudal lords frivolously consumed surpluses either produced
from estates managed according to "time-honored custom" or extracted from
their tenants by various noneconomic means—have to be seriously questioned
(Snooks 1995:47).

Of course, one cannot completely deny that a small minority (the nobility) in a given territorial unit did impose substantial financial extractions on
the majority (the peasants) without much reinvestment occurring in the countryside (e.g., Maddicott 1975; Thoen 1988b:636–637). Nor can one say that
"surplus extracting by non-economic compulsion" (Brenner 1985:232) did *not*
take place.[13] But it is fundamentally important to acknowledge that strong cities
dominated their hinterland and exploited the countryside just as well as did
the feudal lords (Harvey 1991:19; Nicholas 1971:93; Epstein 1992:124–133;
Hilton 1974:212). Cities simply cannot be excluded from the analysis of power
relations in the Middle Ages (Cherubini 1990:129–130), something that Brenner fails to comprehend as he equates "all feudal exploiters as lords" (1986:28).
Throughout his entire "narrative of socioeconomic change" on the transition
from feudalism to capitalism (1985, 1986), Brenner—along with other Marxists like Katz (1989:74–75)—fails to discuss the importance of trade and cities,
reducing the latter to mere passive entities (Boone 1996b:162).[14]

---

in England had increased to about 20 percent (Britnell 2001:5). All over Western Europe, "as
peasants paid out more in cash and less in labor service, their need for monetary income increased.
Turning to merchants and town markets to sell their produce, they deepened their dependence on
extra-regional trade. Manorial autonomy declined sharply" (Seccombe 1992:140). For the presence
of a variety of "alien merchants" in late 13th- and early 14th-century England, see Lloyd (1982,
1991).

13. On a more abstract level, it is important to note that often, "terms of trade unfavorable to
peasant producers turn market exchange into yet another channel of exploitation of the peasantry
by urban society at large" (Shanin 1973:76).

14. It is "no coincidence that Marxists addressing the problem of the crisis and the transition to
capitalism have generally concentrated on the least urbanized areas in medieval Europe" (Epstein
1991b:4) in order to make reality fit their model of productive relations defined through access
to land. Even when requested to refine his analysis at a more recent conference on the Low
Countries, Brenner (2001) failed to address the dynamics of commercialization and urbanization
on the region.

It is, however, the important division of labor between town and countryside and the competition between city-states to access different markets (see infra) that shatters Brenner's overly simplistic narrative of feudalism's grip on economic growth. That many important markets were often located in an urban setting and that many peasants were involved in this activity (whether induced to trade or forced to sell) cannot be denied (Fritze 1985:21–22). Yet, by relegating the market's importance to a secondary position, Brenner and his fellow travelers (e.g., Wood 1999) completely overlook the crucial importance of medieval cities and their urban markets.

The Modernization Theory

The modernization theory[15] is thought to be based on either the emergence of "modern" (i.e., spiritual or religious) values, which are then said to form the basis of the emergence of capitalist accumulation (e.g., Landes 1998:516; Lal 1998; Park 1995; Tawney 1926; Weber 1930; Werner 1988; Stark 2005),[16] or the technological innovations that led Europe on an unavoidable teleological path of dominance over the 'rest of the world' in subsequent centuries (e.g., Ashtor 1992:IV; Gimpel 1976; Jones 1981:45–69; Labal 1962:32–39; White 1962). Either way, this theory too is problematic.

In constructing a developmental/modernization model to explain the steady rise of putting-out systems (in symbiosis with the emergence of capitalism), one must be careful not to reify concepts, as historical misconceptions loom everywhere.[17] A typical misconception inherent to the modernization theory is the tendency of many contemporary scholars (e.g., Farr 1997:24) to dismiss medieval corporations and guilds, as though they were synonymous with socioeconomic stagnation, decline, and archaism (Boone 1994:3–5; Lis and Soly 1997:228; Munro 1994:IX:44). Guilds and corporations all too often become the victims of this historical misinterpretation primarily because their presence is framed in a "period of transition," whereas capitalism—identified as the "real progress" within the modernization theory—is described as having replaced the "decadent" pre-Renaissance medieval structures while "installing modernity" (Boone 1994:4). The classic example of this traditional

---

15. This theory is sometimes associated with a "commercialization approach" (Persson 1988:64), but given its obsession with situating modernity in the postmedieval era and its prejudices vis-à-vis everything associated with the "Dark Ages", I prefer to label it the "modernization theory."

16. For an elaborate criticism of Landes (1998) and related "cultural" arguments, see the useful discussion in Goody (2004:19–49).

17. For instance, the expansion of the Verlag system in Western Europe (the main commodity chain flowing from the Low Countries through Germany toward Northern Italy) was not universal in time and space, nor was its appearance uniform (Holbach 1993:207–250).

modernization/development point of view comes from the most famous prop-
agator of modern economics, Adam Smith:

> One objective of the craft guilds was to exclude competition. A craft
> guild was an association in a given town of the masters of a trade who
> combined to control prices, wages, and the standards and conditions of
> sales of their products, and to monopolize their manufacture. (1976:69,
> 139)

Ever since, the guilds have been depicted as conservative medieval remnants
and "socially inefficient cartels" (Hickson and Thompson 1991:127), obstruct-
ing the "route to progress" with their regulations and prohibitions (which, according to the modernization theory, are detrimental to the increasing wealth
of nations within a "free" market) (Stabel 2004:188).[18] Contributing to this
misconception is the fact that from the late 15th century onward, the guilds
were the losing forces against the ongoing processes of centralization. Finally,
the 19th- to 20th-century liberal industrial nation-state was always significantly
more interested in illustrating its own vibrant dynamism than in giving credit
to its predecessors, the medieval craftsmen and guilds (Braunstein 1994:23).
Surely, it is said, capitalism could not have originated in the midst of this "archaic pre-modern" world (Boone 1994:4).

For modernization theorists then, it seems as though nothing novel or
important happened in the 16th century; as in Marxist theory, the Industrial
Revolution of the late 18th and early 19th century is looked on as the historical
watershed that opened up the gates of modernity (Cantor 1973:298–301). And
like Marxists, modernization theorists predominantly focus on England in order
to understand modernity (e.g., Wrigley 1988). As a result, the economic historian's principal interest in preindustrial economies lies with understanding the
constraints that actually prevented those economies from becoming modern.

Needless to say, this stagnant interpretation of medieval economic history had an impact on the course of historical debates and the assumptions
that many scholars shared about the state of the premodern world in general.
Only premodern factors such as the availability of land and population growth
were considered necessary to understand the premodern world,[19] relegating

---

18. See Lis and Soly (1994:366–369) but also Persson's well-founded critique of Mickwitz's (1936)
view of guilds and competition (1988:50–54). Orthodox Marxists such as Dobb (1947:155) were also
convinced that guilds retarded the appearance of capitalism. "The customary dismissal of the role
played by craft-based apprenticeship and innovation in British and continental industrialization
may need to be revised" (Epstein 1998:707).

19. See, for example, Postan (1966, 1973) and Postan and Hatcher (1985). For the supposed
nonexistence of technological progress, framing "pre-industrial agrarian economies in a sort of
Ricardo-Malthus trap," see Persson (1988:3–4, 24–32). For a dismissal of pessimistic assessments
regarding late medieval agricultural productivity and proficiency common to both Malthusian-
ists and Neo-Marxists, see Verhulst (1997:91–92). For an excellent revision of the ideal typical

commercialization, specialization, and technical change to the periphery (Britnell and Campbell 1995:8). Unfortunately, the terms *feudalism* and *Middle Ages* have been "weighed down with every conceivable implication of evil" (Heers 1974:625), which explains why many still associate the Middle Ages with an age of ignorance, backwardness, and general "underdevelopment" (Pernoud 1992:16).[20] In doing so, theorists continue to uphold a "traditional picture of medieval society as feudal, hierarchical, deeply conservative and religious and the economy as a self-sufficient subsistence economy" (Fryde 1998:207) dominated by passive, self-subsistent, Chayanovianesque peasants (Bois 2000:41).

With regard to technological progress, dynamism, and inventiveness, medieval labor formations should not be dismissed as being premodern, as though a major gap divides them from our "modern" world. Their dynamism and innovation actually reveal that they were anything but incarnations of conservative, stagnant, and unproductive economic entities (Boone 1994:16). In fact, preindustrial (i.e., pre–19th-century) markets were much more complex and varied than is usually envisaged (Epstein 1993:470) and it was the guilds that were at the heart of urban medieval society and its political institutions. Thus one should not only rethink the concept of the Industrial Revolution—praised (and conceptualized) by the modernization/development theory (Wallerstein 1984:179–80)—but also the term *Agricultural Revolution* (Verhulst 1989b:71–95; 1990:17–28).[21] Unfortunately, not only does the modernization theory dismiss the guild's infrastructure, but at times it ends up dismissing the entire medieval era, "consigning it to a pre-industrial limbo of gloom and inertia" (Dyer 1991:7), a period only waiting to be swept away by the triumph of laissez-faire economics.[22] Like Marxism, which also emphasizes the Agricultural and Industrial Revolutions in its stagist perspective, the modernization theory is dismissive of the premodern 16th century as well as the Medieval Era. Therefore, the modernization theory is similarly incapable of assessing the importance

---

"lymphatic peasants" à la Postan and the "lackadaisical lords that sapped the agricultural sector of dynamism" à la Brenner, see Campbell (1995c:76–108) and the brilliant overview provided by Hatcher and Bailey (2001).

20. See also Black (1997:67), Geremek (1994:15), and Le Goff (1998b:7–8). On the problematic usage of the word itself, see Reuter (1998).

21. Some even situate the Agricultural Revolution in the 13th century (e.g., Dowd 1961 for Italy).

22. Many refer to medieval features as "obsolete remnants from the past" (Howell and Boone 1996:305). Blickle rightfully states: "Most historians build their interpretations on the experiential basis of two separate spheres—one urban, industrial and modern, the other rural, agrarian and traditional—and impose upon Ancien Régime Europe a dichotomy that artificially separates the Third Estate into the bourgeoisie and the peasantry. The city becomes a bourgeois shrine and serves, so to speak, as a laboratory of capitalism; the peasantry, meanwhile, is under control of noble seigneurs and thus is dispatched to the fate of a dying world" (1992:98). The narrative embraced by modernization theorists thus often explains capitalist modernity as (inevitable) progress as opposed to the "backward" way of life of the premodern era or areas (cultures).

of early modern urban networks and their creation of self-sustained growth. Many Marxist and modernization theorists tend to forget that "the industrial revolution was *not* the source of modern economic growth" (North and Thomas 1973:157) but rather, the *outcome* of different processes that must be traced back to the period before the Industrial Revolution.

Findlay (1992:160–161) rightfully states:

> The view that only England, with its Industrial Revolution on domestic soil and with home-grown technology, was truly able to initiate the modern industrial world is fundamentally mistaken since it adopts a "national" instead of a "systemic" perspective. One must not look at the consequences for individual nations or states, but for Europe or the West as a whole.

While most (not surprisingly, European) scholars continue to focus on the Industrial Revolution as the key historical moment (e.g., Grassby 1999:63; Vries 2003) that brought about real growth in terms of a rise in per capita income, there is ample historical evidence that this occurred much earlier than the 18th century (Jones 1988:38; Van der Wee 1988:343–344; cf. Snooks 1994). As Douglass North (1979:251) put it: "There is nothing new about sustained economic growth, despite the myth perpetrated by economic historians that it is a creation of the Industrial Revolution." Some scholars (e.g., O'Brien 1990, 1991, 1992) choose to explicitly dismiss the profits derived from international trade *prior* to the Industrial Revolution. This is not surprising as moderniza- tion theory has a long history of denying imperialism (Omvedt 1972). But in reality the Western European core was able to industrialize precisely *because* it was able to specialize in the production of goods with a higher added value, whereas the periphery's industrialization process was thwarted. Admittedly, the periphery's production was geared toward supplying raw materials for the core, as its markets were opened to the refined products from the core. Thus, while the importance of an internal market in creating sustained growth should not be underestimated, the external market and interregional trade, both as sources of raw materials and as consumers of services and finished products with a higher added value, are also crucial for *any* economic growth (Van der Wee 1988:321, 337), even before the 18th century.[23]

---

23. Or as Hobsbawm put it in his now-classic study *Industry and Empire*: "The British Industrial Revolution cannot be explained in purely British terms, for this country formed part of a wider economy, which we may call the 'European economy' or the 'world economy of the European maritime states.' It was part of a larger network of economic relationships, which included several 'advanced' areas, some of which were also areas of potential or aspiring industrialization, and areas of 'dependent economy,' as well as the margins of the foreign economies not yet substantially involved with Europe. These dependent economies consisted partly of formal colonies (as in the Americas) or points of trade and domination (as in the Orient), partly of regions which were to

World-Systems Analysis

A world-systems analysis attempts to explain the emergence of a capitalist world-economy in Europe in tandem with the incorporation of regions through domination and colonization, which in turn resulted in an international division of labor and an interstate system. At the same time, it debunks the notion of modernity and the importance attributed to the Industrial Revolution. While a world-systems analysis does not deal effectively with the "transition" problem, unlike the modernization theory and orthodox Marxism it at least brings the Medieval Era back into the picture. It does not disregard medieval Europe in its entirety since it has to "reopen the question of how and when the capitalist world-economy was created in the first place; why the transition took place in feudal Europe and not elsewhere; why it took place when it did and not earlier or later; why earlier attempts of transition failed" (Wallerstein 1979:135).

Another positive element about a world-systems analysis is its illustration of how the "Brenner Debate," pitting class history against the so-called "objective economic forces, particularly those deriving from demographic fluctuations and the growth of trade and markets" (Torras 1980:253), can be overcome by emphasizing that "the exploitation of labor is not only determined by the wage bundle and the extraction of labor from labor power in the production process, but in substantial measure by the prices at which goods are exchanged between the economies that make up the world-system" (Bowles 1988:434). In this sense, a world-systems analysis attempts to explain the emergence of capitalism by integrating the Marxist focus on production with the Smithian focus on the circulation of goods in the market.[24]

---

some extent economically specialized in response to the demands of the 'advanced' areas (as in some parts of Eastern Europe). The 'advanced' world was linked to the dependent world by a certain division of economic activity: a relatively urbanized area on the one hand, zones producing and largely exporting agricultural products or raw materials on the other. These relations may be described as a system of economic flows of trade, of international payments, of capital transfers, of migration and so on" (1969:35).

24. Brenner's claim that a world-systems analysis is "circulationist" should be rejected, as Sanderson (1995:178) rightfully points out: "While it must be admitted that much of what goes on among Wallerstein's zones of the capitalist world-economy involves exchange, much also involves production. When, for example, core capitalists peripheralize a region in order to extract surplus value from it, they are doing so through the direct establishment of productive activities that they ultimately control. How can such an economic relationship between core and periphery be regarded as based only on exchange?" It is indeed important to note that it is the combination of profits based on the exploitation of wage labor as *well as* those derived from unequal exchange that constitute a capitalist system. Profits derived from surplus value are *not* necessarily "of greater historical significance" (Heilbroner 1985:66) than those derived from unequal exchange. If one insists on measuring the number of people within a specific polity who are "fully dependent upon wages as landless laborers" (Brenner and Isett 2002:631) in order to determine the degree to which a polity can be classified as *truly* capitalist when compared to others, one should realize that many of today's

As Thomas Hall observes, many agree that a "World-System Theory cannot be applied wholesale to pre-capitalist settings, before approximately A.D. 1500" (1996:444–449). This then leads to the question: Was there no capitalist system before the 16th century? The answer to this question depends on whether one tends to agree with a *spatial* predisposition, namely that in one part of the world there was a period of transition from feudalism to capitalism wherein the existence of multiple systems converged into a single world-system (i.e., a world-economy centered around Europe or Western Asia), or a *temporal* predisposition, namely that this transition from feudalism to capitalism occurred somewhere between 1450 and 1650. Let us focus first on the temporal predisposition within world-systems analysis.

Temporal Predisposition

For Immanuel Wallerstein, perhaps the most renowned world-systems scholar, capitalism evolved in Europe out of the 16th century's feudal crisis. With the emergence of the modern world-system, one single new mode of production came into existence. Notwithstanding his lengthy writings on the 16th century—the "period of the world-economy in creation" (1974:356)—his summary explanation of the transition (1974:37) remains unsatisfying. As Cornelis Terlouw notes:

> During this long transitional phase, feudalism was slowly transformed into, and superseded by, capitalism. This can only mean that during at least two centuries feudalism and capitalism coexisted in one world-system. So what Wallerstein explicitly denies (the coexistence of two modes of production in one world-system) he implicitly assumes for the period between 1450 and 1650. If one accepts that during a very long period, several modes of production coexisted in one single system, it is a small, and completely logical, step to admit that at any moment in the history of the world-system several modes of production could exist simultaneously. (1992:57–58)

Like Marx, Wallerstein is more interested in the functioning of today's capitalist world-economy. But this interest has some unfortunate theoretical implications:

---

countries would then have to be classified as "precapitalist," stuck within some kind of "Asiatic" or feudal mode of production. This Marxist position also ignores the fact that wage labor in the core emerges in tandem with greater exploitation of coerced labor (e.g., slavery) in the periphery, a consequence of more intense commercialization. Awareness of this fact does not, however, automatically translate into a Smithian paradigm in which the market will inevitably "grow of its own accord," as Hindess and Hirst (1975:262) point out, in order to bring about capitalist modernity.

By focusing his attention on the emergence of the present world-system, Wallerstein inadequately theorizes about the temporal borders between world-systems. His fixation on the unity of the present world makes him blind to the intertwining of different social systems in the past. (Terlouw 1992:57)

Wallerstein was, of course, very aware of this problem.[25] But describing the transition at a given moment in time as complete (in the sense that capitalism has superseded other modes of production or that its logic appears to be predominant) is hard to do since "it is always easy to find presumed instances of 'non-capitalist' behavior in a capitalist world—all over Europe in 1650 and 1750 and 1950. The mixture [of 'non-capitalist' and 'capitalist' behavior] is the essence of the capitalist system as a mode of production" (Wallerstein 1980:32). Who can really specify the exact moment when one system significantly takes over (incorporates) the other(s)?

To completely dismiss any distinction between bulk and luxury goods from as far back as 5,000 years ago up to the present would seem to imply that no transition from feudalism to capitalism occurred. Frank and Gills (1991; 1992; 1993a; 1993b; 2000), for example, completely dismiss the notion of a transition in the Middle Ages, or for that matter, even in the 16th century; for them, no sharp break or transition occurred around 1500 (Frank 1990:243; Frank and Gills 1993b:297). In seeking to make their analysis "as holistic as possible," they instead envisage the contours of a world-system that existed 5,000 years ago (1993b:45). Ironically, in doing so, a "frozen history" narrative is constructed; that is, that since time immemorial, trade has linked peoples and tribes, providing some with profits while others were exploited. They are convinced, for example, that "the labor of the ancient lapis lazuli miners of Afghanistan and the textile workers in urban Sumeria was all surely interlinked in a world economic system division of labor even in the fourth or third millennium BC" (1993b:299). According to their theory, mankind has always lived (and perhaps always will?) in a world capitalist system.[26] Needless to say, their

25. "To analyze the period from 1450 to 1750 as one long 'transition' from feudalism to capitalism risks reifying the concept of transition, for we thus steadily reduce the periods of 'pure' capitalism and sooner or later arrive at zero, being left with nothing but transition" (Wallerstein 1980:31). This criticism could also be applied to the more recent work of historian Jean Baechler (2002), who, in his attempt to present us with a "universal history" starting in the Paleolithic, does not mention capitalism at all.

26. Frank claims that "this economic and interstate world historical system already exists for at least five thousand years" (1990b:212). I do not deny that some regions were—at different points in time—interconnected through trade, which had profound social consequences in the long run (Wallerstein 1990:221). But this does not mean that they were all integrated in one *system*. Although I do not agree with Wallerstein's periodization of "modernity," I do agree with his important critique of Frank's extreme position: "Only if we keep the caesura [from proto-capitalism to the emergence of a capitalist world-system] in mind will we remember that this historical system, like all historical

position is somewhat extreme and remains among the minority in the world-systems school. Unlike Frank and Gills, Wallerstein at least uses the concept of a transition, but unfortunately the confusion surrounding world-system theory does not end there.

Wallerstein's reluctance to apply concepts such as *core* and *periphery* before the 16th century is a result of his interpretation of the importance and impact of long-distance trade (Wallerstein 1990:221). The dichotomy that he creates (and which many in the world-systems school follow) between precious commodities (luxuries) and essentials/utilities (bulk trade) must seriously be questioned, particularly prior to 1500 (Schneider 1991:48). First of all, how does one define luxury versus bulk goods? Does one focus on the quantity of goods exchanged, or instead emphasize the nature of the goods? And if certain luxury items become mass commodities after some time, widely bought and sold due to a rising demand in the market (as occurred with wine,[27] sugar,[28] and salt[29]), when does this "critical" transition from luxury to bulk goods

---

systems, not only had a beginning (or genesis), but that it will have an end" (1993:295–296). For an interesting intermediary position between Wallerstein and Frank, cf. the more recent interventions by Beaujard (2005).

27. "In some years around 1300, England exported up to 15 million pounds of raw wool, and a year's export of about 25 million gallons of wine from the Garonne valley was recorded. The wine trade found markets in Tunis and the Black Sea. Exotic commodities were more and more moved in bulk" (Mundy 1991:91). See James (1951), Craeybeckx (1958), Rénouard (1968), Sivéry (1969), and Maguin (1982) who demonstrate the significance of both regional production and long-distance trade. One should not underestimate the impact of wine production on the "monetization of the rural economy and the accumulation of profit" (Mousnier 1997:327; see also Childs 1978:126–136). As an example, let us examine the massive production of wine for the market in the medieval era: "The annual average, in the first half of the 14th century, was between 747,000 and 850,000 hectoliters (c. 1308–1309). When we compare this with 1950, the total export of wine from the whole of France was about 900,000. And these figures only refer to some areas of the Gironde: Bordeaux and Libourne" (Pernoud, Gimpel, and Delatouche 1986:195). For the importance of the "regular, large-scale, well-developed trade between distinct but relatively integrated economies," of which the wine trade was illustrative, see Menard (1997:236–248) and Verlinden (1962). Pauly clearly demonstrates that wine in the early 14th century cannot be dismissed as a luxury commodity; the consumption of wine was so widespread—even prisoners were given wine—that it should be considered as "basic and of primary importance" (1998:297–298). For a striking example of a 14th-century source that provides clear insight into the existing class conflict revolving around wages in the wineries of rural Auxerre, see Stella (1996).

28. For the sugar industry in late medieval Sicily, see Epstein (1992:210–222). For the structure of the Levantine sugar industry in the Later Middle Ages, "a true capitalistic enterprise, with big trusts which systematically pushed the small enterprises aside," see Ashtor (1992: chapter 3, esp. p. 237).

29. The salt trade asserted itself as "one of the unifying elements of the western economy" (Mollat 1993:65) as it became the target of special taxes all over Europe (Bautier 1992:V–VI; Mollat 1968, 1977:VI–VIII; Abraham-Thisse 1988; and Hocquet 1979a, 1979b, 1985, and 1987). For the significance of the salt trade in Northwestern Europe, see Bridbury (1973:22–39).

occur?[30] In other words, when do "luxuries" become "necessities" (Wallerstein 1993:294)?

Furthermore, to what extent is it analytically useful to draw such a dichotomy between the two prior to 1500? Could the growing wealth of Europe be measured by its increased demand for luxuries (Cheyney 1962:10)? Is it impossible to retain the importance and impact of luxury trade without conceptually reducing it to the same analytical level as bulk trade? Is it not conceivable that luxury trade (and certainly, the serious profits that it involved) could have provided essential financial leverage for the same merchant entrepreneurs/families who also engaged and invested in bulk trade, particularly before 1500? And could one not argue that this leverage was necessary, if not essential, to further increase the trade in mass commodities, thus stimulating the actual expansion of capitalism in this "era of transition from feudalism to capitalism"?[31] A medieval "super company" such as those managed in Italy by the Peruzzis or the Bardis around 1300 invested in and made notable profits from both textile (luxury) and large-scale grain (bulk) trading (Hunt 1994:244; Britnell 1993:123; Wolff 1959; Bradley 1994:57–58; Papacostea 1973:601; Balard 1989:VI; Balletto 1977; Yver 1968:104–126).[32] While Chase-Dunn and Hall

---

30. One might pose the same question about some of the other commodities that were traded in bulk in the 14th century, such as the beer produced in Northern Germany and exported to the Low Countries (Unger 1989; Aerts and Unger 1990; van Uytven 1988:548). Beer gradually replaced wine as a major consumption item (Unger 1998; Peterson 2000). Even more important was the trade in herring; in one single year a city like 14th-century Lübeck imported 90,000 tons of it (Stark 1993:191). The significance of the timber and fur trades should also not be underestimated (Martin 1978, 1986). In short, by the early 14th century, a wide variety of commodities was shipped in bulk all across Europe (Mollat 1988b:13; Ashtor 1981:261; Balard 1989:VI:64).

31. This is especially so if one realizes that in this period, commercial expansion and industrial specialization both required unprecedented investments of capital (Schumann 1986:107). For the importance of both bulk and luxury trade in the medieval economy, see Bozorgnia (1998). Clearly luxury trade in and of itself does not constitute a world-system even though from the point of view of state formation in the external arena—that is, areas outside of the modern world-system proper—it can be of major importance. As this study will show, luxury trade can have an impact on certain processes within the (emerging) system but does not in itself constitute a *capitalist* system; it is at best a prestige goods-based trade-network system (Chase-Dunn and Hall 1997:54).

32. One should note that "since the latter part of the Middle Ages, the range of articles in long-distance commercial circulation was already a very diverse one, and encompassed consumer goods which were relatively commonplace, [while] it did not absorb very high transaction costs" (Torras 1993:202). According to Unger (1980:191), Miskimin (1975:125), Scammel (1981:48), and Lewis and Runyan (1985:134–135), bulk trade *dominated* commerce in northern Europe. See also Romano (1954), Sapori (1970), and Cherubini (1993:282–283), who reject the implicit Sombartian perspective that Wallerstein seems to follow: "While recognizing the fact that we are not dealing here [the market in medieval Italy] with quantities comparable with the figures brandished for the days leading up to the Industrial Revolution, the circulation [of commodities] did not only involve products of specifically high value, but also the most run-of-the-mill goods ... we must reject the image of Italian commerce during this era as being centered around products such

(1997) and Modelski and Thompson (1996) are proponents of the existence and importance of various long-distance trade patterns and cycles prior to 1500, the dichotomy between luxury and bulk trade is not as important to them as it is to Wallerstein.

I would therefore argue that it is a serious exaggeration to claim that industrial production in the Middle Ages was "scattered, small-scale, and mostly geared to a luxury market" (Wallerstein 1974:123) and that "there was no middle-distance division of labor as local zones did not generally depend on or count on 'regional' (i.e., middle-distance) supply sources" (Wallerstein 1993b:5). Such thinking makes it seem as though medieval trade was nothing more than "local trade and exchange in which goods moved within restricted regions [while] long-distance trade was characterized exclusively by valuables produced for the elites" (Wolf 1982:32; Mandel 1962:127). Although local production and consumption of grains and textiles remained important (Munro 1998:275), regional as well as international markets were at the heart of the economy in medieval Western Europe; the city-states' dependence on both the grain trade (for the urban proletariat's consumption)[33] and the textile market clearly illustrate this. Indeed, the export of grain from the Baltic to the Low Countries from 1250 onward (Slicher van Bath 1963:156) and to England in the 14th century (Fourquin 1979:317), or from the Black Sea region (Manolescu 1981; Balard 1989:VI) to cities such as Genoa (Karpov 1993; Unger 1980:183; Day 1981:637), Venice (Nystazopoulou 1973:560), or Montpellier (Reyerson 1998:269) constituted an *essential* feature of the urban system (van Uytven 1985). Increasing amounts of raw materials (furs, timber, cattle) and grain were transported from "Eastern Europe" to the cities of the Low Countries (Tits-Dieuaide 1975:150–166; Sosson 1977:102–111; Lewis 1978:IX:33–35; Samsonowicz 1975:668), and occasionally to Italy (Balard 1975:21–30; Favier 1996:172–173). In return, the "bulk of the [western] cities' growing exports was directed to Eastern Europe" (van Uytven 1983:181; see also Berza

---

as spices and other highly-priced items." Nor should one forget that the "medieval usage of the term spice could be highly elastic" (Modelski and Thompson 1996:178). Essentially, "one becomes increasingly convinced that most of the commodities transported in the Mediterranean consisted of grains, wine, oil, and copper, wood, iron, alum and other goods part of people's daily lives. One should therefore pay attention to these bulk goods—and especially grains—rather than spices" (Bautier 1992:VI:224). According to Iorga (1914:297), the grain trade was so important that wars erupted over its supply routes. Furthermore, "the mass traffic of heavy products, such as salt and grain, and of cumbersome products, such as wood, also corresponded to a certain division of tasks between the sea and land routes" (Mollat 1993:65; see Heers 1965b:44–48). For the magnitude of profits from Italian trade with England from 1270 to 1530, see Fryde (1974, 1983:XIV–XVI).

33. Estimating that the "average inhabitant of a northern European town in the Middle Ages consumed 300 kg of grain annually" (Samsonowicz 1998:306), one can imagine the logistical problems for a city of a certain size (Schneider 1955:427), especially when many workers only had low wages to rely on to feed their families (Boone 1984:88).

1941:419–420; Bratianu 1944:47; Nystazopoulou 1973:563; and Giurescu 1976: 592–594).

What made the world-system from the 16th century onward *modern*, when compared with mini-systems or world-empires, was precisely its emerging single division of labor between large geographical areas interconnected by trade. Some might regard the division of labor between the urban inter-city-state system of Western Europe and the countryside of Eastern Europe and the Black Sea area (Balard 1983:45, 51) as an embryonic form of "peripheralization," culminating in the transformation of "East Central Europe into a virtual colonial appendage of the European heartland, supplying raw materials in exchange for finished goods" (Rowan 1994:197–198; see also Turnock 1988:209; Asdracha and Mantran 1986:348; Scammell 1981:87; and Tits-Dieuaide 1975:160). This is illustrated quite well in Hungary's trade deficit (Malowist 1974:348), which arose due to the massive import of cloth produced in the Low Countries (Abraham-Thisse 1998:133), and by the socioeconomic developments in Poland, where the local textile industry could not flourish in the long run due to the continuous inflow of textiles from the Western European city-states (Malowist 1957:578; Wyrozumski 1981:301; Kloczowski 1996:471–473). This, of course, had political ramifications in that the Polish urban bourgeoisie's power was limited (Wyrozumski 1978:37) and it could not grow as strong as its counterpart in the West as "the producers were drawn into exchange with economically advanced Western Europe [which] strengthened the political privileges of the Polish nobility who disposed of the crop production" (Gieysztor 1978:211). In turn, the much more powerful nobility was able to implement a socioeconomic policy that peripheralized the country vis-à-vis the West (Samsonowicz 1981; Bogucka 1985:101; Makkai 1975:236–238; Samsonowicz and Maczak 1985). From the 13th and 14th centuries onward, the Baltic area became more and more important as a source of food and other raw materials (e.g., timber) for the major urban centers in the Low Countries (Verhulst 1963:74–75; Gunst 1989:62; Malowist 1974:330–333). While this European division of labor did intensify in the 16th and 17th centuries, as Wallerstein (1974) points out, "certain aspects of the one-sided economic development of Eastern Europe were already evident" prior to this period (Malowist 1974:356–357).

In my opinion, the emerging European division of labor in the period from 1300 to 1500 is an adequate explanation for the relation between the "unidirectional development towards increased agricultural production" (Tarvel 1990:71) in Eastern Europe, and the increasing number of nonagricultural workers in West European cities (Wunder 1983:270–271; Pàl Pach 1994:IX–XI; Van der Wee 1988:338). It is not surprising then that most Polish craftsmen did not become very specialized (Samsonowicz 1988:180), unlike those in Western European cities. While admittedly, one should not "homogenize" Eastern and Western Europe, the late Middle Ages nevertheless have to be regarded as the "crucial turning point [that] led to divergent agrarian development in East and West" (Rösener 1994:106), when the balance of trade shifted in favor of Western Europe (Samsonowicz 1975:665). The fact that cities were more powerful in Western rather than Eastern Europe can be regarded as a crucial reason for this divergence (Kahan 1973:97).

Thus the emergence of Eastern Europe as "the granary of Western Europe" and its integration "into the Western European market system was the result of prolonged evolution" (Loewe 1973:23, 35) that started in the 13th to 14th centuries. As Szúcs points out, the Western European city-states were the first to suffer from the mid–14th-century feudal crisis, but also the first to rebound from it "because one could find new markets and metal producing zones in Central and Eastern Europe. *For a long while the regions situated to the East of the Elbe had to pay the price of the convalescence of Western Europe*" (1985:70, emphasis added). The emerging division of labor within Europe (Samsonowicz 1996:50–52; Szúcs 1985:74; Bauer and Matis 1988:101) was then part of the systematic construction of a colonial periphery (see infra), which in turn, is crucial to explaining the emergence of capitalism. It makes the claim of "internal" transformations within a single nation-state (a "capitalism in one country" phenomenon) quite absurd as well as presumptuous.[34]

The transition to capitalism that Wallerstein eventually situates around 1500 only becomes more problematic, however, if one examines other (non-world-systems) literature. Many describe the late Middle Ages as either a period of *transition* (particularly between 1300 and 1520) (Ferguson 1962), or a period of *acceleration* (particularly between 1270 and 1520) (Fossier 1991:337–441). Some have even used the phrase "commercial revolution" to describe the period between 1100 and 1350/1500 (Lopez 1954:615; 1976:56–84; Jones 1997:152–332), which in turn initiated the era of capitalism (and in the long run, made the "rise of the West" possible). Those who use this term, however, debate whether various forms of technological innovation (e.g., White 1962; Mokyr 1990; Balard 1991:113–123; Carus-Wilson 1941) or a form of agrarian development and surplus extraction—itself an outcome of specific class relations (Brenner 1985:11–12)—are at the heart of the matter.[35]

Snooks traces the decline of feudalism to some time between the 11th and 13th centuries (1996:191, 304). The late French agricultural historian Alain

---

34. See, for example, Wood: "The English economy in the early modern period, driven by the logic of its basic productive sector, agriculture, was already operating to principles and 'laws of motion' different from those prevailing in any other society since the dawn of history" (1999:96). As Duchesne (2002b:136) politely put it: "The capitalism in one country of Robert Brenner and Ellen Wood will no longer do."

35. Some have attributed events outside Europe as crucial to "the rise of the West" (e.g., technological stagnation resulting from the fiscal policy of despotic governments) (see Ashtor 1992:III:266, 273–280).

Derville agreed, stating that the transition from feudalism to capitalism in the countryside took place around A.D. 1150 (1995:243–250). Several studies that focus on urban[36] and agrarian[37] production and trade, bulk and luxury goods alike, clearly indicate a historical continuity on all levels between the late Middle Ages and the 16th century. This then explains the political, economic, and technological evolutions within the transition from feudalism to capitalism.[38]

Even the change in mentalities, notably, the rational drive to achieve a ceaseless accumulation of capital, can trace its roots back to the Middle Ages (Le Mené 1977:160–190; Jorda 2002).[39] Martin referred to this as "Marx in practice, 600 years before the appearance of 'Capital'! One's failure or success in life is indicated by the magnitude of accumulated capital" (1996:357–370). Le Goff considers the theological controversy surrounding usury in the 13th century as "the labor pains of capitalism" (1988:9–10). He explains: "The instigators of capitalism were usurers: merchants of the future, sellers of time; the hope of escaping Hell, thanks to Purgatory, permitted the usurer to propel the economy and society of the thirteenth century ahead towards capitalism" (1988:93).[40]

Although prohibited by the church, "the church's condemnation of usury did nothing to shackle the development of capitalism" (Le Goff 1979:25). Whatever the Church may have thought, many urban authorities in the 12th and

---

36. See the essays on 14th-century urban economies and putting-out production in Boone and Prevenier (1993). For descriptions of the putting-out system implemented by medieval merchant capitalists, see Reynolds (1961:236–243), von Stromer (1991), Holbach (1985, 1994), Friedrichs (1975), and Kellenbenz (1973). For a comparison of urban industries in the Low Countries and Italy, see Van der Wee (1988).

37. For example, the studies in Van der Wee and Van Cauwenberghe (1978) and Thoen (1992, 1993).

38. In emphasizing historical continuity throughout this study, I do not intend to simplify the complex history of certain conjunctures related to particular products bought and sold in the marketplace, as discontinuities did occur (see Munro, 1997, for the "new draperies"). What I want to stress, rather, is the *overall* continuity of economic growth from the 13th to the 16th century and the nature of the capitalist exploitation inherent to it.

39. See also Heers (1965:51). Cipolla notes that by the 15th century, "Western glass too was widely exported to the Near East and a telling symptom of the European 'capitalist' spirit, unhampered by religious considerations, was the fact that the Venetians manufactured mosque lamps for the Near Eastern market and decorated them with both western floral designs and pious Koranic inscriptions" (1994:210). With regard to medieval Bruges, Murray states that "the term medieval capitalism should not be rejected out of hand, for despite its tint of anachronism, capitalism does indeed describe the workings of the Bruges economy in the 14th century" (1990:25). See also Murray (2005).

40. "With the development of the monetary economy in the 12th century, usury will become an important issue for the Church. It is during the 13th century that the issue becomes a crucial one, when capitalism is making its first steps, using exactly those practices condemned by the Church up to that point in time" (Greilsammer 1994:810). See also Heers (1992:253–256) and Mundy (1997:196–202).

13th centuries "turned a blind eye" (Erner 2005:471) if not "defended the practice of usury altogether. . . . Synods that denounced canonical infractions such as usury hardly installed any fear in the business community" (Wyffels 1991:870–871) since "money-lending was freely practiced in the Middle Ages among the poor as well as the rich. Usury was still forbidden by canon law, but there were all kinds of subtle devices for cloaking usurious transactions" (Du Boulay 1970:59; see Little 1978:180–183). One such disguise was the carrying on of banking activities "under the cloak of exchange" (de Roover 1969:29):

> Medieval lawyers and their clients became spectacularly adept at circumventing the laws by disguising interest payments. The church itself was a borrower and a lender and it, too, made use of the ingenious methods of casuistry that had been developed for paying interest without appearing to pay interest. In short, credit financing had become too pervasive and integral a part of economic life that no amount of theological argument was going to make it go away. Although theologians continued to argue the moral fine points of the usury problem, by the mid 14th century there was a marked decrease in the Church's actual prosecutions of usury, and it even began to change its laws to allow moderate interest rates. (Barnett 1998:60)

According to Little, "what was once deviant behavior, which by definition is marginal, was [by the mid-13th century] becoming standard practice and thus simultaneously, from an official point of view, increasingly difficult to define as deviant, particularly as more and more of those in positions of authority had a mercantile background. This is self-evident in the case of the urban patriciate, but it was also true of the ecclesiastical hierarchy" (1978:212). Of course, the existence of money-lending predates the European medieval era/area and is not unique to Western Europe (e.g., Habib 1964). As Bois points out, "one usurer in purgatory does not create capitalism. An economic system only replaces another one after a long period in time" (2000:30).

Another important development related to the rise of capitalism and dating from the beginning of the 14th century was the appearance of mechanical clocks on churches and town halls in Western Europe (Barnett 1998:80). Indeed, "the rational outlook of the merchants and bankers was fundamental to the installation of mechanical clocks in the West. With their capitalistic mentality they had observed the value of time" (Gimpel 1976:170).[41] Thus began "a historical

---

41. Or to quote Barnett: "God's time began to grant space to the new secularized idea of time required by a money economy" (1998:61) As Rossiaud (1990:172) points out, bells on churches and belfries as well as clocks became "fundamental to collective life" as "theological time was replaced by technological time" (Gurevich 1990:279). On the diffusion of clocks in medieval Europe and its implications ("Merchant's Time" and "Work Time and Hourly Wage"), see Dohrn-van Rossum

revolution in the measuring of time, with far-reaching intellectual, commercial and industrial consequences" (Gimpel 1976:165; Pernoud 1992:140). Time became a compartmentalized and rationalized commodity (Le Goff 1991:46–79; Martin 1996:168–174) and the clock an increasingly important instrument to *control labor*: "Everywhere workers had to submit to the new instrument that measured time, to the watch, to the clock on the belfry, the church or the city hall and that from now on rigorously determined rhythms and time of work and leisure" (Rossiaud 1998:471).[42]

Could it also not be argued that "l'esprit d'entreprise" of merchants like Jacques Coeur in the middle of the 15th century (Mollat 1988), Jean Boine-broke (Espinas 1933; Bernard 1976:311; Koenigsberger 1987:223–224) and the Genoese 'capitalist' Symon de Gualterio (Face 1969:75–94) in the late 13th century, or even Guillaume Cade in the mid-12th century (Derville 1994:52–54), were all linked to the emergence of capitalism? According to Bernard:

> The capitalistic nature of major commerce and international finance becomes clearly apparent in the fourteenth and fifteenth centuries. The volume of medieval trade and the amount of business conducted was negligible by comparison with present-day trade, but this means very little. It was substantial considering the size of the population, and the relative importance of other sectors of the economy. In tonnage, some figures actually surpassed those of Seville's trade with America in the first half of the sixteenth century. (1976:309–310)

In answer to the question "was the medieval economy capitalistic?" the economic historian Heaton responds: "Fourteenth-century merchants were conducting complicated businesses with intelligence, foresight, and a detailed

---

(1996). Whitrow even goes so far as to claim that unlike in China or Mesoamerica, "in Western Europe the mechanical clock first appeared and with it a new type of civilization based on the measurement of time" (1988:96). The point of this book is not to engage in a discussion about which part of the world was the first to invent a mechanic clock or organize maritime expeditions to the New World. While interesting for historicist speculation and as a means of debunking a certain amount of Eurocentric historiography (cf. Hobson 2004:21), the first invention of a certain technology or the first 'discovery' of a certain area of the world does not, in itself, lead to any kind of intrinsic claim regarding the origins of a capitalist system. Obviously the abovementioned variables were all part of such a system, in which an axial division of labor based on unequal exchange was the engine for ceaseless capital accumulation and further colonialist expansion, but were themselves insufficient conditions or indicators.

42. See Epstein (1988), Crosby (1997:75–93), Cipolla (1977), and Haverkamp (1998). For the far-reaching implications of changes in the perception of time between 1300 and 1650, see Thompson's "Time, Work-Discipline and Industrial Capitalism" (1993:352–403). Landes (1983:72–76) explicitly links the large-scale production of the textile industry to the diffusion of work bells in medieval urban communities. By the mid-14th century, "the division of hours into 60 minutes and minutes into 60 seconds became common" (Hallam 1976:34).

knowledge of their financial position. There was no lack of capitalistic spirit, organization, or technique in the management of great estates during the 13th century" (1948:185–187). Although I do not want to stress the emergence of a Weberian capitalist *spirit* and do not agree with the claim that "what made European expansion different and 'special' was derived from a series of religious and cultural factors which were largely peculiar to European society" (Phillips 1998:243), a new commercial mentality did occur in the educational field (Dahl 1998:67–68; Wolff 1989:58–59; Prevenier 1994:13; 1996:353). What was so unique about the 16th century then, as far as the features of capitalism are concerned?

The concept of an "age of transition" can be interpreted as requiring the operation of at least two coexisting modes of production, and the eventual domination of one over the other. If we want to analyze the rise of one mode of production and the demise of another, at some point we have to acknowledge them as working together. If not, one is left with the argument that feudalism simply disappeared within Europe during the 16th century. But as Britnell has said, "The transition needs analyzing as a much longer process than most traditional accounts imply" (1993b:359). Why not argue that the feudal system and some of its social structures were very much alive in the 19th century? Wallerstein insists that the creation of the modern capitalist world-economy took place no earlier than 1450 and no later than the 16th century. And yet, he is very much aware of major changes in Europe prior to 1450, stating that "the crisis of feudalism in Europe in the period of 1300–1450 [was] a crisis whose resolution was the historic emergence of a capitalist world-economy located in that particular geographic arena" (1984:23). Despite his acknowledgment of the existence of some capitalistic features in the late Middle Ages, Wallerstein does not note any fundamentally important historical continuity in Europe between the period 1300 and around 1500 that might help to explain the transition from feudalism to capitalism:

> There were no doubt other times throughout history when such a transformation [into a capitalist world-economy] seemed to be beginning, such as in the Mediterranean basin between 1150 and 1300. And there were parallel occurrences at other moments in other regions of the world. But for various reasons all the prior transformations were abortive. (1979:142)

This is a very important statement, signifying that unlike Europe, other regions did not witness the emergence of capitalism. It also implies that what happened between 1150 and 1300 did not impact the emergence of capitalism in Europe in 1450, since he dismisses it as "abortive."[43]

---

43. An "earlier attempt of transition [that] failed" Wallerstein (1979:135).

Is there really such an extreme break with the past?[44] Because several features of capitalism were already strongly apparent in Europe prior to 1500—more precisely between 1100 and 1350[45]—and because of their growing importance, is it not plausible that the feudal system sunk into a crisis, rather than being suddenly and completely replaced by an entirely new system of accumulation? Or to put it another way, that the feudal system fell into a slow, agonizing period of decay and was eventually superseded by the dominant "logic" of capitalism? In this regard, historical continuity is revealing.

In the 14th century, there was already a valid money market wherein the banking and trading companies had branches that dealt in paper currency and which was, like every market, governed by the laws of supply and demand and subject to various seasonal and cyclical fluctuations (Bernard 1976:327). As the economic historian John Day points out:

> By the mid-fourteenth century, merchant capitalism has already perfected the instruments of economic power and business organization that were to serve it for the next four hundred years: foreign exchange, deposit banking, risk insurance, public finance, international trading companies, commercial bookkeeping. (1987:199)[46]

In Braudel's conceptualization of the "économie-monde," forms of capitalism (e.g., commercial, industrial, and banking[47]) existed in 13th-century

---

44. In a more recent article, Wallerstein claims that there is a fundamental difference between "proto capitalist" systems with capitalist features (investments of capital, extensive commodity production, wage labor and weltanschauungen consonant with capitalism) on the one hand, and the "genesis of a radically new system" after 1400 out of the "crisis of feudalism" on the other (1999:34). It is my position that one should be careful not to overlook the development of the embryonic European capitalist system in the period 1200 to 1400, precisely in order to understand the developments in the world-economy in a much more intensified pattern, and on a larger scale, in the period 1400 to 1600. Unfortunately, in Wallerstein's model, the 16th-century capitalist world-economy is "virtually a creation ex nihilo" (Sanderson 1995:159).

45. With regard to continuity from medieval merchant capitalism originating in Italy and the Low Countries, cf. Sée (1928:7–56). For a more recent synthesis in general, see Jorda (2002).

46. See also Bouvier and Germain-Martin (1964:21–22) or Lane (1977). For the importance of credit instruments in 14th-century overseas trade, see Munro (1994:X:67–79). Using transfers of credit by exchange instruments, "inter-city exchange bankers" could avoid moving bullion over long distances (Blomquist 1994:345). For a discussion on the usage of bookkeeping by urban governments in Western Europe, see Samsonowicz (1964). For a comparison of the medieval and 16th-century price revolutions, see Fischer (1996:11–38).

47. With regard to medieval banking, Le Goff concludes: "Taking into account the amount of money he controlled, the geographical and economical horizons he was familiar with, and the commercial and financial methods he used, the medieval merchant-banker was a capitalist. But he also is it in spirit, because of his way of life and his place in society" (1962:41). See de Roover (1948, 1971) and Blomquist (1979). In the late 13th century, Genoa introduced maritime insurance contracts, which were rapidly adopted elsewhere (Heers 1959:8–14; Wolff 1986:136–139).

Florence[48] and have since tightened their grip on the economy. Thus unlike Wallerstein, Braudel is not reluctant to apply the term *capitalism* to the Middle Ages,[49] nor is he unwilling to apply the concepts of a world-systems analysis (e.g., periphery, semiperiphery, core, etc.) to that period.[50] Indeed when discussing the emergence of capitalism, why not use such world-systems terminology before the 16th century (De Wachter 1996:51–57)?

Regarding the temporal origins of capitalism, Wallerstein considers the "axial division of labor involving integrated production processes" a conditio sine qua non for identifying a system that is capitalistic in nature (1993:294). From the late 11th century onward, energetic merchant-entrepreneurs[51] in Flanders started to produce standardized textile goods intended for large scale export (Verlinden 1976:104; Ammann 1954).[52] This export industry drew its

---

For the links between insurance practices and the availability of credit, see Leone (1983). For a general history of corporate finance from the Middle Ages onward, see Baskin and Miranti (1999).

48. The functioning of the 14th-century Florentine economy is discussed by Brucker: "The merchant-entrepreneur would buy the raw materials (wool, dyeing substances, wood and alum) and market the finished product once the wool had passed through the various stages of cloth production. [First] the imported wool would arrive at the wash house, it would then proceed to the factory to be carded and combed; out to the country to be spun; back into the city for weaving and dyeing; once again into the country to be fulled and then back to town finally to be stretched, packed, checked, sealed and retailed or exported . . . during this process he would have recourse to workers directly answerable to him . . . he would always remain in charge and retain ownership of the wool, as it progressively became transformed into cloth . . . spinners and weavers remained financially dependent on the lanaiolo: the looms were borrowed or sold on a pro rata basis of payment by installments of work, or else they were pledged to the lanaiolo in return for work" (1998:105). On the power of the setaiolo, the merchant-entrepreneur in the Italian silk industry, see Piergiovanni (1993). See Borlandi (1954) for the power of the merchant in the fustian industries.

49. Nor is Henri Pirenne (1937:19) or André Sayous (1934).

50. See Braudel (1992b:70).

51. The 13th-century merchant-entrepreneur was very active. "Disposing of lots of capital, he controls the import of raw materials, the export of the finished product, bears the risks created by the disparity of markets and controls all the stages of the production process while determining the rhythm of it" (Sosson 1991:280).

52. For the importance of Champagne and Flanders cloth in the Genoese market of the 12th century, see Krueger (1987), Reynolds (1929, 1930), and Laurent (1935:1–20). For the significance of Scottish and Spanish wool production for export, see Ewan (1990:68–91) and Childs (1978:72–106). For the impact of market fluctuations on transformations in the textile industry, see Munro (1991). For evidence that cheap Northern cloths exported to the Mediterranean in the 13th century exceeded those of luxury woolens, not only in volume but also in aggregate value, see Chorley (1987). The importance of the trade in cloth is confirmed by Malanima (1987:351): "In the 13th century, large scale trade became increasingly linked to the trade in textiles: of all the goods that traveled across the Mediterranean these were the most valuable. In comparison the spice trade had become a secondary affair, with not only a more limited scale but also a much lesser value since a sack of Flemish cloths was equivalent in value to between three and five sacks of

strength from a far-reaching division of labor, employing both semi-skilled and unskilled workers in large numbers[53] (Van der Wee 1988:320; Heers 1965:57). As an example, in the Flemish textile industry from the 12th century onward, each of the tasks described was performed by a specialist: breakers, beaters, washers, oilers, carders, combers, spinners, weavers, fullers, tenderers, teaselers, shearmen, dyers, pressers, pickers, greasers, and so on (Munro 1988:1–27; Cardon 1999). Further specialization within a single manufacturing process also took place: "The dyers, for example, subdivided themselves into groups which concentrated on a particular color" (Van der Wee 1975:204; see Heers 1976:219). Braudel is convinced that the boom of the 13th century arose out of the proliferation of the newly created division of labor (1992:315). This increasing division of labor, particularly apparent in the textile industry but also found in the mining industry,[54] had a significant impact on social stratification and

---

spices." Indeed, according to Ashtor, "the [long distance] trade of bulky commodities, like cotton and alkali ashes, yielded much more than that of spices" (1985:376). Interestingly, the significance of canvas-type cotton cloths during the 12th-century "birth of the European fashion industry" (Abulafia 1994:8) is evidenced by the etymology of the English words "jeans" (from Gênes) and "denim" (referring to "de Nîmes") (Abulafia 1998:342).

53. From 1356 to 1358 (after the great plague) between 59 percent and 67 percent of the population in Ghent (pop. 65,000) was involved in the cloth industry (Prevenier 1975:276–279; Lis and Soly 1979:10). The situation was more or less similar in Tournai, Maubeuge, Valenciennes (Bruwier 1992:261), and even higher in Ypres (Galvin 2002:136). In 14th-century Florence, a minimum 40 percent of the working population was employed in the textile industry (van Uytven 1981:292; Franceschi 1993:103). Jacoby claims that in 15th-century Catalonia, "between 40 and 60% of the population was engaged in the manufacturing of woolens" (1994:551). For 15th-century Leiden and Oudenaarde, one report estimates 34 percent and 50 percent of the population, respectively (Prevenier 1998:82) and for early 14th-century Dendermonde (pop. 9,000), about 40 percent (Prevenier 1983:261). In early 14th-century Bruges (pop. 46,000), more a commercial than an industrial city, the professionally active population employed in the textile industry fluctuated between 31 percent (Dumolyn 1999:53) and 37 percent (Blockmans 1997b:263). This was probably the case for other, smaller villages as well (Favreau 1989:172). On average, 34 percent of the population in the Low Countries resided in cities (Prevenier 1983:273). On recent population estimates of medieval Italian cities, see Hubert (2004:116).

54. See Braudel (1992:321–325), Pounds (1994:329), Molenda (1989), Braunstein (1987, 2001), and Sprandel (1968) for a long-term view of iron production in the Middle Ages. By the early 14th century, the impact of private capital from urban merchants investing in the countryside in order to extract minerals in Tuscany can be deduced from key clauses of mining laws that indicate "the separation of land ownership from the rights to the subsoil (which allows the deposits to be exploited by a person other than the owner of the property) and the possibility that exploitation can be undertaken by several persons in a partnership, who adopt a capitalistic structure comprised of partners, salaried workers, and 'magistri' or directors of the enterprise" (Piccinni 1994:225). While many mines were initially exploited by the nobility, the medieval bourgeoisie took over this role in the early 14th century (Hesse 1986:437–438; van Uytven 1988:552); "the prospection and exploitation of mines was conducted completely by private initiative and the local bourgeoisie" (Menant 1987:786–787). By 1400, leading mining towns such as Kutna Hora in Bohemia employed 4,000 to 4,500 miners (Pollard 1997:179) although even higher figures have been suggested (Koran and Vanecek 1962:32). Most importantly, "during the 13th to the 14th century the mass of

polarization.[55] The leather and metal industries (lead, tin, copper, bronze, silver, gold, and iron and their finished products) were also affected: "Metal-working guilds had divided as early as the thirteenth century into several dozen independent professions and trades" (Braudel 1992:v.2:315). Metal-working gradually ceased to be a part-time occupation of the farming community and became the full-time pursuit of professional iron-workers: "Medieval Europe witnessed a mass production of metals that, due to the nature of the enterprise, the modalities of work, and the functioning of markets, cannot be interpreted in the framework of mere artisanal production" (Braunstein 1994:23).[56] Merchant capitalists who dealt in bar iron first invested in ironworks and then leased and operated them (Pounds 1994:327).[57]

At the same time, the steadily increasing population in Europe[58] during the economic upturn of the mid-13th century resulted in massive land reclamation.

---

working miners were freemen working for a weekly wage" (Koran and Vanecek 1962:37). In less economically advanced regions such as Poland, foreign merchants (acting as Verlegers) controlled much of the profits derived from ore mining (Molenda 1976:157–166).

55. Thus Flanders and northern Italy had developed a genuinely capitalist mode of "production in which the workers had effectively become wage earners, a proletariat, owing nothing but their labor, even though there were as yet no factories and the workers worked in their homes ... the employment of these workers was subject to the fluctuations of the international market which they did not understand and over which they had no control. It is not surprising therefore, that both areas were beginning to experience industrial strife: strikes and urban revolts" (Koenigsberger 1987:225). For an overview of working conditions in the Western European Middle Ages, see Wolff and Mauro (1965) and Fossier (2000).

56. Metal-working contributed significantly to international trade, such as in Huy and Dinant in the Low Countries (Jansen 1989:360–361). By 1430, the expansion of the metal industry in the areas of Namur, Liège, and the Haut-Palatinat (due to the construction of ever larger "hauts fourneaux"), lead to a takeover of the industry by merchant capitalists (Gillard 1971; von Stromer 1991:46–47). For the metal industry in Northern Italy, cf. Braunstein (2001). For the putting-out system in the Low Countries in the 14th and 15th centuries, cf. Arnoux (2001).

57. Paper, glass, mirror, and crystal making and shipbuilding were also important industries (Wolff 1989:49–53; Favier 1996:188; Ashtor 1981:279–280). According to Modelski and Thompson, the Venetian Arsenal, "where standardized galleys were constructed along an assembly line, can probably claim to be one of Europe's first modern industrial factories" (1996:237). For the importance of capitalist relations in the medieval building industry, see Hodgett (1972:135–136). For medieval international trade and the "rise of an English merchant class", see Miller and Hatcher (1978:79–83; 1995:181–254).

58. One cannot deny the impact of the considerable population growth in the 13th century. One result was that not everyone could live from his own land, which in turn led to more "self-employment, dependence upon trade and a greater availability of wage labor" (Britnell 1993:104). The latter is, of course, very important. According to Goldthwaite, the labor contract in medieval Florence was "thoroughly monetized. The employer calculated wages entirely in precise monetary terms, he rarely paid in kind ... paid no more for longevity on the job, and provided no social and health benefits for unemployment, accidents or old age ... that even the humblest of men thought about their wages and daily purchases in the abstract language of moneys of account rather than in

As the new expanding urban centers placed greater demands on the agrarian economy (Mackenney 1987:78–79), reclamation of land from the sea, particularly around great river estuaries, became very important. Once the sea had been excluded from the area, the land proved to be excellent, fertile, flat and stone-free soil (Ponting 1993:125). Such reclamation of land was very impressive in Flanders and Holland (specifically in the areas of peat moors),[59] although the greatest progress was made in Northern Italy (Pounds 1994:170). Investments were also made in reclaiming the wet and fertile valley of the Po River and in creating polders in the Low Countries (Alberts and Jansen 1964:74–79; TeBrake 1985). For the merchants in 14th-century Milan or Venice, and for the burghers in Bruges or Ypres, the idea of land as a commodity that one could acquire, improve, and profit from was quite natural (Pounds 1994:109–110; Ponting 1993:154). Thus land reclamation (Verhulst 1990b:54–55) became, in its turn, an important aspect of capital formation (Smith 1991:100).

Where then does the "incorporation" of new arenas—defined by a world-systems analysis as the "historical process by which non-capitalist zones are absorbed into the capitalist world-system, [and where] inhabitants of territories that have been outside are brought into the system through colonization, conquest, or economic and political domination" (Dunaway 1996:455)—fit into this discussion? Could the creation of the Crusading states in the Levant in the 12th century—a region that was strongly interlinked with intercontinental trade—or the Reconquista of the Iberian Peninsula (ending in 1492) not be interpreted as an *identical* form of expansion, subjugation, domination, and exploitation as Spain's conquest of the New World, albeit on a smaller scale?[60]

It is clear that the colonialism practiced by city-states such as Venice in the Eastern Mediterranean (Wolff 1986:214–215; Luzzatto 1954:117–123; Dennis 1973) or by Genoa in the Black Sea area (Balard 1978, 1992; Scammell

---

terms of medium of exchange is a mark of the extent to which their attitudes were conditioned by the practice of offsetting [or giro transfer on private accounts] within the framework of a written accounting record" (1991:649).

59. The production of peat was important in the Low Countries from the 14th to the 17th century (Leenders 1989:251–271).

60. See Bernard (1976:292–293) in general. See Thiriet (1977:XIII, XV), Jacoby (1999), and Laiou (1992:X:177–198) for medieval Crete; Poisson (1995, 1997); Abulafia (1993:I:28–29), Tangheroni (1995), and Day (1983:198–200; 1984:700–701) for medieval Sardinia (which primarily exported grain, salt, and metals); Cancellieri (1989) for Corsica; Hocquet (1989) for certain parts of Dalmatia; and Ashtor (1978:VI; 1978b), Jacoby (1979:VII), and Prawer (1972) for the Levant in the Middle Ages. The case of medieval Sicily (Abulafia 1977), however, is more doubtful (Epstein 1989), while the North African states in the Western Mediterranean were simply too strong for the Italian city-states to colonize outright (Jehel 1993:66; Dufourcq 1990:III).

1981:162), was not simply political but also financial (Day 1985; Astuti 1970).[61]
For instance, the steady "colonization of the Byzantine Empire" by the Italian
city-states (Thomson 1998:63–96), resembling the political and economic dependence of the 20th-century third world (Oikonomidès 1979:130), cannot be
separated from the acquisition of raw materials such as alum—"indispensable
for textile production in western Europe" (Verhulst 1998:110; Dahl 1998:40),
cotton—vital to both the textile and candle industries in Lombardy and South
Germany (Mazzaoui 1981:43–44, 102–103; Ashtor 1992:II:263–264), or cheap
alkali ashes—for the European soap and glass industries (Ashtor 1992:II:269;
Jacoby 1997:IX:69). In a steady process that lasted two centuries (1150–1350),
the power of the once-formidable Byzantine Empire was gradually undermined, its "manufacturing and commercial potential drained by the dominance
of the Italian capitalist city-states" (Angold 1985:37), forcing more and more
of the Empire into a subordinate position within the unfolding inter-regional
division of labor.[62]

Laiou concludes that the Italians who controlled the market "did not allow
the Byzantines to develop their own manufactures. It is not insignificant, nor
accidental that the textile industry which had flourished in the Morea until
the 12th and early 13th century declined, for the most part, in subsequent
centuries."[63] The glass industry in Greece was "replaced by imports from the

---

61. This is particularly evident when one scrutinizes the relation between the Byzantine Empire
and the Italian city-states:

> As to the question of the division of labor, the answer is to some extent evident from the
> description of the economic function of the [Late Medieval] Eastern Mediterranean; this
> is an area whose main exports are food, raw materials, or the re-export of eastern luxury
> products, while its primary imports are manufactured articles from Western Europe. It
> was Western traders, especially the Italians, who ran and dominated this market; for they
> had the access to the Western markets, they controlled the sea lanes and therefore com-
> munications with their ships, they created and controlled the information mechanism,
> and their needs dictated the currency transactions. (Laiou 1992:VII:182)

62. The city-states' commercial colonies in the Eastern Mediterranean had, "because of their
nature and administration a striking contrast with the feudal world around it" (Halpérin 1950:30).
Nevertheless, the Eastern Mediterranean colonies were slowly but steadily integrated into the
expanding division of labor of Western Europe, which imported food and raw materials from the
East and re-exported its manufactured commodities in return (Laiou 1982:13). Despite this, one
should also not forget to take into account the practices of colonialism implemented by the city-
states vis-à-vis their respective hinterlands/contado, which was equally important for the supply
of food and raw materials to the city (Blomquist 1969:69) since "the creation of urban wealth
through the monopoly of the sources of raw materials" (Nicholas 1976:28) was generated in this
socioeconomic/political periphery.

63. "The connection indeed, was seen by some contemporaries. . . . Cardinal Bessarion complained
that even in the Peloponnesus, the Byzantines had allowed themselves to become importers of
manufactured goods and had even lost the art of making woolen cloth" (1992:VII:187). Furthermore, "Byzantine governments failed to deliver sufficient essential force and projection of political
influence to enable Byzantines to compete on equal terms with the entrepreneurs of the West"
(Pryor 1997:211).

West" (Laiou 1982:15) during the latter's 13th-century economic upturn, while the Byzantine Empire's provinces "became increasingly specialized in form of production, [yet] less closely tied to Constantinople and more connected to other parts of the Mediterranean world" (Pryor 1997:206). These developments coincided with specific policies implemented by the Italian city-states; according to Jacoby (1994:558), the government in the Venetian metropolis "focused on the immigration of specific professional groups, with a clear emphasis on textile craftsmen, in order to promote industrial development," while in its colonies no industries were allowed that would compete with those of Venice (Scammell 1981:122). Not surprisingly, "ship-patrons were warned not to accept as passengers skilled artisans who wanted to emigrate from Venice and craftsmen who emigrated were threatened by many [Italian] governments with heavy punishment" (Ashtor 1992:VIII:20). In Genoa as well, drastic laws were issued "against any attempt at establishing competing workshops in her own colonies" (Lopez 1964:527).

In the long run, the balance of payments between the city-state and its colonial territories was favorable to the metropolis (Balletto 1976:123). Richard even goes so far as to claim that by the late 14th century, a city-state such as Venice "is increasingly becoming a colonial rather than a commercial power and her riches come above all from the exploitation of her insular domain" (1977:I:23). Essentially, the sustenance of major merchant capitalist city-states in Europe and the preservation of their "recurring growth" cannot be separated from the continuous (re)construction of the colonized periphery that served as a source of foodstuffs and raw materials (Jacoby 1979:I:45; Balard 1985:259), and as a market for the city-states' industries. Many similarities exist between these forms of colonialism in the Eastern Mediterranean and later forms in the Atlantic (Balard and Ducellier 1995, 1998; Balard 1989, 1990; Verlinden 1970).[64]

If all of these parallels exist, what is it that originates around A.D. 1500 that is so modern (Verlinden 1984)?[65] This criticism is not only directed at the

---

64. A close investigation of sugar production in Cyprus and Crete in the 14th century, as well as on the Madeira Islands, the Canary Islands, and the Azores in the 15th century, reveals that this strategy of capital accumulation was copied and transplanted on a much wider scale in the "New World" after 1500 (Heers 1981:12; Solow 1987; Galloway 1977; von Wartburg 1995; Verlinden 1972), as was the slave trade—a growing source of profit during the Middle Ages (Verlinden 1977)—that went hand in hand with it (Thiriet 1977:XIII:63–64). Although the transformation into an exploitable colony was quite gradual (Richard 1983:VIII; Mercer 1980), insisting on a *fundamental difference* between forms of "medieval" and "modern" colonialism, as Bartlett (1993:306–313) does, is not warranted (Lewis 1978:IX:37).

65. In other words, "Forms of investment which one can already qualify as capitalist were largely known and used, both in rural and urban environments, at sea and on land.... it is important to realize that the system of capitalism that existed in Protestant countries during the Early Modern Era, originated in forms of capitalism that had developed considerably during the Late Middle

Wallerstein version of world-systems analysis but also, to a certain extent, at Arrighi (who takes the story back to approximately A.D. 1400).[66] Venice may indeed have been the first "true prototype of the capitalist state," as Arrighi (1994) points out, but why does he only look to the Italian city-states to explain the origins of capitalism (Cistozvonov 1978; Meyer 1981:58)? Thus the concept of commercial capitalism is applicable to the Late Middle Ages throughout the entire Western European inter-city-state system (Chaunu 1969:311) and its historical continuity is undeniable (de Vries and van der Woude 1997:159–165; Hunt and Murray 1999; van Uytven 1974). Consequently, a rethinking of the temporal predisposition put forward by the world-systems analysis is needed. Let us then discuss the spatial predisposition of world-systems theory; that is, the emergence of capitalism within Europe.

Spatial Predisposition

For Wallerstein (1984:23), the transition from feudalism to capitalism took place on the European continent. Such a conclusion begs the question: Should we attribute the transition to internal or external transformations? Wallerstein (1974, 1980) focused on the transition within Europe, as it coincided with Europeans' impact on others (i.e., 16th-century colonies) and subsequent contributions to European economies in general (Wallerstein 1983). But the emergence of capitalism can hardly be explained by focusing exclusively on certain transformations within Europe or more particularly Northwestern Europe (Sweezy 1976; Takahashi 1976:74), or on the "internal contradictions" in England and France (Dobb 1976:59 and Brenner 1985). Consequently, other world-systems literature has attempted to analyze the impact of external factors on Europe prior to the 16th century. According to Abu-Lughod, for example, the linkages that existed in the 13th and 14th centuries constituted a system since "all these units were not only trading with one another and handling the transit trade of others, but had begun to reorganize parts of their internal economies to meet the exigencies of a world market." The effects of this interdependence were so great that a decline in one region contributed to a decline elsewhere. In comparing a cluster of interlinked regions with one another and in analyzing their common commercial network of production and exchange, one cannot help but wholeheartedly agree with Abu-Lughod when she states that

---

Ages" (Contamine et al. 1993:403–409). That said, I do not deny the qualitative shift that occurred in the 16th century when a *global* division of labor took place and when the inter-state system replaced the inter-city-state system. City-states were simply too small for the ceaseless accumulation of capital on an ever-wider scale; Genoa and Venice could colonize and exploit their rural hinterland or their colonies (Scammell 1981:106; Laiou 1982:16) within a core–periphery relationship, but not the Americas (Boris 1991:108).

66. As does Rénouard (1949:197–250) in his studies on 15th-century capitalism.

"it would be wrong to view the 'Rise of the West' as . . . an event whose outcome was attributable exclusively to the internal characteristics of European society" (Abu-Lughod 1989:355–361). This coherent holistic approach, which undermines the nation-state as the exclusive unit of analysis, is one of world-system theory's most valuable contributions to explaining the emergence of capitalism.[67] But it still leaves the question: Why did capitalist features occur in Europe and not, for example, in West Africa (Sanderson 1996:512)?[68]

The Inter-City-State System of the Middle Ages

Certain specific phenomena within medieval Europe may have stimulated the emergence of capitalism there, and not elsewhere. Although some in the world-systems school have advocated *civilizational underpinnings* as the reason for the emergence of capitalism in Europe, I prefer to stress the importance of the European inter-city-state system.[69] In this part of the chapter then, I propose an alternative theoretical framework[70]—that is, that capitalism was appearing in Western Europe from the late 12th century onward.

As discussed earlier, most capitalistic phenomena found in the 16th century were already apparent in the urban centers of medieval Western Europe; for example, wage labor, the specialization of industries, a complex division of labor, class struggles, profits from trade (derived from the fact that entrepreneurs who own the means of production are involved in specialized production and competition), complex financial techniques, and the systematic construction

---

67. In this perspective, it makes no sense to claim that one single nation-state was "the cradle and nursery of capitalism" (Macfarlane 1988:185).

68. The critics of Eurocentrism raise the question: "Why speak of transition to capitalism only for Europe? Indeed, why not abandon the notion of transition altogether in favor of a constant evolution of a system in existence for a long while?" (Amin 1993:251). Blaut contended that between 1000 and 1500, the whole world was moving in the direction of capitalism (1993). For an interesting case study of Japan, see Sanderson (1994).

69. Merrington refers to the "independent growth of urban capital" in the Western city in contrast to the Eastern one: "In China 'city air' made nobody free" (1976:178). See Bairoch (1989:227–231).

70. It is not my intention to merely deconstruct theoretical perspectives and plea for nothing more than historical research in order to come closer to an "objective Truth" (e.g., Grassby 1999:61–73). Historians' incessant warnings of "imprudent generalizations" (Sosson 1990:348) and "pretentious and ill-founded grand hypotheses launched by some sociologists" (Dyer 1991:1) should not, however, be taken as absolutes—for what is history without theory? As Hardach put it: "Economic history without theory is just as little thinkable as theory without empirical foundation and verification" (1972:46). Equally problematic, in my view, is the notion that "interconnections" and "exchanges," whether cultural or economic, are somehow separate from power and domination in the real world (e.g., Berg 2004 and to a certain extent Pearson 1998).

of an exploitable periphery to further the ceaseless accumulation of capital.[71] These capitalistic features became more and more apparent in Europe after A.D. 1100 and the mutual existence of feudalism and capitalism was entirely possible up until about 1350. All of this took place within an inter-city-state system, before any sort of crisis caused one type of logic (the capitalist one) to dominate the other (the feudal one). Similar to the inter-state system that came into existence later, there was constant competition in the Middle Ages due to the "absence of a unicentric polity, that is, the existence of a multicentric political structure over most its space" (Mandalios 1996:283). In recognizing the importance of the political nature of the city-state system, together with the existing economic system of merchant capitalism (e.g., Epstein 1993), one disarms the criticism that a world-systems analysis entails "viewing political processes as epiphenomenal in relation to economic causation" (Zolberg 1981:255).

For Hicks, "the fact that European civilization has passed through a city-state phase is the principal key to the divergence between the history of Europe and the history of Asia" (1969:38). In focusing on the European medieval inter-city-state system, I do not wish to homogenize the European town because it existed in different forms (Delumeau 1998). But it should be emphasized that all over Europe, the cities at some point reached a very high degree of autonomy, sometimes independence, ruled by a small minority of their population—their elites (Prevenier 2002)—resulting in a patriciate (Stouff 1992; Boone 2005:12). This is what distinguishes them from, for example, Chinese (Deng 1999:108, 199) or Islamic cities (Udovitch 1993:792; Labib 1974:237; Abulafia 1987:405), where merchants could not acquire significant political and military power to the same degree.

True, the inter-city-state system of the 12th to the 15th centuries had more interregional trade characteristics (Holbach 1993b) than the predominantly local, autarchic productions that characterized Europe prior to the 12th century or the more international flows that would shape the world-economy in the 16th century. But one should not forget that "many aspects of the commercial exploitation of property that have been identified for the early sixteenth century had interesting equivalents two centuries earlier, at a time when the volume of commerce was probably greater" (Britnell 1998:115).[72] Therefore, I

---

71. It is the *combination* of these features that constitutes a capitalist system. Profits derived from surplus value are *not* necessarily "of greater historical significance" (Heilbroner 1985:66) than those derived from unequal exchange. Mollat spells out the similarity between 16th- and 14th-century profits: "The intensity and the frequency are new during the 16th century, not the phenomena themselves" (1977:I:45). Or as Mauro notes: "As far as financial, commercial and industrial techniques is concerned, nothing new happens after 1500. The difference is the multiplication of phenomena" (1988:758). See Lopez (1952:320), Bratianu (1944:57), and Jehel (1993:438–440).

72. Therefore, "the assumption that English society was commercializing more rapidly [in the 16th century] than during earlier centuries" (Britnell 1998:115) has to be abandoned. One should

suggest analyzing the qualitative shifts that occurred in Europe in the 12th century and the shaping of the political inter-city-state system within the mostly interregional trade networks, as it was these factors that eventually resulted in the 16th century emergence of the capitalist world-economy, one which had an interstate system with international—indeed intercontinental—trade networks.[73]

In acknowledging that the commercial specialization between the 12th and 14th centuries was a feature of regional development (Britnell 1995:16, 24) and of growing regional markets, which can in turn be linked to processes of state formation (Malanima 1983, 1986), I suggest looking to regional studies (e.g., Derville 1996; TeBrake 1985; De Wachter 1996; Terlouw 1996; and others) to help situate and analyze the emergence of capitalism within the Middle Ages (Morimoto 1994:17). Drawing on the Brenner approach, one can also investigate the extent to which class formations constantly changed over time and when, during the Middle Ages, the juridical basis of economic power within the feudal logic gradually became less significant and capital accumulation became the logic of an increasing number of merchant-entrepreneurs. Another very important and related issue is the correlation between the power of a certain area's nobility vis-à-vis its peasants and the location of that area within the geographic, socioeconomic, and geopolitical realities of the early modern European region.[74]

---

note that the rural population of England and France was potentially greater in circa 1300 than in the early 18th century (Titow 1961:218; Delatouche 1989:36; Bois 2000:65). The volume of trade prior to the outbreak of the plague in the mid-14th century should not be underestimated, *even when compared with* the early 16th century. Scholars may make much of the banking activities of the Medici in the late 15th century, but the capital at their disposal—their economic power—was clearly inferior to that of the Peruzzi of the early 14th century. This is also reflected in the fact that "their employees numbered well below those of the Peruzzi and were not much more numerous than those of the Acciaivoli, the third ranking bank in the pre-plague period" (Lopez and Miskimin 1962:424–425).

73. The qualitative shift from an inter-city-state system to an inter-state system cannot be separated from the creation of a capitalist world-economy. Within the emerging European nation-states, the merchant class not only aspired to occupy crucial posts in the bureaucracy and the administration (e.g., Prak 1992:192; Galland 1998; Glete 2000:64; Dumolyn 2001), but it regularly used the (mercantile) state's strength to support its own colonial and capitalist strategies all over the world, as these practices were rooted in the policies of medieval city-states (e.g., Baratier 1970:338; Lopez 1970:347). Although it is not true that the phenomenon of city-states is unique to Europe (as is claimed by Bauer and Matis 1988:92)—since they can be found elsewhere, such as on the littoral of the Indian Ocean throughout the Middle Ages (Lombard 1988:15; Curtin 1984:121)—it was only in Europe that merchants managed to retain such political power in the transition to an interstate system (Rodinson 1970:32). This explains the emergence of medieval Western Europe capitalist societies "that had been constructed on the resources accumulated within international commercial networks" (Berza 1941:430).

74. In 13th-century Britain, peasants could run away from the land that they lived on to escape a nobleman's oppression. But as Britnell (1993:75) points out, this implied "exchanging the likelihood

It seems clear that the medieval inter-city-state system (12th–15th centuries) had a specific political framework: local authorities (i.e., the oligarchy—essentially a commercial capitalist class from A.D. 1200 onward; Derville 1997:125; Boone 1997:44) created deliberate poverty-relief policies that kept in check the poor, who often "were not willing to jeopardize their miserable allowance" (Blockmans and Prevenier 1978:56), thus maintaining them in a perpetual state of dependence (Gonthier 1978:340).[75] It is not surprising then that in urban revolts "we find among the ringleaders craftsmen in well defined categories who had suffered loss of income or status . . . it was not paupers who led the fray but groups with a certain level of prosperity which they felt was threatened" (Blockmans and Prevenier 1978:56–57; see Rotz 1976). Indeed, the aforementioned governmental policy of the urban merchant elite determined the urban workers' maximum salaries. With regard to cloth production (the economic backbone of city-states in the Low Countries), the "magistrate worked hand in glove with the entrepreneurs" (Brand 1992:17; see Jansen 1982:176 or Van der Wee 1975:208), determining a wage that was to the advantage of the employers (Prevenier 1978:418). The same is also true in the Italian city-states (Mollat 1986:200) and in some German city-states (Halaga 1983; von Stromer 1991:44).[76] In most of Holland, the established elite succeeded in preventing the guilds from becoming powerful pressure groups; Count William III even forbade the formation of guilds in 1313 (Brand 1992:25).[77]

---

of economic security for the certainty of insecurity [since] even if he was sore pressed by the exactions of his lord, custom would normally ensure that a hereditary tenant could feed his family from year to year. To abandon that hereditary right was to commit himself to a life dependent upon wage-earning." While such actions were risky in 13th-century England, they were less risky in 13th-century Flanders where the socioeconomic and geopolitical reality of the peasants living in proximity to the urban core was very different. The far-reaching division of labor in Flanders and the employment of large numbers of skilled and unskilled workers (especially in the textile industries) significantly lowered the risk for peasants as far as rural migration to the city (and wage-labor) was concerned. This in turn had an impact on the power of the nobility. One can then question the extent to which English peasants' opportunities were altered according to the hierarchical core–periphery relation between, for instance, England and the Low Countries in the 13th century on the one hand, and the change in England's socioeconomic and geopolitical position within the early modern European region in the 15th century on the other (see infra). The same question can be raised regarding the freedom of peasants in Eastern Europe and the urban core of the Low Countries from the 14th to the 17th centuries (see supra).

75. This "social policy was clearly inspired not by Christian charity but by those of capitalist enterprise . . . public poor relief controlled the relative surplus of population in the towns and exercised supervision of the labor-market" (Blockmans and Prevenier 1978:56). Cf. Soly (1975:584–597) and Maréchal (1984).

76. In France, the existence of a merchant oligarchy that had taken economic and judicial control over multiple French cities can already be observed in the writings of Philippe de Beaumanoir in 1283 (Bove 2004:21).

77. A common feature in the 13th century was "a steady multiplication and fragmentation of guilds, [which was] deliberately fostered in places (Venice, Siena) by a calculated merchant policy to divide

The strict wage policies in the textile industry were not surprising; it was precisely because of the fierce competition in the regional and international markets that the only effective way to make a profit was to keep wages down while increasing production (Carrère 1976:489). This was done by exploiting the fullers and to a lesser extent, the weavers, who even in periods of economic upturn could hardly make ends meet (Brand and Stabel 1995:203–204, 219; Boone and Brand 1993).[78] In general, the medieval working class was a readily

---

and rule" (Jones 1997:250). According to Brand, drapers in the Dutch city of Leiden "were the only people with sufficient capital to purchase raw materials, pay wages and to run some risks [while] spinning, carding, combing, fulling and dyeing were done mostly by unskilled laborers. . . . First, the producers, descendants of the circle of small independent artisans, managed to climb to the position of merchant and capitalist. Second, some traders began to control production directly and thus became capitalist industrial entrepreneurs. Wealthy artisans focused on the concentration of labor, i.e. they invested in central workshops where laborers were put to work for low wages in order to market the final product at the lowest possible price. But entrepreneurs centralized production and divided it into a broad spectrum of treatments. Since the various stages of production could be done by relatively simple means, and much of the work was done within the family, investments were low. This system had many advantages for the drapers and strengthened their power over the part manufacturers; it was also a result of the differentiation of tasks which resulted in little mutual solidarity among the waged laborers, so that any attempt to revolt could easily be suppressed . . . the entrepreneurs (industrial capitalists working in close co-operation with the urban government) frustrated the emancipation of artisans by way of the putting out system and a repressive wage policy. The artisans' way to the market was cut off and they were robbed of any possibility of organizing in politically influential guilds" (1992:26–32). Howell (1986) incorrectly classifies the textile industry in Leiden as "small commodity production" (Brand 1996:169–180). The suggestion that small commodity production was supported by some urban elites who preferred a "moral community" (DuPlessis and Howell 1982:80) over profits and capitalist relations, hinges upon the erroneous dismissal of subcontracting on the one hand, and the view that corporatism would somehow be antithetical to merchant capitalism on the other (Lis and Soly 1997b:12–17; Derville 1987b:723; von Stromer 1991:35–38; Schneider 1955:404). Merchant capital's control of the "productive sphere" (Heers 1965:66–68) was more impressive in the early modern period than some are willing to admit (e.g. Bois 2000:201).

78. "In the Low Countries, textile guilds had very limited powers in controlling the supply and cost of their inputs, including labor, and thus in setting most wages. Furthermore, their price-setting powers were limited, since they could not prevent competition in their major markets" (Munro 1990:44). "The so-called weaver-guild was in reality an association dominated by master weavers who, as the chief industrial entrepreneurs, organized production by a domestic putting-out system. Most of their employees were unprotected, defenseless females whose piecework wages the weaver-drapers controlled without difficulty" (Munro 1994b:383–384). Not only merchant-entrepreneurs, but even some 14th-century German city-states (ruled by the commercial elite) acted as "Verleger" in employing poor unemployed women as textile workers (von Stromer 1989:877). The drapers' employees were subject to the regulation of the urban industrial "police," who guaranteed the quality of the product (Yante 1984:432). The raw materials were owned, and the work directed by businessmen, making the day laborers little more than the kind of proletarian factory workers of the 19th century (Gutmann 1988:28–29). Effective resistance by the working poor within the city-states was difficult though violent strikes did occur (Boone, Brand, Prevenier 1993). According to Geremek, "the cost of raw materials and the instability of the market, coupled with increasingly complicated technology demanding specialized skills and an extensive division of labor, often forced the craftsmen to submit and work for the merchants and entrepreneurs who organized production" (1994:64–65). In addition, many workers had no control

available pool of (often seasonal) extra labor, exploited when it was seen fit to do so. Furthermore, it was a labor pool whose numbers increased thanks to child labor:

> Journeymen worked in shops that had a number of boys or girls [working] for meals and a place to sleep at night. These children served also to remind the journeymen that they had competition for work, especially in the unskilled trades. (Epstein 1991:120)

Although many children performed low-skilled work in the textile industry because they were easily exploitable, many women—although this was not an absolute—were also relegated to the bottom of the occupational hierarchy (cf. Pelizzon 1999). A 12th century text by Chrétien de Troyes clearly reflects the complaints expressed by young female textile workers about their working conditions:

> We will always weave silken cloth, and be no better clad thereby; we will always be poor and naked, and we will always be hungry and thirsty; never will we be able to earn enough to be better fed. We have only a very scanty supply of bread: not much in the morning, and less in the evening, for from the work of our hands each of us will never have any more than four deniers out of each pound to live on; and from this we cannot have enough food and clothing, for she who earns twenty sous in a week is in no way at the end of her troubles. And here we are in poverty, and he for whom we toil is rich from our earnings. We stay up large part of the night and every day we work to earn our bread . . . we suffer so much shame and harm that we cannot tell you the fifth part of it. (Ackerman et al. 1977:88–89)[79]

Some 13th-century merchants were also able to concentrate their power in the workplace (Hodgett 1972:137–156; cf. Derville 1972:360–361); they bought the raw materials to make cloth, controlled and supervised its fabrication, and preoccupied themselves with the selling of the finished product in the marketplace (Haquette 1997:882).[80] It should be noted that capitalism not only

---

over the price of primary resources (wool), since it had to be imported from distant countries. (In the case of Flanders, it first came from England and Scotland, and eventually, Spain.)

79. For the complex sexual division of labor in the Middle Ages, see Howell (1997), Kowaleski (1995:153–154), and Stabel (1999).

80. This also occurs in late 14th-century Holland (Kaptein 1998:43) and 13th-century England, where entrepreneurs "bought wool and had it washed and dyed; they gave it out to carders and spinners; they employed weavers and fullers throughout the town, under stringent supervision,

intensified in the cloth industry of the Low Countries, but also in the Italian city-states that were competing in the expanding European market,[81] which in turn was part of a larger world-economic system (Abu-Lughod 1989:356–361).

---

at piece-rates fixed by themselves; and they sold the finished cloth at the great fairs of eastern England" (Miller and Hatcher 1995:112). In a study on trade in Exeter, Kowaleski points out that "a closer look at the commercial relationship between cloth merchants and cloth workers suggests that the capitalist clothier so common in the 16th and 17th centuries had begun to emerge by the late 14th century" (1995:150). Indeed, even small English towns such as Stratford-upon-Avon were affected by the international textile trade: "the monks of Winchcombe Abbey, who held three manors within easy carting distance from Stratford, contracted to sell the wool of their whole estate in the early 14th century to Italian merchants" (Dyer 1997:56–57). According to Lis and Soly, in 14th-century Cologne and Florence the "overwhelming majority" of weavers were working directly or indirectly as subcontractors for wealthy merchant-weavers who "controlled all stages of the production process" (1994:372–373; see also Favier 1998:185). The practice was also widespread in Flanders and Brabant (Lis and Soly 1997:229). In late 14th-century England, the practice of dyers working for merchants (or weavers and fullers for local gentry and clergy) *on a contractual and subcontractual basis* was quite widespread. The resulting "dependence of cloth workers on wages or payments from clients who contracted for their labor [through task work or piece work]" (Kowaleski 1995:153) is striking. The practice of subcontracting not only took place in the textile and construction industries (Small 1989), but was also extended by the Italian city-states into the realm of warfare (France 1999:134).

81. Strengthened by larger profit margins, the greater firms swallowed up the smaller, reducing many petty masters and independent craftsmen to the penniless status of wage-workers, proletarian *sottoposti*. And as the workforce expanded, terms of employment hardened. "Under the pressure (or pretext) of competition, working hours, including night hours, were stretched to the limits of endurance, wage rates lowered to what in many places by the 14th century was near starvation level, and wage earnings depressed by payment in debased coin or by truck in overvalued goods, and by loans and pay advances which tied workers to employers as much as peasants to landlords by rigid bonds of poverty and debt" (Jones 1997:251; see Ferguson 1962:271–272). Fullers in 14th-century Ghent were mostly paid by the piece (Boone and Brand 1993:173), as were wool combers and carders in 13th-century Genoa (Epstein 1988b:120) and weavers in 13th-century London (Britnell 1993b:369). This, of course, made their income unstable since it was subject to economic conjunctures and price fluctuations (van Uytven 1982:208; Derville 2002:106). In 14th-century Florence, one can also see "the contours of the 'modern' wage laborers emerge: people who are neither artisans, nor serfs, but employed en masse, interchangeable, controlled by a foreman, and 'free' to sell their physical strength for a paycheck. Their contemporaries did not call them salaried workers but instead labeled them Ciompi to indicate their miserable condition" (Stella 1989:544). The lowest social strata of the agricultural workforce were no better off than the urban proletariat, since landless laborers were also "dependent only on wage income: . . . sawyers were employed on a flat daily-wage and at a piece-rate paid per 'hundred' feet of board sawn" (Clark 1991:234). Although most studies focus on the exploitation of urban-based wage laborers who often constituted a majority of the population within the city limits (Luzzatto 1954:135; Sosson 1979:232), wage labor in the countryside was anything but exceptional; in 14th-century England, "the proportion of people who obtained most of their living from wage work must have exceeded a third of the whole country, rising to two-thirds in parts of the east" (Dyer 1989:213). Only after the Black Death did wages go up (Gavitt 1981), although this increase should not be exaggerated (Perroy 1964:244–245; Brucker 1972:161; Bois 2000:98, 136) since most workers continued to spend at least half of their wages on bread (Ashtor 1970:19–20); a considerable increase in purchasing power was only notable among the more skilled workers (Sosson 1979:259, 268).

   In addition, due to the restructuring of markets and a deliberate policy of the entrepreneurs, capital was constantly "reallocated from urban centers to the countryside (Heers 1963:121–124; Saey and Verhoeve 1993:107) as the latter "offered more abundant and cheaper part-time agricultural labor, with a lower cost of living, virtually tax-free production, and an escape from specific guild and urban regulations" (Munro 1994b:378; see Geremek 1994:116).[82] This capital reallocation (i.e., investments in the countryside), which continued unabatedly up to the 16th century (e.g., Prevenier, Sosson, and Boone 1992:164–166), also caused increased investments in technology such as wind and water mills, the use of which was often opposed by urban guilds (van Uytven 1976:93).[83] This "shift to lower wage zones and the possibility of further intra regional diversification" (Van der Wee 1993:205–208) was generally in direct competition with the urban proletariat (Brand and Stabel 1995:220), causing the guilds of larger towns such as Brussels and Ypres to organize futile "warlike expeditions to destroy looms in the rural areas around the towns" (Van der Wee 1993:209).[84] The guilds, however, were only able to eliminate

---

82. Holbach notes: "Labor costs were the main motive for the relatively early transfer of weaving into the countryside. The transplantation of labor intensive tasks to cheaper centers of production intensified in the late Middle Ages [and] jeopardized the economy of the older centers.... In drawing the countryside's resources into the production process, 'putting-out' presented (merchant and wealthy artisan) entrepreneurs with considerable competitive advantages. Older cloth towns could lose jobs to the countryside [while] entrepreneurs had more elbow room and could always transfer production to other places in order to evade unpleasant stringent regulation" (1993:238–243). According to Stabel, "average wages in the countryside were only 60 to 70% of those in the towns of the same region" (1997:131). Van der Wee (1998) notes there may be a correlation between increasing "reallocation" processes in the Low Countries and the implementation of an "import-substitution" strategy in 14th-century England; as the island was transformed from a raw producer of woolens for the Low Countries' textile industry to a producer of textiles, there was an increase in competition and a subsequent need to reduce wages within the Low Countries. Nevertheless, not all "production sites" were reallocated to the countryside since urban locations offered some advantages: e.g., better coordination and supervision of the specialized labor required for high quality luxury cloth; urban financing (Munro 1990:45); and lower transaction costs (if the textiles were made in an entrepot like Bruges—an entrepot/"gateway city" crucial for the international trade flow into the Flemish urban network (Stabel 1995, 1997)—and linked directly with the international market.

83. According to Pacey, "By 1250–1300, the foundations had already been laid for the later technological ascendancy of Europe" (1978:39). These technological innovations and techniques (e.g., mechanical fulling displacing labor power where water power was available) became widespread in the early 14th century (Carus-Wilson 1952:410–411; Heers 1965:64) and their socioeconomic implications should not be underestimated. In 14th-century England (pop. 6 million), there was a mill for every 400 to 600 people; in 14th-century France (pop. 17.6 million) it was 440 persons per mill (Langdon 1997:284–285). For the impact of wind and water mills on textile production in the Low Countries, see van Uytven (1971).

84. In the Low Countries, only Ghent was successful in controlling its immediate rural hinterland (Thoen 1992:56–57; Boone 1990:191–197). For an overview of military expeditions organized by urban militias against the competing drapery production in the countryside, see Nicholas (1971:75–116, 203–221).

competition from those rural surroundings located within a radius of a couple of miles (Thoen and Verhulst 1986:54).[85]

The expansion of a putting-out (Verlag) system beyond the town walls was primarily characteristic of labor-intensive tasks like combing, carding, and wool spinning (Holbach 1993:235–236). While many urban-centered industries eventually managed to adapt to the changing socioeconomic situation—for instance, by specializing in higher quality products—(Munro 1977:231), it is likely that in several cities (especially those that had no right to store grain), the wages of many unskilled and unorganized workers remained structurally insufficient (Sosson 1979; de la Roncière 1982:381–461; Blockmans 1983:88). For most urban-based unskilled wage laborers, the fear of massive "downsizing avant la lettre" and long-term unemployment was also a daily reality (Jones 1997:253). Clearly the cities' dependence on the market for textiles made them vulnerable to social unrest, especially given the "unbending interests of exploitative capitalism" (Mackenney 1987:29). Not surprisingly then, social explosions could be sudden and extremely violent during periods of economic recession (Milis 1989:68; Cohn 2004). Thanks to inflation, the social discontent in urban centers was specifically focused on wages (Epstein 1991:116; Prevenier 1998:83; Munro 1979:111) and workplace abuses such as the length of the work day (Geremek 1968:103–104) and the truck system (Munro 2003:2002).[86] Occasionally, the protests even took the form of vague socialist and communist

---

85. The way Ypres and Ghent terrorized their hinterlands in the early 14th century in order to protect their cloth production monopoly resembles Wallerstein's core–periphery model (Prevenier 1997:196). The Italian city-states were generally the most successful at subjugating and dominating their rural hinterlands, the contado (Stabel 1997:73; Redon 1994), although the same can be said about cities with a "vignoblium," the equivalent of a "territorium" (Le Goff 1998:238–239). But since, within a hierarchical division of labor, the countryside was subordinate to the city-state, and since the city-state enforced its virtual monopoly on the distribution of goods to urban and rural populations alike (Stabel 1992:352), the rural industries were at times more complementary to rather than competitive with their urban counterparts. Undesirable work, such as tanning, was often performed in the countryside because of the "annoying smells and pollution generated by the process" (Kowaleski 1995:160). At the same time, one should consider the extent to which the so-called upper class (*buitenpoorterij* or *bourgeoisie foraine*; i.e., people who migrated from the city—whilst retaining their citizenship—to the countryside or wealthy countrymen desiring citizenship) strengthened (juridically, socioeconomically, and politically) the city's control over its surrounding hinterland (Thoen 1988a:480–490; 1988b:448–449; Boone 1996:715–725) and similarly, the extent to which the "landowning rural membership of an urban guild linked the town with the political life of its hinterland" (Carpenter 1997:63). By the mid-15th century, about one in four inhabitants residing in the Flemish countryside had obtained this status.

86. In 14th-century Paris, artisans worked up to sixteen or seventeen hours per day in the summer and around eleven hours in the winter (Geremek 1968:81), a very harsh work regime indeed. "Social strife was rampant and workers attempted to increase their salary or reduce the length of their working day. In Paris and Auxerre workers in the textile industries or in the wineries stopped working at the agreed-upon signal and organized strikes, but mostly in vain" (Rossiaud 1998:470). English workers were expected to "be at their posts before 5 am, take breaks of no more than two hours in total, and remain at work until 7 or 8 in the evening" (Woodward 1994:14). See Yante

aspirations, as when the weavers and fullers of Valenciennes in 1225 deposed the government, despoiled the plutocrats and declared a commune (Carus-Wilson 1952:399).[87]

According to Pirenne (1939:226–245), the 14th century brought about something of a revolutionary climate. Thanks to its trade connections, Flemish radical doctrines spread and influenced Wat Tyler's movement in England at the end of the 14th century (Pirenne 1947:199). Although some of Pirenne's writings have been meticulously questioned in the last twenty years,[88] it is hard to deny the significance of the social strife related to living and working conditions in the Middle Ages (Roux 1994:102–117).[89] The Ciompi revolt in Florence is probably the most renowned revelation of the deep social and political grievances (Hay and Law 1989:249–251; Stella 1993) and the popular

---

(1990:372), Boone and Brand (1993:184), and Rosser (1997:27), but also Holbach (1993:229) and the literature cited therein.

87. The most violent demonstrations occurred in economically advanced cities: Douai in 1245, Arras in 1253, Genoa in 1258 and 1276, Siena in 1257, Ypres in 1280, Viterbo in 1281, Bologna in 1289, and Florence in 1293–1295. Interestingly, most protests were located in Flanders and northern Italy (Mackenney 1987:2; Pirenne 1963:94–109; Leguai 1976).

88. For example, Despy and Verhulst (1986).

89. Britnell points out that, as far as medieval England was concerned, one should "reject the supposition that standards of living improved for the whole population between 1180 and 1330. . . . The subdivisions of holdings and competition for employment pushed living standards downwards for the poorest families. Piece rates deteriorated during the period of commercial growth between about 1270 and 1320 [while] the merchant class was larger and wealthier in 1330 than in 1180" (1993:125–126). This is precisely what occurs on a *global scale* in today's capitalist world-economy: a minority's (located in the core) standard of living increases, while the majority in the periphery faces relatively more poverty and deprivation. This is no coincidence. Between 1100 and 1350, those parts of England that were peripheral to the urban nexus in the Low Countries provided the core with grain on a regular basis (Adams 1994:147). Some scholars even describe England as having been an economic colony (Rosenberg and Birdzell 1986:76; Cazel 1966:110; Van Houtte 1974:392) since it was essentially "underdeveloped, a primary producer, lacking the expertise and infrastructure to process its rich natural resources effectively" (Raban 2000:56; see Munro 2000:108). It was only after "import substitution" took place in the late 14th century (Ashtor 1992:VIII:17) that its textile production for the international market increased, while its wool exports gradually decreased (Gutmann 1988:36; Prevenier 1973:494–495; see Ramsay (1974) for this transformation). Another important example from the late 14th century onward was how the urban core of the Low Countries turned to the Iberian Peninsula to sell more of its textiles (Verlinden 1976:110) and to extract raw materials (wool) for these industries (Van Houtte 1974:392). This had profound implications for the Iberian Peninsula's socioeconomic development; in Castile, 1.5 million sheep were estimated to have produced wool circa 1350, while a century later the number was 2.7 million (Favier 1996:181) and by circa 1500 it was about 10.5 million (Alonso 1997:65). Thus considerable parts of Spain supplied raw materials, which the Genoese and Flemish industries "turned into profitable products marketable elsewhere" (Fernández-Arnesto 1987:115). For Castile, this eventually brought about "a colonial economic structure characterised by the sale abroad of raw materials, the most important of which was wool [while] economic growth did not entail a significant expansion in the production of finished products" (MacKay 1977:170).

element in those revolts is undeniable (Mollat and Wolff 1973:7). For Lestocquoy (1952:131–137), the social struggles and the "egalitarian social visions"
(Howell and Boone 1996:322) that emerged in the second half of the 13th
century resemble those of the period 1830 to 1848.[90] The existence of "class
consciousness" should not be dismissed either (Prevenier 2002).

The effect of international competition due to market pressures was very
real, ultimately inducing the urban textile centers to shift their production to
more exclusive luxury goods (for which demand was less elastic), while the
countryside took over the role of producing the lower-quality bulk products
(Stabel 1997:144; Abraham-Thisse 1993b:172–173). However, the question
remains: To what extent was the 14th century "international urban network"
(Bartlett 1993:176) truly integrated (Stabel 1997:72), when traces of "inter-
urban specialization" could already be found (Van der Wee 1975:205)? Regional
economies were certainly interconnected (Masschaele 1997; Kowaleski 1995;
Wolff 1995:65), while concurrently, regional "identities" were in the making
(Babel and Moeglin 1997). International trade was also becoming more important.[91] What remains to be explored, however, is the degree to which the
economies of scale and economic differentiation in the Middle Ages had a
considerable impact on uneven regional development *in the long run* (Ashtor

---

90. With regard to the "social struggle" in the medieval Ages, Heers (1963:315) warns us not
to interpret the warring factions as the expression of social classes. Indeed, like all other social
constructs, the emerging bourgeoisie should not be treated as a static phenomenon but as a
class in the process of perpetual re-creation and hence, one which constantly changes its form
and composition (Wallerstein 1979:224, 286). While the social strife of the Middle Ages cannot
be simplified as class warfare between the urban "proletariat" and the "bourgeoisie", as if they
were homogeneous entities (Prevenier 1988:57; Heers 1974:647), and given that workers did
not perceive themselves solely in terms of "social and economic distinctions" (Rosser 1997), it
is undeniable that the "social issue," symbolized by the serious tensions between the lower and
higher social strata, was extremely important (Jordan 1998:132–133) since "the dependence of city
economies to international markets made their stability sensitive to external disturbances" (Britnell
1991:29). For a recent useful overview of urban rebellions in medieval Flanders, cf. Dumolyn and
Haemers (2005).

91. It should be emphasized that Western European city-states not only had to import their
foodstuffs from increasingly greater distances, but that the urban industries also often depended
on long-distance trade to provide them with vital "supplies of wool, cotton, silk, alum and dyestuffs"
(Britnell 1991:29; see Heers 1958). One example is the English wool produced for the textile
industries in the Low Countries and the Lombard towns (Lloyd 1977). "To take a single commodity:
by the opening of the 14th century lords and peasants were directly or indirectly selling abroad the
wool of over seven million sheep" (Campbell 1995b:553). In the following years, "the demand for
English wool increased" (Lopez 1952:329), while from the 15th century onward more wool from
Spain and the Balkans was imported concurrent with the demand of the Northern Italian industries
(Van Houtte 1974:392–393). The existence of medieval villages specialized in the production
of ceramics that were in turn exported hundreds of kilometers also testifies to the remarkable
specialization and expanding interregional if not "international" division of labor (Chapelot and
Chapelot 2000:124–125,138–139).

1978b; 1983:375–433, Mokyr 1990:44 or Meyer 1981:66).[92] Exploring the long-term impact of the inter-city-state system on the evolution of Western European economic history is a necessary endeavor. Ultimately the medieval city, existing "in the margins of the feudal system" (D'Haenens 1982:42) with its "division of labor and its impulses on the monetary economy brought about a fermentation process in the feudal mode of production that destroyed it in the long run" (Le Goff 1998:15; see Dobb 1947:70; Tuma 1979:89). The medieval city therefore needs to be understood because it is a crucial variable in the long-term history of Western Europe.[93]

Tentative Conclusions

Like later nation-states (Giddens 1981:12, 148), medieval cities were essential to the development of capitalism (Crone 1989:167). In my view, it was the city-states' political system(s) that had a crucial impact on long-term European socioeconomic processes; it was these political systems that enabled capitalism to grow, thrive, and ultimately expand into a world-economy. Therefore, it is necessary to recognize the importance of early modern cities as the "power

---

92. Cf. the critical tone of Abulafia (1997:36–39), Galloway (1977), Epstein (1991b:50), and Day (1981), and the tentative conclusions of Balard (1998).

93. In referring to an inter-city-state system, I do not wish to downplay the importance of the countryside in the Middle Ages or in the 'transition debate' (Hoppenbrouwers and van Zanden 2001). After all, 80 percent to 90 percent of all Europeans lived there (Bois 2000:138). Although I would not go as far as Szúcs who claimed that "the dense medieval urban network exercised an absolute form of domination over the whole existing socioeconomic structure" (1985:26), it is clear that "the modernization of the commercial infrastructure was only possible after the emergence of European cities who created ever more, new and optimal conditions for an increase of productivity and thus allowed successive series of increasing growth" (Van der Wee 1981:14). Cities are the key to the "international commerce [that] had become an extremely dynamic sector, of a vital importance to the growth of the European economy" (Van der Wee 1981:10). Cities were labeled by some as the "nodes of capitalism" (Rosenberg and Birdzell 1986:47) and the "hot spots of growth in the pre-industrial world" (Horlings 2001:97) since in many regions of Western Europe "a shift of economic emphasis from the countryside to the towns and cities [occurred]" (Tuma 1979:58). Much of the socioeconomic changes in the countryside were, after all, "fueled by urban demand [which] stimulated an intensive and highly commercialized agriculture" (Yun 1994:116; see Menant 1993:293; Derville 2002:96). Without cities, it would not have been feasible or sensible for agricultural producers to specialize and commercialize (Halpérin 1950:32–33; Wrigley 1978:301). Last but not least, it was primarily within cities that capital accumulation took place, since in the countryside "the margin between incomes and outcomes was just too small to leave room for a significant accumulation of capital" (Toch 1986:180). Moreover, the rural nobility spent most of its surplus on urban-based goods or services, thus redirecting a lot of the cash flow back into the city (Spufford 1981:622; Lopez, Miskimin, and Udovitch 1970:98). Ultimately, I have to agree with Rodinson that "the origins of capitalism cannot be explained, as Marxist dogma considered, by means of a unilinear evolution of agrarian relations of production. It is from an essentially urban development that one needs to start" (1978:67).

containers" of the bourgeoisie. The same policies and techniques of domination and exploitation experimented with and implemented by elites in the medieval European city-state system were later used by the elites of nation-states during the 16th and 17th centuries to foster their ceaseless accumulation of capital.

The comparative analysis of European and non-European regions (China, India, and Northern Africa) developed in the following chapters will hopefully bring about new insights on how socioeconomic history was profoundly affected by different political systems. In order to avoid Eurocentric biases, one must stress the impact of medieval non-Europe on Europe (as opposed to the idea that European "medieval development" was nothing but "auto-development" [e.g., Delatouche 1989:26]). At the same time, one has to be somewhat Eurocentric in order to pin down the specifics[94] that contributed to the qualitative shift on the European continent between A.D. 1000 and 1500. This comparison is not meant to imply that other regions were less successful at trade, waging war, or achieving technological innovations throughout the Middle Ages. Nor is it a judgment of these other civilizations. It is, however, an attempt to examine how the convergence of *both* internal and external (thus *relational*) developments can provide a sound analytical basis to explain why and how capitalistic features came into being in certain parts of Europe[95] or West Asia and subsequently spread over the world.

I do not challenge the fact that after 1500, capitalist logic intensified because of the "the great maritime discoveries" (Sée 1928:41)[96] and the subsequent profits based on increased trade and exploitation of "non-Europe."[97] Nor do I deny the emergence of an inter-state system after 1500 or the shifts between different hegemonies (e.g., Arrighi 1994). How then can one accept general concepts of the world-systems analysis and explain the emergence of

---

94. The historical evolution of Europe cannot be "copied" in the Third World, as some modernization theorists would argue.

95. It is only for hermeneutic convenience that I use the word *Europe*.

96. The link between world accumulation in the 16th century and capital accumulation prior to the 16th century has been acknowledged by Frank: "The production and concentration of merchant capital which had originated within the Italian cities proved to be essential to accomplish the voyages of discovery and the creation of the first global commercial network" (1977:32). This nevertheless leaves us with the question: How did these capitalistic features first appear in medieval (Italian) city-states?

97. It is clear that after 1492, "the combined output of central European and American mines supplied the treasuries of western Europe with large quantities of precious metals. The accumulated resources induced them to increase their commercial activities with the East. In due time, the influx of silver, coupled with the high value placed on this specie in the East, enabled Europeans to monopolize the trade of Asiatic countries and subordinate their economies, thereby laying the foundations of European domination and colonialism in the region. This domination ultimately enabled the Europeans to [channel] wealth and resources from every corner of that continent back to Europe" (Bozorgnia 1998:180).

capitalism in the late Middle Ages?[98] If one accepts the fact that merchant capitalism was already maturing in Europe prior to the 16th century, the development of a true *world*-system after 1492 is not empirically challenged. What needs to be rethought and explored is the emergence of capitalism in medieval Europe before it expanded into a world-economy. This emergence could be seen in the exploitation of wage labor; class struggles; the reallocation of capital; the exploitation of a peripheral countryside by an urban core; the substitution of labor power with technological inventions (e.g., wind and water mills) in order to minimize labor costs and further the endless accumulation of capital; the commoditization of the material world; and the rationalization of the spiritual world. In short, modern features of contemporary capitalism found their roots in the Middle Ages. "As the high Middle Ages unfolded, European societies experienced impressive rates of economic growth in terms of real GDP per capita" (Snooks 1996:305). And it was precisely within the urban nexus of medieval Western Europe that this self-sustained economic growth was accomplished (van Uytven 1987:127).[99]

Such recurring growth was not, however, an isolated phenomenon located within one city-state and its countryside; to claim that Western Europe managed to create some kind of take-off solely due to its internal features would be a gross exaggeration. The presence of a large number of industrial activities such as mining, textile production, glass-making, shipbuilding, and so forth throughout the whole urban nexus (i.e., Southern England, the Low Countries, parts of France and Germany, and Northern Italy) substantially enhanced "the demand for both foodstuffs and land" (Hatcher 1969:217) and thus created the possibility for deepening interregional trade networks (Richard 1974;

---

98. This must be done without using the extreme form of holism embodied in Frank's post-1990 research. When he claims that "our world system began thousands of years earlier," he does not seem to realize that while most of the historians he is quoting in his lengthy review talk about trade linkages prior to A.D. 1500, they do not claim that the Eurasian market "rested on a truly international division of labor with a unified monetary system" (Frank 1990:165, 197).

99. For Blockmans (1997:30), the 11th century is the moment that brings about recurring growth: "The eleventh century gave Europe a new face and set in place a dynamic which was never interrupted and is still maintained on a global scale. . . . The continuous growth of production and of population, together with the formation of states and the development of a capitalist market economy, started in that period. In some areas these developments took place earlier than in others, but the trend was established. . . . Here and there there was stagnation and regression, but the dynamic of the system continued to be operative over the long term, and still is." Blockmans presents convincing evidence in his magnum opus on the longue durée. What is problematic, however, is his Eurocentrism. In dealing with ten centuries of European history, Blockmans hardly pays any attention to other civilizations or even to the issue of colonization, a neglect he legitimizes by stating that "with the exception of the effects of Arabic science in southern Spain and Sicily during the Middle Ages, influences from outside Europe only became decisive in the twentieth century" (1997:30). Given that this was written in the late 1990s, it is an extreme "internalist" position.

Weczerka 1982).[100] Therefore the growth of its urban economies cannot be properly understood without capturing the vital importance of the international long-distance trade between Europe and non-Europe, as Abu-Lughod (1989) pointed out.[101] Nor can one separate the ceaseless accumulation of capital in the core from the creation of multiple peripheries (colonial or neo-colonial overseas territories that provided cheap labor, raw materials, and markets). Furthermore, although "economists have customarily excluded fraud and coercion because we have thought that they are not empirically significant elements in the ordinary economic transactions of an enterprise economy" (Stigler 1982:24)—which would explain why "economists generally loath contemplating the uses of violence in the economic sphere [as] there seems to be a feeling that it cannot be a 'true' or 'fundamental' basis for any sustained economic gain" (Findlay 1992:159)—the *historical reality* of capitalism proves otherwise.[102]

As I have attempted to demonstrate, the modernization theory, orthodox Marxism, Brennerism, and world-systems analysis all have certain problems with regard to explaining the emergence of capitalism in the medieval period. A recurrent theme among them is the "backwardness" of the Middle Ages: a stagnant artisan economy, a "feudal system in crisis," waiting to be swept away by modernity disguised as capitalism. This theme often points to the easy, yet misleading, dichotomy of a "feudal" versus a "capitalist" era (Heers 1992:35–36). Unfortunately, as Britnell puts it, the "distinction between medieval and modern times, entrenched in pedagogical tradition since the dawn of formal

---

100. Hatcher's example of medieval ports in England is quite illuminating. Precisely because of their integration into a wider regional economy, they seem to "have weathered the economic storms" of the post-plague period much better than others (1969:226). See Carus-Wilson (1973) for 15th-century Coventry.

101. Because of the expansion of the Pax Mongolica over the Eurasian landmass, the markets expanded for Western European city-states and the division of labor in most of their industries subsequently increased between 1250 and 1350 (Bratianu 1944:38–42; Balard 1983). Nor can the remarkable growth of a commercial city such as Lajazzo, for instance, be separated from the Pax Mongolica (Jacoby 1989a:VIII:148; Racine 1972:202). Only when trade across Eurasia became more difficult after the disintegration of the Pax Mongolica (Nystazopoulou 1973:571) did the Europeans revive attempts to circumnavigate the African continent (Richard 1970:363). The interest in gold and slaves was also crucial to the Portuguese/Genoese efforts to bypass Muslim intermediaries and explore Africa in the 15th century (Phillips 1985:135–136; Favier 1996:198–199; Scammell 1981:164).

102. "Classical trade theory is utterly divorced from the historical realities of slave ships and silver argosies. The international division of labor did not result from the operation of the law of comparative costs because the world's trading nations were *never* equal partners. On the contrary, it was *centuries of unequal exchange* that created a 'chain of subordination' and led to the division of the planet into developed and underdeveloped regions" (Day 1999:114; emphasis added). Thus, "Europe's miracle can not be disentangled from its military and economic domination of more populous quarters of the world" (Reid 1999:1).

history teaching" still exists (1998:113). Instead, one should attempt to look at the Middle Ages without prejudices and see how, why, and to what extent the embryonic forms and features of capitalism came into being, matured, and were capable of transforming themselves in the 16th century. In attempting to comprehend the political and economic structures crucial to explaining the transition, I hope to move beyond the limited focus of the nation-state as unit of analysis (Subrahmanyam 1998:42). Only then will we be able to better comprehend the essential, yet complex, features of the capitalist world-economy in which we live today.

CHAPTER TWO

The Political Economies of China
and Europe Compared

HAVING LEARNED more about medieval Europe, the curious reader will undoubtedly ask: What about China? China has long been regarded as one of the most ancient and glorious civilizations. In the Middle Ages, China was probably the most developed of *all* regions—socioeconomically, politically, and militarily. Around A.D. 1100, it had a population of approximately 100 million people and the largest cities likely had up to a million inhabitants (Elvin 1973:159; Kracke 1969:11). "Medieval China witnessed considerable economic advance" (Hall 1988:22) such that it outshone anything in Europe. The economy certainly had a high level of monetization; for example, usage of paper money (*huizi*) issued in A.D. 1160, written contracts, mercantile credits, checks, promissory notes, bills of exchange, and so forth. Militarily speaking, the Chinese emperor was probably the strongest overlord in the entire Eurasian landmass; in the 12th century, he could easily mobilize nearly 1 million soldiers. In comparison, when at the end of the 12th century, Britain's King Richard I wanted to maintain a "regular army of 300 knights supported by taxation, [his attempt] sank without trace" (French 1999:230) due to insufficient means.

As far as socioeconomic, military, and technological developments were concerned, anyone around in A.D. 1000 comparing medieval China with its European counterpart would have staked his or her bet on China (Lippit 1987:37–38; Deng 2000). China was considered the wealthiest country in the world during the Middle Ages, even by the most extensive travelers (Ibn Battuta in Gibb 1994:814). Yet only 800 years later, it was Europe that dominated the globe politically, militarily, economically, and technologically.

Therefore, the crucial question that needs to be asked is: Was the Chinese empire *incapable* or *unwilling* to develop (socioeconomically, militarily, etc.) in such a way that it might conquer, subordinate, and systematically exploit its peripheries, as was done by Western Europe? For those who are only willing to study Europe in order to understand the emergence of capitalism, this question remains unanswered (e.g., Duplessis 1997; Lachmann 2000; Jorda 2002).[1] To find an answer, one not only has to delve into the structural constraints (e.g., geographical, climatological, demographic, geopolitical) then facing China,[2] but also the agency, political choices, and routes taken by the elites in charge of the Chinese empire when faced with particular internal and external challenges.

The Chinese Socioeconomic Revolution during the Sung Dynasty (circa 900–1280)

The era of the Sung dynasty (A.D. 960–1279) is often labeled "China's greatest age" (Fairbank 1992:88).[3] The scale of trade networks and the multitude of goods exchanged in Asia from 900 to 1280 are dazzling when compared with those of Europe. Long-distance trade from China to India, Indonesia, and even East Africa had been in existence for centuries. During the T'ang dynasty (A.D. 618–907), Chinese nautical technology had developed to such an extent that even the larger Chinese ships (about 550 tons) could trade as far as the Persian Gulf (Ray 1993:111). The exchanged goods at that time, however, were often luxuries such as precious stones, pearls, rhinoceros horns, tortoise-shells, and cowrie shells.[4]

Prior to the 10th century, it was the Arabs who acted as middlemen in the Indian Ocean, but from the 10th century onward, the Chinese took to the seas in

---

1. This Eurocentric approach considerably limits the analysis of scholars (Blaut 1993).

2. Unlike Weber, I do not consider the Chinese religion an explanatory variable. "The attribution of virtually unchanging cultural characteristics as the key to discriminating between China and Europe as regards patterns of long-term economic growth must be ruled out" (Elvin 1988:103; see Elvin 1984).

3. "The best economic performance of the Sung as measured by per capita production was probably not surpassed in China before the 20th century" (Feuerwerker 1992:765). While some assert that the degree of economic expansion during the 16th century surpassed the commercial revolution under the Sung (e.g., Zurndorfer 1988:154; Dixin and Chengming 2000), the former is beyond the temporal scope of this chapter and it is not necessary to elaborate on it in the context of the arguments presented here.

4. Cowrie shells were also widely used as a monetary device in different regions (Labib 1974:236; Jain 1990:157). One crucial question, however, is: When did they make the transition from luxury to bulk goods?

increasing numbers with junks that weighed approximately 200 tons.[5] Although some have suggested that the Chinese merchants in the Indian Ocean during the Sung dynasty mostly transported luxury products (e.g., Lewis 1978:XI:462), it appears that significant amounts of bulk goods such as "rice, porcelain, pepper, lumber, and minerals" were also transported overseas (Shiba 1983:104; Ray 1993:111–126).[6] During the Sung dynasty, joint ventures in shipping and the leasing of vessel services had become "quite common" (Deng 1997:102; Shiba 1970:27, 198–200) and "crude forms of commenda and societas maris" also came into use (Shiba 1983:108). Although the roots of the Sung dynasty's economic boom can be traced back to the late T'ang dynasty (Balazs 1969:16), and although maritime commerce between the Indian Ocean and the Chinese coast had always been of some importance (Aubin 1964), Chinese governmental revenue obtained from the taxes on trade reached an unprecedented peak under the Sung; by the mid-12th century, as much as 20 percent of the state's cash income was derived from a tariff on maritime trade (Chen 1991:217).

With continued improvements in maritime technology during the Sung dynasty (Shiba 1970:5–6) and the Chinese government's decision to embark upon massive shipbuilding programs (Dawson 1972:167), a "major upsurge in trade" occurred (Hall 1985:194) followed by a "change of commodity structure" (Chen 1991:220–221). Under the Sung, people were "gradually induced to turn to commercially oriented farming or to take to nonagricultural pursuits" (Shiba 1975:39). During both the Sung and Yuan (A.D. 1279–1368) dynasties, the production of "immediate material means of subsistence" and the transport

5. During the T'ang dynasty, the Arabs and Persians controlled much of the trade between China and the Indian Ocean (Tibbetts 1957:43) but from the Sung dynasty onward, the larger Chinese merchant ships "dominated the route from India to China" (Chen 1991:221; Dawson 1972:174). Under the Sung and the Yuan, Chinese merchants, "under government aegis, managed to wrest from their Muslim rivals their monopoly in the carriage of cargoes and passengers" (Filesi 1972:10; Lo 1969:24; Needham 1954:I:180). Certainly in Southeast Asia, the role of the Arabs decreased because of the increasing number of Chinese merchants (Morley 1949:154; Hall 1985:196–197). According to Chen, large ships took forty days to get from Canton to Sumatra, and sixty days from there to the Arabian peninsula (1991:220).

6. Within the internal Chinese market (which was itself, as big as the entire European continent), many bulk commodities such as rice, tea, and salt were exchanged over long distances (Golas 1980:299), most likely due to a series of impressive technological innovations that in turn stimulated both market activity and rural productivity (Rawski 1972:96–98). Despite this vast internal market, I focus on the exchange between China and other countries throughout this chapter. In doing so, a comparison can be made with Europe regarding the capture and dominance of international markets crucial to the establishment of a capitalist system. I do not mean to imply that local or regional markets were in any way less significant, but when examining the creation of a capitalist merchant class, one has to focus on the highest levels of profit, i.e., long-distance trade networks (Ptak 1994:35).

of these bulk commodities had become central to overseas trade (Kai 1991:232).[7]

The fact that trade flourished as much as it did was a direct result of the fact that the Imperial government actively fostered it: "An active foreign trade policy was formulated to promote trade relations with overseas countries" (Ma 1971:33). Consequently, "the relationship between the state and the merchant associations during the Sung was more intimate than at any other period in the history of China": "the attitude of the officials towards commerce changed from condemnation to approval" (Ma 1971:90, 125). This was probably related to the fact that although officials "were prohibited from participating in any form of trade, privately many of them engaged in commercial ventures [as] they exploited their specially favorable position and carried on businesses" (Ma 1971:129).[8]

Under the Sung, China's principal wealth was the result of commerce and craftsmanship (Gernet 1982:323). Whereas in the early Sung period revenues were mostly derived from the taxation of agriculture, "after the middle of the Northern Sung period, the state drew an increasing proportion of its revenue from trade" (Shiba 1970:45). By the end of the 12th century, some have estimated that nearly 70 percent of total state revenues were due to indirect taxes on tea, salt, and wine (e.g., Deng 1999:316). Despite the growing might of nomadic incursions (Cartier 1982:495–496), China was not a state subsisting on the extra-economic coercion of its peasantry, but, rather, one attempting to survive by fostering trade. Chinese mercantile activity proliferated during the Sung period when the expansion of trade led to increasing urban development and growing divisions of labor, such as in the mining, porcelain, and salt industries. This urban development and expanding division of labor in turn developed capitalistic features identical to those found in Europe's textile and

---

7. Together with the increasing silk trade (Ma 1999), the trade in porcelains was most likely the main export commodity loaded onto oceangoing ships (Chen 1991:221), although large quantities of perishable foodstuffs were also transported overseas to Japan and Korea (Shiba 1970:88). Archeological studies have demonstrated that large amounts of Chinese porcelain were transported all over the Indian Ocean to India (Ray 1996:67) and the Eastern coasts of Africa (Filesi 1972; Gernet 1982:322), and, thanks to the Pax Mongolica, to Europe (Berza 1941:421) and the Maghreb (Gibb 1994:889).

8. Ma states that because of their position, governmental officials "evaded taxes in business transactions, cornered their commodities, and paid no transportation cost on their goods by using government boats and free labor. They even invested government funds as private capital." Since officials were legally forbidden to partake in any form of business (Dawson 1972:176), it was "common practice to put the ownership of [their] commercial establishments under the names of the official's close relatives or even his servants" (Ma 1971:130, 134). During the Sung dynasty, not only officials but also "members of the court held shares in shipping and manufacturing companies" (Lo 1969:24). In 11th-century Quanzhou, for instance, "local officials traded privately with the merchants" despite the fact that international trade was prohibited in that port (Clark 1995:58).

mining industries, but on a much larger scale (Cheng et al. 1992). This is confirmed by the fact that the commercial activities in Chekiang, Kwantung, and Fukien occurred "on a far larger scale than that of the European countries" (Gernet 1982:326). Accordingly, the standard of living during this period must have been much higher in China than in Europe (Needham 1969:171).[9]

Related to this upsurge in international trade was the growing threat from the nomads, which created a "Sung mercantile policy [that] sought by all means to increase the national wealth through the expansion of trade" (Shiba 1983:110).[10] In this respect then, the Chinese government became very successful; trade with Champa and Srivijaya flourished and commercial contacts with other parts of the world also grew more intense, most notably with Arabia (Chou 1974:103), the Philippines (Hall 1985:227), Southeast Asia (Willmott 1966:23), South Asia (Dawson 1972:174), East Africa (Chittick 1970:99; Wheatley 1959:37; Wheatley 1975), and even Egypt (Scanlon 1970).[11]

It is no coincidence that Chinese naval power was very impressive, if not at its peak, in the 13th and 14th centuries (Lo 1955). This growing power was a direct result of nomadic incursions (Dars 1992:10–11). Since the conquest of Northern China by the Jurchen (1126–1127), the caravan routes through Central Asia were inaccessible (Hall 1985:196) and the Sung were cut off from their "last good Asian pastures." This forced the Chinese government to "compensate for its irreversible shortage of horses by creating a powerful navy" (Smith 1991:306). Thus, it was the growing threat of nomadic incursions that "encouraged the Southern Sung to build a navy in order to man all waterways which stood between them and their northern competitors. This construction produced techniques and skills which proved beneficial to the economy"

---

9. This is not surprising, given the fact that in Sung China "wheat and barley yield/seed ratios were about 10:1, and a good deal better for rice, [while] the typical medieval European yield/seed ratio for wheat was 4:1" (Maddison 1998:31). Chinese agriculture, however, was "persistently self-sustaining" (Maddison 1998:32) while the Europeans, in order to achieve a division of labor, found it expedient to construct a periphery through a systematic colonization process—first within Europe, and later abroad. Moreover, Europe's structural bullion drain to the East (see infra) resulted in a shortage of capital, which often caused high interest rates and in turn, considerably limited agricultural yields (Clark 1988). On the importance of the comparative yield per worker in terms of agricultural output, see Duchesne (2002). Although comparative data are difficult to find, it seems that under the Southern Sung, and probably under the Yuan, labor was commercialized on a larger scale than in Europe (Fu Chu-fu and Li Ching-neng 1956:239–240, 243). For a detailed analysis of Fukien's socioeconomic prosperity, see So (2000).

10. The Southern Sung were particularly dependent on trade to survive (Deng 1999: 314) and because of the threat of nomadic invasions, they "constantly turned for help to the big merchants" (Balazs 1969:19).

11. This trade route was probably used by the Karimi merchants (Di Meglio 1970:107). The amount of medieval Chinese ceramics found on Egyptian soil to this day remains astonishing (Francois 1999), but they can also be found in South India and Sri Lanka (Karashima 2004).

(Hall 1985b:46; Dawson 1972:164). According to Gernet, because China was "blocked in its expansion towards the north and north-west by the great empires which had arisen on its frontiers, the Chinese world turned resolutely to the sea and its center of gravity shifted towards the maritime regions of the south-east" (1982:328; see also Lo 1969:22). The growing threat of the Chin and Mongol invasions forced the Sung government to stimulate trade in order to increase its revenues, thus allowing it to counter military dangers. Given that the buildup of a large cavalry was no longer an option, the Sung had to expand its navy into a formidable force in order to counter the nomadic threat. Another outcome of the state's interest in trade was a decrease in protection and transaction costs (e.g., through the state's building of canals and provision of security within the realm), which then allowed the formation of a national market (Modelski and Thompson 1996:163; Elvin 1996:25) that was capable of achieving intense growth (Curtin 1984:110).

As part of the economic boom (agricultural specialization, commercialization, increasing urbanization, and industrialization) that occurred in the South after 1127, one must also discuss the enormous and unprecedented mass migration from Northern to Southern China in the 12th and 13th centuries (Dars 1992:35; Elvin 1973:113–179) and its effect on the increase in maritime trade (Ebrey 1996:141–144). The prosperity of the South, combined with the nomadic warfare in the North, led to an enormous influx of migrants from North to South (Shiba 1970:181), which in turn increased the demand for all kinds of commodities (Lippit 1987:39) and propelled technological innovations (Jones 1988:77).[12] In 13th-century Fujian, for instance, the regional economy was "transformed from a subsistence economy based on the cultivation of rice and hemp into an export-oriented economy producing luxuries [as well as] a range of finished artisan goods, including stoneware, porcelain, and metal" (Clark 1995:70). The region became so commercialized that rice had to be imported "from areas of surplus production, such as the Jiangnan provinces of the Yangzi River valley and Guangdong" (Clark 1995:70).

Despite the enormous profits that merchants made during the Sung dynasty, the empire remained in firm control of certain sectors of the economy. Trade had become so vital for the survival of the Sung government that the state began to directly interfere with several economic activities. Besides the state's promotion of foreign sea trade in order to open up new markets (Hui 1995:31), bureaucratic agents were sent out "into the countryside to take over

---

12. Because of the massive migration from Northern China, "the sudden increase of population in Southern China, where cultivable lands were limited, had forced people living in the southeast coastal areas to participate in marine trade to earn their living" (Hui 1995:31). The population growth in Southern China is estimated to have grown from about 4 million households in A.D. 750 to nearly 12 million in A.D. 1290, while the population in Northern China fell from about 10.5 million households in A.D. 1110 to below 1 million in A.D. 1235 (Kracke, Jr. 1955:480).

key economic functions—transport, rural credit, wholesale and even retail distribution" (Smith 1991:308). Also, according to Lo:

> During the Sung period, not only did foreign trade flourish under private management, not only did officials and members of the court hold shares in shipping and manufacturing companies, but the government itself operated monopolies in domestic trade and various productive enterprises. (1969:24)

Unlike what was happening in Western Europe, the Sung government controlled profitable industries through the imposition of state monopolies on the most lucrative commodities: salt, liquor, tea, and incense (Shiba 1970:111). The Chinese government "did not allow private enterprise to touch these trades except in areas where it could not itself supervise transport and distribution." Despite this competition from the state, "private traders flourished during the twelfth and thirteenth centuries" (Gernet 1962:77, 81).

It is not an understatement to label the 11th and 12th centuries as an era of Chinese commercial revolution (Fairbank, Reischauer, and Craig 1973:132; Elvin 1978:79), one in which Sung bronze coins had become a widely used monetary standard in the East as well as in large parts of Southeast Asia (von Glahn 1996). This revolution was based on a division of labor, regional specialization, and overseas trade, and was more impressive than anything in Western Europe at that time. In several areas (e.g., Shantung, Hopei, Kiangsu), factories existed that "employed a permanent and specialized labor force. Thus at Likuo, in Kiangsu, there were 3,600 wage-earning workers. These big enterprises worked for the state" (Gernet 1982:320; see Fu Chu-fu and Li Ching-neng 1956:239). Because of its wealth, the Imperial state was a driving force for much of the socioeconomic development; the state "turned itself into a merchant and producer, by creating workshops and commercial enterprises run by civil servants and by systematically developing the state monopolies in order to provide for the maintenance of its armies" (Gernet 1982:323). The state, for example, propelled the production of weapons, coinage, and construction materials, leading to an immense increase in the output of iron (Hartwell 1966). As Curtin states, "it was partly because of the large internal market that the Chinese iron and steel industry was capable to increase its scale of production" (1984:110). The state also built roads and canals, printed paper money, and implemented a policy of "strict currency control designed to prevent as far as possible any flight of Chinese currency beyond the confines of the Empire" (Filesi 1972:9). Unlike Europe, the Chinese Imperial state was capable of pacifying the national (i.e., internal) market.

During this era, the balance of long-distance trade was unquestionably in China's favor (Lo 1958:154). Its imports (with the exception of cotton textiles) (Ray 1996:52) were mostly raw materials (e.g., horses, hides, gems, spices, medicines, and some luxuries) (Deng 1997b:271). Meanwhile its exports were mostly manufactured commodities (e.g., porcelain, silk textiles, books, art objects, and iron and steel products) (Fairbank, Reischauer, and Craig 1973:136) together with tea, lead, tin, and other precious metals (Balazs 1972:63; Deng 1997b:272–273). At the time, the biggest Chinese ships were approximately 550 tons (Chen 1991:218).[13] Nicolo de Conti, who in 1437 traveled to China on a Chinese vessel, claimed that the Chinese constructed ships of approximately 2,000 tons—much larger than anything in Europe (Chang 1974:349).[14] Thus up to the mid-15th century, China's maritime capabilities were technologically superior to those of Europe (Chang 1991b:21).[15]

The fact that the Sung government had relied on overseas trade resulted in something of a rise in merchants' societal status from the 12th century onward (Ma 1971:125). Clark even goes so far as to speak of an exceptional "cultural transformation: the growing acceptance of merchants and merchant careers among elite society" (1995:71).[16] What is even more striking is that during the

---

13. Under the Yuan, some grain carriers were as big as 1,350 tons (Deng 1997b:263).

14. For instance, the 13th-century Hanseatic cogs generally had a loading capacity of 130 tons, which by circa 1400 had increased to 300 tons (Schildhauer 1985:149; Gille 1970:196). It is probably due to state intervention that the Chinese ships were much larger than their European or Arab counterparts. Ibn Batuta noted that these ships could hold up to a thousand men, consisting of approximately 400 soldiers accompanying 600 merchants and sailors (Chen 1991:222).

15. It is estimated that in the mid-15th century, the entire Hanseatic League numbered about 1,000 vessels, which represented a freight capacity of circa 60,000 tons (Schildhauer 1985:150). Just one of Zheng He's larger ships is said to have had a cargo capacity of 2,500 tons, although some archeologists have questioned the size of the biggest ships on his expeditions (e.g., Gould 2000:198; Church 2005). When I refer to Europe's technological inferiority as far as naval power is concerned, I do not mean to imply that European city-states could not construct huge ships; 1,000-ton-nefs were used by Venice in the Eastern Mediterranean at the beginning of the 13th century (Hocquet 1995:549) and by the 15th century, their usage was quite common (Heers 1979:IV:140). By the 15th century even 2,000 ton carracks were not ucommon in Genoa (Spufford 2003:398). It was the *multitude* of ships that China could construct that was so impressive (Gernet 1962:72; Cordier 1967:180). In 1257, in just three prefectures, the Sung dynasty mobilized a staggering 20,000 ships for warfare against the Mongols (Lo 1970:171). Some individual Chinese merchants must have been enormously wealthy since the wealthiest traders could own eighty or more seagoing vessels (Shiba 1970:188; Deng 1997b:278), something that was unprecedented for 13th-century Europe (Luzzatto 1954:154). It seems erroneous and disturbingly Eurocentric, then, to claim that private businessmen in China were incapable of "accumulating capital on as large a scale as European entrepreneurs managed to do in early modern times" (McNeill 1992:119).

16. Before the 11th and 12th centuries, merchants had been excluded from elite circles; orthodox Confucianism had designated them the least prestigious members of society. In a society experiencing soaring prosperity so clearly derived from commerce, however, such stigmas were no longer viable and were increasingly ignored (Clark 1995:71). While Clark's assessment is correct, he most likely refers to the coastal provinces around Fukien and Kwantung and not the whole of China (Ptak 1994:42) since merchants continued to be "legally ranked at the bottom of society" (Chang 1994:65; Kracke, Jr. 1955:485).

Sung dynasty, "wealthy merchants were permitted to buy rank to assist the depleted treasury and, by usurping the right to wear official dress, they ate into the unique position of the mandarinate" (Dawson 1972:176).[17]

Despite all of their accomplishments, however, the Southern Sung were impeded from transitioning to a capitalist society because their impressive socioeconomic developments did not result in China's growing political and military might within Asia (Ma 1971:86; McKnight 1971:182; Morton 1995:103).

China and the Mongols

China's impressive socioeconomic growth was not able to prevent the Mongols' conquest of the whole of China in the late 13th century (Davis 1996) and the subsequent creation of the Yuan dynasty (A.D. 1279–1368). Thanks to a massive collection of cavalry forces bound together by unprecedented "iron discipline and central control" (Barfield 1994:174), the Mongols were able to steadily conquer China as they forged their world empire. According to Rodzinski, for all of the countries and peoples that were victims of Mongol invasions, "the effects were truly disastrous" (1984:128); the destruction was enormous, particularly in Northern and Central China (Smith 1992:670–672; Roberts 1996:171; Mote 1999:450), as well as in Persia (Lambton 1988; Marshall 1993:53–57)[18] and "Transoxiana" where, according to archeological studies, 30 percent of the population lived in urban areas prior to the Mongol invasion (Garcin et al. 2000a:170). Jones estimates that "35 million Chinese were killed by the Mongols [which was] one-third of the population in the thirteenth century. . . . The death toll in China alone at the time of the Mongol

---

17. Under the Sung, the state was so desperate for governmental revenue based on trade that "honorary ranks were awarded to merchants who were especially successful in promoting foreign trade and inducing foreign merchants to bring their wares to China" (Dawson 1972:166).

18. While certain regions were more harshly affected than others (Soucek 2000:114), "the great cities of Khurasan such as Balkh, Harat and Nishapur were razed to the ground . . . in the Mongols' steppe-oriented minds, the destruction of cities and agriculture was still a matter of little or no real consequence . . . for Persia, the Mongol period was a disaster on a grand and unparalleled scale" (Morgan 1988:57–58, 82; Chaudhuri 1990:274; Bélénitsky 1960:613–614). "The swarming hordes of Hulagu's armies finally destroyed all the magnificent public works and the wonderful irrigation system of lower Mesopotamia" (Mansfield 1992:60), which were "unprecedented disasters with long-term effects" (Wink 1997:14). Cahen (1977:436) is also convinced of the negative long-term impact of the Mongols in the Middle East: "Ce seront la conquête mongole puis l'équipée timuride qui auront les effects les plus irrémédiables. L'ampleur des destructions, l'installation de types de nomades entièrement étrangers à toute tradition agricole entraînent des conséquences qui ne paraissent pas niables." For an in-depth study of the Mongol occupation of Russia, see Halperin (1986). Szeftel goes so far as to claim that the Mongol invasions can be considered as the cause of the decline of the Russian parliaments (vetche) (1965:345). Gammer (2005:485) also emphasizes the devastating material effects of the occupation.

conquest was so large that it must have obliterated economic life over wide areas" (1988:109–110).[19] The Mongol invasion of Sung China has even been referred to as a "crisis of capitalism" (Jones 1988:110).[20] Smith goes so far as to claim that "after the overthrow of the Sung dynasty by the invading Mongols in 1276 ... China never regained the dynamism of its past" (1991b:27–28), while Buell considers the Mongol invasions "an unparalleled disaster for the sedentary states and empires surrounding Mongolia" (1992:2). Thus, it is quite common to blame the Mongols for later economic failures (Jones 1988:113).

While the Mongol conquest of Sung China cannot be the *sole* reason for the area's failure to transition to capitalism, it should be considered an important variable (Hartwell 1962:162; Gernet 1962:18). Some scholars, however—such as Abu-Lughod (1989), for whom the Pax Mongolica plays a central role in the world-system of 1250 to 1350—have questioned this interpretation. I would argue that one of the key questions that should be asked is: Who benefited from the Pax Mongolica? In the short term, the Mongol rulers obviously benefited from their military conquests and many merchants also saw their protection and transaction costs decrease once the Mongols established their rule (Rossabi 1990:356). But in the long run, were Europeans not the most fortunate?

Western merchants benefited tremendously, both directly and indirectly, from the Pax Mongolica "qui avait créé les circonstances politiques favorables à l'expansion économique des Occidentaux" (Nystazopoulou 1973:570). This is confirmed by Balard (1992:29): "La consolidation des khanats mongols allait faire des Latins les principaux bénéficiaires de l'héritage économique de Byzance dans [l]es régions [de la mer Noire]." Initially it was predominantly Turkish Muslim and Uighur merchants who profited as they, more than any other group, were "employed" as tax farmers in the Mongolian Empire (Endicott-West 1989:146; Allsen 1989:116; Brose 2002).[21] But some Western

---

19. While the combined population of Jin China and the Southern Sung likely exceeded 110 million in A.D. 1200, by 1300, official records indicated a population of less than 70 million (Ebrey 1996:184; Wink 1997:381; Mote 1999:504). The figures for Northern China are even more indicative; according to Barfield "a Chin census of 1195 showed a population of 50 million people in north China [whereas] the first Mongol census of 1235–36 counted only 8.5 million" (1994:176–177). Exact figures are, of course, impossible to obtain, but what does seem to be clear is that "the campaigns of Chinggis Khan and his successors down to the 1250s were murderous to a degree recent history can scarcely equal" (Dreyer 1982:14). Even to 13th-century contemporaries, "the extent and frequency of massacres committed by the Mongols were profoundly shocking" (Phillips 1998:67). Admittedly, some of the population decline in Northern China must also be attributed to the large migration to Southern China (Mote 1994:662), but exact figures are hard to find. For a comparative assessment of population levels across the Eurasian landmass, see Adams et al. (2000:270, 334).

20. Kirby claims that Mongol rule "did little to encourage the positive forces making for social development in the direction of capitalism" (1954:153). In some cases, the payment of tributes to the Mongols led to serious economic problems (Bendix 1978:97).

21. *Ortogh*, or merchant associations, also received government support (Rossabi 1994b:449).

European merchants also benefited by obtaining offices under the Mongols (Richard 1976:XXX; Togan 1991:219), while others penetrated deep into Asia and made significant profits (Lopez 1975:83–186). Because of the Pax Mongolica, a rare period of political unity came into existence in Central Asia (Adshead 1993:78), resulting in an "uninterrupted flow of European traders" (Ray 1991:83)—primarily Italians, of whom Marco Polo is the most famous— as well as envoys, artisans, and missionaries (Needham 1954:188; Morton 1995:120–121; Rossabi 1997:81; Dauvillier 1953:70–71; Richard 1976:XXIII; Ryan 1998).[22]

Along with the lowering of commercial protection and transaction costs (on which the city-states depended for their survival), increasing amounts of knowledge, such as navigation techniques and gunpowder, were transmitted from East Asia to Europe (Needham 1995; Chou 1974:115; Needham 1964:236). Even in terms of geopolitics, Europeans benefited in the form of an indirect weakening of their Muslim enemies in Egypt. For instance, the Mongol Il-Khans, who ruled over Persia and Mesopotamia, sent some fifteen missions to the West between 1262 and 1320 (Boyle 1977:XIII) to forge an alliance against the Mamluk state with whom they were at war (Amitai-Preiss 1995), and Western embassies were sent in the hope of creating a joint expedition to reconquer the lost Crusader outposts (Paviot 2000:315). These alliances, however, never materialized (Richard 2003:XXIII), dooming the Levantine possessions in the long run (Sinor 1956:51) But the Mongol invasions of Mesopotamia and Syria in 1260 and their subsequent unsuccessful attempts to overrun the Mamluk regime in Egypt nevertheless delayed the fall of several Crusader outposts in the Eastern Mediterranean. More importantly, the Mongols twice saved the Byzantine Empire from collapse, first with their defeat of the Seljuks in the 1240s and then of the Ottomans in 1402 (Morgan 1989:201–202).[23]

---

22. Although the Pax Mongolica was regularly interrupted by hostilities between different Khanates from 1260 onward (Endicott-West 1990:349–350), its overall beneficial impact on international trade relations cannot be denied (Berza 1941:428; Sinor 1956:60; Labib 1974:231; Balard 1999:201). The Pax Mongolica enabled "for the first time in history something like regular trade and diplomacy [to] be carried out over a territory ranging from Eastern Europe to Southeast Asia" (Waldron 1994:XXVI; see Bentley 1993:115). Indeed, by the early 14th century, European "commercial expeditions to Asia had become fairly common" (Toussaint 1966:91; see Balard 1973:681 and Richard 1983:XIV:90–92).

23. Mongol incursions into Europe did occur from 1236 to 1242 and it was the Russians who suffered the most; their territories were ravaged and their principalities occupied (with the notable exception of the Hanseatic city of Novgorod) (Blum 1972:57–69). The traditional explanation for the Mongols' sudden withdrawal from Europe in 1241–1242, after their successes against European armies in Liegnitz and Sajos, is attributed to the death of the Grand Khan (Fletcher 1986:47). Yet the logistical and geographical problems that plagued the Mongol armies in their failed attempts to conquer Syria (Smith 1998:61; Morgan 1985; 1988:63) may have also been a variable (Sinor 1972; Morgan 1986:141; Amitai-Preiss 1999b:138). After all, a campaigning Mongol army of 300,000 would have had to find pastureland for 1.5 million horses and 9 million sheep (Smith 1984:308).

During this same period, the main fiscal brunt of the Mongol campaigns directed toward Burma, Vietnam, Japan, Java, and Central Asia (Dars 1992:328–343) fell upon the Chinese population (Dreyer 1982:14). For example, throughout that part of the Eurasian landmass conquered by the Mongols and their nomadic allies, elaborate networks of postal relay stations were installed, which ensured rapid communication between various parts of the Mongolian Empire (Rossabi 1994b:450). These stations, part of "the greatest and most efficient communications net known to the pre-modern world" (Alef 1967:4), surely reduced the expenses of many foreign merchants as they were sources of safety, supplies, and lodging (Rossabi 1990:354). Ultimately though, their maintenance "was a heavy burden on the sedentary populace" (Allsen 1983:264), particularly in Northern China (Schurmann 1967:72) and to a lesser extent in the South (Mote 1994:661).[24] Thus, along with the increasing commerce across the Eurasian landmass and the continued large-scale maritime trade with Southeast Asia (Ptak 1998; Christie 1998) came the increased exploitation of the Chinese peasantry under the Mongol Yuan dynasty. This is no coincidence as the increased levies exacted upon the sedentary population gave the Mongol overlords "a sizable surplus to exchange for products, which they needed" (Schurmann 1967:5).

Although stimulated by the greater demands of the Mongol rulers, increasing economies of scale, a decrease in transaction costs, and the "introduction of a nationwide system of paper currency which replaced the local currencies which had been in circulation" (Schurmann 1967:8), the economic upturn could not last. Initially, the intensified exploitation of the peasantry had augmented

> the surplus available for the Mongols and thus reinforced the basis
> for the great expansion of commerce. However, since in the long run
> neither agricultural production nor productivity increased, the material
> basis for continued commercial expansion was lacking. (Schurmann
> 1967:8)

Together with the outbreak of war between the Khanate of the Golden Horde and the Ilkhans (Jackson 1978:234–238), this supply problem was likely an important factor in preventing further rapid Mongol expansion into 13th-century Western Europe (Sinor 1999:20; Khazanov 1994:27), more so than any military weakness (May 2006).

24. Despite being unauthorized to do so, "Western merchants" used the official mail horses to further their own commercial interests (Lopez 1943:172–173). In addition, foreign merchants could easily make up charges of theft or robbery, thereby "defrauding the local population [since] by Mongolian law the locals were made collectively responsible for all goods lost by travelling merchants" (Allsen 1989:99). In addition, laws were passed that "punished foreigners less seriously than native [Chinese]" and at least a third of all civil service posts had been reserved exclusively "for Mongols and Central Asians" (Smith 1998:5).

Another major problem was that "almost the entire trade was in the hands of foreign merchants" (Rodzinski 1979:185) and the significant profits from trade were exported out of China (Dars 1992:49).

The Mongol empire ultimately disintegrated in a typical pattern of overextension (Collins 1992:379), with increasing warfare thanks to internal sedition and diminishing returns (Unger 1987:107). In the end, the Mongols had simply squeezed too much out of their subjects to the point where the latter finally rose up in rebellion.[25] By 1368, after seventeen years of bloody wars and uprisings (Mote 1988), the Mongol Yuan dynasty was finally driven out of China. The long-term effect of Mongol rule on China was ultimately negative (Dawson 1972:209; Dars 1992:46–48); it was "not only a handicap to the further growth of the country's economy, but also, in fact, the cause of its regression" (Rodzinski 1979:184). For Western Europe, however, the "pacification" of the Eurasian landmass was nothing but beneficial. Because of its increased contact with the East, the West became familiar with the superior Eastern nautical technology[26] (e.g., compasses), gunpowder (Ling 1947; Goodrich and Chia-Shêng 1946), printing (Morton 1995:104; Chou 1974:115; Drège 1994), and much more (Needham 1969:213).[27]

Although replaced by a Ming dynasty (1368–1644) preoccupied with maintaining power, the Mongol threats remained alive and well under Tamerlane (right up until his death in the early 15th century), and similarly under the Oyirat Mongols (particularly in the mid-15th century) (Wang 1991:61). The Chinese emperor's interests were thus focused on protecting the Middle Kingdom from recurring nomadic invasions and on stabilizing the countryside as many peasants had suffered tremendously during the uprisings against Mongol rule (Mote 1977:197).[28] The Ming dynasty was subsequently less preoccupied with naval power as with adequately defending the areas near the Great Wall,

---

25. Di Cosmo claims that the Mongol government "was plagued by the proliferation of an extraordinarily wasteful administration ... the Mongols' attitude to governance remained erratic and negligent" (1999:34).

26. This is very well demonstrated by the fact that in the second decade of the 15th century, one of Zheng He's flotillas was capable of making "a direct crossing from Sumatra to the East coast of Africa at Mogadishu in Somalia, a straight run of 3,700 miles" (Morton 1995:128; see Needham 1964:295).

27. According to Kuhn, the water-powered throwing mill was introduced in Europe at the end of the 13th century thanks to its diffusion from China (1981:52). See also Dobson's (2004) summary of more-advanced Eastern "resource portfolios" (ideas, technologies, etc.), which diffused to the West, either directly during the Pax Mongolica or via the Islamic world (cf. Lieber 1968; Watt 1972).

28. Crone is incorrect in claiming that "the elimination of the barbarian [nomadic danger] on the one hand and the preservation of imperial unity on the other hand meant there was no inter-state competition" (1989:173). Not only did the nomadic threats persist (which implied an important shift in foreign policy decisions), but the representation of China as a unified Empire that did not

which had re-emerged in importance (Mote 1999:610–611). It is ironic then that it is the famous maritime expeditions of Admiral Zheng He, promoted by the early Ming dynasty, that have attracted so much recent scholarly attention.[29] It should be noted that "the climax of the Chinese sea- and ocean-going activities occurred in Sung-Yuan times, not in Ming" (Deng 1997:57).[30] Furthermore, the nature and goals of Zheng He's short-lived expeditions must be interpreted within the context of the resurgent Chinese Empire.

Ming China and Europe: Divergent Paths

Although the maritime voyages of Zheng He in the early 15th century had an economic component to them (Fairbank 1953:34–37; Ju-kang 1981), they were not dominated by an interest in trade or monopolistic rights (privileges) to the marketplace. Rather, they were dominated by a political component (Wang 1970b:375–401; Morton 1995:128); that is, to bring the "barbaric" people living on the fringes of the Middle Kingdom into the tributary trade system (see Rossabi 1983). This is in sharp contrast to the European practices of inter (city) state competition for commercial routes and access to, as well as *domination* of, markets; outright territorial notions such as the "Mare britannicum" speak for themselves. In the late 15th century, Henry VII of England gave John Cabot the advice to "discover, explore, conquer, occupy and take into possession" all the lands he would find overseas (Mollat 1988b:16–17), a mission quite different from that received by Zheng He from Emperor Yung-lo. According to Abu-Lughod, "the impressive show of force was intended to signal to the 'barbarian' nations that China had reassumed her rightful place in the firmament of nations and had once again become the 'Middle Kingdom' of the world" (1989:343):

> Selling desired products such as silk, porcelain and lacquerware, to barbaric peoples was viewed by the Chinese as a manifest demonstration

---

experience any competition is a profoundly Eurocentric one, with Europeans represented as the "agents of change" who forced competition upon Asian state polities (Crone 1989:175), with the latter depicted as part of an immutable/stagnant East.

29. For an updated Zheng He bibliography, see Ptak's (1996) revised edition of the "Hsing-Ch'a Sheng-Lan." For an extensive analysis, see Ray (1993). For a popularized version, see Levathes (1994).

30. "The Ming court had no sustained interest in seafaring, no grasp of the possibilities of seapower. The Ming voyages were not followed up but remained isolated tours de force, mere exploits" (Fairbank, Reischauer, and Craig 1973:199).

of cultural superiority ... Chinese culture itself was China's greatest commodity, while valued wares were testimony to that culture's excellence. (Finlay 1991:6)[31]

What is striking is that "the Ming expeditions were not seeking territory to conquer or sea lanes to monopolize" (Finlay 1991:8), although they could have easily done so (Mote 1999:616).[32] Instead, notions of diplomatic and cultural prestige (through demonstrations of Chinese wealth and power) were central to Zheng He's voyages (Dawson 1972:230).[33] The tributary trade system, however, constituted "a serious drain on the economy: it must have cost the Ming enormous sums of money to pay for tribute articles of little value. The satisfaction felt by the Chinese court at the presentation of tribute articles of little or no intrinsic value by foreigners who themselves did not 'feel' tributary in any way or dependent of China, was an expensive honor" (Serruys 1975:35).

Such was not the case for the ships sent out by the tiny European city-states (later, nation-states), which from the Late Middle Ages onward systematically designed and implemented a foreign policy of direct conquest, political control, and commercial exploitation in order to ceaselessly accumulate capital from a constructed periphery.[34] The Chinese, however, "thought in terms of

---

31. For the importance of culture in the tributary trade system, see the example of Korea (Chun 1968).

32. It is estimated that on Zheng He's seven voyages, an average of 27,000 men traveled with him on sixty very large vessels (Chou 1974:127). This far exceeded "anything Europeans were able to dispatch to the same waters in the next century" (McNeill 1998:229). The ships were also very impressive in terms of armaments: "Already during the reign of Hong Wu around 1393, each Ming warship was required to carry four guns with muzzles the size of rice-bowls, twenty guns of smaller caliber, ten bombs, twenty rockets, and a thousand rounds of shot" (Ray 1987:116).

33. Emperor Yung-lo, a usurper in the early Ming dynasty, felt the need to publicly demonstrate that the new dynasty had obtained the Mandate of Heaven to rule over China. In this respect, the "tributes" obtained from distant countries played a key role (Chou 1974:128; Roberts 1996:185). The reasons for the expeditions may well have been the personal "desire of a vigorous emperor ... to assert the greatness of China at this early stage in the dynasty" (Dawson 1972:231), which would explain why "after his death the motivation of seeking recognition no longer applied" (Roberts 1996:185–186). In addition, the "low return" of Zheng He's voyages also likely led to the eventual abandonment of the project (Deng 1997b:256). Atwell (2002:92) recently concluded that "few if any of the expeditions could have been operated at profit."

34. As Toussaint (1966:79) reminds us, what is ironic is that "it was the European navigators, guided by the compass known to the Chinese, and equipped with arms invented by the Chinese" who eventually established colonial thalassocracies throughout the Indian Ocean. The Portuguese, and later the Dutch, were successful in capturing their vital emporiae and crucial strategic locations throughout the Indian Ocean because huge Chinese vessels like those of Zheng He no longer patrolled the seas. In this sense, "China's abdication was Europe's gain" (McNeill 1992:113). When the Chinese naval power withdrew, the Portuguese had a "clear technological superiority over all Asian competitors" (Ptak 1999:VII:105). The maritime superiority of the European powers,

ritual submission, ceremonial barter and formal recognition as developed for centuries within the context of a superior, powerful civilization condescending to a host of distant, petty and relatively undeveloped principalities" (Finlay 1991:7). Of course, Europeans had notions of religious superiority vis-à-vis the "heathens" or "infidels" they encountered, but in the European inter-city-state system, territoriality was primarily framed in the context of economic exploitation. In 1204, for example, Venice used the crusaders to obtain the Byzantine Empire's wealth when the latter was profoundly weakened by internal strife (Cheynet 1996).[35] The Hanseatic city league fought wars with the Dutch because it wanted to preserve its trade monopoly in the Baltic Sea (Abraham Thisse 1988:136–137).[36] The same was true in the Mediterranean where city-states fought bloody wars for the monopolization of trade routes (Budak 1997:166), markets (Hocquet 1999:509), and the maintenance of colonies on islands that were considered strategically and commercially significant (Argenti 1958; Balard 1983; Pistarino 1990:245–280).[37] Thus the "pursuit of monopoly rent for its merchants" (Spruyt 1994:123) was central, if not the raison d'être, for these European city-states.[38]

---

combined with their skillful exploitation of internal strife among South Asian powers (Scammell 1995:XI:8), enabled the former to control ever more maritime trade routes and thus reap enormous profits in East Asia.

35. According to Krueger, the crusades in the period 1100–1270 "were the strongest influence on the development of medieval trade and industry, [they provided] the Italian cities much of the liquid capital that was needed in the capitalistic developments that were just beginning . . . and promoted the capitalistic cycle of capital, investment, profit, and reinvestment of profit for further profit and capital" (1961:71–73). The Mediterranean city-states not only played an important role in the success of the crusades in the Middle East, but also in the conquest and colonization of the Balearic isles. Interestingly, unlike the warfare in the Levant, the conquest of Ibiza and Formentera materialized through private enterprises that bore all the costs and risks. This is an example of the deliberate conquest strategy of private enterprises, infused by "private speculation for gain: investments [for warfare that] would be recouped from the spoils of conquest" (Fernández-Armesto 1987:16, 31–32).

36. For an analysis of the conflicts between the Hanseatic League and the Dutch, see Seifert (1997).

37. It is true that competition among merchants involves "a need to eliminate others, to win the race for favorable production factors—cheap labor, including women, children and slaves—and to increase productivity by enforcing longer working hours and stricter supervision" (Sprengard 1994:17). The use of state legislation and state violence to guarantee and safeguard monopolies is one of the most profitable and overlooked practices. Not surprisingly, Europeans were most successful in Asia when they were able to establish monopolies (Wong 1999:228), similar to the way in which the most powerful city-states attempted to do so in Western Europe (Hocquet 1979:168–176).

38. The Hanseatic League made most of its profits from the resale of diverse commodities across the Baltic area (Holbach 1993b:184); the preservation of their monopoly was thus crucial if they wanted to maintain serious profit levels.

As Wallerstein noted: "When the Turks advanced in the east, there was no European emperor to recall the Portuguese expeditions" (1974:60). Similarly, the death of a doge in Venice could not have reversed existing policies given the city-states' strong competition for access to their lifelines (i.e., colonies and Eastern markets). With the death of Emperor Yung-lo, however—the Emperor who had initiated Zheng He's naval expeditions (Wang 1970:376)—all further excursions but one were halted. By the mid-15th century, "the landlord-bureaucrat faction at the Ming court was able to have the operations discontinued and the maritime activity severely curtailed" (Findlay 1992:4). When the eight-year-old Emperor succeeded his father in 1435:

> the Confucian bureaucracy came to dominate policy even more. The Treasure-ships were allowed to deteriorate and the shipyards were starved of labor . . . within a generation, the Chinese lost the knowledge of how to build Treasure-ships, and private Chinese vessels ceased venturing beyond the straits of Melaka. (Finlay 1991:12)[39]

Such Ming policies were a clear break from those of the Southern Sung and the Mongol Yuan dynasties, both of which had actively promoted and developed maritime trade (Deng 1997; Hui 1995:31–32; Ptak 1993:8; Ray 1993:111); the Sung did so out of sheer necessity, for its political survival, while the Mongols did so for their military expeditions against Japan and Java.[40] The Sung built warehouses for merchants and lighthouses on the coast (Dawson 1972:166) and provided various kinds of financial and technical support to shipbuilders who, in turn, pledged ships as military assistance to the government when called on to do so (Lo 1969c:68–91). For the Sung, commercial expansion and state protection went hand-in-hand. According to Filesi, "the Mongol invaders were soon fired up by the Sung example to make the navy an instrument of expansion and conquest" (1972:26). The Mongolian nobility later implemented a policy of "financial aid and protection" for the merchants (Schurmann 1967:6).[41] Zheng He's famous maritime expeditions during the Ming dynasty would prove to be exceptional.[42]

---

39. This had profound consequences for the balance of maritime power; by the early 17th century, the Chinese junks, which contemporary Chinese considered "huge," were no longer a match for the Dutch vessels (Ng 1997:249).

40. The scale of these naval expeditions was enormous, especially when compared with those in Europe. According to Chen (1991:226), about 4,400 ships with 140,000 soldiers invaded Japan in 1281.

41. The Mongols were even more inclined to foster overseas trade after war broke out between the Yuan dynasty and the Chagatai Khanate (Dawson 1972:200).

42. Rossabi goes so far as to label Zheng He's voyages an "aberration" of Chinese history (1997:79). Mote refers to them as "the great anomaly" (1999:616). More recently, Atwell (2002:84) has claimed

According to Fairbank (1965:51), Chinese merchants at that time were not considered important enough to be supported by the military power of the state; instead, the Chinese state, and particularly its bureaucrats, upheld the agrarian sector at the expense of systematic development and support for the merchants. This may even be an understatement. As Needham pointed out:

> A predominantly mercantile order of society could never arise in Chinese civilization because the basic conception of the mandarinate was opposed to the value-systems of the wealthy merchants. Capital accumulation there could indeed be, but the application of it in permanently productive industrial enterprises was constantly inhibited by the scholar-bureaucrats, as indeed any other social action which might threaten their supremacy. Thus, the merchant guilds in China never achieved anything approaching the status and power of the merchant guilds of the city-states of European civilization. (1969:197)[43]

Having expelled the Mongols after almost a century of rule, China simply wanted to symbolically reassert itself by restoring its prestige throughout the entire region (Chen 1991:226). Once this was achieved, there was little sense in further pursuing the matter, at least from the perspective of the elites who were in charge (Wang 1970:224–225). "The costs of this expansion," notes Snooks (1996:318), "into a world less developed than itself, far exceeded the benefits, and therefore it was brought to an end ... from this time forward China became increasingly introspective, isolationist, and relatively backward technologically."

This last comment is quite an exaggeration. In 1450, the Chinese Empire was actually a formidable power, certainly when compared with some of the weak emerging nation-states in Europe. Admittedly, it was not able to conquer everything that it wanted[44] and the defense of its northern frontier against the nomadic threats remained a major preoccupation for the Chinese "agrarian-minded, land-oriented officials" (Mote 1999:652). But what should be noted is that the elites who were in charge, particularly the Confucian

---

that an unprecedented collection of *agricultural taxes* due to more benign climatic conditions provided the new Ming government with the resources to finance the great maritime excursions of Zheng He, as well as other military campaigns in the region.

43. See also Southall (1998:149). The lack of societal prestige for merchants is illustrated by the fact that from the time of the Sung dynasty, merchants were "prohibited from taking the civil service examinations" (Ma 1971:125). This legal prohibition continued up to the Ming dynasty (Elman 1991:12).

44. The bloody battles that were vainly fought for many years against the Shan (in upper Burma) and in Annam (Vietnam) throughout the 15th century are indicative of the limits of its strength (Lo 1969b:60; Whitmore 1985).

bureaucracy, strongly opposed foreign interventions (Mote 1999:615) since, from their perspective, the "colossal expenses did not justify the paltry returns" (Willetts 1964:38). Given that the Middle Kingdom already claimed "material and moral superiority" over surrounding tribes and kingdoms—all secondary in wealth and technological prowess—what would China have gained from a policy of expansion (Fairbank 1968:15)?[45]

Even with the increased demand for goods that resulted from the continuous massive chain migration from southern China (mainly Kwantung and Fukien), the Chinese government did not offer the "overseas" Chinese (i.e., traders) any backing or protection, nor was there the political desire to assist the "abandoned subjects of the Celestial Dynasty" (Sun 2001:72; see Hudson 1964:354). Instead, after 1371, the Ming attempted to "reduce the size of the growing overseas Chinese communities [because it] branded private sea merchants 'bandits', 'thieves'" (Hui 1995:35), or "pirates" (Chang 1991b:26). All Chinese who wanted to build ships and venture overseas in pursuit of trade were outlawed from doing so (Mote 1999:720). By 1410, the Chinese Imperial court had even "requested a Javanese tribute mission to help send Chinese immigrants back to China" (Chang 1991b:17). In contrast, European powers offered their nationals protection wherever they traded, and often used their distress as a pretext for various military interventions.[46]

Perhaps the most important factor for China's socioeconomic development (or lack thereof), then, was this absence of state support for its merchants. During both the Ming and Ch'ing (1644–1912) dynasties, Chinese merchants were not permitted "to travel abroad for trade [because] abroad the government could not define normative or expected behavior patterns" (Mancall 1968:81). As mentioned earlier, bans were imposed against building private ships and "a lot of merchant ships were destroyed by the authorities" because the early Ming "advocated a state monopoly on foreign trade." The Ming emperors also "cut down on the construction of warships and armaments. Along with the reduction of the provincial fleets, the large-size warships were gradually replaced by small flat-bottom barges, which were inferior in construction" (Chen 1991:226–227).

---

45. "Beyond the lands that were culturally Chinese were the realms of the barbarians. In theory, they too were under the empire, but undeserving of full membership in Chinese society, and not worth the trouble it would take to enforce their full submission" (Curtin 1984:91).

46. These territoriality practices used by the European mercantile states find their origin in the inter-city-state system phenomenon of the "bourgeoisie fouraine" or *buitenpoorterij* of the Late Middle Ages. The city-state had extraterritorial powers in the sense that those of its citizens who lived in the countryside could only be tried by urban magistrates. Thus, from the 12th century onward, those in the countryside who were well-to-do purchased city-state citizenship, even if they never lived there, precisely to enjoy all kinds of juridical and economic benefits. During the peak of the European inter-city-state system (1250–1400), many cities consistently implemented these extraterritorial prerogatives as instruments of their imperialist strategies (Van Uytven 1982:250–252; see Fedalto 1997:209).

Although the Ming government began to legalize some overseas civilian undertakings in 1567 (Chang 1991:246), throughout most of the Ming dynasty, foreign trade remained outlawed (Huang 1969:99; Lippit 1987:39) and laws on maritime trade appear to have been strictly enforced throughout the coastal areas (Ptak 1999:III:33; Demel 1994:98; Ng 1997:224). Nevertheless, given China's immense coastline and because an all-controlling, smoothly operating despotic government simply did not exist, the ban on seaborne trade (or for that matter, along the Mongolian border) could not be completely enforced and illegal maritime smuggling continued on a large scale (Deng 1997b:270).[47] Thus, contrary to traditional thinking (e.g., Kennedy 1989:8–9; Baechler 2002:116), China was not completely 'cut off' from the world, nor had actual trade dramatically diminished between China and its neighbors Ptak 2004:I, 275).[48] But the exclusion policies nevertheless had an effect in that they:

a) deprived the government of great amounts of revenue that might have been obtained from imports and exports (Huang 1969:99);
b) made it difficult for some Chinese merchants and seamen to return home, for fear of punishment (Reid 1999:63);
c) seriously affected the economies of the coastal provinces in a negative way (Ts'ao 1982:232);[49]
d) limited the overall magnitude of maritime trade (Sun 2000:137); and more importantly,
e) deprived the Chinese merchants of vital governmental support (McNeill 1998:229).

Unlike the Europeans who were about to start their overseas expansion, from the mid-15th century onward Chinese commercial activities were increasingly confined to a relatively small area of the globe (Hall 1985:197); despite the growing private (illegal) trade, Chinese merchants ceased to venture further west than Malaka (Ptak 1991:211; 1999:V:148; Bouchon and Lombard

---

47. Chinese merchants were prepared to take risks and to challenge governmental authority, as evidenced by the illegal Chinese maritime diaspora and the extensive trading networks that relied on it (Ptak 1994:36–37). It is therefore unfair to state that the Chinese commercial classes "remained so thoroughly subject to an imperial bureaucracy as to inhibit large-scale independent enterprise on their part" (McNeill 1992:113).

48. During the Ming dynasty, some countries or tribes linked with China via land routes were also temporarily excluded from tributary trade, which resulted in similar clandestine smuggling activities on the Chinese border (Serruys 1975:40).

49. A major port such as Ch'uanchou "fell on evil times from which it never fully recovered. Though some trade was still carried on during the Ming and Ch'ing dynasties, the city as an international port declined" (Ma 1971:46; see Clark 1995:73; So 2000:181).

1987:54). A similar withdrawal from the seas was impossible in Europe, where no central authority could have imposed such a measure on merchants. This confinement was also in sharp contrast with the governments of both the Sung and Yuan dynasties, which had implemented "policies to encourage oceangoing shipping and trade" (Chen 1991:218). But after the defeat of the Mongols in the late 14th century, the Ming imperial court felt that it no longer needed the merchants. Along with its expulsion of the Mongols, the early Ming dynasty expelled all other foreigners (Petech 1962:558; Phillips 1998:112) as it reinforced its control within the realm (Dardess 1973:169).[50] While some foreign traders did attempt to continue to travel through China, the attitude of the Ming and Ch'ing dynasties toward these foreign merchants was quite different from that of the earlier Sung and Yuan dynasties (Lopez 1943:181). Indeed, foreign merchants who had been used by the Mongols to collect taxes in certain areas faced a backlash of xenophobia.[51]

These exclusionary policies were not, however, simply a matter of "Oriental Despotism." Many scholars have repeatedly turned to the importance of "the multiplicity of partly autonomous and competitive local economic power networks" (e.g., Mann 1986, 1988:18; Findlay 1992:4; Chirot 1985:183; Snooks 1996:318) to explain long-term socioeconomic and technological developments. Suffice it to say that "political fragmentation was a necessary, not a sufficient condition" (Hall 1988:24) for the transition to capitalism. For example, Pearson is convinced that:

> the Chinese state, controlling a uniquely efficient administration, was able to enforce policies that did hinder innovation and economic change. This is not to say that there was no trade, nor indeed growth,

---

50. The Ming dynasty's "isolationist" policy was not exceptional, but simply a return to its previous preoccupation with nomadic threats.

51. "The deep resentment against the Mongols' ... alien rule had inspired hostility toward alien things in general. Gradually this view hardened into a lack of interest in anything beyond the pale of Chinese civilization. This turning away from the outside world was accompanied by a growing introspection within Chinese life ... Chinese xenophobia was combined with a complete confidence in cultural superiority" (Fairbank, Reischauer, and Craig 1973:178). This is confirmed by Modelski and Thompson: "When the Ming expelled the Mongols, China turned in upon itself and shut itself off from the outside world, hardly a recipe for fostering adventures of ideas or enterprise" (1996:175). Since the Mongols had used many foreign merchants for tax farming (Schurmann 1967:89–90; Franke 1994:VII:62) and for governmental positions such as governors, local officials, advisers, and other civil offices (Eberhard 1969:240; Morton 1995:119; Chou 1974:122; Lipman 1997:33–34), the backlash against foreign traders in the form of temporary xenophobic reactions is comprehensible (Roberts 1996:175). But as local studies about Muslims in Yunnan (Wang 1996) or Northern China (Lipman 1997) demonstrate, the intensity of this backlash should not be exaggerated.

but overall the state was too effective [as] the state put into effect policies that hindered growth. (1991:68–69)[52]

Such impediments could not only be observed under the Ming, but also during the socioeconomic miracle of the Sung dynasty. An example from the latter was the growing involvement of the state and the growing power of "bureaucratic entrepreneurs" (*shan licaizhe*); they were involved in the creation of different state agencies that could at times "stimulate rapid short-term economic growth [but] over the long run bureaucratic entrepreneurship degenerated inexorably into confiscatory taxation" (Smith 1991:308).[53] To a certain extent, private Chinese merchants therefore had to outmaneuver the nuisances created by their own government if they wanted to accumulate capital (Serruys 1975:50).

In contrast, the European city-states and emerging nation-states fully backed their traders with as much power as possible. Venice, for example, was a "commercial republic that systematically used state power, not merely to increase state income, but also to increase the income of the Venetian merchants as a socioeconomic class." For typical city-states like Genoa and Venice, "commerce and coercion were closely linked, if not inseparable" (Curtin 1984:116). While piracy did occur (Saletore 1978:11–40; Labh 1996:1–23), the generally peaceful nature of Asian trade in the Indian Ocean prior to the arrival of the

---

52. For Bin Wong (1997:77; 2002:455), Europe (as a "conglomeration of small units with sometimes overlapping jurisdictions") and China (as a unified agrarian empire) are juxtaposed as two extremes within Eurasia. Holton notes that "capitalism of a modern kind developed rather in the relatively decentralized West, where political structures were far from monolithic, allowing internal differentiation" (1986:134). Balazs is even more critical of the Chinese bureaucratic state, which prevented the emancipation of the merchants who "never dared to fight it openly in order to extract from it liberties, laws and autonomy for themselves" (1972:23; cf. Bin Wong 1997:92; Southall 1998:148–149). His negative assessment of the Chinese bureaucracy's role in economic development is likely overstated (Bergère 1984:329). After all, one should not exaggerate the poly-nuclear competitiveness vs. the perceived "monolithic structure in the East" (e.g. Snooks 1996:314–324). The Southern Sung dynasty was an exceptional period in that the imperial government had to take seriously revenues from maritime trade. China's impressive and unprecedented socioeconomic (and cultural) development during the Sung dynasty coincided with the exceptional existence of a multipolar political system (Snooks 1996:318; Modelski and Thompson 1996:151; Rossabi 1983). It follows that the commercial successes of the Sung were exceptional—"an episode of extraordinariness, an epiphenomenon outside China's mainstream" (Deng 1999:322). In contrast, "for most of imperial history, the state's principal source of revenue was land taxes" (Wong 1997:90).

53. Smith clearly points out that "as Sung fiscal agents penetrated ever more deeply into the commercial economy, . . . state intervention destroyed the normal relations between merchants and producers, restricted merchant's freedom of management, seized the merchant community's rightful profits . . . thereby impeding the normal development of a commercial economy" (1991:311–312). See Kracke Jr. 1955:484.

Portuguese and the Dutch stood in sharp contrast to the latter's aggressive policies (Lewis 1978:VII:264; Curtin 1984:128).[54]

While the merchant-controlled European governments prepared the way for a system of capitalism based on commercial imperialism,[55] the same did not occur in China (see Fairbank, Reischauer, and Craig 1973:195). Was it because of ideology (Southall 1998:155), culture, or religion that the Chinese merchants remained unaware of themselves as a class? East Asians certainly were not fundamentally less prone to accumulating wealth. But as Abu-Lughod (1989:340) points out, "unlike their European counterparts, [the Chinese merchants] could not use the state to advance their interests" and thus could not enforce on the region a highly exploitative capitalist system. The fact that the machinery of government in East Asia was not controlled (or even heavily influenced) by merchants (Wang 1990:401–402; Pearson 1991:76) had far-reaching consequences; the economic growth and monetization of the entire Southeast Asian region from South China to East India was embedded in an interregional division of labor "determined more by geographic and ecological considerations than by political or organizational desiderata" (Lieberman 1990:86). In order

---

54. One should not idolize the nonviolent Chinese maritime ventures in the Indian Ocean since they clearly did have an intimidating component (Wade 1997:154–156), and violence was used by Zheng He's forces when necessary. Nevertheless, the Chinese in the Indian Ocean did not operate in a way identical to that of the Europeans—far from it (Mote 1999:616). Prior to the arrival of the Europeans in the Indian Ocean in the 16th and 17th centuries, the Asian seas could essentially be called a "mare liberum" (Pearson 2000:42; Ptak 1994:36). Needham illustrates this well: "In dominating no principality, in setting up no forts or bases, in trading peaceably by and large with all the peoples among whom they came, the Chinese were clearly the inheritors of, and participators in, a millenary tradition, which was broken only by the irruption of European capitalist imperialism in the Asian seas" (1970c:40–70; 1970b:214). Because of the relative lack of monopolies based on violence, most commercial ties "were built upon a mutually beneficial and flexible framework of 'tribute and trade' that allowed participants from either side to interpret the nature of their relations in different ways to suit their own purpose" (Ng 1997:212). However, because the revenues from long-distance maritime trade were central to Europe's competing mercantile city-states and nation-states, once they penetrated Asian waters they "built fortresses and set up maritime trading networks to claim whole kingdoms, [while attempting] to exclude unwanted competitors from access to overseas resources" (Sprengard 1994:8). The colonization policies pursued by Europeans in the Mediterranean from the 14th century up to the "scramble for Africa" in the late 19th century were essentially part of the same process. Internal European competition "fueled the ongoing geographic expansion of European monopolistic control over scarce resources and key strategic locations" (Sprengard 1994:10).

55. In 17th-century England, for instance, "the central government came increasingly under the dominance of the mercantile elite and its associated groups who established a parliamentary regime advancing their specific interests" (Baumgartner, Buckley, and Burns 1976:59). See Rodinson (1970:32). This was obviously not yet the case in early Tudor England, where mercantile interests remained firmly subjugated by royal diplomacy (Grzybowski 1969:216–217). But eventually, the most successful European states were those "governed with, and usually in the interests of, the capitalist class" (Mann 1987:133).

to explain *why* the Chinese Empire gave up its interests in maritime trade
and essentially abandoned its merchants (Wong 2002:457), in stark contrast
with events in Europe, we have to compare Chinese cities with the European
city-state system where the oligarchy of merchant-entrepreneurs wielded significant power.

Although Europe was not more urbanized or commercialized than China,
the political power of the merchant-entrepreneurs vis-à-vis the monarchy was
entirely different. For example, England's King Edward III could never have
financed his war against France without the conditional financial support of Italian businessmen. And Charles V would never have become Emperor without
the critical support of German bankers.[56] While international bankers were
vital to most major military campaigns that a European monarch wanted to
undertake from the Middle Ages to the 16th century (Brady 1991:145; Mc-
Neill 1992:119; Van Gerven 1999:191), of even greater importance was the
taxation of his citizens. In most places this taxation was scrutinized by local
estates and assemblies or city-leagues in which the merchant-entrepreneurial
class wielded significant political—and even military—power (Bois 2000:125;
Nicholas 1997b:103–105).[57] It was precisely the institutional structure of the
city-states, then, that provided the merchants with their continual power, per-
mitting them to struggle against confiscation by powerful lords or, on a more
abstract level, through their representation in the state's decision-making institutions (Chirot 1985; Van Caenegem 1991:133).

Such was not the case in China. Peasant revolts could overturn a dynasty, but
the merchant class could not challenge the gentry, let alone Imperial authority.
Unlike in Europe, Chinese merchants could not carve out an institutional niche
that would secure them long-term political power.[58] Yet, such a niche was

---

56. Since parliamentary strength limited their taxation power (Harriss 1966), the European monarchies essentially depended on the credit of merchants to engage in extensive warfare. The Portuguese venture in the Atlantic, for instance, cannot be understood without the investments of
Genoese capital that had been "forced out of the eastern Mediterranean" by the Ottomans (Padfield 1979:24). And the Spanish conquest of the Eastern Mediterranean cannot be grasped without
taking into account the "alliance of king and merchant or capitalism and chivalry" (Fernández-
Armesto 1987:53).

57. For an overview of *medieval constitutionalism,* see Lyon (1978:VII–VIII), Marongiu (1968),
and Graves (2001). In large regions of early 14th-century Western Europe, the bourgeoisie was so
strong that it could establish "a political culture in which princely power was submitted to the rule
of law, and subjects were entitled to withdraw their loyalty" (Boone and Prak 1995:105) if fiscal
demands did not remain "modestes et raisonnables" (van Uytven 1978:472).

58. Most powerful landlords in the Eurasian landmass were, at some point, in debt to merchants
in their realm. The Mongolian princes, for example, "incurred enormous debts to merchant-
moneylenders" (Endicott-West 1989:128). With the exception of those located in Western Europe,
most merchants never had the political and military power necessary to punish those borrowers who
defaulted on the repayment of debts or engaged in the practice of "confiscatory taxation" (McNeill
1992:120) or "underhand expropriation" (Epstein 1997:169). In Asia, "powerful rulers and military

essential for the preservation of the riches that they had obtained in their quest for a ceaseless accumulation of capital. One such crucial institutional niche is the city-state (Boone 1996:167–169).[59] As Deng (1999:199) summarizes:

> The merchant class was actively involved in the establishment of European cities, while in China cities were built by the authorities [so] China did not have a history of city-states [which was] one of the main reasons that China did not produce an independent bourgeoisie.

Although one should abandon the notion that Chinese cities were more "political" than "commercial" (as if in Western Europe they only had a commercial and never a political component to them), large Chinese towns were generally "dominated by officials who represented the Imperial government, particularly insofar as judicial and fiscal matters were concerned and unlike [European] towns it did not embody the idea of emancipation and of liberty" (Balazs 1969:16).[60] From the Sung dynasty onward, wealth, political power, and social status in the Chinese Empire were virtually synonymous with the gentry (Eberhard 1965), whereas in Europe the merchant class was often able to forge a coalition with the monarchy against the parasitical landlord class whenever the latter threatened to become too powerful (Feuerwerker 1984:301–316).

It may very well be that in China, "the advent of a 'city bourgeoisie' created its own culture" (Shiba 1975:42): urban-based merchants and artisans

---

invaders did not hesitate to enslave whole communities of craftsmen to suit their exceptional needs" (Chaudhuri 1996:113) and many cities were often under the imperial control of posting scouts and garrisons (Humphrey and Hurelbaatar 2005:31). In China, those few wealthy individuals who managed to purchase entry into an administrative office were despised by most bureaucrats and were limited in terms of the amount of power they could accumulate (Gernet 1997:20). In Western Europe, however, the urban merchant-entrepreneur not only had the European nobility at his financial mercy, but was able to control the working population in the cities as well. In some cases, workers were forced to repay their debt by working for the merchants for free (Geremek 1968b:559).

59. As Brenner (1986:37) stated: "merchants do tend to be systematic profit maximizers, *to the extent they are able.*" By ignoring the existence of cities in his ideal-typical model of a precapitalist society, however, Brenner (1985, 1986) is unable to grasp the socioeconomic transformation that was brought about in Europe. For neo-Marxists like Brenner (1986:37) and Wood (1999), merchants are nothing more than luxury traders who sail back and forth on ships, buying cheap and selling dear, and are unable to bring about any change in society as their trading activities are limited to just a few immediate surpluses. The fundamentally important exploitative core–periphery relations between city-states and their colonies, as well as the city-states and their surrounding countryside (and the imposed division of labor that this entailed)—strategies later pursued by European mercantile states—appear to be of no significance to them. Yet institutions are crucial power containers that cannot be ignored if one is to understand social relations within states or the long-term historical developments of states.

60. This is also reflected in Merrington (1976:178). See Bairoch (1989:227–231).

constituted "the majority of the inhabitants" (Shiba 1970:127; Lippit 1987:36)
and some forms of urban identity may well have come into being during the
Ming dynasty (Zurndorfer 1983:308–309). But "unlike the guilds of medieval
Europe, the hang [guilds] in China were politically never very strong in the
cities and they were always under the control of the state" (Ma 1971:83; see
Gernet 1970:85). Consequently, "the Chinese merchant guilds never achieved
anything approaching the status and power of the merchant guilds of the city-
states of European civilization" (Needham 1969:197). Ma Keyao clearly spells
out the consequences:

> Because the [western] medieval town existed and acted as a political
> independent entity, it reared its citizen. The burgher, as a social group,
> played the role that Chinese town people did not . . . the craftsmen and
> merchants in China were weak strata, depended on the monarchy and
> were controlled by it. (1992:66–67)

Thus, despite China's advance on Europe throughout the Middle Ages, in
the long run the Imperial "centralized autocratic system exerted a negative influence on historical development" (Ganquan 1992:82). The notions
Stadtluft macht frei, bürgerliche Rechtssicherheit, or *Freies Eigentum*—
intrinsically linked with western urban institutions and subsequent capitalist development—were alien to China (Schurmann 1956:516; Needham
1969:185). Medieval Chinese towns, gigantic when compared to those in
Europe, dominated their countryside socioeconomically (Ganquan 1992:81)
but did not foster the rise of a politically independent merchant-
entrepreneurial bourgeoisie (Wong 1999:221; Maddison 1998:22).[61] This is
also true for Central Asia and its majestic cities, such as Samarkand or Bukhara
(see Ashrafyan 1998:340), or even the urban centers of the Ottoman realm
(Aricanli and Thomas 1994:27).

Given the Chinese example, then, it is important to emphasize whether
or not a merchant elite was in full political, economic, and military control of
the (city) state,[62] capable of implementing important structural strategies and

---

61. As Day puts it, "the spread of the market economy should not be confused with the rise of
capitalism, as the example of China—a country with an organized market network but without
a capitalist bourgeoisie—testifies" (1999:113–114). Nor should one confuse "free" city-states—in
which a merchant class uses its military and political power—with the emergence of a "free" market
(e.g., Mojuetan 1995:72), which is subsequently often juxtaposed with supposedly "despotic" or
patrimonial polities, which in turn limit economic growth. It is one thing to claim, as Hobson does
(2004:117), that the Smithian paradigm centered on Western free city-states and free trade is an
erroneous depiction of reality. It is something else to assert that distinctions between Chinese and
Western European cities simply did not exist.

62. For instance, the 14th-century city-state of Dubrovnik had two elected senates in which traders,
manufacturers, and shipping guilds were represented but no trace can be found of the presence

reinvesting in the political-military and commercial realm without having to worry about extraeconomic coercion and the imposition of tariffs and taxes by overlords, emperors, or even a rural aristocracy that could limit their power. In China such city-states—the "initial havens for capital accumulation" (McNeill 1992:120)—were notably absent (Needham 1969:185, 196). While different cities were designated as "capitals" by different Chinese dynasties (Chan 1992:648), this does not mean that they were politically independent entities. The Northern Sung capital of K'aifeng, for example, was the administrative and political center of the Chinese Empire and is thus somewhat comparable to Constantinople in the same century. However, it was certainly not a city-state. The citizens of K'aifeng "had no independent city government as their organ of expression, and their guilds were subject to government supervision" (Kracke 1975:53).[63]

The transfer of a capital from one region to another had enormous socio-economic consequences for a Chinese region (Hartwell 1967; 1982:379–386), if not for the entire Empire. When the Ming finally regained North China from the Mongols, China's focus shifted toward the North and away from the South (and the maritime trade associated with it).[64] After all, throughout most of its

---

of a rural aristocracy. I tend to agree with Pearson (1991:69) who asserts that "controllers of small political units typically have to take much more interest, for better or worse, in overseas trade than do rulers with large peasant populations that can be taxed relatively easily." This is exemplified in a comparison of China and Europe: "In contrast to the Chinese state's success with agricultural revenues, many European states could not extract much revenue from the land" (Wong 1997:134).

63. This was also the case in other Chinese cities: "Unlike the craftsmen in medieval cities in Europe, Chinese artisans never formed a viable economic force in the city because the most skillful craftsmen were forced to serve the government and its bureaucrats . . . virtually all lucrative businesses had already been monopolized by the state. Heavy taxation and other extortive practices spared no one but the scholar-official, resulting in extremely scarce capital for people to invest in industrial or commercial ventures" (Ma 1971:137). Ibn Battuta, who traveled through the Empire in the early 14th century, claims that the confiscations enacted by state officials were "a kind of extortion I have seen in no country, whether infidel or Muslim, except in China" (Gibb 1994:893). According to Elvin, "cities played a limited role in pre-modern Chinese political history [due to] the maintenance of a continuous centralized imperial authority and the absence of political fragmentation" (1978:85).

64. As Braudel suggested: "When in 1421 the Ming rulers changed their capital—leaving Nanking, and moving to Peking, in order to face the dangers of the Manchu and Mongol frontier—the massive world-economy of China swung round for good, turning its back on a form of economic activity based on the ease of access to seaborne trade. A new landlocked metropolis was now established deep in the interior and began to draw everything towards it . . . in the race for world dominion, this was the moment when China lost her position in a contest she had entered without fully realizing it, when she had launched the first maritime expeditions from Nanking in the early 15th century" (1992:III:32).
Interestingly, Wallerstein (1974:55) also considers this an important event, which Ray (1987:119) confirms. From that moment on, the Chinese government saw the sea as a "natural defensive barrier" against foreign intruders, while for the small European powers it was "a

existence, the Chinese Empire had drawn most of its revenue from the taxation of land (in contrast to various small European city-states) and its economy was "basically self-sufficient" (again, unlike the European city-states) (Findlay 1992:159).[65] Therefore the Chinese state had no intrinsic need to support its merchants, as did the European city-states and subsequent nation-states in the age of mercantilism. Once the external nomadic dangers had subsided somewhat, the merchants lost what relative importance they had enjoyed before the Ming dynasty came to power (Schurmann 1967:7). Under the Ming and subsequent Ch'ing dynasty, foreign trade became a "potential threat to the political order and, given the size of China and the extent of its domestic trade, [it] felt little need to acquire things unavailable domestically" (Lippit 1987:43).

It seems incorrect to continue arguing that somehow Western Europe was more commercialized than East Asia (e.g., Chirot 1994:70). What is important is the fact that the Chinese imperial state essentially brought about "commercialization without capitalism" since it controlled "large-scale finance, production and much foreign trade while the war-driven European state system allowed, enabled and required those activities to be controlled by private persons, thus producing capitalism" (Marks 1997:12). The idea that private interest groups, such as a collection of powerful merchants, would be able to make decisions about state affairs or foreign policies ran counter to the Chinese conceptualization of statecraft (Gernet 1997:20). If anything, since the Chinese merchants could not manipulate the state for their own goals (Wong 1983:248–251), they actually faced an Imperial state that acted more as an annoying marketplace competitor than as a tool that could be used to further their own commercial interests (Dawson 1972:236).[66] Moreover, whenever political and military

---

means of access to lands elsewhere" (Ng 1997:252). For Wang (1991:41–78), however, it seems that the focus on the nomadic threats in the North was more important than the capital's shift. Up to this day, "historians are divided to the necessity and value of [the] removal of the Ming capital from Nanjing to Peking" (Morton 1995:125).

65. Although the coastal regions of China were always affected by maritime trade, if one looks at China as a whole, its foreign trade (with a notable exception during the Southern Sung dynasty) "still weighed insignificantly with reference to the nation's total economy which was basically self-sufficient except for luxury items from tropical lands" (Chang 1974:357).

66. As an example, the Sung government discouraged investments because it "did not want the private merchants to have too much money pooled together so to compete with government resources" (Lo 1970:175). Lane spelled out the consequences of this policy: "Merchants who gained protection rents from international trade and colonization" had an advantage over those who could not. Throughout the entire history of the capitalist world-economy, one of the main concerns for merchants in their quest to ceaselessly accumulate capital is to construct and maintain a system that enables them to achieve "lower profits for governments and higher profits for trading enterprises" (1958:413). In other words, the "maximization of corporate capital and the minimization of corporate risks and costs" (Sprengard 1994:17) are intrinsically linked with the way merchant-entrepreneurs are able to use (or abuse) the state and its public funds to their own advantage

expansion of the Chinese Empire occurred, the incorporation of "new frontiers committed the government to a shift of resources to the peripheries, not extraction from them" (Wong 1997:148) (often the opposite of what occurred in the European mercantilist tradition).

One should also not forget that one of the reasons the Chinese were incapable of systematically developing, pursuing, and implementing a strategy of socioeconomic subordination, colonization, and exploitation vis-à-vis the non-Chinese, was the incessant warfare that drained the Empire's resources and made China the target of immense and continuous destruction. Chinese military activity had to be "directed at defense rather than conquest" (Snooks 1996:320). This incessant warfare—mostly along the frontiers, but at times, also within China—was generated by two crucial variables not at play in Europe: incessant peasant uprisings and the devastation and warfare brought about by the nomadic peoples living on the frontiers (of which the Huns, Kitans, Uighurs, Jurchen, Tanguts, and Mongols are the most renowned) (Wang 1970:222; Di Cosmo 2002).[67] The number of massive peasant rebellions in medieval and early modern China was enormous (Deng 1999:363–376) when compared with the relatively few uprisings in medieval Europe.[68] While canals were built and large-scale commerce of food was encouraged by the authorities

(Boone 1984:104). This is more important than the opening up of markets and the removal of impediments for growth, as Smithians would have us believe (e.g., Epstein 2000b). Archival sources clearly indicate that as long as the Pax Mongolica lasted (and its decreased protection, information, and transportation costs), European merchants (with some exceptions, like the Vivaldi brothers) had little interest in circumnavigating Africa to access the wealth of Asia (Richard 1970:363). Yet, when the Il-Khanid Empire disintegrated after the mid-1330s and the Pax Mongolica broke down (Kwanten 1979:244–246; Jackson 1975:130), together with the dissolution of the Chagatay Khanate in the 1340s (Forbes Manz 1983) and the deterioration of Mongol control over China after the 1330s, European merchants used their respective city- and nation-states to gain access to (and eventually dominate) Eastern markets (Sprengard 1994:14; Golden 1998:43). Thus, the commercial contacts under the Pax Mongolica "led to the European age of exploration of the 15th century, which culminated in the discovery of the sea route around the Cape of Good Hope to Asia" (Rossabi 1997b:56). In contrast, the Ming actually increased costs for merchants since maritime trade was illegal from the Ming dynasty onward. Chinese traders "could hardly do without a minimum of bribery" (Ptak 1994:41). This is important because in the early modern period, "the most significant expenses of the long-distance trader were transportation and protection costs" (Allsen 1989:97). In addition, "the lack of a reliable commercial code and justice in the court deprived merchants of legal protection for their enterprises" (Chang 1994:66; see Maddison 1998:14). This is again in contrast to the existent practices within the European city-states (North 1991:24–25).

67. William McNeill claims that in the early 15th century, a direct link existed between nomadic warfare and the end of the Chinese maritime activities in the Indian Ocean: "Chinese imperial authorities prohibited sea voyaging on the ground that it diverted valuable resources from the more urgent tasks of land defense against a threatening nomad power across the northwest frontier" (1992:111). Linck confirms this: "The Ming dynasty's self-imposed isolation occurred under the traumatic impact of Mongolian foreign rule and continued Mongolian harassments" (1997:116).

68. Those that did occur were related to the overall weakness of the Western European nobility.

in order to prevent famines (Hsü 1972) and subsequent social unrest (Wong 1983:248), the strong Chinese state provoked systematic armed rebellions by subjecting its peasants to heavy taxation. Repressing these peasant rebellions was not always a sound policy since the uprisings could be interpreted to mean that the ruling dynasty's mandate from heaven had been removed. The ensuing political and military turmoil contributed to a struggle in which merchants could not play a significant political role.[69]

In his *Afterthoughts on Material Civilization and Capitalism,* Braudel stated that due to its totalitarian control, "the Chinese state showed constant hostility to the spread of capitalism" (1977:72). This statement needs to be modified and explained. The Chinese state was not totalitarian in the modern sense of the word. It is erroneous to claim that "the rulers of Ming China differed from almost all their west European counterparts in that they positively discouraged economic growth" (Bonney 1995:3), that Ming China "withdrew from world trade and declined economically, short circuiting the advance toward capitalism" (Sanderson 1994:52), or that "the unified empires of India and China crushed all economic progress" (Macfarlane 1988:191) since Chinese state support for a market economy and economic growth were very much a reality. Such support, however, was not synonymous with an approval of "concentrations of wealth through market manipulation" (Wong 1999:225). The crucial element is that Chinese governmental officials "supported commercial exchange without promoting concentrations of merchant wealth" (Wong 1997:137). Because China was "a huge continental empire sustained by taxes on land, bureaucratically governed with minimal concern for the interests of its own mercantile class" (Hudson 1970:167), it was only natural that the Chinese state "supported the principles of market exchange and sought to protect buyers from monopoly power" (Wong 1997:139), thus resisting the merchants' desires to accumulate wealth at the expense of others (Wong 1983:251), as was done in Western Europe. The latter differed from China, both on the continent and its overseas colonies, because of its "non-Smithian features of European economic expansion represented by sugar and slavery" (Wong 2002:453–454).[70]

---

69. The policy of preventing peasant unrest was the central preoccupation of any Chinese administration since a failure to do so could (and occasionally did) result in massive peasant uprisings that could overthrow the dynasty. Nevertheless, a close examination of the Imperial bureaucratic system reveals that since the lower classes (i.e., peasants) "were able to be represented at all levels of the bureaucracy" (Deng 1999:67), the Confucian bureaucrats allied themselves with the peasants in an antimerchant coalition (Deng 1999:199). Furthermore, Chinese agricultural development was highly successful (Weulersse 1996:794–795); "increased land revenues made income from other sectors of the economy less necessary, [which] reinforced Confucian prejudices in favor of agriculture" (Dreyer 1982:243).

70. Abrams rightfully states: "It was not really the towns that caused the West to advance but the peculiar inability of western feudalism to prevent these people [in them] from maximizing their advantages" (1978:25). In the Chinese state, the gentry were always considerably more powerful

Most significantly, "the potentially disruptive consequences of both concentrated wealth and the pursuit of such wealth" (Wong 1997:146), which cannot be separated from the construction of a capitalist society, was successfully opposed in China by the ruling strata because "China had a mode of operation radically different from that of the European system" (Hung 2001:474)[71].

Conclusions vis-à-vis European Capitalism

While a 20th-century modernization theory and Smithian historiography may look upon the origins of the modern capitalist world-economy as a natural outcome of economic processes, the historical reality of capitalism proves otherwise.[72] The length of urban networks, the flow of goods, the division of labor

---

than the urban merchant elite and this had a considerable impact on how merchants were regarded throughout society. It was not so much that there was, at least compared with Western Europe, an absence of "entrepreneurs eager to make profits" as Braudel (1993:195) claimed, but that for the Chinese state, "enrichment of merchants was viewed as having been achieved at the expense of peasant welfare and government revenue" (Deng 1999:96). As Ho (1962:259) points out, "success in trade, industry, finance, science, and technology, which has for centuries been socially esteemed in the west, was viewed in traditional China as secondary achievement." This is also admitted by Abu-Lughod: "An independent and powerful bourgeoisie was not likely to develop in a society in which merchants were not accorded as much honor as government functionaries and in which a centralized state set the terms for money and credit" (1989:332). Needham confirms this: "In China affluence carried comparatively little prestige. The ideal of a merchant's son was to enter the imperial examination system and to rise high in the bureaucracy" (1969:202). Maddison also praises the Chinese bureaucracy for its "very positive impact on agriculture" and blames their hostility toward merchants, but does not clarify the link (1998:23). There has been a long tradition within the Chinese Imperial Administration and the Court regarding the well-being of the people, especially the poor, which explains specific public policies detrimental to wealthy merchants (Lamouroux 2002; Lamouroux 2003:115; 131–132; 142). These policies cannot be separated from the fact that most power in the Chinese polity had been historically derived not from within cities (as in Europe) but against them (Gernet 1997:19).

71. An analysis of the edicts promulgated by Hong Duc, who ruled over Vietnam (1460–1497), is quite similar. The government appeared to be suspicious of *excessive* concentrations of markets as well as merchant wealth and attempted to achieve a just redistribution of merchandise and better control over transactions and markets in order to protect the common weal against various manipulations undertaken by traders (Yvon-Tran 2002:16–18). Gernet (1997:21) argues that "the contemporary notion that translates the concept 'economy' in Chinese as in Japanese, Korean and Vietnamese is derived from the ancient Chinese expression which means 'to put order in the world and bring help to the people' which explains why state functionaries consider this to be their primary responsibility."

72. One might take into account that "descriptions of the historical markets [are] opposed to the market of economic theory" (Steensgaard 1991:9) since "the separation of economic and political structures is regarded by most commentators as a crucial part of capitalism" (Mann 1980:176). Indeed, speculations on Smithian extensive, and evolutionary growth across Eurasia (Lieberman 1997:498) miss a crucial point: In whose interest did certain state polities intervene (cf. Lane 1979)?

in cities, and the size of the cities were not unique to Europe. In fact, the European variants of these factors cannot compare with those that existed in the Eurasian landmass. I tend to agree with Stavrianos' assessment:

> Western European cities were insignificant in medieval times compared to those of China, India or the Middle East, both in population and in volume of trade. But they were quite unique because of their growing autonomy and political power . . . as the burghers/citizens acquired power and financial resources, townspeople could usually get the king to give them a royal charter licensing them to unite in a single commune. The commune had the right to act as a corporation; to make agreements under its corporate seal; to have its own town hall, court of law [with its election systems] and dependent territory outside its walls. (1999:233)

But, as discussed earlier, the Chinese "political and social structure did not favor the development of capitalism" (Rodzinksi 1979:162). The political power of the wealthy merchant class, an urban-based bourgeoisie, was a sine qua non for the creation of a capitalist system.

In Europe, if a serf escaped and lived in a city for a year and a day without being apprehended, he was freed (and, ironically, free to be exploited by the merchant entrepreneurs within the city). Possibilities like this altered the structure of Western European society (Rietbergen 1998:133), undermining the historical cycle of "primitive accumulation" that had been primarily based on the nobility's extraeconomic coercive practices. From the 12th century onward, many peasants could reduce or even abolish their services on a lord's land by paying him a fixed sum (Cherubini 1990:124–125), which, due to inflation, eventually made the lord even more vulnerable (Bozorgnia 1998) and thus more dependent on the fortune of the successful urban-based merchant class.[73] In China, however, it was the other way around. In the Yuan Dynasty, "the actual rent was calculated in percentages of the crop yield rather than in absolute amounts—a condition hardly conducive to increased production" (Schurmann 1967:26). But it did safeguard the grip of the "rentiers" (be they the gentry or the state) on the peasants, preventing a potential coalition of merchant and nobility. In addition, since the agricultural productivity of rice in China was much higher than dry grain–producing Europe, it is likely that

---

73. It is no wonder that the *noblesse de robe* appears all over Western Europe from the 14th century onward (Crouzet-Pavan 1997:16; Blockmans 1983:68; Miller 1990:240; Cuadrada 1991:292), if not earlier in the most commercially advanced regions where the *homines novi* grew in importance most rapidly while part of the nobility became further impoverished (Halpérin 1950:146; Bonenfant and Despy 1958:57–58; Dumolyn and van Tricht 2000:200–201).

higher levels of surplus extraction occurred in China (Palat and Wallerstein 1999:25). This may explain why the Chinese state and the Chinese nobility in the Ming dynasty did not pursue revenues from maritime overseas trade (and conquests), as was the case in Europe.

By the early 14th century, a political structure had unfolded within the larger European cities in which "the legislative and executive rights that had been grudgingly granted were concentrated in the hands of mercantile elite" (Holt and Rosser 1990:8) who used the city's political power and public finances—generated by taxes—for their own interests (Boone 1984:104). Not surprisingly, it is particularly in the larger cities, whose exports were geared toward long-distance markets, that we most clearly find the embryonic appearance both of capitalist exploitation and class formations (Friedrichs 1975:45). The political structure of European city-states was a major influence since it created the backbone for the urban elite's political representation in "national" consultative assemblies (parliaments), also known as *estates*, which by the early 14th century had emerged all over the continent (Rietbergen 1998:135–136; Smith 1991b:61–62). In the long run, this representation strengthened the bargaining power of the urban-based merchant bourgeoisie.[74]

In my opinion, it was the European nobility's relative poverty (when compared with the Chinese gentry) that restricted their political power; their need to call on credit and financiers was structurally unavoidable. Militarily incapable of building a large empire (unlike the Chinese), the "most common and benefiting thing to do for a prince, when in need of cash, was to borrow from his towns or burghers/citizens" (van Uytven 1996:220). This in turn resulted in the weakening of the prince's political power, as charters and concessions had to be given in return for the financial (and at times, political or military) support of the urban-based elites in charge of the city-state politically, economically, and judicially (Blanks 1998:188).[75] More often than not, this support meant

---

74. As Anderson correctly points out, "few Estates ever yielded to royal rulers the right to raise permanent or general taxation without the consent of their subjects" (1974:46).

75. One should not only think of the city-states in the Low Countries or Northern Italy or in the various urban leagues throughout the Holy Roman Empire, but also of a city such as 13th century Montpellier: the "overlord" King Peter II of Aragon "owed the burghers enormous sums of money in exchange for which he left them free to run their own affairs" (Caille 1998:68). In 1311, "le duc Otton de Bassse-Bavière reconnut l'union conclue par les nobles et les bourgeois pour se défendre contre les abus de l'administration et leur accorda expressément le droit de résister à son autorité au cas où il romprait ses engagements," essentially illustrating the birth of the *Ständestaat* (Folz 1965:178–179). In the city, as Rossiaud (1990:148) points out, "the urban social model was the burgher and the essential criterion of differentiation was money." Speaking of the latter, the bourgeoisie was perfectly aware of the European nobility's (and even monarchy's) financial difficulties, and offered them much-needed loans in exchange for all kinds of privileges and monopolies (Cuadrada 1991:292; Nazet 1978:446; Rodrigues 1997:21)."Efficient interest aggregation around centralization of resources for the armed forces was best achieved in states where the representative institutions and the groups they represented were brought into the decision making process

increasing conditional, juridical autonomy in the form of all kinds of privileges, in return for an increase of specific taxes (Benevolo 1993:60).[76] The nobility's continuous wars of attrition—which they could not afford to wage without relying on merchants' loans (Strayer 1977:274)—also facilitated the bourgeoisie's increasing influence as city-states became critical agents in the existing Western European balance of power (Blockmans 1983).[77]

One must be careful to avoid the construction of a new and more sophisticated version of typical Oriental Despotism vs. European free-market oriented and democratic urban communities (von Sivers 1993; Soullière 1984; Vries 2003:28). It seems unlikely that the European nobility as a whole was less "despotic" than the non-European nobility.[78] Instead, the "extreme dispersal

---

and compelled to share responsibility for its security policy. Their degree of active participation in the state formation process might be of crucial importance. If the social elite were given a stake in the success of the central state they were likely to use their social influence, their capital and their patronage to further the interests of the state" (Glete 2000:64).

76. Because of their relative weakness, European governments often had to tolerate and legitimate the monopolistic activities of the wealthiest merchants, which is in stark contrast with the situation in China. Essentially, the European state and its wealthy merchants were mutually dependent on each other (Wong 1997:127–146). Thus the emerging European nation-state in the early modern period was anything but absolutist, nor was it just a vehicle for repressive extraeconomic ambitions of a feudal class, as Anderson (1974) claimed. Anderson also fails to explain how his "absolutist state" would have furthered capitalism (Lachmann 1987:8).

77. As Strayer duly noted, the "economic consequences of war certainly contributed to the great European depression of the later Middle Ages" (1977:291). The question is, to what extent increasing cycles of conflicts between various layers of the impoverished aristocracy were expressions of the long-term decline of the *feudal system* as such.

78. Chang (1994:68–73) emphasizes the predatory nature of the Chinese state and claims that it resulted in the general feeling that it did not make sense for merchants to continue their successful accumulation of capital beyond a certain point because the state would "milk it away" from them, thus inhibiting the growth of capitalism. Whenever it could get away with it, the European nobility would also default on their loans (e.g., Emperor Charles V) or attempt to confiscate mercantile wealth. Because of a different institutional structure in Western Europe, however, the nobility got away with it less often than did their Asian counterparts. Indeed some cities (Bruges or Ghent) "possessed privileges stating that the property of their citizens could not be confiscated" (Dumolyn 2000:519). Chang also argues that the Chinese extended family (as opposed to the Western "individual" nuclear family), would have drained the merchant of precious revenues. This is confirmed by Mote who states that "successful merchants tended to dissipate wealth rather than accumulate it, and in so doing adopted the prevailing pattern of the bureaucratic social elite" (1999:391). Both the modernization theory (Parsons 1952; Belshaw 1965) and Marxist perspectives (Engels 1972) have often used the argument that large extended families were at odds with capitalist modernity, the latter represented by the prominence of individualism (Crone 1989:154). But one could easily reverse the argument and discuss the advantages of extended family households. Frankly, it is impossible to assess the impact of individualistic vs. collectivistic cultural values on different societies (Hofstede 1997:49–78; Young 1976:31). But one should not forget that excessive spending on nonmercantile activities also occurred on a large scale in Europe. Not that there existed anything like the "betrayal of the bourgeoisie," because for genuine capitalist entrepreneurs, real estate acquisitions are strategies of capital accumulation that complement

of power" within Europe (Crone 1989:156)[79] proved to be an important variable, both as a weakness—any major Asian army could have easily beaten any European army, as happened with the invasion of the Mongols—and also as a strength. As Stavrianos (1999) and Findlay (1992) point out, no European emperor could have ordered the withdrawal of the Iberian vessels out of the ocean for the sake of imperial policy. Because of the nobility's weakness, division and inability to adequately (re)generate primitive accumulation based on extraeconomic coercion, the elites in charge of the European city-state system were capable of constructing and implementing strategies that furthered the ceaseless accumulation of capital (with subsequent reinvestments in their companies). The urban merchant elite's exploitation of the population external and internal to the city-state was necessary to feed the city and to trade with the East.

Throughout most of the 13th and early 14th century, the division of labor within the European cities and their countrysides continued to expand. Specialization within guilds increased unabatedly. Is it a coincidence that these phenomena occurred precisely when the Pax Mongolica—which Cahen (1983:201) referred to as the "golden age" of Eurasian trade relations—was established (1250–1350)? The substantial decrease in transaction and protection costs resulted in an unprecedented expansion of the market for Western European city-states, which in turn increased the division of labor in most of the European urban industries (Ma 1999:45).[80]

The international textile trade in the Middle Ages is sometimes overlooked or underestimated as most scholars tend to focus on bullion flows or the spice trade. However one should not forget that textiles were sometimes more

---

their commercial activities (see Furió 2005:50); but the emulation of Chang's "parasitic rent-seeking literati by the merchant class" is similar to the emulation of the Saint-Simonian parasitic rent-seeking nobility of the European merchant class who often invested profits in land and other real estate (Budak 1997:166). It appears that in every society, merchants had to invest resources to a certain extent, in what Pierre Bourdieu aptly coined social and cultural capital.

79. In this text I have emphasized the institutional space carved out by merchants, but the Church was also very powerful in medieval Europe, which was also in sharp contrast with China. As Adshead points out, in Plantagenet England, "15,000 monks owned between a quarter and a third of the lands, rents and dues of England [while] under the T'ang 350,000 monks owned only 4% of the cultivated area of China" (2000:57). Thus, the Church was another institutional force that prevented the construction of an Empire like that in China (Spruyt 1994).

80. Thus, it is Eurocentric to claim that "medieval development" in Europe was nothing but "auto-development" (e.g., Delatouche 1989:26). The opening up of the East Asian market due to the Pax Mongolica was of an unprecedented scale and provided enormous opportunities for the Western city-states (Balard 1983). The expansion of the textile industry in the Low Countries, for example, was intrinsically linked with "the increased demand for woolen cloth in interregional and international commerce" (Van Werveke 1954:237–238). Reference to the "cloth of Tartary" can be found in Chaucer, Dante, Boccaccio, and many other European texts (Allsen 1997:2).

valuable than spices in the international market (Malanima 1987:351), and
that by the 14th century the export of textiles to the Middle East (and also to
a certain extent, East Asia) was vital, compensating to a certain degree for the
constant loss of bullion to the East created through the unequal balance of trade
maintained by the Western European cities (Day 1978:5, 39; Cahen 1970:36;
Spuford 1988:146–147).[81] Without the export of textiles to the Middle East and
East Asia (Lopez 1943:176; Lopez 1977:450)—where textiles were in high demand (Allsen 1997), especially under the Mongols, and often served as a means
of exchange (Serruys 1982)—recurring growth in Western Europe would have
been impeded (Stearns, Adas, and Schwartz 1996:468; Wolff 1982:509).[82] The
"commercial efflorescence" between the European merchants in the Black Sea
area on the one hand, and Central and East Asian markets on the other, should
not be underestimated (Di Cosmo 2005:392).

The 13th and 14th centuries changed many European merchants' views of
Asia (Bouchon 1999:311–318) as more economic and cultural contacts were
established (Togan 1991:218). Whereas prior to the early 13th century the
non-Christian world, including East Asia, was perceived and symbolized as
chaotic at best, if not outright demonic, the Mongol explosion replaced it with
"un reservoir de richesses fabuleuses et de toutes merveilles ... d'un monde
désiré" (Mattoso 1988:105). When the Mongol empire was more or less stable
in the period circa 1250–1340, East Asia offered merchants enormous opportunities.[83] The first half of the 14th century can be considered "the Golden

---

81. It is estimated that by the 15th century, approximately 40 percent of the goods coming from
the East were paid for with Western goods and 60 percent with precious metals (Pamuk 2000:23).

82. "The inadequate supply of bullion was one reason for the permanent deflationary depression
lasting from 1390–1460, and most likely it was also the reason for the political instability of those
days" (Von Stromer 1981:24). As Atwell (2002:88) points out, the scarcity of bullion in Western
Europe cannot be separated from the trade with East Asia.

83. It has traditionally been assumed that since the Eurasian silk route was an overland trade, it
could not have been as important as maritime trade and thus its impact was probably minimal.
Yet, as Palat and Wallerstein state, "it is unwarranted to assume that land routes were always
eclipsed by sea traffic" (1999:33). The overland trade route to China started from the eastern part
of the Caspian Sea because Italian ships were not only active on the Black Sea and the Sea of
Azov (where settlements were located), but also on the Don, the Volga, and the Caspian (Cordier
1967:105; Richard 1970:362; Nystazopoulou 1973:562). Chinese silk—one of the main objects
of trade with the Orient—was greatly sought after in the European market due to its low price
and was imported on a significant scale as long as protection costs remained low. Although the
Genoese sold some Chinese silk in Italy and France prior to the destruction of Baghdad by the
Mongols in 1258 (Petech 1962:550), it was only after the Mongols crushed the Muslim domination
of Mesopotomia that the Italians started to regularly "import Chinese silk directly from its country
of origin. This direct import of Chinese silk evolved into mass commerce, which was sustained
not by its great quality but by the [enormous] quantity of it, and its relatively low price" (Lopez
1975:104). Not only was the northern route (from the Caspian to Urgench) important in the
territories controlled by the Golden Horde (Grekov and Iakoubovski 1939:143), but so was the
southern route (Heyd 1959). With large settlements in Trabzon, Lajazzo, and Tabriz (Richard

Age of western penetration into Mongol Asia" (Richard 1977:I:17).[84] Thus, the desire for ever more luxuries from the East, facilitated by the Pax Mongolica, generated an incentive among European urban merchant elites to implement strategies to acquire recurring growth, based essentially on colonial exploitation (Verlinden 1970; Balard 1989), unequal exchange, exploitation of wage laborers, and the subsequent commoditization, subjugation, and exploitation of the natural realm.

This was quite unique to Western Europe. While city-states could be found elsewhere throughout the Middle Ages,[85] they never experienced a transition to an inter-state system where merchants retained so much institutionalized political power. In fact, the European private (but state-supported) colonial enterprises stood in sharp contrast to the more peaceful Asian free-market economy (Needham 1970; Thomaz 1988:31; Chang 1991b:24). Therefore, the qualitative shift from an inter-city-state system to an inter-state system cannot be separated from a discussion of the transition from feudalism to capitalism. Within the emerging European nation-state, the merchant class could not only hope to occupy crucial posts in the bureaucracy and the administration (Prak 1992:192; Galland 1998), but it could regularly use the mercantile state's strength to support its own colonial and capitalist strategies.[86] Although many

---

1977:I:12; Lopez 1975:108; Pistarino 1990:192–193), the Italians were able to import much silk from Persia (Matthee 1999:16) and China up to the mid-1340s when the chanates of the Il-Khan and Chagatai dissolved into anarchy (Akhmedov 1998:267). At that time, the silk route across the Khanate of the Golden Horde became less safe (Balard 1989:XII:85) and Lajazzo was sacked by the Mamluks (AD 1347). But the Northern route from the Don River to Urgench and the Amu-Darya remained quite safe up to the 1360s (Phillips 1998:113) and was often used by Italian traders (Petech 1962:559–560). For a splendid overview of trade routes from Europe to East Asia and the people who used them, see Reichert (1992).

84. Even after the mid-1340s, western (primarily Italian) merchants continued to penetrate the East (Richard 1977:I:21; Lenhoff and Martin 1989; Balard 1989:XIV:158–159), but the amount of traders and the volume of commodities transported back to the West shrank remarkably (Balard 1983:38). For a useful collection of testimonies, see Gueret-Laferte (1994).

85. See Pearson (1991:70–74); Snellnow (1981); Brett (1995); Horton and Middleton (2000:157–178).

86. For administrative practices and the Chinese gentry, cf. the discussion on the work of Patricia Ebrey, John Chaffee et al. by Xiaonan and Lamouroux (2004). At the very least, merchant capitalism was "an essential preliminary of the decisive change that took place with the advent of European industrialization" (Goody 1996:223), which in turn widened the gap between the West and the non-West more rapidly. As stated above, some scholars (e.g., O'Brien 1992) tend to dismiss the profits derived from international trade prior to the Industrial Revolution. But the indirect influence of commercial profits derived from overseas (colonial) profits on the industrialization process should not be underestimated (Leuilliot 1970:620–621; Inikori 2002). The long-term construction of a periphery in South and East Asia through an imposed system of commercial capitalism was *primarily* for the benefit of European core powers. This does not imply that Europe was the "only active maker in history" (Washbrook 1990:492), as the technological and commercial link with Asia also was crucial for its development. One of the questions I simply want to raise is: Why did

Chinese ventured out into the entire Southeast Asian region during the Sung and Yuan dynasties, they were not supported by the Chinese Empire (Wills Jr. 1993:87). This was in contrast with "European maritime merchants who were large traders with state support" (Hui 1995:28)—support crucial to their ability to trade and subsequently colonize in the long run (Andrade 2004:443–444).[87] Had European merchants also lacked this state support, "they would have probably established connections with Asian traders in some of the major emporia and thus participated in the network of emporia trade" (Rothermund 1991:7). But with state support behind them, Portuguese, Dutch and ultimately British merchants were able to act quite differently (Vries 2003:59-60).

Unlike China, the Portuguese state "promoted overseas trade and gave incentives to its subjects to participate in it" (Ptak 1994:44). The same can be said of the Dutch state, as early 17th-century eyewitnesses observed that "the Dutch government was vitally interested in promoting the welfare of its merchants wherever they might be engaged in commerce" (Wertheim 1993:50). Ptak does not hesitate to call the early modern Portuguese state "a kind of huge entrepreneurial institution which wanted to improve its position in international trade and politics by establishing the Estado da India" (1994:44–45). In the long run, the Portuguese state was not the real benefactor of its activities in Asia after "royal bankruptcies and debts transferred control of exchequer and trade to foreign merchant-bankers" (Pearson 1988:34), namely Genoese and Florentine capitalists who aspired to outflank the joint Venetian–Mamluk monopoly over trade routes to East Asia by financing the Portuguese exploration of the Atlantic (Unger 1997:513; Melis 1969) and by sustaining it with

---

Europe eventually dominate and colonize almost the entire Eurasian landmass (a process that lasted several centuries), with far-reaching consequences for its own path of development, while the far superior early modern Asian powers did not pursue such a strategy? If events in East Asia had occurred differently, it may be plausible that "Europe could have become very much a periphery of a system centered in Asia" (Fitzpatrick 1992:513) and not capitalistic. When the Portuguese forces besieged Malacca in 1511, its Sultan appealed to the Chinese Emperor, of which he considered himself a vassal, for aid (Bouchon 1999:81). In the competitive European context of state formation, imperialism, and colonial expansion, in which war was a crucial factor (Tilly 1992; Spruyt 1994), it is doubtful that such a call for help would have gone unanswered, especially since there was a substantial Chinese community living in the city (Ptak 2004:X:179).

87. "The qualities we associate with commercial activities, risk-taking, entrepreneurial activities, the search for foreign markets, the mobility and the desire to accumulate and reinvest, were widely distributed [throughout Asia] and cannot be looked upon in the framework of European developments alone" (Goody 1996:222). Such a statement is self-evident but it is not the same as being a professional merchant who can use the advantages of state power on the one hand (by externalizing certain costs, such as protection rent), and who has sufficient freedom (through institutional and legal protection) from states and rulers on the other (Andrade 2006). The full development of modern banking and credit facilities, for example, was hindered in China because of "the lack of a legal and political framework which protected wealth from the state itself and some of its rapacious officials" (Wang 1970:222).

experienced sailors and navigational expertise (Verlinden 1969). Thus, it is erroneous to claim that "up to the voyages of Columbus the Italian merchants
did not have any interests in looking for a new route to East Asia" (Grzybowski
1969:219). It was precisely the inter-city-state competition for access to Eastern
markets and the threat of the expanding Ottoman Empire that led to the discovery of the Americas. What is more important to note is that the Portuguese
methods of colonization and subjugation represented a continuation of Italian
practices in the Mediterranean (Pearson 1991:106; Scammell 1981; Verlinden
1984) discussed earlier. The way European merchant capitalists could com-
bine the state's political and economic power to their own advantage (Baskin
and Miranti 1999:29–88) is in striking contrast with the non-Western European powers that had access to the Indian Ocean. The Karimi merchants, who
accumulated much more wealth than did their European counterparts by controlling the trade from Egypt to the Indian Ocean during the Late Middle Ages,
are a good example. Though one can indeed consider them "merchant capitalists" (Garcin et al. 2000b:120), their lack of political power was, in the long run,
their undoing (Arenson 1996:117) because the Egyptian state, which was not
under their control, eventually turned against them (Labib 1970:214; Fischel
1958:172–173; Ashtor 1992:VI:322).[88] The unwillingness and at times inability
of several non-Western maritime powers (e.g., Mamluk Egypt and Ming China)
to support their overseas merchants enabled the small, weak European powers
to occupy "small posts of commercial and defensive potential at selected strategic points all along the coasts of the Indian Ocean" (Keswani 1970:544). Their
military supremacy by sea, essentially an expanding "network of trading posts
and fortresses on the fringes of the continent" (Malefakis 1997:173), ultimately
resulted in the establishment of ever-more effective commercial monopolies
(Reid 1992:458). These incrementally small steps were, to the disbelief of
the great land-based empires of Asia, nothing more than a prelude to world
domination (Katz 1989:90). These different policies can be explained by the
fundamentally divergent hierarchical social structures in China and Western
Europe, which in turn helps to clarify why Western Europe was, in spite of its
lesser achievements, the cradle of capitalism.

---

88. Cf. the recent study by Meloy (2003) who argues that the Mamluk Sultan Barsbay did attempt—
albeit temporarily—to implement a more mercantilist strategy favoring Egyptian merchants than
has been previously acknowledged. Due to the nature of the Sultanate, however, this was not a
sustained policy.

CHAPTER THREE

The Political Economies of South Asia and Europe Compared

Trade and Commodity Flows in the South Asian Region

The more traditional gloomy representations of South Asia as a subcontinent that suffered from economic self-containment with trade primarily composed of high-valued luxuries (e.g., Gopal 1965:157; Palat 1988:283, 447), has been increasingly challenged over the last thirty years (Prakash 1971:203; Subrahmanyam 1994:12–13).[1] The relative lack of South Asian sources on long-distance trade in the period A.D. 1000 to 1400 (Wijetunga 1968:497) should not imply that foreign trade was insignificant. Instead, Chinese and Arab sources confirm (Jain 1990:71–72; Gibb 1994:813) that the South Asian subcontinent's "expansion of overseas trade was an important factor in, as well as a reflector of economic growth" (Indrapala 1971:101) during the 10th to 13th centuries (Hall 1980:111). After all, the South Asian subcontinent was "the midway location

---

1. Chandra claims that from the 10th century onward there was a notable "revival of towns in north India" (1997:169) that can be related to the concurrent (albeit partial) monetization of the economy in South Asia (Deyell 1990:112–132; Champakalakshmi 1995:289) and Southeast Asia (Wicks 1992:134). Throughout the Indian Ocean, "new networks of exchange, formation of trade guilds and a new phase of money production and circulation" occurred (Chattopadhyaya 1995b:325), reflecting intense interregional trade (Lewis 1976). According to Ibn Hawkal, in the 10th century, the majority of the inhabitants of the city of Daybul lived from commercial activities; al-Idrisi also noted intense trade with Oman and China in the middle of the 12th century (Kervan 1996:56).

between west Asia on the one hand and southeast and east Asia on the other" (Prakash 1998:12).

After a severe economic downturn in the post-Gupta period (circa 600–900) (Thakur 1989:25; Chattopadhyaya 1974), parts of the South Asian peninsula (especially the southwest) experienced "rapid urban growth and an upsurge in maritime trade" by the 11th century (McPherson 1993:107; Indrapala 1971:102). This upsurge in trade was not 'confined to the regional market' (Jain 1990:35).[2] From the 11th century on, the Malabar and Gujarat coasts benefited from an intense trade with the Arabian peninsula. Trade from the South Asian coast to Eastern Africa was also of tremendous importance from at least the 11th century onward—from Egypt in the North (Gotein 1954) to Kilwa and Sofala in the South (Newitt 1987; Pearson 1998).[3]

Like in Europe, bulk commodities were widely bought and sold across various regions; grains, sugar, oils, salt, potteries, leather, timber and metal goods, rice,[4] and more importantly, textiles,[5] were transported in considerable quantities over large distances (Jain 1990:57–70). Trade from South Asia to Aden, for instance, included "rice, kichree, sesame, soap, cushions, pillows, table cloths, arabi cloths manufactured on the Malabar coast" while trade to South Asia included "Arabian horses and madder" (Shihab 1996:

---

2. Yet the regional market should not be underestimated. In the late 13th century, the South Asian continent was probably more populated than either China or Europe and the market demand this generated was considerable. Interregional trade was particularly impressive: from foodstuffs, dyes, yarn, iron, and textiles to horses, elephants, spices, and pearls (Abraham 1988:64, 123–128, 156–181).

3. In the early 13th century, "porcelain, cotton and copper were brought on Gujarati, Arab and Persian ships to Oman and the Persian Gulf and exchanged for African commodities" (Varadarajan 1987:101). These in turn were mostly "gold, ivory, and mangrove timber" (Chaudhuri 1985:57) as reflected in the 12th-century writings of al-Idrisi (Ferrand 1913:1:177). The slave trade from Northeastern Africa to South Asia was also considerable prior to the Portuguese intrusion (Pescatello 1977:26–29).

4. According to Pearson, rice was traded by sea "within the Bay of Bengal, in Indonesia and up and down the west coast of India: Indian rice even went to Aden, Hormuz and Malacca" (1987b:75).

5. Textiles in particular were exported from South Asia to the South Arabian coast (Smith 1997:XIII:36) as well as from Gujarat to Malabar and then to China, but metals, timber, and cereals were also frequent export commodities (Jain 1990:99–104). "Artisanal production of handicraft articles, metal-working and cloth production [became] important features of the economy" in southern South Asia (Heitzman 1997:219). Gujarati, Coromandel, and Bengal cloth was sold "in substantial quantities" as far away as Malacca, Indonesia, and the Ryu Kyu islands (Das Gupta 1987:248). Contrary to Stein (1982:42), Ramaswamy even claims that during this period, "the foreign trade in textiles was perhaps of greater importance than the internal trade" (1985b:70). For a detailed overview of specialization and large-scale production in the textile and ceramic crafts in Vijayanagar, cf. Sinolopi (1988).

25–26).[6] Some of the exchanged commodities were handled by large traders, not just peddlers (Meilink-Roelofsz 1970:152; Gunawardana 1987:88; Chandra 1997:196). Recent archeological evidence suggests that commercial linkages between South Arabian coastal towns and South Asia, and to a certain degree even East Asia, were much more intense from the 12th to the 15th centuries than previously envisaged (Hardy-Guilbert 2004; Rougeulle 2004; Bing 2004).

This notable "increase in the tempo of trade" from the 11th century onward (Gommans 1998:8–9) was also evidenced by the presence of South Asian traders in Java (Varadarajan 1987:105), in China (Guy 2001), a notable resurgence in urbanization (Kulke 1995:13), and the increased activities of several South Asian merchant corporations (Champakalakshmi 1996:224, 312). A considerable number of people in coastal areas were capable of living entirely by maritime trade (Gibb 1994:803; Chakravarti 2000). But the impact of international trade was not limited to the coastal towns as various products sold and resold in South Indian ports—perfumes, pearls, rice, nuts, spices, and cotton, to name but a few (Bouchon 1999:82–85)—permeated various hinterlands, thereby allowing locally produced commodities to reach coastal areas and vice versa. During the Cola era there was "considerable commercial activity in the South Indian hinterland and well-organized trade networks supplied the commodities demanded by foreign traders" (Hall 1977:208).

It was also during the 11th and 12th centuries that forced labor in South Asia decreased as more of it was "commuted into money payments" (Sharma 1965:243), while the sophistication of credit and banking increased (Jain 1990:201–207). As the economy expanded in the northern and southern parts of the subcontinent, it gradually affected the entire Indian Ocean region (Palat 1988). As far as the textile trade was concerned, the relatively peaceful trade that characterized the Indian Ocean (that is, until the intrusion of the Portuguese)[7] caused the region to become more and more integrated through an

---

6. Since excellent horses were rare in South Asia and very important to the armed forces, it follows that these were regularly imported on a massive scale (Sinopoli 2000:377). Chakravarti notes that "the Vijayanagar king alone ordered 13,000 horses from Ormuz every year" (1996:155) since horses bred in South Asia were inferior to central Asian ones (Chandra 1997:15). This trade occurred on overland routes (Gopal 1965:113) and by sea (Wink 1997:83–87; Nizami 2002:351).

7. "The arrival of the Portuguese in the Indian Ocean abruptly ended the system of peaceful oceanic navigation that was such a marked feature of the region. For the commercial communities of the Indian Ocean the challenge in competition in transcontinental trade was as wholly exogenous as the timing was sudden and unexpected" (Chaudhuri 1985:63). The peacefulness of the Indian Ocean prior to A.D. 1500 should not be exaggerated as Abyssinian mercenaries were used "as the best means of ensuring security from pirates" (Gunawardana 1987:84). Of course, the occasional pirate attacks, particularly near Indonesia and the Andaman islands (Krishna 2000:50) and in the vicinity of Calicut (Bouchon 1999:87) were of a different scale and nature than the Portuguese efforts to monopolize and eventually tax maritime trade routes. Chaudhuri correctly points out: "In Asia commercial traffic was in the hands of highly skilled professional merchants,

expanding division of labor (Gibb 1994:827). This is clearly illustrated by the extensive specialization of the industry's workers (tailors, weavers, and dyers) as described in the Gujarat (Jain 1990:63) and Bengal (Ray 1993) case studies, or even those of the deep South (Hall and Spencer 1980:131). The South Asian textile industry was probably more technologically advanced than that in contemporary Europe (Ramaswamy 1985b; Vanina 1989:279).

In addition to their fertile tracts and rich handicrafts, the areas of Gujarat and Bengal carried on a brisk overseas trade (Bouchon 1999:90). The Gujarati traders had a large role in Middle Eastern and African trade while Chittagong in Bengal was a flourishing port for trade with China. Indeed, ample fragments of Chinese ceramic potsherds exist in the southern part of the subcontinent (Karashima 1992:174–176), primarily dating from the 13th and 14th centuries (Jacq-Hergoualc'h et al. 1998:283). Urbanization increased even more in the 13th century; Delhi became one of the largest cities in the world[8] and Multan, Lahore, Kara, and Cambay also grew considerably. The multiple Mongol invasions had a negative impact on some cities located in the northwest (Chandra 1997:64–73), but in general, the period 1200 to 1400 was that of a flourishing urban economy characterized by widespread usage of bills of exchange and joint trading (Islam 1996:238–239), as well as a concurrent increase in craft production (through the use of spinning wheels and treadle looms) and commerce (Ramaswamy 2002). Textiles, wine, paper, and sugars were produced in Bengal (Ray 1993:83), and both Chinese (Ray 1993:92) and Egyptian (Goitein 1973:190) silk was imported into the area. The trade in cotton textiles from Bengal to China during the Sung and Yuan dynasties was also significant. By the early 15th century, "Bengali ships carried their exports to China. Bengal served as a link between China and Malacca and contributed substantially to the growth of Malacca as an entrepot" (Ray 1993:130–132).

---

who operated as private individuals with little substantive state support [whereas] in the Christian Mediterranean, with the rise of the Italian city states, the institutional basis of world trade underwent a new development. The commercial rivalry between Genoa and Venice, erecting into open naval conflicts, and the Venetian encounters with the Muslim fleets *fused together the interests of the merchants and the state*. The Italian experience was reproduced later in Seville, Lisbon, Amsterdam, and London" (1985:16; emphasis added).

Some claim that the Cola naval expeditions were an indication of state interest in foreign trade (Abraham 1988:152) and were of "mutual benefit" to both Cola merchants and rulers (Abraham 1988:130). Nevertheless, the degree of mercantile influence over royal diplomacy and military intervention was very limited when compared with that in Western Europe (Keay 2000:222; Lewis 1976:469–70).

8. Its rapid population growth was not simply an endogenous phenomenon: "The city became the natural refuge for those in Khurasan and Central Asia—whether bureaucrats, soldiers, scholars or mystics—who fled from the Mongol terror.... Delhi's growth during the 13th century is largely attributable to this influx, which was swollen, after the outbreak of civil war within the Mongol Empire around 1261, by groups of Mongol fugitives also" (Jackson 1986:19).

Given the considerable wealth accumulated on the basis of the above-mentioned trade and the sheer size of commerce within the South Asian region, as well as between its cities,[9] it has often been asked why capitalism did not "spontaneously" emerge in the area (e.g., Habib 1995b). Much ink has been spilled about the impact of colonialism—either at the merchant capitalist stage or the industrial capitalist stage—on South Asia's own "potential for capitalism" (Washbrook 1988:63). Some authors (e.g., Pearson 1976) have dismissed the Portuguese intrusions in the Indian Ocean as mere "piracy," only occasionally affecting trade routes and markets whenever they could muster enough force to wage war in the immediate area, but without important implications for the regional economy as a whole (Perlin 1980:274).[10] (There is no question that from the 16th century onward, the Portuguese attempted to disrupt the spice trade to the Levant—from the European point of view, the most profitable commodity—which had been controlled by Muslim traders for several centuries. But most of their efforts failed to achieve their ambitious aims; see Meilink-Roelofsz 1964:189).[11] Others, such as Steensgaard (1974) and Reid (1993), have pointed to the fundamental changes brought about by the intrusion of European chartered companies (like the Vereenigde Oostindische Compagnie or VOC) into the Asian trade networks and their success at establishing monopolistic control over the commercial routes in 17th-century Southeast Asia.[12] But the reality is that in the period 1250 to 1650, Europeans

---

9. The capital city of the Vijayanagara Empire is estimated to have had about 100,000 inhabitants in the early 1400s (Sinopoli 2000:370).

10. This was actually the misguided opinion of the Mughal governors in South Asia (Chaudhuri 1981:224). For the indifference of Emperor Jahangir toward Europeans, see Digby (1999:249).

11. Given that some merchants who traded in spices made profits of up to 300 percent (Bouchon 1999:231), it was not surprising that the Portuguese attempted to control the spice trade. This was of course very difficult to achieve as Portuguese power in the Indian Ocean area was virtually nonexistent on land and very tenuous at sea (Cowan 1968:6), and most of their attempts to control routes or subordinate cultivators in the Indian Ocean failed (Kieniewicz 1991:81). Although the Portuguese attempted to construct a monopoly, they only managed a very tenuous hold over the spice trade (Boxer 1969:418–419) as reflected in the fact that Venice did not suffer much from the Portuguese trade around the Cape (Romano, Tenenti, and Tucci 1970). It is therefore a great exaggeration to claim they "seized control of the commerce of the Indian Ocean" (Chirot 1994:69). The rulers of the large territorial states in the South Asian peninsula did not undertake any action to destroy the Portuguese intruders as they were not considered a serious threat to the aristocracy's power in the region.

12. The relative success of these companies has been contested by scholars such as Subrahmanyam (1990) and Perlin (1993:284–285). Understandably, European scholars often focus on the (presumed) impact of Europeans and their joint stock companies in East Asia. Asian scholars tend to highlight the activities generated by the South Asian hinterland outside European-controlled ports, the different levels of "indigenous resistance" (Datta 2003:287), or the many ingenious strategies of Asian merchants to repeatedly outflank and outmaneuver the European powers' attempts to impose a system of monopolistic control over port cities (Vink 2004:48) (e.g., by regularly altering commercial routes and outlets).

were not in a position to dictate anything in most Asian markets. Although more European merchants than previously recognized were able to penetrate the Eastern markets, once they were faced with the "powerful Asian states on the mainland" (Meilink-Roelofsz 1972:172), their freedom of action was extremely limited. Another problem that European merchants faced on the South Asian subcontinent during this period was the lack of South Asian interest in the commodities offered (Richards 1993:198). In fact right up to the late 18th century, when the European powers were able to establish more direct colonial rule on the ground and affect production quotas, at least 80 percent of the cargoes originating from Western Europe contained mostly silver and gold (Meyer 1982:301; Attman 1991). There was, of course, a way around these problems: a gradual increase of power in the region.[13]

The settlement of the European colonial powers on the diverse islands and archipelagoes across the Indian Ocean littoral was not coincidental; rather, it was a logical copy of the colonization of the Byzantine Empire's insular possessions[14] (and a response to the consequence of unequal bullion flows

---

13. These problems were not a new phenomenon, having already been raised in the 13th century by European merchants who ventured into East Asia (Lopez 1973:445). At that time, Europeans were unable to exercise *any* form of coercion on the Asian continent. This changed when the first Europeans started to penetrate the Indian Ocean world economy in the 16th century. The decline of the central Asian caravan trade and the increasing importance of the maritime routes after the breakdown of the Pax Mongolica (Reid 1999:64), followed by the political turmoil within Central Asia itself, raised overland transportation and protection costs considerably (Rossabi 1990). Ironically, this shift from land routes to maritime routes strengthened the European position in the Indian Ocean geopolitical and commercial arenas.

14. Although K. N. Sastri was chastised by a multitude of scholars for having had the audacity to compare the Cola state to the Byzantine Empire (1975:447–448), I think the historical comparison is essentially correct *insofar as* the Empire's relation and subsequent subjugation to European city-states and South Asia's relation and subsequent subjugation to European chartered companies is concerned. At the risk of being similarly chastised, I believe it is relevant to quote Haldon at length: "Leading elements [of Italian city-states] were at the same time businessmen whose wealth and political power was often dependent as much on commerce as on rents [from the agricultural hinterland]. Therefore the economic and political interests of the leading and middling elements were identical with the interests of the city, its political identity and its independence of outside interference. State/communal and private enterprise were inseparable. The economic and political well-being of the city-state was thus to a large extent coterminous with that of the social elite and its dependents. The Byzantine state, in contrast, played no role at all in promoting indigenous enterprise . . . and viewed commerce as simply another minor source of state income" (2000:107–108).

Haldon then quickly reminds the reader that this does not imply that there was no successful Byzantine merchant class. Rather, "the interests of commerce were subordinate to the relationship between the political and ideological structure of the state on the one hand and the interests of the dominant social-economic elite on the other" (Haldon 2000:108). Once nomadic incursions and tribal outbreaks at the margins of the imperial polity disrupted the existing order, "the reduced income derived from the appropriation of surplus through a tax on a smaller and constantly shrinking territorial base; the fragmentation of territory and political authority; and the lack of serious naval power with which to defend its interests" (Haldon 2000:110) led to the Empire's

to the East), legitimized by a neomercantilist strategy propagated at home.[15] The enormous textile production in South Asia, exported to the entire Indian Ocean region but especially to Southeast Asian markets, was intrinsically linked with the massive import of spices from Southeast Asia (T'ien Ju-kang 1981); these spices were either consumed in South Asia, or later resold to the Middle East and ultimately Western Europe (Sen 1962:92). The European merchants were bound to immerse themselves in the inter-Asian trade not only to make ends meet, but to obtain the spices "and the fabulous profits expected" (Sen 1962:93). But if profits were to be made, the Europeans *had* to obtain naval bases and strategic locations from which they could hope to dominate the sea and, consequently, a very large segment of the trade flows.

It is impossible to compare the amount of overland trade during this period with the amount of commodities exchanged by sea, but since transportation over water was much cheaper, most commodities (especially bulk goods) were probably transported by ship (Tampoe 1989:114; Krishna 2000:44). There is probably some truth in the statement "whoever controlled the sea, controlled most of the trade" (Jain 1990:90). Nevertheless, the impact of overland trade in certain areas should not be underestimated (e.g., Stargardt 1971) and it would be a gross exaggeration to claim that in Asia, "already before 1400 long-distance trade went almost entirely maritime" (Wink 1988:43).[16] It seems equally doubtful to claim, as does Borsa (1990:9), that the Europeans had already obtained a "dominant share of the inter-Asian trade" by the early 17th century; the

---

gradual destruction. Despite a difference of five hundred years and a different geographical zone, the processes in South Asia appear structurally similar.

15. Guérreau correctly observes that "l'assimilation du commerce à la guerre est un des traits de la pensée mercantiliste" (1996:99). Vries (2002:74) remarks that "mercantilism was a partnership between capital and coercion, in which capital did not always have things its way. It was a dangerous liaison in which both parties could gain and lose." Fair enough. But then he proceeds to claim that these policies existed "in all corners of the world," which is an incorrect interpretation of world history. Duchesne (2004:71) even claims that "mercantilist trade was not as beneficial economically as the world-system school has insisted." Obviously, some colonial mercantilist policies and strategies provided more of a windfall than others; some were even very costly and were undertaken in the imperialist scramble to colonize remaining areas of the world. What is significant, however, is the fact that this mercantilist competition was an intrinsic part of an expanding capitalist system and was beneficial to merchant traders who often externalized their own (transaction and defense) costs onto the emerging nation-state. The question is not so much to what extent an *entire* nation-state consistently benefits at a certain point in time from a particular policy, but to what extent a certain capitalist elite benefits from the implemented strategy. As Duchesne (2004:71) later admits, "Western Europeans were willing to finance a costly transatlantic expansion under the mercantilist belief that military power and security could be obtained." Unfortunately, he does not elaborate on this important statement.

16. After all, "a great deal of the trade volume with Central Asia was transmitted through pastoral nomads, who traversed the pastures between the Indus and Oxus" (Gommans 1991:55). For evidence concerning the importance of overland trade in medieval Southeast Asia, see Sun (2000).

European share in Asiatic trade was probably only minor up until the early 1800s (Wink 1988:65). This limited trade was primarily due to the Europeans' inability to effectively dominate all major maritime trade routes, let alone any of the land routes.[17] Nevertheless, one can hardly deny the negative impact of Western colonialism as it gradually tightened its grip on the region over a period of four hundred years (Habib 1995:22).[18]

Once the tragic consequences of western colonialism are acknowledged, one is still left wondering: To what extent was South Asia on the verge of developing a merchant capitalist system prior to the intrusion of the European powers? In order to answer this, one has to take into account the specific nature of the existing polities and the diverging power relations between the different social strata.

States and State Structures in South Asia

The traditional Marxist model associated with the Asiatic mode of production (Gough 1981) has always assumed that South Asia's sphere of the market must have been limited (Pryor 1980) as it had to exemplify the stereotypical, or rather, the ideal-typical precapitalist society (Subhramanyam 1994:7). But as O'Leary (1989) brilliantly pointed out in his critique of Marxist and Wittfogel's (1957) claims, the image of such a state (traditionally defined as *Oriental despotism*; e.g., Breton 1982:454; Pavlov 1983) clearly has to be relegated to history's dustbin.

Historical materialism, on the other hand, should not be discarded. Rather, it should be used to challenge the recent reappraisals of cultural or religious frameworks that attempt to explain the rise of the West (e.g., Lal 1998; Landes 1998; Stark 2005) or the failure of non-Western societies (Morris 1967). There is little point in having the image of contemporary India projected into the past and then declaring that they could not have developed in the long run because

---

17. While it was only toward the middle of the 18th century that the inter-Asian maritime networks—the so-called *country trade*—were increasingly dominated by Europeans (Toussaint 1964:304) and it was "no longer possible to conceive of Indian states as functioning independently of the influence of European intervention" (Perlin 1983:83), I want to focus on the long-term political, social, and economic factors that facilitated this process.

18. The presence of European merchants in the Indian Ocean world economy from the 16th century onward did not immediately result in a mass commodity trade between the Indian Ocean and Europe. But this does not imply that the trade within the Indian Ocean was that of mere luxuries (Wallerstein 1989:132). Only from the 17th century onward, in a small cluster of areas such as the Moluccans, did Europeans muster enough naval power to impose a formidable exploitative system upon the existing population, and the commodity flows controlled by the Europeans increased as the route around the Cape became more popular.

of their cultural values or because of a notable "absence of freedom of thought and of science" (Habib 1974:79).[19]

The mainstream sociological explanations have tended toward discussions of how the caste system's *cultural values* prevented modernization in the South Asian subcontinent, a theory that is quite indebted to Max Weber: "The hereditary caste system of Indian society with its ritualistic segregation of the professions, excluded the emergence of a citizenry and urban community" (1958:84). Ever since Weber's argument that religious acceptance of the existing strata precluded dynamic social change (1958b) (unlike Europe, which experienced the protestant ethic and individualism), the specificity of cultural values related to the acceptance of the caste system has been a major variable used to explain why technological change was inhibited (Qaisar 1982:138) or why capitalism/modernity did not emerge within the South Asian peninsula (e.g., Moore 1966; Hall 1985; Baechler 1988;2002:174–183). A recurrent theme is the claim that religious and cultural values specific to South Asia supported a caste system that in turn limited socioeconomic developments (Subrahmanyam 1996:24–30). The depiction of homo anthropologicus—and particularly in South Asia, homo hierarchicus (Dumont 1966)—as fundamentally different from the European homo economicus (cf. Madan 2001) is another deplorable outcome of this line of reasoning (Subrahmanyam 1996:22–23; Washbrook 1997:415–416). All too often, scholars have claimed that as opposed to Western Europe, the concept of the individual did not exist in the normative framework of South Asian culture or that "material accumulation or exchange is subjugated to social or spiritual goals, that exchanges are used more for solidarity than for profit, and production of goods is integrated into religious or social ceremonies" (Mukerji 1983:8). Although forms of ritual sovereignty (in the case of the Cola and Vijayanagar Empires) and specific cultural features were important (Stein 1985:396), when assessing them one has to be careful not to reconstruct an artificial "supposed duality between materialist and spiritualist civilizations" (Thapar 2000:51).[20]

One of the problems with this strong emphasis on religious and cultural values as the primary characteristics differentiating the West from the non-West is that it cannot be analytically separated from the categorization of South Asian society as essentially "stationary in character" (Srinivas 2002:187) and

---

19. Eurocentric scholars continue to assert that Europe—because of its unique cultural features—experienced a different path than did South Asia or other Asian regions, which seemed incapable of providing secure property rights for their merchants (Weede 1990:372–373). While I consider the first claim outlandish, the second part of the argument is a traditional one (e.g., Issawi 1970:251; Kuran 2004) that has, to a certain extent, been undermined by empirical evidence (Kumar 1985; Palat 1988:241:ff.).

20. As Kulke points out, "the existence of ritual policy and ritual sovereignty was an important partial aspect of genuine policy rather than a substitute of it." (1995:43). Cf. Thakur (1989:xxii–xxiii).

its polity as weak, underdeveloped, and incapable of implementing strategies that facilitated capital accumulation (Vink 2004:66). It is therefore no surprise that Stein's famous model of the segmentary state (1980; 1995)—based on a typology for early modern African states (Southall 1956)—depicts rulers as exercising their authority in purely ritual and symbolic, rather than political, terms (Christie 1986:68; Veluthat 1993:250–254).[21] Similarly, Geertz's (1980) model of Southeast Asian political structures depicts a weak polity where religious and cultural values are much more important than actual material conditions. Geertz's assessments are particularly suspect given the manner in which they depict Asian trade as a bazaar economy of petty commerce (1967:372). Not only are these statements factually incorrect (Christie 1986:69; Kathirithamby-Wells 1990), but this "anthropological" approach tends to depict South Asian polities as practically stateless (Kulke 1986:4; Chattopadhyaya 1995:225); this seems to imply that the European state formation process was somehow uniquely dynamic, relegating the South-Asian and Southeast Asian historical experience to one in which castes were more important than states (Inden 1990:208–209). Even a Braudelian like Reid has recently claimed:

> Although the military power of the Dutch was far beyond that of their Iberian predecessors, they used it for calculated commercial advantage, never for symbolic victories. In effect, if not in deliberate intent, they encouraged Southeast Asian rulers to retreat from economic and military concerns to symbolic and spiritual ones where they did not compete with Dutch ambitions. (1999:176)

Clearly then the nature of the early modern South Asian state has been perceived by many as a crucial element in explaining the different political and socioeconomic trajectories within South Asia. But a consensus on the processes of South Asian state formation cannot be found in the existing academic literature (cf. Subrahmanyam 2002; Champakalakshmi 2002); indeed, most of the theoretically informed debates revolve around the acceptance of "Indian feudalism" (Sharma 1965, 1995; Yadav 1973, 1974; Thakur 1989; Veluthat 1993; Jha 2000; Mukhia 2000), the acceptance of the aforementioned segmentary state (Stein 1980), or a variant of the relatively weak patrimonial state model inspired by Weber (Blake 1979; Hardy 1986; Sinopoli 2003:38–62).[22] The image

---

21. Approval of the segmentary state model is also found in Spencer (1983:98) and Fox (1971).

22. A combination of the above might read: "The Asiatic Mode of production should be considered a feudal mode of production which was linked with a self-sufficient economy in its initial phase" (Sharma 2001:29). Due to the size of the South Asian subcontinent and the wide variety of different polities (Grewal 2005), historians are particularly hesitant to choose among different typologies (e.g., Talbot 2001). More recently, Indian historians have expressed their discontent with European (or African) models relating to the South Asian experience (Habib 1995; Subrahmanyam 1986:375) and many were keen to point out the impossibility of coming up with any

of South Asian development as "trapped" in a fundamentally weak state polity is, of course, as erroneous a depiction of historical reality as the traditional Western image of Oriental despotism (cf. Madan 1979) which portrays "Indian civilization as being static, despotic in its orientation and outside the mainstream of relevant world history" (Thapar 2000:6). A necessary corollary of the alleged fundamental weakness of the early modern South Asian polity in the segmentary state model is the implication that unlike Western European powers, South Asian states were not powerful enough to impose a form of peripheralization on the territories that they conquered:

> The emphasis upon long-distance plundering expeditions [most notably those of the Cola state into Bengal, Southeast Asia and Ceylon in the 11th century] must have been largely compensatory, offsetting a weakly integrated political system . . . these expeditions were nothing more but brief raids. (Spencer and Hall 1974:59)

The Colas' "lucrative military escapades" (Heitzman 1997:235) or those in Southeast Asia (Hagesteijn 1989:59, 91), though grandiose at first glance, are said to have been rather limited at creating dependencies because they themselves were the outcome of a relatively weak state formation (Wink 1990:318–327); at best they lead to temporary forms of nominal and ritual claims of sovereignty and to occasional tributes from the intimidated areas (Spencer and Hall 1974:59). The temporary predatory expansions of the Colas and the Nayakas, it is argued, were central to the South Asian state's inherent constraints as these campaigns signified an attempted "direction of common enterprise among the diverse elements of a markedly decentralized socio-political system" (Spencer 1976:406).

What is most important, however, is not so much the characterization of or the functions attributed to the South Asian polity (Inden 1990:265) but rather, those who were in control of the state apparatus, using it to achieve certain ends. In Western Europe, for instance, monarchical dynasties had to battle

---

one model for the South Asian subcontinent because of its inherent diversity. Any "received" "alien" model is especially prone to attacks from specialists defending the "uniqueness" of their respective region of specialization, as if it were a chasse guardée (e.g., Subrahmanyam 2001:93, 98; Ptak 2001:402). But the corollary of providing no theoretical alternative whatsoever (aside from a "let one thousand micro-studies bloom" narrative) is to be deplored since it implies a return to a form of histoire événementielle (Bois 1995), if not outright "inevitable historiographical anarchy" (Chattopadhyaya 2002:120). And as Moosvi (2005:49) put it, "meaningful history cannot do without theoretical frameworks." Chaudhuri also correctly reminds us that "it is not enough to be an archival mole, for a mole is blind" (1981:225). Given the paucity of data available for this period, it is admittedly difficult to present an "ideal-typical" model of the early modern South Asian polity. Nevertheless, important issues regarding state formation and its impact on long-term socioeconomic development have to be assessed.

city-states but were unable to do so effectively (circa 1200–1450) until the increasing economies of scale, territorial enlargement, and military innovations enabled them to accumulate more power. The early modern South Asian polity was similarly restrained, but instead faced an organized local nobility (*nattar*) in their collective body (*nadu*) (Chibber 1998:24). Gradually, the South Asian state (which was actually quite powerful—more so in the Vijayanagar period than under the Colas—but far from despotic) was able to weaken the local power of the *nattar*. It did so by undermining the rural *nadu* (Chibber 1998) and by developing a relatively well-organized central administration[23] and a powerful standing army (Ludden 1985:74). This was also true in the North where the Delhi Sultanate was capable of maintaining "a strong standing army, centrally recruited, centrally administered and centrally paid" (Nizami 1985:73). As in the emerging Western European polities, elites from the local territories who resisted had to be effectively incorporated into the state structure, appeased with offices, functions, annuities, and a new status. They were coerced to accept the newly imposed sovereignty in the short run, and made dependent on the enlarged state polity in the long run (Chibber 1998:28). A similar process took place in Europe, but there it was the urban merchants who grafted themselves onto the power structures of the most important capitalist states (Prak 1992; Isaacs and Prak 1996). After painstakingly difficult prosopographical research, Bulst concludes that in late medieval France, "la plupart des officiers royaux était issue de la bourgeoisie, particulièrement les lieutenants et les receveurs" (1996:115). If anything, the bourgeoisie was the *primary* beneficiary of the construction of an emerging early modern state (Bove 2004:589, 632). And according to Brady, "already in the late 15th century Emperor Maximilian favored burghers over nobles in his administration" (1997:249).[24] In South Asia however, "merchants had no access to the powers of the state" (Parthasarathi 1998:94).

Furthermore, despite the long-entrenched practice of handing out tax-farming duties to the nobility—who also made up most of the state officials

---

23. See Subbarayalu (1982:295–301), Karashima (1984), Palat (1988:440), Veluthat (1993:72) and Heitzman (1995:174) on the administrative apparatus of the Colas.

24. See also Hoppenbrouwers (2001:59) and Dumolyn (2001:83–84) on the Low Countries. A gradual fusion of merchants and gentry, the latter increasingly involved in trade, also occurred in late medieval England (Nightingale 2000). Over time, this kind of "cooptation" (cf. Collins 1997:633) created the foundation for the construction of a "modern" nation-state with a new "state nobility" (Dumolyn 2006) which would attempt, in light of the experiences of city-states, to create and establish, on an even larger scale, clear demarcations of "sovereignty" over land as well as over the sea. Similar attempts were not pursued by the elites in charge of South Asian polities (Chakravarti 2004:315), and one could explain this by the differential organization of their social structure. Blockmans (1990) argues that the latter also has implications for political stability, which furthers a specific state formation process.

(Ojha 1993:35)—the South Asian polities were unable to obtain a long-lasting allegiance from the powerful upper social strata (Richards 1993:294).[25] Although the development of a coherent supraregional power was more successful on the South Asian subcontinent than in Southeast Asia, the Delhi Sultanate's policy of granting temporary prebendal territorial assignments (*iqta*) to collect the land tax (*kharaj*), house tax (*ghari*), and cattle tax (*charai*) (Habib 1978:295–296) did not prevent the state's relatively rapid fracture and disintegration once external pressures became too strong (Heitzman 1997:218).[26] In the South, the "iqta system was adopted mutatis mutandis by the Vijayanagar emperors [and known] as the nayankara system" (Kulke 1995:32). Since the state was unable to maintain the temporariness of the land assignments over the long run,[27] "the ensuing heritability of territorial assignments was bound to lead sooner or later to a fragmentation of political authority" (Kulke 1995:32).[28] Centuries later, the Mughal dynasty's similar but improved assignment of land (*jagir*) along a highly elaborate ranking system (*mansab*) would not fare much better: "The mansabdari system did not remove its structural weakness: a strictly enforced temporariness of the jagir assignments led to a nearly unlimited exploitation of peasants, and thus to agrarian unrest and social crisis" (Kulke 1995:32).[29] In both the 13th and 14th centuries and the 17th

---

25. Ojha also refers to the aristocracy's widespread and pervasive disloyalty towards the state (1993:137). In Southeast Asia, "most supra-regional political systems lacked organic solidarity [and] continual coercive power" (Hagesteijn 1989:141, 144). For a more recent overview of the volatile state formation processes in early modern Southeast Asia, cf. Colombijn (2003).

26. Sinha and Ray also refer to the failure of the empire: "the all-India character of the empire was never a reality; it remained throughout a loose fabric of virtually separate units ruled by Muslim governors or Hindu chiefs over whom the central government could wield no authority except by military coercion" (1986:257).

27. "The wide distribution of land grants (iqta istighlal) with rights to land revenues, [was] supposed to be temporary and revocable but tended to become de facto hereditary holdings, highlighting the land-based nature of resources and power" (Risso 1995:31–32). Sultan Firuz Tughluq, for instance, had to appease the nobility by "granting the iqta of any incumbent to his sons after his death" (Chandra 1997:120). This is symbolic of the imperial structure: more prebendal in its heyday and more feudal as its power waned (Champakalakshmi 1995:301). Similar prebendal rights could be found in the Deccan (where they were known as *mokasa*) and in the Mughal empire (where they were known as *jagir*) (Perlin 1985:458), but in most cases the office became hereditary (Farmer 1977:438), creating military conflicts and political crises in the long run. Garcin et al. (2000a:196) claim the institutionalization of the iqta "encouraged the sacrifice of [socioeconomic] development in the long run to immediate profit."

28. "The empire was divided into a number of fiefs. The military officer in charge of an iqta was known as a Muqti. So long as powerful and vigorous monarchs presided over the center the provincial government was kept under control but the presence of a weak ruler on the throne of Delhi invariably encouraged the provincial chiefs to take on the airs of a de facto sovereign" (Sinha and Ray 1986:281).

29. "The mansabdar who had received a temporary revenue assignment knew that he was to be transferred to a fellow mansabdar in 3 to 4 years felt no incentive to invest in the future prosperity

century, peasant rebellions brought about by heavy taxation (Stein 1985:401; Palat 1986; Nandi 1987:274–275) occurred on such a scale that they contributed to the breakdown of the various South Asian "imperial" systems (Habib 1985:49; D'Souza 2002:12). The latter were caught between increasing levels of taxation—provoking the aforementioned rebellions—on the one hand and by territorial expansion—necessitating further military expenditures and taxes— on the other (Palat et al. 1986:178).

Chibber's (1998) ultimate dismissal of South Asia's failure to experience a transition to capitalism hinges upon the dubious assertion (inspired by Brenner) that South Asian peasants were not market oriented and were fundamentally risk averse. Equally unconvincing is his position that "increases in artisan production were propelled by elite consumption and therefore incapable of generating an endogenously driven growth trajectory" (1998:32), ignoring the fact that the overwhelming majority of textiles produced were exported throughout the entire Indian Ocean region. A more plausible argument is that, unlike in Western Europe, merchants were kept outside the structures of institutionalized power and the processes of decision making.[30] (In the Northern part of the subcontinent, the political position of merchants was even weaker; Mahajan 1963:98–100). While taxes in South Asia were often collected by local bodies, merchants' leverage was quite limited; taxation, for instance, was a royal prerogative not subject to institutionalized and extended forms of negotiation and conditionality (Shanmugam 1987:8, 141; Vanina 1989:274). The South Asian merchants' lack of power can also be illustrated by their weak control over the labor process in the textile industry (Palat 1988:263), unlike the mercantile power that existed in Western Europe (see Chapter 1).

Arasaratnam's (1980:267) study of late 18th-century India presents convincing evidence that even during that period, weavers who had received cash advances for their work (as most did) retained considerable control over the

---

of his jagir. On the contrary, it was in his interest to squeeze the maximum profit out of it in the shortest possible time. For this reason the jagirdari system, excellent as it was as a political device for preventing the growth of local bases of power among the mansabdars, was ruinous for agriculture" (Farmer et al. 1977:439).

30. In his study on the trade and statecraft of the Colas, Hall pays great attention to the merchants' success at resisting state centralization and subsequent tax increases (1980:75, 83, 205). Although one cannot deny that the merchants' control over local militias and armed mercenaries (not to mention their considerable wealth) sometimes gave them some autonomy and power over local assemblies (Hall 1980; Ramaswamy 1982:314), their political importance in the Cola polity should not be exaggerated (Vanaja 1982:331; Chibber 1998:15). Heitzman concludes that the major political figures in the Cola state were "the several layers of nobles and landowners, resting on the fruits of peasant cultivation, who interacted with the kings and constituted state institutions" (1995:193). The locally dominant landowners, organized into chittiramëllis, were thus capable of shifting most of the taxation burden to the rest of society: smaller peasants, tenants, artisans, and merchants (Palat 1988:89; Chaudhuri 1990:386).

production process. This is confirmed by Parthasarathi (2001). Earlier, Parthasarathi summarized his remarkably pertinent findings:

> Both [Indian] weavers and merchants were free to cancel the contracts at any time. But while the weaver bore no cost for canceling (he simply had to return the advance to the merchant) the merchant forfeited his advance if he canceled . . . weavers possessed the freedom to accept advances at will and sell completed cloth to any buyer [that] gave [them] great power to set cloth prices, which, naturally, adversely affected merchant profits. The asymmetry of contract also made it difficult for merchants to enforce cloth quality standards [and] the lack of institutionalized and legally enforced systems for debt repayment made it extremely difficult for merchants to recover debts. (1996:97)

In conclusion, Parthasarathi states that in the 18th century, "merchants were excluded from the state within the south Indian political order. Unlike many parts of Europe where the economic power of merchants was supplemented by political power, in south India merchants had no access to the powers of the state" (1996:98). Indeed, they rarely tried to capture political power (Chakravarti 2004:315). Even Subrahmanyam and Bayly, some of the most ardent defenders of South Asian political and economic dynamism right up to the early 19th century, have to admit that in South Asia "there is little evidence to show that merchant guilds controlled production or defined and defended regions of mercantile activity against rivals" (1988:406). Ramaswamy (1985b:81, 144) and Hall (1980:115) remain rather noncommittal about the existence of a putting out-system.[31] The latter nonetheless states that under the Colas, "there is no evidence that merchants exercised wage controls over artisans or for that matter that production standards were set or that fines were levied for poor craftsmanship." This is confirmed by Qaisar, who refers to the "the feeble hold of merchant-capital over the production process during the 17th century" (1982:131). Alavi is even more specific:

> The relationship between the creditor and the weaver inherent in the Indian system is quite distinct from that of the putting out system in England where the merchant was directly involved in the purchase and provision of materials and even equipment (that he often hired) to weavers [whereas in India] with the system of cash advances there was no such involvement by the merchant in the organization of production and provision of materials and equipment. (1982:49)

---

31. Similarly for East Asia, Pomeranz (2002:563) refers to the growth of merchant control in the marketplace as "debatable," referring the reader to an unpublished paper by Gary Hamilton.

It is quite clear that in South Asia the "tools remained those of the artisan" (Habib 1980:38). Although the political and—especially financial—power of early modern South Asian "portfolio capitalists" should not be underestimated, merchants who wielded significant political power in state polities or over textile workers (e.g., Dasgupta 2000:68) should be seen more as an exception rather than as the rule, as demonstrated by the overall absence of European-like putting-out systems (Pearson 1998:102).

It was precisely this variable—the power of the merchants—that ultimately transformed Western Europe into a core area within an expanding global division of labor. In Western Europe, the combination of the merchants' growing power over the proletariat due to a highly unusual alliance between the state and the bourgeoisie (Crone 1989:167) and the *subsequent* increasing revenues from the financial windfall of overseas colonial conquests—first in the Mediterranean and eventually in the New World—explains why specific polities were capable of eventually achieving world domination.[32] This explanation is not meant to replicate "the image of the eternal East, as a counterpoint to the vibrant, dynamic and therefore dominant Occident" (Chakravarti 1998:98).[33] But it does stress the fact that in South Asia, merchants lacked the institutionalized political power structures to effectively proletarianize their workers at home and effectively peripheralize other geographical areas within the Indian Ocean region.

While there is evidence of occasional contact between merchants and aristocratic rulers (Pearson 1972:125), or of some merchants serving specific rulers as "ministers" (Buchon 1999:219), and ample proof that some of these South Asian merchants were indeed "enormously wealthy" (Gopal 1965:142; Pearson 1972:122; Bouchon 1973:42; Krishna 2000:88, 108), especially when compared to their European counterparts (Digby 1982:135; Chandra 1997:196), the "European fusion" of state and mercantile interests, of which the VOC was a logical outcome,[34] simply did not occur. Certainly "some merchants used their

---

32. As Glete points out, "there is nothing in capital and capitalism that make them inherently hostile to big structures and complex organizations, provided that capital owners remain in control" (2000:199). This was obviously the case in the city-states of medieval Western Europe and among the multiple "India Companies" in the early modern period, but not among the South Asian polities.

33. While it is true that the merchant class' possibilities to successfully accumulate capital were greater in South Asia than in China (due to the lack of a unified Imperial structure), and that this was exemplified by the fact that, unlike in China, "big merchants (*vaisyas*) were on a pedestal higher than peasants (*sudras*) and artisans" (Jain 1990:210), I doubt that one can go so far as to claim that in South Asia "a prosperous and powerful class of merchants, which on account of its opulence, tended to dominate the political, social and economic fabric of the region [and that] these merchants attained a status as high as that of the brahmans in learning and politics, and as that of the Ksatriyas in war" (Jain 1990:209).

34. As Van Dyke (1997:42) put it: "Company shareholders and members of government were often one and the same." This fusion of political and economic power comes out of the city-state

power to participate directly in the political activity at a courtly level" (Pearson 1972:128) and "even if a merchant lacked the desire or opportunity to enter the noble class, or the service of a noble, he could still be influential, for money meant power" (Pearson 1972:129). Of course to a certain degree, money meant power and influence everywhere in the early modern world, including early modern South Asia (Bayly 1983; Datta 2003:263–264). The question however is: Where did it structurally wield *more* power and, most importantly, why? The power of the European merchant class was institutionalized in a variety of ways, as described in Chapter 1. The lack of such institutionalization on the South Asian subcontinent meant that although "states often called on merchants to serve in their administrations" (Beaujard 2005:457), in the long run, quite often "sections of population engaged in productive activity—*particularly the mercantile classes*—were to a lesser or greater degree treated as milk cows by those having the power and the authority to coerce them" (Prakash 1972:280; emphasis added). Conversely, "those who built their wealth through commerce rarely seemed to have acquired land in order to use it as a base for political power" (Thapar 1974:119). Political power for merchants could—to a certain extent—limit extortion by the nobility or imperial bureaucracy, but this was less apparent in South Asia (Spodek 1974:462; Mahapatra 1987:259). These are crucial variables that one needs to take into account when analyzing the manner in which, during the Late Middle Ages, "the economic stage was being set for the world-wide exploitation of the 'riches of the East' by upstarts of the far West" (Hodgson 1963:247).

The Strategies of Elites
in South Asia and Europe

Although abundant city-states existed across the littoral of the Indian Ocean— from the East African coast (Pearson 1998) to the Indonesian archipelago (Kathirithamby-Wells and Villiers 1990)—a very different entity existed in Europe: city-states ruled by coalitions of merchant-entrepreneurs and noblemen. While city-states like Malacca and Hurmuz "controlled key nodes" of maritime trade (Subrahmanyam 1993:13–16), they were fundamentally different from those that existed in Western Europe (Aubin 1973:145).[35] Even

---

tradition where governments were controlled by the wealthiest merchants, who continuously lent money to the state in wartime. This debt was of course to be paid back with interest by the general public (Spufford 2003:44).

35. As Bin Wong (2002:455) notes: "It is certainly true that Southeast Asian states tap an expanding commerce for revenues, but there doesn't appear to be the mercantilist logic of competition and expansion driving any of the rulers to have their merchants venture out beyond the networks of

Meilink-Roelofsz concedes that in Southeast Asia—one of the most commercialized regions in the world—the position of the mercantile community was

> in no way comparable to that of the contemporary, late medieval merchant magnates of Europe. In Malacca as elsewhere in South-East Asia, the merchants were entirely at the mercy of the ruler, who could dispose capriciously of their property. Although the merchants of South-East Asia sometimes were able to seize political power by means of force, they were bereft of all those autonomous rights and civil freedoms which are such an intrinsic feature of medieval European society and which consequently exercised a definitive influence on the development of European politics. (1970:152–153)

Within South Asia there were some institutionalized local and regional concentrations of power (e.g., the *nadu* or *nagaram*) or port city-states in the Indian Ocean region (e.g., Malacca, Calicut, Hormuz) that *did* obtain some autonomy (Pearson 1987:13; Subrahmanyam 1995) and in which the mercantile class had some degree of administrative power (Hall 1978:83, 90).[36] Though upward social mobility certainly occurred in certain "artisan-cum-trading communities" (Kanaka Durga 2001), these classes were unable to funnel their energy into enlarging their territorial base (e.g., port city) at the expense of others (Aubin 1973:145). The European city-state structure, characterized by its institutional autonomy, was simply absent in South Asia (Heesterman 1980:87), and consequently merchant republics like those found in Europe did not come into existence (Bouchon and Lombard 1987:61; Pearson 1987b:82) as the political and economic realms were, generally speaking, separated to a much

---

exchange that they are already establishing . . . we do not seem to find a European kind of desire for expansion based on the wedding of profit and power." Basa, however, goes so far as to claim that Southeast Asia was in essence a periphery experiencing unequal exchange as a consequence of its early trade relations with South Asia (1998:408–410).

36. This autonomy, however, should not be exaggerated. The Western European "city-state" resembled the urban centers of Southeast Asia (Manguin 2000) more than those of Central, South, or East Asia. But in Southeast Asia, the gradual transition toward a nation-state did not occur and the significance of citizenship was not as clear cut. While in Western Europe walls surrounding a city had not only a military purpose but also a strong symbolic element, the mid–15th-century city of Calicut was not strongly fortified (Bouchon 1999:229), and even though others were, it did not always constitute an expression of urban independence (Deloche 2002). On the South Arabian coasts, and on islands in as well as near the Red Sea and the Persian Gulf, plenty of quasi-independent emirates emerged for whom commercial activities as well as piracy were significant windfalls (Ducatez 2004:174; 186–187). Despite the fact that these were, at times, quasi-independent from larger polities, such settlements did not have the same characteristics as Western European city-states and were not transformed into nation-states, which could wield even more power.

larger degree than in their Western European counterparts (Bouchon 1999:88, 223).[37]

One of the most important things to keep in mind is that together with this lack of mercantile power, the nobility on the South Asian subcontinent was much stronger than its Western European counterpart. For example, it was the natural propensity of all rural nobles, wherever they may have been located, to extract as much wealth as possible from the rest of the society (from their point of view, the peasants, merchants, and clergy) through extraeconomic coercion.[38] Because of the weakness of its nobles in relation to the urban-based merchant class, Europe was exceptional in this regard. (The Danish King Waldemar IV, for example, mobilized all of his resources against a coalition of Dutch merchants and the Hanseatic League for a nine-year war but was ultimately forced to submit to his financially superior enemy in the humiliating Peace of Stralsund in 1370; Malowist 1972:93; Van Klaveren 1969:77.)[39] All over Western Europe, many of the citizens in each city-state were armed and trained to fight. This situation was intrinsically linked with defending their privileges (monopolistic rights) and urban autonomy—if not outright independence—against other city-states (Putseys 1994) and more importantly, against the economic claims formulated by the nobility or territorial overlords in the vicinity. Such urban militias were an important leverage for institutional power vis-à-vis the nobility (cf. Zylbergeld 1984; Boone 2005) as well as an illustration of symbolic capital vis-à-vis the overlords (Powers 1971; Van Gerven 1999).[40] While the urban population in Central and South Asia

---

37. Even Bayly (2000:96) admits that "Indian fortunes and Indian commercial operations seem to have been relatively short-lived by comparison with those of Europe ... Indian cities were cities of burghers but not 'burgher cities.'"

38. A consequence of the nobility's or state's increased revenue demands was usually an intensification of monetization and commercialization, as peasants were forced to sell their produce in order to pay their taxes (Hall 1999:442). This is quite a uniform phenomenon in the early modern world. Despite the degree of monetization and commercialization in South Asia, however, it appears that wage labor in the countryside might have been somewhat more prevalent in Western Europe (see Rudra 1988:390, fn 7).

39. Another example of the mercantile city-state's strength and of the nobility's weakness in Western Europe during the Late Middle Ages is illustrated in a comparison of the military capacities of the King of England and of the city of Firenze: the former could muster about 3,000 knights and approximately 25,000 foot soldiers for his campaign in Scotland in 1298, while the latter was able to mobilize about 2,000 knights and 15,000 foot soldiers for a war against the city-state Lucca in 1325 (Mundy 2000:254). By contrast, in the late 16th century, Abbas's Persian army—including provincial troops—"consisted of 70–80,000 combatants, of whom 40–50,000 could be mobilized for use on any one campaign" (Morgan 1988:135).

40. The European guilds' military significance cannot be separated from the institutionalized power of the cities vis-à-vis the nobility (Wyffels 1951:144): "During a revolt of the Bruges' city militia, who, returning from a military campaign in 1411, refused to enter the city until the Calfvel, a hated charter degrading their privileges, was canceled, a grain tax abolished and the city

had more autonomy than that in the Chinese Empire, as is evidenced in the erivirapattinam (Abraham 1988:111–112), it would be something of a stretch to equate them with their European counterparts (e.g., Barendse 2000:209–210). Inhabitants of most Central and South Asian cities were not expected to arm themselves and in the process, acquire institutionalized political power in the long run (Aigle 2005:102).[41] This lack of citizen armies was symptomatic of large, semi-imperial polities dominated by their nobility.[42] In medieval South Asia, most often "the general population—Muslim or Hindu—was aloof from the political power struggle and was usually its victim" (Shokoohy and Shokoohy 2005:338).

Nevertheless, it is important to challenge the Eurocentric assumption of "inevitable growth of European settlements on the Indian coast from tiny beginnings to vast sprawling metropolises of trade" which ignored the obvious "dynamism and flux in the Indian world of that time." Even if one looks at the 18th century, "when there is undisputed evidence of decline in Indian mercantile activity," one cannot teleologically assume that the ports controlled by the multiple European (colonial) powers would have been able to supersede the commercial network of the South Asian ports (Arasaratnam 1989:75–94). Yet, when it came to enlarging their power beyond the borders of their city-states, the European armed mercantile bourgeoisie (in alliance with the weakened nobility) mostly benefited from their maritime ventures to outflank,

---

government replaced, Duke Philip the Good conceded most of their demands, after deliberating with his chancellor and council. He realized that his military position was too weak to enable him to react forcefully against Bruges" (Dumolyn 2000:510).

41. Cook illustrates this well in his account of 11th-century Balkh, a major metropolis in medieval Central Asia under the rule of the Ghaznavids: "While the Ghaznavid ruler was away making war on the Indians, Balkh was taken off him by the Qarakhanids, a typical tribal state. Soon after this, the Ghaznavid ruler returned and repossessed Balkh. Now the people of Balkh—perhaps unusually—had not remained passive through these events. They had vigorously resisted the Qarakhanid invaders, with considerable loss of life and property. What then was the reward they received for their loyalty when the latter returned? What the Ghaznavid ruler did was to treat them to a homily on the importance of minding their own business. Warfare, he admonished them, is for rulers, not for subjects; it was their duty to pay taxes to whoever had them in his power. The notables of Balkh duly apologized for their misconduct, and promised not to repeat it. The Ghaznavid ruler, I suspect, spoke for Muslim rulers as a whole" (1988:134). Although Balkh is not located in South Asia, the Delhi Sultanate "bore an indelible stamp" of both Sassanian and Ghaznavid traditions (Nizami 1985:142–157; Nizami 2002:98–109), making Cook's remarks relevant (see Kumar 2005:261). As Saberwal (1995:29) put it: "Indian merchants have not had much appetite for running the apparatus of government on their own account openly . . . merchants had difficulties in mutual cooperation even on a much smaller scale; making a bid for something like urban self-government would have been a far cry indeed."

42. Although certain mercantile towns in South Asia were protected (e.g., erivirapattanas) and some itinerant trading communities were linked with the existence of mercenary groups, it was not uncommon for imperial forces (e.g., the Colas) to station army units in big trading centers (Champakalakshmi 1995:289, 292).

outmaneuver, and frequently raid a Eurasian land power whose main strength lay in its armed cavalry and infantry. A prime and early example of this was the Western mercenaries' systematic exploitation and plunder of the Byzantine Empire (Burns 1954). But in the more distant Asian waters, similar attempts were much more difficult as the companies were plagued with high mortality rates (due to the different climate) and regular desertions (De Vliegher 1999). Furthermore, a profound conquest of the South Asian interior (and subsequent large-scale transformation of production sites) involved enormous amounts of time, energy, and significant costs. It is therefore a gross exaggeration to claim that in the 16th century, the European naval forces were already capable of "dominating the Indian Ocean [as] they imposed their own restrictions. . . . The ancient Indian Ocean system was modified in order to suit the new colonial masters" (Nag 1987:157).[43] Given that Europeans were "just one more strand in the already complex fabric of Asian maritime trade" (Reid 1999:155) throughout much of the 16th and 17th centuries, many debates then revolve around *when* the European powers were able to achieve the upper hand in the Indian Ocean world economy. Or, to frame it using world-system terminology: When was the Indian Ocean "incorporated" and ultimately "peripheralized" (Wallerstein 1987)?[44]

European colonial supremacy in East and South Asia—or as Pomeranz (2000) coined it, the "great divergence"—is considered by some as a relatively recent (late 18th or even early 19th century) phenomenon (e.g., Kieniewicz 1981) and therefore viewed as nothing more than a footnote in history (e.g., Frank 1998). Indeed, the traditional focus on the Industrial Revolution as the watershed event that brought about the European powers' colonization of the world (e.g., Bairoch 1997; Vries 2002) is a prevalent one, though to a certain extent misguided.[45] Others believe that their colonial experience was so unique

---

43. Because a profound conquest of the interior (and subsequent large-scale transformation of production sites) involved such enormous resources, *effective* control over more than just the South Asian coastal areas (Murphey 1996:195) did not take place until British rule in the late 18th century (Arasaratnam 1995). With regard to Ceylon, Arasaratnam notes that "the Dutch appear as a foreign power grafted on to the superstructure of Sinhalese/Tamil society, a new dynasty that had seized power" (1971:70). Nevertheless, it should be noted that even the Dutch were only capable of seizing power over the island as well as other parts of the Indian Ocean due to the massive state support given to its overseas merchants (Barendse 2002). Similar state support for South Asian merchants was not readily made available (D'Souza 2002:25).

44. I want to emphasize that the Indian Ocean region, despite its splendor, was not a capitalist world-economy (Pearson 1988:61). Although South Asia is geographically and socioeconomically central to the Indian Ocean (partially because of the monsoon winds), its merchants did not peripheralize the areas with which they were trading.

45. The ongoing debate regarding the extent to which "the industrial revolution does and does not represent a break with earlier history" (Pomeranz 2002:551) is an important one. Yet by focusing specifically on the Industrial Revolution as the watershed event that transforms a nation's history

that similarities between Western (and imperial) encroachment in Asia and elsewhere should be ignored, indirectly leading to the proposition that Western powers almost *accidentally* ruled most of the world up until the mid-20th century. Indeed, Subrahmanyam sarcastically refers to the "inevitable triumph of the European capitalist core [that] was played out once more, as South Asia was 'incorporated' into the capitalist world-system" (1996:24). He even goes so far as to wonder whether unequal exchange even existed in "his" region (1989:146). While one should pay attention to the multiple existing colonial models and consider the way in which local structures were "disrupted and dismantled in favor of the increasing hegemony of Europe" (Perlin 1983:90), while keeping in mind how the different "nature of states and societies in the external arena made a big difference in terms of how they responded to Europeans" (Pearson 1988:31), it is an altogether different matter to critique any Western theory, in the name of history, by insidiously suggesting that it merely "substitutes superficial secondary material for authentic documentation" (Subrahmanyam 1989:142).[46]

My point is that prior to the Industrial Revolution—according to Pearson (1988:45), long before 1750—Asia was on the road to peripheralization as "European companies began to assume an increasingly dominant role, gradually subverting the Asian trading nexus and local Asian economies to an international division of labor and commodity circuits centred in Western Europe itself" (Perlin 1983:60).[47] But the fact that Europeans eventually ended up dominating the maritime trade routes in the Indian Ocean does not imply that Asians were "static" or fundamentally "landlocked" (Chakravarti 2004). Thus, Pomeranz is correct in claiming that the scale of trade networks, the multitude of exchanged goods, and the wealth accumulated in Asian urban centers were dazzling when compared with those in Europe prior to the 19th century (2000). From the vantage point of the longue durée, there is no question that "Asia and not Europe was the leading maritime continent of the world" (Chakravarti 1998:99) and that the merchants engaged in it were not "mere peddlers," as European scholars once claimed (Pearson 1987b; Guo 2004:96). Therefore, it

---

thereby ushering in modernity, and which can be replicated elsewhere, one has long neglected the preconditions for technological innovations, which are rooted in economic power and political constellations.

46. Historians often lament that sociological models and exercises in comparative as well as world history are useless enterprises undertaken by "professional Jacks-of-all-trades, such as Immanuel Wallerstein, Janet Abu-Lughod, Jack Goldstone and André Gunder Frank" (Subrahmanyam 1994b:133).

47. This ultimately resulted in "their maritime economies increasingly imposing their will [in Asia] leading to de-industrialization" (Perlin 1983:90). For an example of de-industrialization in the salt industry in colonial Bengal, see Ray (2001).

is all the more surprising that the Europeans—a minority of the world's population to this very day—were capable of dominating Asian trade routes and eventually colonizing most of the continent.

European attempts to control these trade routes and to eventually engage in a systematic policy of colonization and conquest within the Indian Ocean region were not, as Goldstone (1998:267) pointed out, "one smooth and steady process," but rather, a very difficult and lengthy undertaking. Whereas in the early 16th century a European adventurer like Cortes destroyed the Aztec Empire with only 600 men under his command, and the Pizarro expedition dismembered the much larger Inca Empire with even fewer men (Williamson 1992:17–28), the more formidable empires in the Indian Ocean region were strong enough to withstand invasions of a similar scale. The outright conquest and colonization that took place in the Atlantic islands and Brazil could not be seriously considered in South Asia (Subrahmanyam 1988:139–140). From the Europeans' point of view, the South Asian hinterland consisted of an open frontier that could not be easily remolded and incorporated into an exploitable periphery due to the inherently limited resources available on the one hand (Desai 1969:504–505), and the enormous military capabilities of the Safavid, Moghul, and Vijayanagar states on the other. Instead, a mixture of peaceful trading by individuals and the use of collective military force to obtain money (e.g., through the imposition of a passport system in the Indian Ocean) had to be relied on to make profits.[48] An essential feature of the latter was virtual monopolistic control of the use of violence over the most widely used maritime trade routes.[49] But perhaps most important to European strategies to dominate the seas was the fact that "even under favorable circumstances Asian rulers were not always able to defend their merchants against attacks at sea" (Labh 1996:9); in the long run, an important factor for Asian merchants was "the absence of a central power strong enough to exert any sort of political influence over overseas countries" (Coedès 1964:12). Indeed, without the Asian governments' weak naval abilities, the European chartered companies would never have

48. This was not a new policy; in the Eastern Mediterranean of the early 13th century, the Iberian powers consistently turned to protection rent, collected through the threat of enslavement. Forcing Muslim communities to purchase indemnity from enslavement or expulsion (fees "pro stando in terra ista") was a common strategy (Fernández-Armesto 1987:22) that may have generated as much revenue as did occasional enslavements.

49. Violence was not a uniquely Portuguese strategy, nor a 16th century one for that matter. In A.D. 1182, the French nobleman Rénaud de Châtillon ordered the construction of seven galleys near his domain of Eilat on the Gulf of Aqaba. From this base his ships raided the Red Sea and the Arabian coast as far as Aden, with the intention of controlling the spice route to South Asia. Saladin's destruction of the Latin Kingdom in 1187, however, brought an end to these early European attempts to penetrate the Indian Ocean (Mollat 1964:249–250), but they were clearly a harbinger of events to come.

been able to impose the cartaz system (Pearson 1987) or been able to let their compatriots plunder South Asian vessels. Interestingly, South Asian merchants' demands for full compensation for losses suffered at the hands of European pirates also "turned out to be unenforceable because of the superior naval strength of the European companies" (Prakash 1979:47), even at the time of the powerful Mughal empire whose revenues "fattened the nobility and fuelled the war machinery" (Ludden 1999:107). So while it was possible for various South Asian polities to retaliate against European merchants whenever they appeared to trade on the mainland, it was impossible for them to directly retaliate against those countries that financed and directed major military naval expeditions in the Indian Ocean.[50] Chaudhuri refers to this lack of naval power as an enigma:

> The successive political Dynasties of the Indian subcontinent were fully occupied in upholding their political and economic power over unbroken terra firma and never seriously considered overseas colonial ventures as logical corollaries of seaborne trade. India of course had a crucial role in Indian Ocean commerce, not only in terms of geographical contours but also in terms of the overall volume and the value of the commodities exchanged. [This makes] the Indian lack of interest in sea power in the pre-modern era distinctly enigmatic. . . . The large territorial kingdoms of India, with their capital cities far from the sea, showed no real interest in maritime mastery. (1985:15)

The "enigma" disappears, however, when one takes into account why the nobility's option to use state power to construct a huge navy and ward off European attacks was never implemented—it simply was not in their interest to do so (Flores 1997:36–37). Although in South and Southeast Asia some noblemen and even the Mughal emperors themselves occasionally participated in commercial activities (Chandra 1987; Sun 2000:193), the majority of revenues had always been derived from the land (Wink 1988:54; Palat 1988:318; Veluthat

---

50. Of course the South Asian nobility could attempt to retaliate by taking European merchants as hostages or by threatening port cities' supplies by withholding commodities produced in the interior. But as Abernethy points out: "Virtually uncontested control of the high seas offered advantages on land as well. Europeans could select among invasion sites, avoiding hostile places and favoring ones in which resistance was known to be weak or nonexistent" (2000:179). Besides the successful use of force by European companies that internalized their protection costs (Steensgaard 1974), another fundamental and often-ignored disadvantage for Asian merchants was the European companies' "ability to gather information and to survey the situation in the whole of Asia (and in Europe as well) [enabling them] to compare market conditions in Amsterdam, Taiwan and Persia" (Van Santen 1991:93).

1993:186).[51] This was not just the case in Northern South Asia (the so-called heartland of the Delhi Sultanate and the Moghul Empire). In Southern South Asia (Palat 1988:71), Safavid Persia, as well as the Ottoman Empire, "land remained their principal resource and customs duties were only a minor item in the state budget" (Wink 1988:57; Pearson 1987b:79). This dependence on revenues from land is in sharp contrast with 13th-century England (Cazel 1966:104), and even more so with a medieval European city-state with policies explicitly designed to increase revenue from trade[52] and which, because of its institutional autonomy, could limit extortion by local rulers (Borsa 1990:10). For example, it is estimated that in 1293, the amount of taxes derived from Genoa's sea trade "postulated a taxable income of nearly 4 million Genoese

---

51. Borsa claims that "not more than 5% of revenue in the Mughal Empire was derived from customs [and] in Gujarat itself, where some major ports were located, it was [only] 6%" (1990:11). "The main source of India's wealth was agriculture and the proverbial fertility of her soil" (Sinha and Ray 1986:283). Agriculture was also considered "the source of all wealth" (Yadav 1974:24) during the Delhi Sultanate. In Southern South Asia, "mobilization of agricultural produce was the primary consideration [of the elite] . . . wealth generated from artisan and mercantile activity was a necessary but not sufficient component" (Heitzman 1997:235) since trade remained relatively "marginal to [South Asia's] economy and society." According to Palat et al. (1986:173), it was the "massive appropriation of agricultural surplus that made feasible the existence of the impressive urban centers" in South Asia where, depending on the region, one-fourth to three-fourths of the agricultural output was extracted as revenue by the state. According to Risso, "in northern India, the Delhi Sultanate derived its most dependable revenues from agricultural production and taxation [and] the self-sufficiency reduced the impulse toward long-distance maritime trade" (1995:42). Steensgaard even claimed that at least up to the 16th century, "long-distance trade still remained marginal to the economies and empires around the Indian Ocean" (1987:129), which is a serious exaggeration. It is more correct to state that "maritime trade became a lucrative source of profit to supplement taxes raised upon agriculture" (McPherson 1993:152). This was, of course, much more the case in Southeast Asia than in South Asia (cf. Hall 2001).

52. In the 13th century, "the revenues of the single city of Acre were about the same as those of the Kingdom of England" (Pryor 1988:123). Trade was also crucial for a city-state like Venice: "Venetian food, Venetian wealth and even her very existence as an independent state depended on her trade with the east" (Robert 1970:147). This statement applies to the overwhelming majority of Western cities where already, by the early 14th century—if not earlier—on average, 75 percent to 80 percent of all incomes were derived from indirect taxes on trade and consumption (Herlihy 1964; Boone 1989:113; Menjot and Sánchez Martinez 1999). In the first decades of the 15th century, the German princes of Cologne, Mayence, Trèves, and the Palatinat received approximately 60 percent of all their revenues from tolls on trade (Pfeiffer 2002:742). Abulafia (1994:23) notes that already in 1302, taxes derived from trade constituted "about half the king's known revenue from Catalonia." This is clearly in sharp contrast with the agrarian rice cultures in Asia (Palat 1995). Though Hobson (2004:54) correctly states that in Asia taxes were increasingly demanded in cash, he does not bother to elaborate upon this very significant difference. Palat and Wallerstein explicitly state: "The possibility of harnessing large agrarian surpluses meant that in contrast to the historical experience of early modern Europe, where political authorities and commercial entrepreneurs were tied to each other in a symbiotic alliance, state-builders in late medieval South Asia were less dependent on merchant-financiers for the resources needed to maintain their coercive forces" (1999:39–40).

pounds, roughly ten times the receipts of the French royal treasury for the preceding year" (Lopez 1975:45).

This does *not*, of course, imply that one should recreate an ideal-typical dichotomy between dynamic "mercantilist" trading states on the one hand and static agrarian "inward-looking" states with antimercantile practices on the other (Subrahmanyam 1993:19; Matthee 1999:89). It would also be erroneous to claim, as does Sanderson (1994:41), that "large bureaucratic empires stifle mercantile activity"—an unfortunate recurrent theme in Western social science.[53] Empires should not be perceived as intrinsically averse to trade (Bang 2003:204): as in Western Europe (e.g., Verhulst 1967b), South Asian rural overlords stimulated the economic growth of agricultural productivity and commerce in various ways (Sastri 1966:328–333). Both the Delhi Sultanate and the Cola state created and supported multiple infrastructure projects (e.g., highways, inns, roads, bridges, canals, aqueducts, dams, water tanks, and other irrigation facilities). These projects, meant to provide a certain measure of safety for itinerant merchants, facilitated commerce considerably (Habib 1982:83–84; Nizami 1985:90; Karashima 1984:20). In the Delhi Sultanate this was also achieved by hunting down robbers and extortionists (Sarkar 1978:20), and by constructing police and postal departments (Sinha and Ray 1986:234).[54] The commercial benefits of safe travel around a large empire should not be underestimated (Lewis 1976:461) (although political stability was less guaranteed than in China). The Vijayanagar Empire also stimulated artisan and commodity production (Chibber 1998:20) and maintained inland transport routes to increase state revenue (Sinopoli 2000:388).[55] One can notice similar policies in Southeast Asia as well (Hall 1992:212).

It was because of the European bourgeoisie's success at achieving institutionalized power[56] and because of specific policies enacted by them that

---

53. Unfortunately, the claim that capitalism emerged within Western societies as an outgrowth of their *rational democratic institutions* also remains a popular narrative, one that enables Western social scientists to completely dismiss the impact of colonization, be it by nation-states (e.g., Baechler 1995:258) or medieval city-states (e.g., Chirot 1985).

54. Thus, one cannot possibly agree with Hall who claims that the nature of the "Islamic state" was "purely predatory," as though—unlike European states—Muslim governments did not consciously encourage trade for a long time (1987:159, 164).

55. The Empire's economic benefits derived from its seaports and other territories seem to have remained limited, however, and do not seem to fit readily into more "traditional core-periphery models of imperial structure" (Sinopoli and Morrison 1995:85).

56. Ramaswamy, hardly Eurocentric or pessimistic about pre-European artisan productivity and commercialization in South Asia, nevertheless admits that "unlike the European guilds, [Vijayanagar guilds] did not attempt to standardize prices or products" (1985a:426). Despite the fact that certain groups of South Asian merchants did unite in various guilds and associations, and at times enjoyed considerable autonomy (Jacq-Hergoualc'h et al. 1998:279–280), European merchant power in city-states was quite different. Recognizing the latter's success at obtaining and

a systematic peripheralization of the external arena occurred. Mercantilism as a strategy, however, was less capable of being implemented by the merchant class in South Asia since—with the exception of Southeast Asian (city-) states such as Malacca (e.g., Reid 1993:71–73)—it failed to create institutional structures from which it could wield significant long-term power. As Hall and Spencer put it: "In South Asia there was no widespread sociopolitical urban 'movement' comparable to that of medieval Europe, no emergent burgher class which directly confronted and undermined existing patterns of urban and rural overlordship" (1980:147). This does not imply that South Asian merchants were passive; the larger merchant organizations[57] performed important functions since they were "entrusted by kings and royal officials with the collection of taxes, dues, tolls, . . . and looked after religious establishments [while] even arbitrating in disputes of a more special type" (Wijetunga 1968:506–507). Even more important was their maintenance of armed troops (sometimes labeled as mercenaries), used to protect their property while traveling across the large Indian Ocean area (Indrapala 1971; Spencer 1976:413; Abraham 1988:78). Merchant "regiments" also assisted "regular" royal troops in the plundering expeditions of South Asian polities, sharing in the royal troops' booty upon their return (Hall 1980:193). Nevertheless, these "large collegial bodies of merchants" remained subordinate to imperial [Cola] power (Palat 1988:85), to a degree unparalleled in late medieval Western Europe.[58]

The Impact of the Perilous Frontier

In South Asia, "imperial expansion was primarily agrarian expansion" (Heesterman 1991:40) and the mercantile class' lack of political and military power weakened its capacities when more and more European intruders poured in,

---

preserving monopolistic power over scarce resources and trade routes (often interlinked with the ability to rely on the use of military force) is crucial to debunking the myth of dominant laissez-faire historiography (Chaudhuri 1981:238; Alavi 1982)—that is, that Europe succeeded in taking off because of laissez-faire policies (Steensgaard 1981:253)—as well as the fallacious narrative in which premodern feudal agrarian violence is juxtaposed with a modern commercialized urban market in which peaceful trade flourished (Maire Vigueur 2003:112–113).

57. The Ayyayole 500 or the Tamil Tis'ai Ayirattu Ainnurruvar are the most renowned examples mentioned time and again (e.g., Abraham 1988:41–71; Krishna 2000:92–93; Karashima 2002).

58. The same can be said about most of the South Asian subcontinent under the Mughals. As Washbrook (1997:429) concludes: "The Mughal state was bureaucratised only in weak patrimonial ways, which made continuity of connections between merchant capital and state power insecure. Also, and ultimately, the state's ambitions centred more on enriching itself and its nobility rather than the commercial classes *per se*. Merchants and bankers . . . were always at risk and individual merchant fortunes seem to have been hard to institutionalise and pass from one generation to the next."

supported by their bases at home.[59] South Asian merchants from the Coromandel Coast may have been able to successfully compete with the different European joint-stock companies "as long as they were able to operate in freedom and stability" (Arasaratnam 1986:143). But given the aforementioned bullion flows and the Asian disinterest in European commodities, this caveat would be challenged by the European merchants *in situ* who realized that substantial profits could not be made simply through peaceful trading in the Indian Ocean as Europeans were unable to supply Western commodities at competitive prices (Vink 2004:51). In order to succeed, the Europeans systematically attempted to create a coercive business environment through the "judicious use of violence" (Prakash 1998:82), which then facilitated the implementation of "monopolistic claims." This in turn would put them in a position to dictate prices in their own interest (Arasaratnam 1969:481). As Jan Pieterszoon Coen wrote in a letter to the directors of the VOC in 1614:

> Your Honours should know that trade in Asia must be driven and maintained under the protection and favour of Your Honours' own weapons, and that the weapons must be paid for by the profits from the trade; so that we can not carry on trade without war, nor war without trade. (cited in Reynolds 1974:145)

To the profit-seeking European merchants, the systematic militarization of the Indian Ocean basin and the subsequent territorial conquests of strategic points across the Ocean's littoral constituted a logical policy (Heesterman 1991:46) which dates back to the medieval city-states for whom warfare and commerce were a "double vocation" (Maire-Vigueur 2003:268).

In South Asia, the clear lack of interest in retaliatory naval warfare and the various state mechanisms and geopolitical choices must be understood in light of the important historical role of pastoral nomadism. As mentioned earlier, nomadic attacks were a constant threat to the Chinese Empire (Barfield 1989) and consequently, an important factor in that empire's decision to abandon the major maritime expeditions of the early 15th century. The historical evidence reveals that nomadic incursions also constituted a formidable threat on South Asia's northwestern frontier (Chandra 1997:19–73).

---

59. This distinction between commercial versus agricultural expansion is also reflected in the distinction between the Portuguese and Ottoman views on naval warfare: "While Portugal rejected the conquering tradition of her warrior aristocracy to lean almost entirely on maritime commerce as the primary reason for imperial naval expansion in the East, the Ottomans, in contrast, sought to conquer territories in order to gain tax revenues from newly acquired agricultural and commercial economies [reflecting the difference between] an empire whose economic aims were largely agricultural and . . . a state whose interests were primarily commercial" (Hess 1970:1916).

A strict dichotomy between "civilized" agrarian states and "barbarian" no-mads in constant conflict would be misleading since both "needed each other for an exchange of the commodities which each had to sell" (Hourani 1991:101); the tribes constantly interacted with the empires situated around them (Golden 1998:20), interaction that occurred both in peaceful and hostile ways, depend-ing on the historical context (Khazanov 1984). The extremely profitable over-land trade from South to Central Asia, for instance, was unimaginable without the nomads who operated in the area and who were themselves attracted to the richness of the South Asian peninsula:

> In their capacity as potential participants in Indian sovereignty and wealth, they did not remain idle behind their Hindu Kush mountain strongholds... It should not surprise us that the official Afghan accounts prefer their eagerness for the jihad against the kuffar of Hind (India) as the main motive behind migration, although even the, in this respect, exemplary classic Khulasat al-Ansab makes mention of the temptation of the rich Indian bait, referring to gismat-abkhwur (share of fortune). (Gommans 1991:55)

The tribal breakouts of the early 18th century, which had enormous repercus-sions from the Safavid Empire in Central Asia to the Mughal Empire in South Asia (Bayly 1988), were not simply a phenomenon of that particular century (Roberts 1980:415). Rather, they were a permanent feature in Central Asia (Singh 1988), a feature that Western Europe no longer had to contend with after the Magyar invasions of the 10th century (Wendelken 2000:244; Crone 1989:150; Wink 1997:24).[60] The extent of the constant nomadic threat in the northern part of the subcontinent is illustrated by the history of the afore-mentioned Ghaznavids as well as the Turkish Ghurids who captured Lahore in 1186 and Delhi in 1193 (Wolpert 2000:108), and even more so by the Mon-gol armies' strength on the northwestern frontiers. These threats were very serious (Jackson 1999) from the time of Sultan Iltutmish (1211–1236)—who was confronted with danger from neighboring Afghanistan (then occupied by Mongol forces)—as well as during the period of Sultan Ghiyas-ud-Din Balban (1266–1287), who also had to remain on the defensive against the Mongols. The permanent danger on the subcontinent's northwestern frontier and the regu-lar military campaigns (Chaudhuri 1990:274–275; Nizami 2002:349) gradually increased and even threatened Delhi under Sultan 'Ala-ud-Din (1296–1316)

---

60. The Magyars overran large parts of Germany, France, and even Italy, whereas the Mongols did not advance beyond the suburbs of Vienna during their offensive of 1241. As Marc Bloch (1966) pointed out, the relative immunity of Western Europe from recurring nomadic incursions after the 10th century probably played a significant role in its later socioeconomic development.

(Wolpert 2000:114), and again in 1327 under the reign of the most powerful Sultan, Mohammed ibn Tughluq (Sinha and Ray 1986:240). The impact of these recurrent nomadic raids cannot be underestimated (Jackson 1999) as they also account for the introduction and wholesale diffusion of a wide range of new technologies throughout the 13th and 14th centuries (Habib 1980:17).

Inseparable from the nomadic element were the multiple raids of the Sultans of Delhi under Muhammad ibn Tughluq (1325–1351) against Hindu princes in the Deccan as far South as Tamilnadu. The Delhi Sultanate's need to defend itself against continuous nomadic (e.g., Mongol) invasions (Wink 1997:202–211) created its own need to raid the empire's outer fringes as the spoils of war constituted a significant part of state income (Sinha and Ray 1986:280).[61] These raids included sporadic attempts to incorporate the weaker parts into the state structure or to at least impose a tributary status over neighboring states and tribal formations (Jackson 1999; Wink 1997:158). Thus, the southward expansion of the Sultanate under both 'Ala-ud-Din and ibn Tughluq (Sinha and Ray 1986:226–244) should be understood not only as an aspect of empire formation (as a second capital was temporarily built in the Deccan), but also for the easily obtainable booty and rewards made available to the Delhi sultanate's armies that had to defend themselves against recurrent Mongol invasions, and which, ironically, often recruited Mongol prisoners of war into their ranks (Chaudhuri 1990:275).

The Sultanate of Delhi achieved its largest territorial expansion during the reign of ibn Tughluq, who was regularly forced to campaign against the Mongols (Jackson 1975:142–143). This gradual expansion rapidly came to an end in the last years of his life, however, as wars on multiple fronts shattered the empire (Asher and Talbot 2006:51).[62] In the south, the Deccan became independent again in the period 1330 to 1347 due to Hindu opposition, and Tughluq's successor, Firuz Shah (1351–1388), felt compelled to abandon the reconquest of the area (Wolpert 2000:118). The Delhi Sultanate's power in the northern part of the subcontinent was ultimately crushed by the successful invasion of the Mongols under Timur, who sacked Delhi (1398–1399). This

---

61. The importance of plunder and booty from campaigns is widely accepted as an additional source of revenue for imperial polities like the Colas (e.g., Shanmugam 1987:59) or the Champa in Southeast Asia (Hall 1992:252–260), but it is not necessarily an indication of weak political centralization (e.g., Spencer 1983:6), or that plundering and tributes were more important forms of income than land taxes (Shanmugam 1987:145). Keay nevertheless claims that the "conspicuous generosity" inherent in the patronage of an imperial polity did "necessitate access to substantial revenue [which made] the rich pickings of predatory warfare essential" (2000:220).

62. Shokoohy and Shokoohy (2004:317) note that his "hectic maladministration and his mistreatment of his army commanders had led to rebellions in most of the provinces of the empire, with the governors declaring themselves independent sultans."

destruction enabled large areas such as Gujarat, Jaunpur, and Malwa, which had been incorporated into the Sultanate, to once again become independent (Wolpert 2000:119). In the short run, the Lodi dynasty (1451–1526), itself of Afghan descent, was able to recover some terrain for the Delhi Sultanate thanks to continuing immigration from Afghanistan (Shokoohy and Shokoohy 2005:353).[63] But the same waves of nomadic immigrants that initially strengthened the sultanate militarily would also cause its demise. Multiple rebellions by these forces eventually brought about a new invasion by the Mongol (Mughal) Babur, a descendent of Timur, who—after having been expelled from his homeland near Samarkand by other nomadic forces—launched a major campaign from Afghanistan that destroyed the Lodi dynasty in the Battle of Panipat on April 21, 1526.

Along with the role of the tribes in the spectacular destruction of states, the states' attempts to annihilate the tribes should not be overlooked. On many occasions, the political authorities of strong Asian states hoped "to force or induce [nomads] to settle down permanently or to expel them beyond the state jurisdiction" (Chaudhuri 1990:266). While the latter was sometimes achieved, the durability of tribal structures in the steppe and on empires' frontiers in South Asia, Iran, and to a certain extent even China, made it very difficult for the states to absorb them:

> Traditional states responded by leaving them alone, the combination of tribal resistance and lack of material resources in the relevant areas making it pointless for them to attempt more than minimal control; and so the tribes were left to further develop their tribal way of life. (Crone 1993:367)

A permanent pacification of the "perilous frontier" (Barfield 1989) was impossible for the state polities, which simply were not strong enough to indefinitely subdue the tribes around them. In addition, the latter were often very mobile and were dispersed over large areas. Lastly, the relative "poverty of pastoral surplus" (Humphrey and Hurelbaatar 2005:20) often made this enormously risky financial and military enterprise not worthwhile. Yet, nomadic invasions that took over a state by outright conquest (as the Mongols did in China) did not solve the problem either. As Saunders pointed out, "pure nomadism could never hold an empire" (1977:59), thus the nomads' absorption into sedentary society was a sine qua non if they wanted to control it continuously (as in the case of the Yuan Dynasty). When they remained:

---

63. Initially, the Lodi dynasty was capable of increasing the Sultanate's territory by achieving military successes against Jaunpur and by dominating parts of the Punjab and the Ganges area.

in the conquered land, they fell victim to the process of socioeconomic and political differentiation that they escaped at home and merged with the conquered population; but those who stayed at home remained tribesmen, meaning that the process could start again. (Crone 1993:367)[64]

An alternative was some form of coalition during the process of empire building, between a state structure on the one hand and one or more tribal formations on the other. The case of Tamerlane, who plundered Delhi in the late 14th century, and the raids by Nadir Shah Afshar from Persia in the early 18th century, are striking examples (Bayly 1988:7). Structurally, however, tribal formations did not make for good governments as they were "oblivious to the long-term demands of the central government" (Crone 1993: 70). A coalition was only a temporary solution, one that existed so long as the bounty and plunder were available and the violence that tribal formations were capable of generating could be channeled outside the state structure that provided the basis for the coalition. Often a coalition would collapse on the death of the sovereign who had kept it together (Paul 2004:1092).

Clearly inherent to the process of empire formation on the South Asian subcontinent then was the wealth generated from raiding and plundering (Spencer 1976, 1983). But aside from these raids and the slow, steady "growth of the monetary economy" (Chandra 1997:161) of the Delhi Sultanate, "the main source of the state's income [remained] land revenue which generally averaged one-fifth of the total produce, though sometimes it was as high as one-half" (Sinha and Ray 1986:280). The growth of the urban economy, though substantial, was still relatively strongly characterized by slave-labor (Habib 1978:293, 297) and not based on a putting-out production system, as in Western Europe.[65] Thus, unlike European polities, income generated by occasional plunder and tribute and regular taxes on land were more important than taxes derived from commerce (Thapar 1966:206). This in turn had profound consequences on state policies and economic development in the long run (Habib 1980:38).

Along with its perilous frontier, attempts to unify the entire South Asian continent (mainly under Ibn Tughluq) in the early 14th century, as well as in the

---

64. See also Chaudhuri (1990:270).

65. This does not imply that in South Asia "slaves were exclusively used for economic enterprises or that the economic life of the times depended upon them" (Gopal 1965:78) since both agricultural laborers and urban residents working for wages existed in Europe as well as in South Asia, and since slave labor in the latter was primarily intended for domestic services (Chandra 1997:171–172). Nevertheless, slave labor in 13th-century South Asia was much more widespread than in Europe and continued to expand (Lal 1994); this is also evident by the widespread use of slavery in the military at the time (Kumar 2005:250–251) and the ongoing vibrant slave trade in the region (Levi 2002:282–283).

years of the Great Moghul Aurangzeb in the late 17th century, ultimately failed since the Empire never succeeded in forcing the powerful Hindu nobility to accept exclusive allegiance. Permanently threatened by nomadic (mainly, but not exclusively Mongol) invasions from Afghanistan and the Lahore area in the period 1200 to 1530, and facing strong Rajput resistance to the imposition of tributary relations elsewhere, the Delhi Sultans were unable to create a strong and enduring centralized empire. The ultimate failure of the Delhi Sultanate under Ibn Tughluq in creating such a firm centralized polity meant that political fragmentation remained "the norm in central and southern India" (McPherson 1993:107).

The lack of a unified empire spanning the entire South Asian subcontinent created something of a conundrum: on the one hand the area was unable to provide merchants with long-term protection, as in the Chinese case, while on the other hand the autonomy of the cities was limited and unable to compete with the military strength of the powerful rural aristocracy (nattar; chittiraméli). The latter, through their crystallization into nadus (Heitzman 1997:16), managed to control the local market centers (nagarams). The power of the rural nobility in turn resulted in attempts to create their own dynasties or to vigorously oppose formal incorporation into an imperial structure, especially whenever a form of imperial overextension occurred (Palat 1988:86). Because of the nature of these often-formulated imperial claims,[66] overextension is bound to happen in polities that desire to construct a world-empire.

Unlike, for example, misguided debates on the failures of protoindustrialization (Coleman 1981; Perlin 1983), the failure of imperial and colonial conquests by the South Asian elites is an important issue that needs to be addressed. One of the crucial features of the South Asian subcontinent's polities was the strong position of the rural nobility. But succession to the throne in South Asia was particularly problematic. Just as the Mongol Empire experienced inherent succession problems[67] whenever a Khan with exceptional charismatic authority (in the Weberian sense) would die (Allsen 1996),[68] the South Asian subcontinent also witnessed considerable instabilities and conflicts due to recurring power struggles between those of the ruler's lineal descendants who attempted to centralize the state and those who wanted to preserve their rule over specific parts of the kingdom (Saberwal 1995:41).[69] Although

---

66. Analyzing the inscriptions and representations of "universal sovereignty" among the Calukyas and the Colas, Davis (1997:72–74) makes quite clear the *intentions* of constructing empires.

67. See Joseph Fletcher's (1986) "tanistry."

68. "As was typical of Eurasian nomadic political formations, the state was viewed as the collective possession of the ruling class" (Golden 1992:288).

69. Interestingly, Faruqui (2005:510) interprets this as a heritage of "Central Asian political traditions that permitted familial, clan or tribal groupings considerable political latitude vis-à-vis the ruling monarch." The uncertainty revolving around entitlements to sovereignty and legitimacy in

one should not exaggerate the negative impact of warfare (as Western Europe experienced its own feudal military chaos), when it came to successful empire building, the constant centrifugal tendencies in South Asia (Veluthat 1993:19; Pouchepadass 1996:706–707) were another destabilizing factor in what one could call a *pyramid of rule*, composed of a "calibrated parceling of sovereignty" (D'Souza 2002:11). Furthermore, since the nobility's armies were generally much larger than those in Europe (Jackson 1999:239–240), not only could they inflict more damage[70] but they were also capable of preventing the merchant class from obtaining institutionalized power; essentially, "the world of mercantile capital occupied a subordinate position in the temple urbanism of South India" (Heitzman 1997:115). Finally, there was the *nayankara* system in Vijayanagar, in which prominent commanders received land grants and privileged status as *Nayakas* (local lords or governors). This system, which resembled a sort of military feudalism on the fringes of the imperial polity, appeared to function quite smoothly when the central authority was strong, but also provided territorial bases from which the *Nayakas* could build semi-independent hereditary holdings in times of imperial weakness (Sinopoli 1994:227; Karashima 2001:41), especially during the recurring and seemingly inevitable succession crises (Karashima 1992:72; Pouchepadass 1996:715).[71] The imperial rulers were aware of the provinces' powers and tried to counter them by appointing members of the royal family as governors of the militarily more important (but not necessarily more lucrative) provinces. On the whole, however, this was not successful because succession rivalries, as in the northern Muslim kingdoms, tended to produce filial disloyalty to the throne and even rebellion or *fitna* (Wink 1984).

Europe experienced similar succession rivalries after the breakup of the Carolingian Empire into petty chiefdoms, as a result of the multiple invasions of Saracens, Vikings, and nomadic Magyars on Europe's perilous frontier. The concurrent parceling of political power in the period 900 to 1100, however, created a political vacuum in which "autonomous urban enclaves" (Anderson

---

the Timurid state system and its legacy in South Asia is also discussed by Khan (2001:19–26) and more recently by Balabanlilar (2007:10–11). This "lack of strict rules of succession" also applied to several Southeast Asian polities (Hagesteijn 1989:112).

70. Gopal (1965:255) gives various examples of several South Asian cities that were completely sacked in wartime. On the significant increase of military conflict through the 13th to the 14th centuries, see Champakalakshmi (1987:101–103).

71. In another example of the multiple pressures generated by inheritance and succession struggles in South Asian polities, such as the Mewar region of Rajasthan, Kapur (2002) considers the aspirations of various kinsmen of the Guhila rajputs as a major factor in the temporary incorporation of their early modern "polity" into the Delhi Sultanate during the early 14th century. To a certain extent, this was also true for Kashmir after 1470, facilitating its incorporation by the Mughals (Hangloo 2000).

1974:422) could eventually emerge (Szűcs 1985:26).[72] This had profound consequences in terms of divergent political and socioeconomic developments in the long run. Unlike the Indian Ocean region, city-states in the Western European region were gradually capable of experiencing economic growth through a strategy of capital accumulation at the expense of their hinterlands and multiple semi-colonial peripheries, as well as the usage of public debt to finance these strategies, practices that were later copied by mercantile states.[73]

Why were the Europeans ultimately able to colonize and "underdevelop" India, and not the other way around (cf. Chattopadhyay 1972:189-190)? In my opinion, the answer lies not in the often-discussed events of 1757 or 1857 (Markovits 1992), but rather, in the combination of these extremely important yet often-ignored events that made peripheralization possible; that is, the prelude to de facto colonial annexation.[74] As Crone (1989:15) correctly points out, in most preindustrial societies, the "vast majority of people *had* to be peasants" and society's overall economic growth was generally limited and/or not recurrent (Wrigley 2004; Lal 1999:211–221). But peripheralization changes this. A systematic policy of colonization and deindustrialization in the periphery (Habib 1985) allowed Western powers to achieve long-term economic growth.[75] This does not imply that the production and export of raw

---

72. This development is in contrast to the weakness of the urban bourgeoisie in Hungary (D'Eszlary 1963:507) and Poland (Samsonowicz 1988:181–182), where the power of the nobility actually increased.

73. The studies by Marc Boone (2002) exemplify the importance of public debt for elites in various city-states that were gradually incorporated into a larger territorial entity, as they allied themselves with princely power. The "financial revolution" that scholars such as Tracy (1985) have noted in the early modern Dutch state, which people have coined the "first bourgeois republic," has to be compared with the practices in city-states in an earlier period (Boone 2002:340–341; for the example of Venice, cf. Hocquet 2005). In addition, the institutional similarities between the European "medieval" city-states and the United Provinces are remarkable and illustrate the continuity of merchant power (Blockmans 1973:26).

74. In doing so one should also pay attention to the extent, as Washbrook (1988:76) has put it, to which "colonialism was the logical outcome of South Asia's own history."

75. Lal elaborates on Crone's statement by claiming that two major types of growth exist: Smithian growth and Promethean growth: "The former [exists] due to the creation of empires which linked hitherto separate economic areas with diverse resources into a closer and more unified economic space through the mechanisms of trade and investment (e.g., Pax Gupta, Pax Sung, Pax Tokugawa)... all led to intensive growth in their regions and to extensive economic miracles. But this type of intensive growth in agrarian economies is inherently limited because it eventually hits diminishing returns because of the ultimate dependence of an agrarian economy on the fixed factor—land. The Industrial Revolution, by substituting mineral-based energy sources based on the seemingly unlimited fossil fuels, removed this constraint on intensive growth. This Promethean growth allows the prospects of unlimited growth, and is of course the major characteristic of the modern era of growth" (1999:211). I do not intend to minimize the significance of the Industrial Revolution as much as does Wallerstein (1989), but his point—which coincides somewhat with that of North and Thomas (1973)—that the Industrial Revolution should not be interpreted as

materials (e.g., agricultural commodities) were not lucrative in the short run; it is stated, for example, that in different periods of the 16th century, the trade balance between Eastern and Western Europe was actually negative for the latter. This simply illustrates the importance of the longue durée: producing commodities with a higher added value and selling them to peripheral areas is a much more successful economic strategy *in the long run*, as evidenced by the relation between Western and Eastern Europe.

Conclusions

While criticizing mainstream Eurocentric presuppositions about the lack of socioeconomic dynamism in South Asia, one certainly has to acknowledge the specific differences that explain its divergent path. It is clear that South Asia did display the emergence of individual capitalists, and witnessed remarkable economic growth over a prolonged period of time, but a capitalist system as such was not in the making due to the subcontinent's fundamentally different political structure.[76]

Given its geographic location, South Asia was the pivot of the Indian Ocean region (Sastri 1972:1), and the itinerant "valiant merchants" (*vira valanjigar*) of the Coromandel coast undoubtedly had a great cultural impact in Southeast Asia, as noted by the influence of Hindu civilization in the 11th through 12th centuries and the spread of Muslim conversions in the 13th through 15th centuries (Stein 1965:50). Despite the depictions of some nationalistic 20th-century scholars, these successful merchant traders did not attempt to colonize these areas in order to systematically exploit them as peripheries. The Cola

---

the major event which brought about recurring Promethean growth, but rather as the outcome of modern economic growth (in the core), is well taken. A much more clarifying position is taken by Wrigley, who points out that "pre-industrial economic growth was, in its underlying nature, more like a movement from one plateau or level to another, than a step onto the moving staircase of exponential growth which has been the distinguishing, even in a sense the defining characteristic of the economic growth of industrial economies" (1979:302). Thus the Industrial Revolution enabled the West to achieve economic growth more rapidly and more intensely (which ultimately widened the gap between the core and the periphery) after circa 1800. (See the debate between Immanuel Wallerstein, John Hicks, Celso Furtado, and others in Guarducci 1983:695–746, and essays in Prak 2001.)

76. I completely disagree with Beaujard (2005:453) who claims that in the Abbasid caliphate, 9th-century southern India, 12th-century Ayyubid Egypt, and the 15th-century sultanates of Bengal and Gujarat, "capitalism came to *dominate* the spheres of production and commerce" (emphasis added). Similarly, Farooqi (1991:120) claims that the new economic policy of the sultans from circa 1296 onward marks the beginning of a capitalist era. It is beyond doubt that *capitalists* existed in all these areas at different moments in time but, once again, this does not equal a capitalist *system* (Bang 2003:207). The usage of merchant *capitalism* (e.g., Mukund 1999) is therefore inappropriate in the South Asian context.

expeditions, for instance, did not lead to permanent annexations of territory, let alone attempts to peripheralize the areas in which they operated (Kulke and Rothermund 1998:117, 127).

In a sense, Kieniewicz (1991:85) is correct in claiming that notwithstanding the considerable variety of commodities traded in the region, the multitude of different societies bordering South Asia did not display many signs of socio-economic integration; for example, while the decline of the Pax Mongolica had an important effect on Europe (and also to a certain extent, China), it did not slow down commercialization in South Asia. Thus Abu-Lughod's (1989) depiction of a 13th-century world-economy that included South Asia as a specific zone within one world-system is a serious exaggeration. In fact, contrary to Abu-Lughod's view, there is no substantive evidence of socioeconomic decline in the 14th century within this particular region (Arasaratnam 1984:112–113), nor is there a decline in urbanization (Barendse 2000:182) ,which implies that by 1400 there did not yet exist a "single world economic system of which all world regions were an integral part" (Frank 1999:26). Though it may be an exaggeration to claim that it was a completely "self-contained trading system" (Abulafia 1994:7), South Asia was clearly a different historical system (Palat and Wallerstein 1999) from which relatively few quantities of bullion flowed out (Bouchon and Lombard 1987:67).

Much of the Eurocentric writing that exists regarding the area therefore needs to be revised. For instance, one can no longer depict Asian traders as mere peddlers,[77] (Pearson 1987c:24–25; Guo 2004:96), or look upon early modern Asian commodity flows as somehow less important in quantity or quality than those that occurred elsewhere (see McPherson 1993:217). To a certain extent, a "reorientation" would be justified (e.g., Frank 1998) in the sense that—at least from the vantage point of the Indian Ocean (but not from the Caribbean)—the world essentially remained polycentric up until the late 18th century. But the claim that Asia was the center of some kind of world-economy (or world-system) from time immemorial up to A.D. 1800 is something completely different; it essentially substitutes misguided Eurocentrism with misguided Sinocentrism or anachronistic Central Asianism (Krader 1992:116). When Ricardo Duchesne (2003:202) aptly refers to anti-Eurocentrism as an explicit ideology designed to encourage the idea that there was nothing particularly different about Europe, both Frank (1998) and to a certain extent Hobson (2004), in their quest to erase capitalism and modernity from its particular emergence in Europe, deny that a cancer has to originate somewhere to subsequently spread out; they create their own arbitrary temporalities—be it

---

77. E.g., Van Leur (1955). This is still implicit in some of Palat's (1991:27; 1995:66) arguments.

5000 B.C., or in the case of Hobson's "oriental globalization," A.D. 500—equal to those of the Eurocentric scholars they criticize.[78]

At its best, anti-Eurocentric scholarship, in its desire to "provincialize Europe" (Chakrabarty 2002), provides a much-needed correction to parochial social science that disguises itself as objective, unbiased and universalist; but at its worst, it celebrates, as Sudipta Kaviraj (2005:501) puts it, an equally problematic "turn towards indigenism." The narrow path between this Scylla and Charybdis, which Pollock (1998:43) characterized as the epistemological trap between "a homogenizing universalism and a ghettoizing particularism," is a difficult, but necessary, endeavor. To illustrate, medieval/early modern Europe was in many ways similar to, and certainly not "more advanced," than many other regions of the world; it displayed its own specific particularities which enabled capitalism to emerge there, without it being a "self-contained" area (Duchesne 2006:79), detached or isolated from other regions of the world. This does not however imply that various non-European regions shared identical characteristics that did not allow capitalism to emerge there, or for that matter, that despite their distinctive features, they were not "incorporated" into the capitalist world system in structurally similar manners.

Although both South and East Asia were the final destinations of massive flows of bullion from Western Europe, this does not imply that the former significantly benefited from this "drain" in the long run (Tucci 1981:125) since the Chinese and South Asian state polities did not attempt to impose a highly exploitative capitalist system of labor control on their respective peripheries (Pomeranz 2000:268, 289). This is one of the main features of a global capitalist putting-out system that continues to exist to this very day. While the significance of bullion flows should not be minimized (Richards 1983; von Glahn 1996), they should also not be interpreted as the prime movers of world history (e.g., Frank 1998). Instead, it is the fundamentally different non-European state polities (and their respective social structures) that explain why areas like China or South Asia did not ultimately "develop" at the expense of other regions and why they did not initiate a distinct mercantilist strategy of their own (Dale 1994:137–139), with tremendous repercussions for the future (Van Santen 1991:93; Parthasarathi 1996:90).

To paraphrase Singh (1993:339), the dissolution of precapitalist modes and the transition to another phase occurred in South Asia as well as in other parts of the world once Western colonialism was imposed upon the region.

---

78. One should also mention the bizarre "essentialist" characteristics imposed on East Asia as when Hobson (2004:70) states that "the fact is that the Chinese could have initiated an imperial mission throughout much of the world had they so wished. Why then did they not? It should be clear by now that this was not a function of inadequate material capacity. It was because they *chose* to forgo imperialism, largely as a result of their *particular identity*" (last italics added).

The remarkable increase in trade throughout the period 1000 to 1500 and the deepening division of labor in the region should not be taken as evidence of a newly emerging capitalist order (Chibber 1998:31, 33). Without the intervention of European capitalism, the indigenous development of capitalism would have been extremely unlikely (Mukhia 1993:79–80), especially given the aforementioned constraints that the merchant class faced within existing state structures. These constraints, which highlight the role of non-market power in capitalist development, or lack thereof (Ludden 2002:238), in turn limited the development of legal codes that facilitated the rise of a capitalist system (Saberwal 1995; cf. Kuran 2003:438). While the region was far from static or stagnant, or economically and technologically lagging behind Europe in any way, the quintessential South Asian tribute-gathering state ruled by a prebendal military elite did not facilitate the development of a powerful indigenous merchant class that could then subsequently wield power to further its own interests. The long-term consequences of this reality enabled Western European powers to gradually take control of the export trade—forcing Indian merchants into a subsidiary role (Sharma 1998:290; Dasgupta 2000:72)—and ultimately to succeed in their colonization efforts, which dramatically changed the shape of South Asian history for generations to come.

CHAPTER FOUR

The Political Economies of Western Europe and Northern Africa Compared

Northern Africa and the Sudanic States (circa 1200–1500 AD)

A major problem with many studies of 13th- and 14th-century socioeconomic history is the complete omission of Africa, with the notable exception of Egypt (e.g., Abu-Lughod 1989). One of the misguided notions inherent to Euro-centric historiography is the view that "with the exception of the effects of Arabic science in southern Spain and Sicily during the Middle Ages, influences from outside Europe only became decisive in the twentieth century" (Blockmans 1997:30), thus implicitly endorsing a belief in European auto-development (e.g., Delatouche 1989:26). Having compared Europe's political economy with that of South Asia and China, it is my contention that Europe's "rise" cannot be explained without also taking into account its trade linkages with the North African region (the Maghreb and its South Saharan empires), which by the 13th century had become increasingly interdependent (Abulafia 1994:4).

While more attention has been paid in the last decade to the trade links with and commercial routes to the east under the Pax Mongolica (e.g., Humphreys 1998:455), the eminent role of northern Africa in Mediterranean Europe's commercial relations during the Middle Ages has surprisingly been relegated to history's dustbin, as if it were relevant only to those few curious specialists of the era/area (Devisse 1974:204; Lacoste 1974:1). Whenever the continent is not neglected, a world-systems analysis often focuses on the 16th century as the initial period of peripheralization (Rodney 1982; Wallerstein 1974).[1] Only a comparison of the political economies of the North African and Western African Sudanic states with that of Western Europe can explain why capitalism did not come into fruition in the former, which is particularly interesting since "when closely examined, all the factors which enabled Europe to succeed, were available to Islam much earlier" (Shatzmiller 1994:405).[2]

In A.D. 772, Ibrahim al-Fazari was already referring to Ghana as the "land of gold" (Burman 1989:112), indicative of Northwest Africa's importance to the Mediterranean Islamic states as a bullion-exporting region. The African kingdoms were also renowned for their export of slaves obtained near Lake Chad, the Niger, and Senegal rivers (Brett 1978:505–506). Although textile production in the Maghreb was the least-productive industry in Dar-al-Islam (Serjeant 1972:177), and most of its trade was very local up to the mid-12th century (Vanacker 1973:674), some of its production was generated by demand from areas located south of the Sahara. Salt was another commodity transported throughout the Sahara from at least the 10th century onward, exported from the Maghreb to Ghana by Islamic merchants—especially those from Ifriqiya[3]— who were also responsible for the proselytism of the region's elites (Brett 1969, 2001:251–254).[4]

From the 9th century onward, commercial activities across the Sahara gradually intensified (Kaké and M'Bokolo 1978:67; Devisse 1988). In Northern Africa, it was mainly Ifriqiya that displayed the strongest economy up to the 11th and 12th centuries, as evidenced by the glass and textile production that was exported to the south (Serjeant 1972:178; McDougall 1985:7). Under the Almoravids, however, Morocco increasingly exported its textiles (such as those produced in Sijilmasa) and horses (Levtzion 1973:178; Fisher 1972; Abulafia 1987:469) to the major commercial caravan center of Awdaghost (Vanacker 1973:661; McDougall 1983:271).[5] These commercial activities raised the gold

---

1. While this periodization has been challenged (e.g., Thornton 1998), this debate does not lie within the temporal scope of this study.

2. North African states also faced some of the same hurdles as Europe. For example, Islam's prohibition of usury is well documented (e.g., Taleqani 1983:105–112). This prohibition, however, should not be seen as an impediment to economic growth or to the development of capitalistic features (Udovitch 1970:61). As in Western Europe, religious leaders and theologians proclaimed one thing, but the reality of daily mercantile activities was quite different (Thiry 1995:469).

3. Approximately present-day Tunisia.

4. From the 11th century onward, the military threat from the Almoravids also contributed to the spread of Islam among local elites, although economic and political factors were sometimes equally important (Paulme 1957:562–563). According to Trimingham (1962:26, 31), conversion to Islam in the Bilad-al Sudan was initiated by merchants and subsequently propagated by force.

5. During the 14th century, Morocco also "functioned as a granary for western merchants" (Abulafia 1994:12). For a general overview of the trade between Morocco and the Sudan during

trade to a new peak, resulting in the creation of the renowned golden African *dinars* (Brett 1969:358; Levtzion 1973:41, 129).

Once Ghana had started to decay, the empires of Mali (13th–15th centuries) and Songhai (from the 15th century onward) constituted the most important polities in Western Africa (Paulme 1957:563–564; Cissoko 1984; Niane 1984b). Regional trade increased in particular under the Mali Empire (e.g., dried fish, yams, millet, grains, vegetables, livestock, malaguetta pepper). The international export of slaves (primarily from the central Sudan), gold (primarily from the western Sudan in the form of powder or currency) (Levtzion 1973:175; Hopkins 1973:60), and textiles (particularly from Timbuktu and Djenne) and the subsequent import of finished copper items, salt, spices, coral, tin, lead, and silver,[6] increased to such an extent that it affected the entire North African region (Devisse 1972). From the 13th century onward, enormous caravans circulated in the Maghreb between Niger and the Mediterranean coast,[7] spurring a demand for metallurgical and textile industries in cities like Sijilmassa, Aghmat, Messa, Tedsi, Taroudant, Teijeut, Tagaost, Marrakech, and Tlemcen.

Although cottons, silks, woolens, and raffia were produced on a substantial scale in Western Africa involving a very specialized and impressive division of labor (Garcin et al. 2000a:216–217), and since some of these commodities were exported to the North (Hopkins 1973:48), one cannot consider the region as having been peripheralized by Northern Africa (although some raw materials were exported, e.g., hides, ivory, and kola nuts).[8] Rather, these industries allowed the region to obtain expensive commodities—most notably slaves and gold—from the South (Magelhaes-Godinho 1969:101; Levtzion 1977:347; Idris 1984:111). After two months of travel from Sijilmassa, one of the largest commercial centers in the area (Messier and Fili 2002), the world traveler Ibn Battuta arrived in Walata (the Western part of the Mali empire) and observed that the people were relatively wealthy and wore clothes made of fine Egyptian cloths (Burman 1989:122). Indeed, several regions became quite dependent

---

the Middle Ages, see Jacques-Meunié (1982) and Devisse (1972). For a model that explains the transition from an agrarian political economy under the Idrisids to a state relying on revenues from long-distance trade under the Almoravids, Almohads, and Marinids, see Boone, Myers, and Redman (1990).

6. Silver was quite rare in Sub-Saharan Africa (Mauny 1961:348) but since it was relatively abundant in the Maghreb, especially in Morocco (Rosenberger 1970), a gold-silver trade developed between the Mediterranean region and Sub-Saharan West Africa (Lopez 1952; Mauny 1961:371; Watson 1967).

7. According to Jacotey (1998:295), about twelve thousand caravans circulated between the Maghreb and the Niger bend every year. Some convoys contained as many as twelve thousand camels (Thiry 1995:462).

8. According to Levtzion, "kola was by far the most commercialized fruit in West Africa" (1973:181). See Mauny (1961:366).

on one another. Salt, for instance, was not a luxury but rather a necessity; because of the extreme temperatures in the Sudan, salt deprivation was a genuine problem, especially in a region where the conservation of food was extremely important (Hopkins 1973:47). Given that it was produced locally in only some areas, much of it had to be transported south across the Sahara in large caravans that could travel 25 to 30 kilometers a day (Garcin et al. 2000a:264). In some kingdoms, such as Gao, salt played such a predominant role that it even functioned as currency and constituted the "best part of the king's treasure" (McDougall 1983:275).

If, because of geographical proximity, cultural affinity, and economic linkages it is acceptable to claim that Omayyad Spain, the Fatimid Caliphate, and its subsequent political heirs (Almoravides, Almohades) were "made" thanks to African gold (Coquery 1965:41), one should not underestimate the economic impact of the bullion flows into Western Europe (Watson 1967) and Egypt (Blanchard 2006). African gold, transported across the Sahara and Morocco, was very important to the European economy. Because of the structural trade deficit, silver was largely transported Eastward, making gold:

the prime metal for international transactions, whether commercial or political, and indeed for all considerable payments. . . . In the last century and a half of the Middle Ages most countries of western Europe had an adequate stock of gold currency, however debased and diminished their silver currency might be. (Spufford 1988:283–287)

As Phillips puts it: "The attraction of North Africa for European merchants arose from such bulky items as high grade merino wool and grain, but above all from gold bullion [which] was of great importance to the development of the medieval European economy" (1998:140). The slave trade across the Sahara (Meillassoux 1982), was equally important: hundreds of thousands of slaves were relocated from the Sub-Saharan region (vaguely referred to as the Bilad al-Sudan by many contemporaries) to Northern Africa, and from there sometimes even to Europe.[9] Austen (1987:36) estimates that between A.D. 650 and 1600, approximately six million slaves were exported from Africa to the Islamic world, most of them forced to cross the Sahara with about 20 percent dying en route (Hopkins 1973:81).[10]

---

9. In the 14th and early 15th centuries, Spanish, Sicilian, and Italian Christians bought slaves in the Tripoli market to use as domestic servants or as agricultural laborers (Malowist 1966b:69; Devisse 1996:865; Abulafia 1987:469).

10. For a more recent interpretation, see Austen (1992). Mauny (1961:379) initially estimated that two million slaves were crossing the Sahara each century during the late Middle Ages, but later (1970:240–241) estimated that it would have had to have been 14 million between the 7th and 19th centuries. All of these figures continue to be disputed (e.g., Malowist 1966b:60; Thiry 1995:511–512; Wright 2007).

The elite's reliance on revenues from the slave trade also created a state of warfare and permanent raids between the different polities of Northern Africa (Jacques-Meunié 1982:260–261).[11] This military aggression was not that different from that which took place in other parts of the world—only the motives were somewhat peculiar. The ironic consequence of the slave trade was that it:

> inhibited economic development because it led to the investment of much of the productive capacity of the state in an activity which was aimed at exporting one of the most important factors of production, labor, in return for goods which, for the most part, contributed little to the growth potential of the importing areas. (Hopkins 1967:154)

Unlike Amin (1972:109) or Halpern (1967:106) then, who praise the "egalitarian nature" and "autonomous character" of African societies prior to the 16th century, while minimizing the importance of the slave trade on the African continent ("a few hundred thousand"), I would avoid the myth of a "Merry Africa" in the period prior to European colonization (see Cohen 1991:116–117).

Along with the slaves, gold, and textiles, other materials—such as alum from the Kawar region north of Lake Chad—were eventually transported to the Mediterranean (Vikor 1982:123; Devisse 1996:866) as the area around Kanem Bornou was gradually converted to Islam (Cuoq 1984:231–256; Lange 1980:176–177). Further evidence of Western Africa's international commercial relations is illustrated by the fact that cowrie shells, initially used as currency on the South Asian littoral, were also accepted in Western Africa (Abulafia 1987:470). From the time of their appearance in Niger in the 11th century, they gradually became a major currency (Johnson 1970; Fisher 1977:283; Hogendorn and Gemery 1988). But gold would remain the most important item, as reflected in the Catalan Atlas of 1375 (Magelhaes-Godinho 1969:29). Between four and ten tons of gold crossed the desert annually (Magelhaes-Godinho 1969:119), at times exchanged for the same amount in weight of salt or copper (Devisse 1996:867 and 869). (The former was a necessity while the latter was a "metal de luxe," also used as a medium of exchange—like gold in Europe—because of its relative scarcity in the area; Herbert 1981:122–123, 127; Fisher 1977:278.)[12]

Unlike their South Asian counterparts then, the elite in this area profited more from the taxation of trade and the resale of imported commodities (e.g.,

---

11. The Arabs' view of blacks in general was negative, comparing them to wild animals that could be bought and sold whereas the area they inhabited was considered a mysterious region filled with gold, where skillful traders could amass a fortune (Diop 1998).

12. In 14th-century Kanem and Takedda, copper was used as currency (Levtzion 1973:120) and, occasionally, so were pieces of cloth.

salt) than from the taxation of agriculture. Because of the climate, agriculture yielded relatively little surplus. Consequently, the acquisition of land was not such an important goal (Mojuetan 1995:17). Given the importance of gold for North African and Western European polities, it is interesting to note that most of the gold-supplying areas were not directly controlled by the Mali empire; much of the bullion was actually obtained as "tribute from animistic peoples inhabiting regions loosely attached to the empire or even situated outside its frontiers" (Malowist 1966:9), for example, in forest areas like Akan (see Cuoq 1984:122–123). More important than direct rule over the gold-producing areas in the south was the ability to control markets, trade routes, and commercial centers (Levtzion 1973:115).

Among the Saharan and Sudanese polities, "the scarce factor of production in West Africa was labor rather than land" (Hopkins 1973:24).[13] As is noted in the "transition debate," "if labor is too demographically scarce, 'free' wage laborers will cost too much" (Gottlieb 1984:30); the ultimate cost of acquiring and maintaining slaves was less than that of hiring workers. The fact that large amounts of slaves were bought and sold in Northwest Africa—not only for domestic work but also as miners, transporters of commodities, and agricultural workers (Levtzion 1973:117; McDougall 1983:276), as well as for some positions in administration and the army (Brett 1969:354; Fisher 1977:269)—appears to have had long-term negative effects. As Hopkins emphasized:

> From the point of view of economic development the chief disadvantage of slavery is not that it is inefficient, but that it limits the expansion of the market by holding down purchasing power and by concentrating effective demand in the hands of a few luxury consumers. This consideration was irrelevant to the aims of West African rulers. (1973:25)

Furthermore, a slave economy coupled with a relatively low population density—related to ecological and climatological variables—is unable to invest in indigenous technological developments (Goody 1971) since the latter are often an attempt by entrepreneurs to offset the costs of maintaining a relatively high-wage labor force. Though economic growth certainly enables technological innovations to occur, "the use of inventions takes place only when it becomes profitable to invest in technological development" (Beaujard 2005:430). Essentially, a political economic system in which slavery is fundamentally important (Meillassoux 1975, 1982; Levtzion 1985:154)[14] does not encourage significant

---

13. "Africans measured wealth and power in men rather than in acres: those who exercised authority were man-owners rather than landowners" since "wealth was achieved through the labor of slaves" (Hopkins 1973:26–27).

14. In the Sudanese states "slave labor, quite apart from that controlled by the state, [was] a critical element of the towns, mines, and oases of the northern trade, freeing traders, clerics and officials

technological innovations (Shatzmiller 1994:401; Austen 1987:47), which are in turn inseparable from the accumulation of power in an emerging capitalist system. Although individual technological innovations accomplished by various (world) empires can be quite impressive, in the long run, cycles of technological innovations are most likely to flourish in those economic systems most conducive to it. In a capitalist system where many wage laborers are present, it is inevitable that private capital—controlled by capitalist entrepreneurs—is (continuously) invested in technological equipment and innovations in order to offset the cost of salaries. This incentive is lacking in a slave economy, where more energy will be devoted to overseeing and coercing the slaves. The construction of the Great Pyramids then is more an expression of the coercive force that a slave state was capable of generating than an indication of the economy's *structural ability* to produce and use technological achievements on a regular basis. At any rate, given the focus on acquiring, possessing, and controlling coerced laborers, the continuous loss of people in Northwest Africa "hampered evolution towards higher forms of political organization" (Tymowski 1987:63).[15]

The polities in the region are therefore appropriately labeled as "early states" (Tymowski 1987, 1991), wherein a tributary mode was predominant (Amin 1991), and were more fragile politically than the aforementioned Chinese Empire or Sultanate of Delhi, making them less capable to pacify large areas of space for a prolonged period of time (Picard 1997:475). The Mali Empire, for instance, was characterized by "spheres of influence, defined not by territorial or boundary lines but by social strata [and] the ruler was not interested in dominating territory as such" (Trimingham 1962:35). After all, *people* were taxed, not parcels of land (Thornton 1998:77–78). This resulted in raids, the accumulation of slaves, and control over the most important trade routes, rather than the "occupation" of specific territories (Lacoste 1974:3) and its subsequent transformation into an exploitable periphery. Some have even questioned whether the structure of the Sudanese state could have implemented such a design:

---

to pursue their special callings, and providing additional goods for trade" (Moseley 1992:530). McDougall (1983:279) also concludes that in southern Sahara the development of "what economic potential there was [occurred] through the purchase of slave laborers." The Saharan salt mines at Taghaza as well as the mines of Taoudeni and Idjil were operated by slaves, as were the mines at Takedda near Air (Mjouetan 1995: 176), though a substantial amount of the miners were free peasants as well (Blanchard, 2006). In the Maghreb however, it appears that wage labor in both urban and rural markets was more common than coerced labor (Mojuetan 1995:37; Shatzmiller 1997:179). In Mamluk Cairo the role played by wage labor was also relatively limited compared to its increasing importance in Western Europe (Sabra 2000:177).

15. Based on an analysis of the writings of Muhammad b. Ali al-lamtuni on the Sudanic states in the Sahel, Ould Cheikh (1991:26) states that "d'une manière générale l'arbitraire, allant jusqu'à la mise en esclavage des individus libres, et la corruption, semblent caractériser l'exercice du pouvoir dans cette société."

> The Sudanese empire was an amorphous agglomeration of kin-groups having little in common except mythical recognition of a far-off suzerain. Within these empires were tribute-paying units of various types above that of the village state called *dyamana* in Mande, over which Mali applied a system of protectorates. (Trimingham 1962:36)

This is not meant to imply that the fate of major Sudanese cities like Timbuktu[16] always paralleled the occasional rise and fall of different dynasties and/or state polities (Saad 1983:11). Cities like Timbuktu, ruled by an elite made up of Muslim scholar-notables from the mercantile bourgeoisie, clearly displayed a large degree of autonomy vis-à-vis the early state or a ruler claiming suzerainty (Saad 1983:224–233). The autonomy of a city of such considerable size, however, did not result in a city-state formation (Saad 1983:23) with all the aforementioned advantages benefiting its mercantile class, as occurred in Western Europe (Abulafia 1987:405).[17] Thus, when examining medieval Africa, one of the fundamentally important questions that have to be raised is the extent to which African towns were "essentially different" from those in late medieval Europe (see infra).

Hopkins chooses to downplay the importance of any structural differences:

> African towns not only sheltered farmers, they housed specialized personnel, such as craftsmen, transport contractors, hoteliers and merchants, they were focal points for the exchange of goods of all kinds; and they were important administrative and religious centers. Indeed, some towns on the Sahara-savanna border concentrated on trade to such an extent that they were almost entirely dependent on external supplies for their basic food requirements. (1973:20)[18]

Despite the fact that cities in the Bilad al-Sudan displayed economic vigor (the prosperity of Gao, Walata, Timbuktu, and Djenné easily come to mind) and were sometimes more dependent on long-distance trade for their basic food requirements than were their Western European counterparts, most were loosely encapsulated in a "steppe empire that displayed structural weakness and

---

16. Tymowski (1994:32) claims that it had a population of about 35,000. Goa's population was probably somewhat larger, while Djenne's was smaller (between 15,000 and 20,000).

17. Similarly, in the Middle East, attempts by the mercantile bourgeoisie to carve out an institutional space for autonomous power occurred in the period 950–1150, but ultimately failed (Ashtor 1956, 1975). In Western Europe, however, "the organization and administration of urban society came to be dominated by an oligarchy which was alien to the feudal structure of the countryside" (Milis 1989:66).

18. According to Al-Bakri, Aoudaghost's market was full of merchandise despite its relative isolation; grain, fruits, and dry grapes were imported (Coquery 1965:50).

instability" (Trimingham 1962:36). For the Almoravids, the Almohads, and the Merinids, control over an urban market center like Sijilmassa was crucial to their expansion—indeed, existence—as a major political force in the North African region (Lacoste 1974:4). But together with various factions' continuous claims on a city (a result of dynastic strife),[19] not to mention the pressures of pastoral nomads, the emergence of city-states was a very difficult endeavor. It was easier for the very wealthy private bankers and money dealers of these early North African states to aspire to individual upward social mobility by becoming ministers of finance, lord chamberlains, or viziers within the structure of the existing polity, than to attempt to create a commune or become a "bourgeoisie" (Lacoste 1974:5–8; Mojuetan 1995:25).

A major gateway city like Timbuktu could be characterized as "an emporium for the people of the Sudan" (Saad 1983:26), an emporium being the spatial manifestation of a commercial node, a "meeting point" (Cissoko 1984:203) that developed more as a consequence of geographical opportunities and economic needs than through political decisions. Such a city, however, was unable to counteract the "diversion of much of its commerce" (Saad 1983:30) caused by resurgent warfare and banditry, unleashed by the nomads who continuously maintained ambiguous relations with the settled zones around them. The prosperity of the 14th-century Mali Empire, for example, should not overshadow the structural weakness of the early state in that region. The allegiance of surrounding vassals and pastoral nomadic groups were tenuous at best (Le Tourneau 1969:59; Cuoq 1984:83; Niane 1984a:160–161). Political fragmentation followed until eventually, an exceptional chief (hunter/warrior) was able to found a strong dynasty that would rule over a successor state that displayed similar dynamics (Levztion 1973:47). "The ruler himself was essentially no more than the chief of a tribe which had become the head of a confederation of tribal groups" (Lacoste 1974:12; see Iniesta 1994). Like most imperial polities, the Mali Empire ultimately disintegrated amidst dynastic crises and nomadic incursions (Levtzion 1977:384–385).[20]

---

19. Dynastic strife occurred everywhere, but according to Tymowski (1994:27) it occurred to a greater extent in Sudanic states than in their European counterparts because of polygamy and the resulting large number of descendants who could claim the throne, leading to a "continual fracturing of power between generations" (Brett & Fentress 2002:75).

20. See Brunschvig 1947:154–170; Mauny 1961:400, 429–437, 461; or Jacques-Meunié 1982:366 on the example of Sijilmassa. The ambiguity of relations between pastoral nomads and state polities is a greatly under-researched subject and one must be careful not to fall into the trap of depicting "the nomad" as a one-dimensional creature bent on destroying civilization or preventing progress of any kind, as can be found in Golvin's study of the medieval Maghreb: "Le véritable nomade, celui qu'aucun intérêt n'attache à un pays si ce n'est celui du moment, celui qui ne se connaît, en fait de propriété, que celle de l'humble logis qu'il transporte de point d'eau en point d'eau au pas mesuré de quelques chameaux, celui-là ne peut avoir le respect de la propriété d'autrui. C'est un anarchique, souvent une sorte de perpétuel révolté qui saisit ce qui se trouve à portée de sa main. Pour lui, l'avenir ne compte pas, il vivra de la rapine et tout ce qu'il rencontre est à

Compared with their Western European counterparts, these gateway cities were much more dependent on the fluctuation of trade routes—not surprising since they "themselves were the creation of these routes" (Anene 1965:192)[21]— but they were also unable to control or maintain these fluctuating routes or the dispersed hinterlands that provided them with essentials. Unlike the citizens of European city-states who were armed and trained to defend their privileges, most of the military power in the Sudan was held by the rulers of the early states and the pastoral nomads who lived with them (Mojuetan 1995:24); it was they and not the merchant bourgeoisie who determined the success or failure of the trans-Saharan trade that was so central to a city's prosperity (McDougall 1985:28).[22] The presence of powerful nomadic forces also limited the development capabilities of the early states in Northwestern Africa (Fisher 1977:249; Lawless 1975:50–53): "The nomadic sphere, far from the reach of government and religious authority alike, was fertile ground for religious dissidence and militant rebellion" (Zubaida 1985:328).[23] Not only could these nomadic forces

---

lui s'il en a besoin [etc.] " (1957:141). Similar statements can be found in Terrasse (1969:7–8) and to a certain extent more recently in de Planhol (2000:158–159). Brett is much more convincing in depicting the North African nomad in relation to the prevailing "conditions of prosperity and strong government, in which nomads might be expected to cooperate to a certain extent with other sectors of the general community; under conditions of declining prosperity they might be expected to resort to violence in an attempt to retain their previous income" (1969:351). Nonetheless, political and socioeconomic instability caused by tribal formations across the Sahara, in the Maghreb, and even to a certain degree in Mamluk Egypt proper, can be considered an important factor in explaining why capitalism did not develop there (Garcin 1988:108).

21. Mauny (1961:479) concluded that trans-Saharan trade both gave birth to and sounded the death knell of southern Saharan towns. Saad also emphasizes that "although Timbuktu owed much to the rich region of the Niger delta to its south, nonetheless the site may have remained marginal to the economics of the area if it had not been for the influence of Saharan commerce, as a first step, and for the influence of trans-Saharan commerce later" (1983:28).

22. Timbuktu was unable to withstand a raid in 1338 by the Mossi, who plundered the city (Davidson 1998:60), a clear indication of the Sudanese cities' military precariousness despite their fortifications (e.g., the walls of Djenne). Within Northern Africa, some major urban settlements like Aghmât and Nfîs were not even fortified (Ennahid 2001:108), whereas others such as Kétama or Sijilmassa were considered major "fortresses" by contemporaries (Gourdin 1996:26–27; Kea 2004). Mantran and de la Roncière depict Timbuktu as an enormous commercial center rather than as an autonomous urban enclave within the Mali Empire, referring to it as "an enormous permanent caravanserai, regorging wares from all parts, where troops of slaves were parked before setting off again" (1986:387). According to Ennahid, "few urban settlements survived the repetitive cycles of political turmoil that accompanied dynastic wars" among the tribal configurations in Northwestern Africa (2001:122). In the post-Idrisid period, several autonomous and militarily self-sufficient cities might have threatened the elite but were subsequently destroyed (Boone, Myers, and Redman 1990:636).

23. This in turn explains the relative fragility of the North African state structure and its inability, in the long run, to establish a centralized nation state (Lacoste 1984:91, 126–128; Roberts 1987:9). Mojuetan (1995:10) explicitly links the "endemic incidence of siba" (dissidence) with the existence of tribal configurations in medieval Maghreb.

shift commercial routes (Niane 1975:201), but they could also threaten the existing polity since "in North Africa the state was, in a sense, a confederation of tribes allied with the tribe of the ruler" (Lacoste 1974:13).

Together with this tribal instability and fluctuating trade routes, the lack of available maritime transport created further problems for economic development:

> Commodities could be traded locally, but not over long distances because transport costs prevented them from competing with acceptable substitutes, which could be produced on the spot in other areas. Local trade, by definition, served a market which was too small in terms of numbers of consumers and purchasing power to justify the introduction of cost-reducing innovations and greater specialization.... The costs of carriage were too great and the number of relatively affluent consumers was too small to permit the development of a mass market in manufactured goods. Consequently, the multiplier effect of long-distance commerce was limited.... Transport costs were higher than in many other areas because the population was small and scattered. (Hopkins 1973:76)

Moreover, local trade routes were affected by a variety of significant ecological constraints in the Sahara and the Sahel (Tymowski 1987:62; Thiry 1995). Although most of the trade was overland (using camels, horses, donkeys, slave carriers), transport by waterways, which was crucial to the development of the European commercial revolution discussed earlier (Bautier 1989), was used wherever possible. While in Europe this may have been the cheapest means of transporting bulky commodities over long distances (Spufford 2003:405), most West African rivers were difficult to navigate; several had dangerous rapids, some were flooded in the rainy season, and others lacked water in the dry season, all of which created an "exceptionally difficult transport environment" (Austen 1991:24).[24]

In the long run these various factors (fluctuating trade routes, environmental constraints, dynastic strife, etc.) limited economic development (Karpinski 1968:82). Using the Sudan as our example, most of the surplus derived from the control over trade routes was not reinvested in productive industries, primarily due to "a lack of more profitable alternatives" (Hopkins 1973:77). Instead, most surplus was spent by the elites on conspicuous luxuries from the Mediterranean

---

24. The use of canoes (some of which could carry as many as one hundred men) (Smith 1970), especially on major rivers like the Niger (Tymowski 1967) and the Senegal, did make some commercial water transport possible (Hopkins 1973:72), which is why Mali's greatest cities were located in that area.

and the Middle East (Mauny 1965:178; Triaud 1973:220). A substantial amount of the revenues generated from external trade were also appropriated by foreign traders and drained to Northern Africa (Tymowski 1987:63), resulting in situations where "external contacts, which originally acted as a strong stimulus to the formation of Western Sudanese states, later created an insurmountable barrier to their growth" (Tymowski 1994:31). Furthermore, regions outside the major trans-Saharan trade routes remained poorly developed, as evidenced in the early 15th-century observations of European traders in Wolof territory where the variety of commodities offered in local markets was quite limited (e.g., cotton, cloth, vegetables, oil, millet, wooden bowls, palm leaf mats, and occasionally weapons) and where goods were often sold through barter since money was seldom used (Levtzion 1973:120; Tymowski 1991:134). The relative weakness of the economies in several areas of the Sudan—most notable for their lack of monetization (Coquery 1965:70)—is also related to the fact that slaves were considered a significant part of the neighboring state's resources (Tymowmski 1991:135–140), causing "tragically destructive warfare and social divisiveness" (Brooks 1993:57).

North African Cities, States, and the Balance of Power in the Mediterranean

Economic prosperity in North Africa had achieved unparalleled heights between the 10th and 12th centuries. New cultivation methods and the improvement of irrigation techniques resulted in a substantial increase in agricultural output (Shatzmiller 1994:47; Watson 1983). There is a large consensus that the development of markets in North Africa also resulted in "regional specialization in industry as well as in agriculture, bringing about relations of economic interdependence that sometimes existed over great distances" (Rodinson 1978:56).[25] Despite this economic prosperity, however, North Africa's naval power began to deteriorate and the 12th to the 16th centuries have often been depicted—vis-à-vis Western Europe—as a period of relatively slow economic decline (Shatzmiller 1994:42).

Muslim powers in the Mediterranean were disadvantaged by the lack of timber resources in the area, which contributed to the deterioration of their naval power (Devisse and Labib 1984:648; Agius 2001:50–52).[26] Further setbacks accumulated in the 10th century when Crete and Cyprus were

---

25. Kably (1986:167) speaks of "maghrebo-africano-european economic interdependence."

26. "Spain was the notable exception to a scarcity of wood in the region" (Shatzmiller 1994:178). By the 15th century, the loss of access to large quantities of wood, iron, and copper created problems with regard to the availability of firearms and cannons in Mamluk Egypt (Irwin 2004:128).

reconquered by a resurgent Byzantine Empire and in the 11th century when Corsica, Sardinia, and Sicily were lost to Islam.[27] This had tremendous repercussions on trade with Northern Africa (Nicolle 2001:142). The loss of these vital strategic outposts[28] across the littoral of the Mediterranean (in the Iberian Peninsula as well as in Palestine) dealt a major blow to any serious attempt to engage in naval warfare, whether by the Fatimids or Ayyubids (Egypt), the Almohads or their North African successors (Marinids, Ziyanids, Hafsids). The commercial consequences were enormous: "from the eleventh to the fifteenth centuries Muslim shipping lost almost completely whatever share of trans-Mediterranean maritime commerce it had prior to then" (Pryor 1988:135; see Walker 1983:45; Heers 1973:355). When Ibn Khaldoun in his Muqqadimah lamented that "the Muslims came to be strangers to the Mediterranean" (Ibn Khaldoun:2:46), he was referring to the fact that from the 12th century onward, Muslims preferred traveling on Christian ships—even between Muslim ports—because of their speed and security (Ragheb 1996:182). Since every devout Muslim at some point in his life wants to experience the *hajj*, many—particularly Arab pilgrims from, for example, Tunis, Morocco, or Granada—journeyed aboard European vessels (Ashtor 1981:282). This in turn provided significant amounts of bullion for the European economy. Given Alexandria's intense commercial activities with the Italians, some of the gold spent by Muslims while passing through that city on their way to the hajj may also have reached Europe.[29]

Another, although minor, reason for the transfer of gold from North Africa to Europe at that time, was the presence of European mercenaries in the Muslim states.[30] From the 12th century onward, the Mediterranean Muslim states

---

27. After Las Navas de Tolosa (A.D. 1212), most of the Iberian Peninsula was lost to the Muslim powers. De Planhol (2000:63) claims that "la société musulmane, au long des siècles, n'a pas, dans sa masse, sécrété de véritables marins, des vocations d'hommes de mer." This is almost tantamount to a "civilizational explanation" as it depicts the image of the sea in Islam as detestable and therefore a good Muslim cannot be a marine (De Planhol 2000:468–469). For a more useful study that attempts to deal with the issue of Muslim naval power and merchant activities at sea, see the detailed exposé in Picard (1997).

28. Pryor (1988:83) estimates that the maximum time Mediterranean galleys could spend at sea without running out of water was about eight to nine days. Water resupply posts were therefore decisive in determining naval power in the Mediterranean.

29. The most famous hajj was of course the one made by the Mali emperor Mansa Musa in 1324, whose wealth became legendary (Fall 1982:183–202). For the socioeconomic impact of his visit on Egypt, see the testimony of Al-Umari in Levtzion and Hopkins (1981:264–272) and the discussion in Levtzion (1994:XIII).

30. "From 1306 the Marinid army included regular Castilian and Portuguese soldiers, whom we know were paid wages. Some of its members gained influence in the court.... In the 14th century al-Umari gave the numbers in the standing Marinid army: Arab tribes, 1500 Ghuz arrow shooting cavalry of Turkish origins, 4000 Frankish cavalry, more than 1000 Andalusi arabaletiers shooting arrows from a footbow and a group of Berber tent dwellers. The Christian mercenaries, French or

were increasingly put on the defensive by European forces. Roger II of Sicily's attempts to carve out an African Norman Empire exposed the relative weakness of North African cities, which could not withstand being attacked and plundered (Djidjelli in 1143, Brask in 1144, Bône in 1153) (Golvin 1957:147). Meanwhile tributary relations were imposed by European powers on some North African islands (Djerba in 1135, the Kerkenna islands in 1145) and cities (Sousse and Sfax in 1143, Tripoli in 1146, Gabes in 1147, Mahdiya in 1148).[31] Although the Sicilian kingdom failed to maintain itself in the face of Almohad pressures and popular discontent over "infidel rule" (Abulafia 1985), this event nevertheless exemplified the Europeans' growing naval power in the Mediterranean. While both sides were known to initiate piracy and raiding, it seems that these 12th-century developments led to a gradual shift in power in the Mediterranean during the 13th and 14th centuries (Hrbek 1984:80) when European powers were able to raid the North African coast to obtain booty and occupy strongholds (e.g., in 1284 Aragonese forces occupied Djerba until circa 1335) (Julien 1964:152). Even Mamluk Egypt, despite its military successes on land against the remaining Crusading outposts in the Levant, was in a precarious position during the period 1250 to 1345 as world trade routes reoriented themselves away from the territory (Heyd 1959; Lapidus 1984:23).[32] Given their reliance on mercenaries (Bovill 1968:100) and the creation of European "protectorates" (Fernández-Armesto 1987:126–134), North African Muslim states—although too powerful to be beaten into submission or a state of colonial dependency (Gourdin 2000)—did decline in the sense that they were less

---

Spaniards, numbered around 5000 under the Marinids, and received payment in cash every few months" (Shatzmiller 2000:127).

31. Bullion flows also reached Europe through the imposition of tribute payments on Muslim states in Spain, the central Maghreb, and Ifriqiya (Julien 1964:131; Lawless 1975:61; Hrbek 1977:26).

32. Instead of attempting to develop its maritime strength in the tradition of the Fatimids (Agius 2001:53), the Mamluk regime implemented "a policy of willful destruction of port cities and installations, leading to unemployment for a multitude of specialists and workers" (Shatzmiller 1994:274). Despite a temporary recovery in the period 1422–1470 (Lapidus 1984:32), the regime was unable to prevent the Europeans from undermining its share of the international spice trade. While this did not destroy the economy, it "removed what had been one of its most reliable and useful crops" (Lapidus 1984:42). Its role as an indispensable intermediary had also been steadily undermined since the 13th century (Cahen 1963:446). While Mamluk Egypt's textile industries continued to flourish in the 13th and early 14th centuries and were exported throughout the Mediterranean, by the late 15th century the declining quality of its production "could no longer compete with the advanced Flemish and Italian industries . . . which outpaced it both in terms of technique and quality" (Louca-Bloch 1998:509–510). From the late 14th century onward, the benefits derived from the surplus balance of payments dissipated (Bacharach 1983:173). Emirs and sultans also mismanaged their lands to such a degree that the population of Cairo was forced to import food from overseas (Fernandes 2003). Ultimately, prolonged policies of European mercantilism set in a gradual process of socioeconomic and artisanal decline (Raymond 1982).

of a military threat than before. Their relative weakness at the time is also exemplified by the European slave raids in the area.[33]

During the 12th and 13th centuries, the Italian city-states intensified their trade with Northern Africa (Krueger 1933 & 1937); growing numbers of Italian merchants established *funduqs* (emporia) along the North African littoral (Bovill 1968:103), while exporting grain (especially from Sicily), copper, beads, wine (Brunschvig 1947:259–268; Bovill 1968:105), and most importantly, textiles (Levtzion 1973:131–132).[34] Because of the multiple trading opportunities, Genoese merchants traded quite extensively in Tripoli, Sale, and Ceuta in the 1160s (Mauny 1961:370), entrepots that were also gateways to the trans-Saharan trade routes.[35] Through the port of Hunayn, Italians could easily obtain goods from Tlemcen, one of the great nodes in the trans-Saharan commercial network (Levtzion 1973:142; Bouayed 1988).[36] Italian, Spanish,[37] and French ships also regularly sailed to Taount, Mazagran, Mostaganem, Brechk, Cherchel, and Algiers (Lawless 1975:59), and European traders flocked to Tunis in the mid-13th century after a gradual shift in the trans-Saharan trade

---

33. Slave raids against the Muslim Mediterranean littoral can only be understood in relational terms, that is, in the need for slaves in peripheral areas on the one hand, and the production of raw materials for the city-states by coerced labor regimes in the peripheral zones on the other. The sugar plantations in late 14th-century Cyprus are a good example of this process. When "the king of Cyprus had captured 1,500 Saracens, who were subsequently employed on the royal sugar plantations, the king claimed that Cyprus had 'grant besoing de laboreurs qui laborassent les terres pour faire sucre'. It is thus in the profitable Cyprus sugar production ... that slave labor must have been particularly remunerative during that period of scarce manpower" (Arbel 2000:IX:161). Arbel is right on the mark when claiming that "as a Venetian colony, Cyprus was undoubtedly exploited" (2000:XII:178), as indicated by its harsh "status servile" (at least when compared with Western Europe). What is so brilliant about his analysis is that he avoids falling into the trap of depicting the colonial situation as a "black legend" of outright misery for all; as with contemporary peripheries, Arbel carefully exposes the Cypriot elite that benefited extensively from collaboration with the Italian city-states.

34. "In 14th century Mali, the king was dressed in a long garment made of a European cloth" (Levtzion 1973:109).

35. Although some Europeans must have traded outside the North African funduqs (Levtzion 1977:368; Bovill 1968:111), e.g., in Tunis or Sijilmassa (de la Ronciére 1938:82), most of their mercantile activities were restricted to the maritime towns (Bovill 1968:107). The exceptions were the merchants of Jewish faith. Jewish communities in Barcelona, Majorca, Tlemcen, and Sijilmassa provided a crucial link for the flow of gold to Europe. This is indicated by the fact that in 1247, the king of Aragon extended his royal protection to two Jewish families in Sijilmassa (Lawless 1975: 60; Levtzion 1994:XI). By contrast, very few Muslim merchants were active in non-Muslim European trading centers across the Mediterranean (Abulafia 1994:11).

36. Records from 13th-century Palma indicate that two ships departed every week to trade with the Sultanate of Tlemcen—and this was in the middle of the winter (January–February 1284). Summer trade must have been even more significant (Lawless 1975:62).

37. For trade between Catalonia and the Maghreb, see references in the classic study by Dufourcq (1966:93–131) and García-Arenal and Viguera (1988).

routes (Walker 1983:37; Doumerc 1999). From the early 14th century, European ships also sailed toward Anfa (modern Casablanca) (Abulafia 1994:15). Since European ships controlled most of the Mediterranean routes in the 14th century (Bouayed 1988:329), spices imported from the Levant were resold to Northern Africa (Abulafia 1998:345). Thus, in addition to Muslims' declining power in the Mediterranean, the balance of trade between Muslim North Africa and Christian Europe favored the latter, which further increased the flow of gold into Europe (Levtzion 1977:369; Dufourcq 1965:520).[38] Even in those areas where the balance of trade may have favored Muslims (such as perhaps Ifriqiya in the early 13th century), gradually "Europe's more advanced maritime skills left a disproportionate share of the business in the hands of merchants from Genoa, Pisa and Marseilles" (Perkins 1986:46).

Ceuta was a major entrepot in the 12th and 13th centuries, linking Italian, Spanish, and French merchants with the port where they then sold cloth and copper and received gold originating from the Senegal area (Dufourcq 1955:70). Even more significant however is the fact that this hub of interregional and international exchange—one of the greatest during this period—managed to achieve outright independence in the 1230s. Free from any overriding power, one of Ceuta's richest merchants, Ahmed al-Hachah Abou-l-Abbas al-Hanasti, controlled the city for several years. But when Genoa found its economic interests threatened, resistance against the 120 warships that were rapidly sent to Ceuta's harbor was futile (Dufourcq 1955:87 and 101) and Ceuta's short-lived independence soon succumbed to Almohad pressures (Picard 1997:503–504). A similar occurrence took place in Tripoli, where a local merchant-aristocracy achieved urban independence during the 12th century. Again the Genoese, whose relations with the Maghreb were driven by economic considerations (Jehel 1995:92), demonstrated their naval power by surprising and capturing the city in 1355. Although at various times many North African cities displayed forms of urban independence similar to those found in Western Europe, they were incapable of achieving much lasting power in the Mediterranean. This is best illustrated by the fact that Abu Bakr ibn Muhammad ibn Thabit, aspiring to take over Tripoli, had to hire Genoese ships to transport his troops from Alexandria to Tripoli (Brett 1986:88–89).

Given these periodic moments of urban autonomy, one of the questions that should be asked is not whether the North African urban community could ever be mobilized to defend the city walls (Brett 1995:117), but whether they were able to provide some type of military support on a regular basis (Brett

---

38. Gradually, Europeans dominated commercial activities around the North African coasts (Garcin 1995:305–306) and the balance of trade turned in their favor (Spufford 2003:349). By the 15th century, if not earlier, "the economy of Islam as a whole was being drawn into dependence upon its north-western neighbor" (Brett and Fentress 2002:130).

1986:119). The lack of permanent militias or armed guilds made it impossible to maintain the existence of a Muslim "city-state."[39] Equally important variables influencing the existence of the Muslim city-state were the encroachment of the European mercantile republics, the expansionist zeal of the Iberian nobility (Malowist 1964; Rosenberger 1993), the administration of the sultans who were keen on preserving their power over North African cities (Hrbek 1977:89), and the nomadic inland tribes who eagerly attempted to force towns into paying tributes.[40] Given that the "villages and small towns seem to have been submerged by the nomad expansion [while] the larger towns survived as isolated oases of urban civilization and commercial activity" (Levtzion 1977:360), one should not equate the relative political weakness of a North African Muslim city with insignificant socioeconomic activity, as the wealth and splendor noted in a city such as Fès testifies to the contrary (Ferhat 2000); the merchants' influence only seems less impressive because "in Islam the salaried artisans frequently owned their means of production" (Shatzmiller 1994:403), as opposed to the Western European experience where the putting-out system gradually gained influence (see Chapter 1). Paradoxically, despite the fact that most Muslim urban areas, and especially their elites, were more prosperous in Northern Africa than were their Western European counterparts (Garcin et al. 2000a:199), they had less political power within their own polities (Picard 1997:508). The relative political weakness of Muslim merchants within North African cities is discussed by Udovitch at length:

> In the trading towns of medieval Italy there was a virtual identity between the merchant class and the state. Merchants exercised great political power and the state apparatus was in many ways an instrument of their interests and needs [but] for contemporary Islamic cities on the other side of the Mediterranean a comparable judgment is inconceivable. While commercial exchange was certainly a major activity in the life of Islamic cities of the medieval Mediterranean, the relationship

---

39. Some large cities in the Muslim world had guild-like organizations (only logical given the existing division of labor) and militias to maintain order (Hamdani 2002:164–165). Nonetheless, the former had much less power than those in Western Europe, and the latter were not systematically mobilized to protect the city's mercantile interests from extraeconomic coercion. In one of the largest Muslim cities, Mamluk Cairo, the significance of guilds seemed "minor compared with similar institutions in Europe" (Sabra 2000:175).

40. Jacques-Meunié claims that the invasion of the Maâqil Arabs in Morocco had "des conséquences désastreuses pour le commerce et l'agriculture et ruina les structures politiques" (1982:66). This is confirmed by Ennahid (2001:93). For the destruction caused by nomadic attacks in 13th-century Libya, cf. Thiry (1998:245–247). Even the more powerful Mamluk polity could not prevent the destruction undertaken by Bedouins (Ayalon 1993:116–117).

of merchants—and of settled urban society generally—to government
and power was of a very different order. (1988:53)

This is a valid argument, but should not be exaggerated to the point of some
sort of despotic rule. Indeed, often associated with the image of (Oriental)
Muslim despotism is the claim that

> the Muslim town bears the marks of an almost total absence of munici-
> pal organization [since] it shows no exceptional privileges, no particular
> rights [and] boasts no municipal official or magistrate, except the muh-
> tasib, who has hardly any responsibility but the oversight and policing
> of the markets. (de Planhol 1980:455)[41]

According to de Planhol, "nothing tempers the absolutism of the ruler"
(1980:455). Given that even the Caliph should be considered as nothing more
than a "primus inter pares" (Cahen 1980:532) because the provincial governors had a large degree of autonomy (Jacques-Meunié 1982:276), de Planhol's
statement appears to be something of an exaggeration. Rather, as Udovitch
points out:

> Merchants . . . were allowed to conduct their business affairs generally
> unhampered by arbitrary barriers and interventions on the part of the
> authorities. They were [however] never able to achieve an identity
> of interests with their rulers sufficiently powerful to use its material
> and military resources to enhance and further their own commercial
> interests. (1988:72)

This is an extremely important element in his analysis and is confirmed by
Shatzmiller in her discussion of North African commercial decline:

> Neither individual merchants nor the Muslim states felt the need to
> devote their resources to developing and protecting merchants' naviga-
> tion. In order to fully appreciate the importance of the political backing
> which rulers or nations provided for trading activities, it is necessary to
> compare these attitudes with the zeal, dedication of resources and po-
> litical power which the Italian city-states invested in the Mediterranean
> trade. Either by lack of power and means or by conviction, the inability
> of the Islamic political powers to act aggressively in the pursuit of trade,
> explains why Islamic states on the shores of the Mediterranean failed

---

41. For a useful discussion of the muhtasib's functions, see Essid (1995:123–150) as well as Berkey
(2004).

to develop a more vigorous and sophisticated system of maritime trade, despite the fact that they could easily have done so, and why, from the eleventh century onwards, they relinquished control and participation to the Italian cities. (Shatzmiller 1994:45)[42]

Conclusions

In analyzing the political economy of Northern Africa, it is clear that capitalist features were appearing in the Islamic world, but their development (when compared with Western Europe) remained limited because the "bourgeoisie never achieved political power as a class, even though many of its individual members succeeded in occupying the highest appointments in the state" (Rodinson 1978:52–55). This is extremely important. As Boutillier and Uzunidis point out in their study—appropriately called the *Myth of the Entrepreneur*— "individual initiative is nothing without the support of the state who provides him security, access to markets and even capital itself" (1999:10). Can one call the large traders who amassed fortunes in the Bilad-al-Sudan capitalists (e.g., Cuoq 1984:91) comparable to the Catalan merchants in Northern Africa (e.g., Dufourcq 1966:58–62) or other European traders (Picard 1997:456)? Certainly, as the socioeconomic splendor of the medieval Islamic society cannot be denied. But the presence of *capitalists* does not necessarily imply the successful creation of an endurable capitalist *system* in the long run (see Rodney 1982:55). Marx had already noted that the development of merchant capital (and by implication, the existence of merchant capitalists) did not *automatically* result in a capitalist mode of production (Gottlieb 1984:16; Coquery-Vidrovitch 1978). And although up to the 19th century the larger cities were located outside Europe (e.g., Baghdad or Beijing), this does *not* imply that Europe "remained inferior and peripheral to the large empires of the Near East and China until the late eighteenth century" (Chase-Dunn and Grimes 1995:395). Instead of focusing on the size of cities, one should examine the capitalist dynamics within a given region. The North African dynamics are perhaps best highlighted when briefly juxtaposed with the European situation at the time.

---

42. Hrbek paints a similar picture of Egypt where its townspeople, "be they craftsmen or merchants, neither attained nor strove to form an autonomous political class, a bourgeoisie in the true sense of the word, that would rule the township freely and according to its own interest as distinct from those of the military feudal class. Thus an important socio-political factor of development was absent, and this situation enabled the perpetuation of the military despotism of the Mamluks, which finally led to the political and economic decay of the whole empire, especially Egypt. . . . Not even the Karimi merchants and bankers were allowed to play any role as an independent or self governing body" (1977:50). The existence of aldermen or consuls was not a possibility (Martel-Thoumian 2001:272). Even in the case of revolts in Egyptian cities, "the urban popular forces could scarcely take on the military forces of Mamluks and war-lords and win" (Zubaida 1985:316).

Chapter 1 already discussed how cities such as Ypres and Ghent terrorized their countryside in the early 14th century in order to protect their monopoly on cloth production (Nicholas 1971:75–116, 203–221). The Italian cities' successful subjugation and domination of their rural hinterland (the *contado*) (Perrot 1983:93–97; Bowsky 1970:225–255; Maire Vigueur 1988) and the creation of their respective "banlieu" (Bochaca 1997) or "kwartier" (Prevenier and Boone 1989:84) was also touched upon. Such exploitative capitalistic power relationships (Heers 1965:82) were an intrinsic feature of the inter-city-state system in medieval Western Europe. It was a system that was exploitative both internally *and* externally.[43]

Indeed, part of the hierarchical division of labor between urban and rural areas was the city-state's "external" subordination of the countryside. For instance, the city-state enforced a virtual monopoly on the distribution of goods to the rural population (Stabel 1992:352), while positioning itself as the middleman between alien traders and the peasants who wanted to sell their commodities (Adams 1994:145 & 154). Such exploitation was also illustrated by the production of grain in the hinterland or in the more remote countryside (Hunt 1994:244; Bautier 1992:VI:224), appropriately termed "dispersed hinterlands" (Horden and Purcell 2000:116–122).[44] But the division of labor between town and countryside was probably best exemplified in the textile industry, which had a truly international character. This export industry drew its strength from a far-reaching division of labor, employing large numbers of semi-skilled and unskilled workers (Van der Wee 1988:320; Le Goff 1999:1142). Given the socioeconomic dynamism in Northern Africa in the same period, it was not unusual in Muslim cities for 18 percent of the city's labor force to be occupied

---

43. The town is "both internally and externally an institutional expression of power" (Abrams 1978:25). Though some Italian cities such as Venice gave precedence to expanding their maritime empires in the 11th–14th centuries, before implementing a systematic policy of exploiting their immediate surrounding countryside as a colonial territory (Chittolini 2005:325), the exploitative relationship was similar.

44. Artois produced most of the grain supply for the larger cities in the Low Countries (Derville 1987), but from the late 14th century on, more grain had to be imported from distant areas such as from the Baltic to the Low Countries (Aerts, Dupon, and Van der Wee 1985:237) and from the Black Sea to the northern Italian cities (Laiou 1992:VII; Karpov 1993). Most city-states attempted to control their hinterlands in order to minimize price volatility in the grain market, as such volatility was closely related to potential social disturbances by wage earners in the city (Epstein 2000:118). It is not surprising, for instance, that "Florentine policy towards the contado followed the well-practiced mixture of paternalism and authoritarianism established during the early 14th century, which combined rural export bans and forcible supplies at fixed prices to the city" (Epstein 2000:112). It should not be forgotten that the urban oligarchy of merchant entrepreneurs who controlled the city's hinterland was essentially the same elite that attempted to control the county's or duchy's foreign trade because of the aforementioned importance of trade (Boone 1997:43). For the city-state, both the surrounding hinterland and its more remote peripheral areas were socioeconomically important (Heers 1976:217).

with the manufacturing of textiles (Shatzmiller 1994:240). Yet these labor force percentages are somewhat smaller than those in Western European city-states, where the distinction between town and countryside was much more prevalent.[45] A putting-out (Verlag) system beyond the town walls was characteristic for labor-intensive tasks in European cities and such reallocations from the city to the countryside occurred regularly throughout the entire European continent (Heers 1963:121–124; Bois 2000:135). Thus, the exploitation of the cheap labor in the surrounding countryside was used to further the commercial interests of the elites who controlled the city-state.

The exploitation of the hinterland is well illustrated in examples like that of Florence where 14 percent of the region's population enjoyed 67 percent of its wealth, but also in the production processes that enabled the merchant-entrepreneur[46] to accumulate ever more capital.

The *threat* of competition and the reality of sudden economic crises made many urban-based unskilled wage laborers vulnerable, which brings us to the system's "internal" exploitative mechanisms, that is, the ruthless exploitation of the underclass, of all of those without property (grauw, gemeen, rapaille, ciompi), who had no stake in the city's political community (van Nierop 1997:278–279). It cannot be overstated that much violence, which spread from cities to their surrounding countryside, was economically motivated; the urban proletariat was often reacting to the attempts of merchant-entrepreneurs to reallocate their capital to the countryside where they could exploit the available labor pool.

The social explosions within European city-states, especially during periods of economic recession (Derville 2002:135–141), were indicative of the urban system's social polarization (Blockmans 1997b:260).[47] Again, medieval Florence provides an excellent example: "Going up the scale of urban wealth, we must pass through 85% of the Florentine households before the total of their holdings equals that of the richest 1%" (Herlihy 1978:138).[48] This exploitation

---

45. This important town/countryside distinction, so characteristic of Western Europe, did not apply to the same degree to Northern Africa (Abun-Nasr 1987:117) or the South Asian subcontinent (Chattopadhyaya 1994:181–182).

46. The "lanaiolo" (see Brucker 1998) can be considered both tradesman and entrepreneur.

47. Similar conditions occurred in a great Islamic urban center such as Baghdad: "The number of individuals occupied in the unskilled services were a volatile force. On the one hand, as a large, available pool of human labor, they were a positive economic factor, when economic activity was vigorous and demand for labor force was growing, as it did during periods of great activity in construction or growing demands for manufactured items. When economic conditions worsened and demand for labor declined, their sheer numbers constituted a threat to the regular conduct of the economy" (Shatzmiller 1994:287).

48. Massive inequalities were of course not unique to European cities; in 18th-century Cairo, as Raymond points out, "3% of the individuals shared 50% of the cumulated wealth and 50% possessed only 4.3%"(1994:14).

of the lower strata, including women and children (Stella 1993:99–125), whose wages were notoriously low (Geremek 1994:66), is linked with the high division of labor in the city and the specialization in the production of cloth for the international market in the inter-city-state system.

It is crucial to note that these internal and external forms of exploitation operated in symbiosis. Much of the medieval "proletariat" was a readily available pool of (often seasonal) extra labor, exploited when seen fit. This reserve labor pool consisted not only of cheap female and child labor, but also of a permanent inflow of impoverished immigrants from the countryside (Heers 1965:69; Day 2002:122–123) who were often employed as bargemen, fullers, or tanners (Thoen 1994:350) and treated "with contempt and hostility" (Geremek 1994:69). Without the constant migration of these unskilled rural workers to the urban center, the city would not have been able to maintain its population—let alone experience any significant growth—because of the so-called urban-graveyard effect (Zientara 1981:200).

Given these external and internal forms of subjugation then, one cannot consider cities as "capitalist non-feudal islands in the feudal seas" (Katz 1989:88), as if their surrounding countryside lived as an autarchy. Nor can one dismiss the importance of the town/countryside relationship by simply asserting that the power relations between lords and peasants were the primum movens of the Middle Ages (Brenner 1985); class warfare between peasants (the exploited) and the nobility (the exploiters) is too simplistic a framework (Epstein 1991:258). When one acknowledges that strong city-states dominated their rural hinterland—the "colonization of the countryside" as Benevolo (1993:91) puts it—just as well as did feudal lords (Epstein 1992:124–133), and that such subjugation was important to remain a central player in the urban network—which was itself hierarchical (Coquery-Vidrovitch 1993:32)—it is clear that within the European feudal system one must give agency to the city-states (Rösch 1999:112–113).

The "refeudalization" of Western Europe after 1350 failed not because the nobility did not want it to happen, but rather because the presence of strong cities prevented it (Van der Woude 1982:202). In turn the city-states constructed a town/countryside relationship that displayed many of the features of core–periphery relations (Prevenier 1997:196; Timberlake 1985:14; Cuadrada 1991:289): the availability and control of cheap "raw" materials in the peripheral areas (including a cheap labor force that was lured to the cities) (Wrigley 1978:306); the existence of more highly coerced labor (thus increasing profits for the capitalist entrepreneur); and higher taxes.[49] These were all

---

49. "In the 13th century the burden of direct taxation on the countryside was frequently much greater than that of indirect taxation in the town. In the 1280s the countryside of Pistoia supported a burden six times as high as that paid by the city [which explains why] the countryside fell into a state of endemic debt to the city. Repeated continuous loans from the city to the countryside, and

essential components of the methods used by large independent European city-states to exploit, transform, and maintain a hierarchical dialectic relationship with their respective hinterlands (Cherubini 1974; Lalik 1978:15), and later on, with their maritime colonies (Balard 1989; Balard and Ducellier 1998). In the "Islamic world," however, "the line between city and countryside was not sharply drawn" (Hourani 1991:113).[50] Independent urban institutions that favored policies that would facilitate capital accumulation were not established (Picard 2000:97–98) and most cities did not envisage implementing a systematic colonization strategy similar to their Western European counterparts. The ones that came closest to resembling a European typology, with an urban patriciat, such as Ceuta, (Garcin et al. 2000b:80–81), were not strong enough to effectively compete with their European counterparts (Picard 1997:347).[51] Usually wealthy North African merchants attempted to influence those who

---

the purchase of rent-charges on the countryside by city-dwellers, only made the situation worse. Contadini were compelled to concentrate on cash crops rather than their own needs, and a cycle of deprivation was set up not unlike that in parts of the Third World today" (Spufford 1988:246–247). Of course, not all of the dwellings and not everyone living in the contado were equally hit by these taxes; inequalities varied from village to village, but inequality in taxation levels was obvious (Ginatempo 2005:210). In 14th-century Florence, "mountaineers and those farthest from the city paid much higher tax rates on their property than those closer to the city and in the lowlands ... the tax on the countryside was highly regressive: the wealthier the peasant, the lower the tax rate" (Cohn 2000:187). Fiscal levies in the city of Milan were also much lower than those in the countryside that it controlled (Chittolini 2002).

50. See also Mojuetan (1995:25) and the important study by Bulliet (1972). Typologies about "Muslim" or "Islamic" cities and generalizations based on them should of course be qualified as they do not refer to a sociopolitical or economic entity as such and constitute therefore more ambiguous units of analysis based on religious demarcations (Garcin 2000b:97–98).

51. At the core of the debate on the relationship between town and countryside within the historiography of Europe, as well as that of Northern Africa or Asia, is the confusion surrounding the criteria that actually *define* a town or a city (cf. Nicholas 2003:6–10). The various criteria used to label a particular site as a "city" or "urban" (differentiating it from the surrounding countryside/hinterland) are important to every theory. Several types of criteria may be used, each with its own complications:

(a) The most obvious type of criteria is likely statistical, i.e. a focus on the size of the urban ratio. But a statistical approach is not without controversy as some population figures are unreliable, making certain extrapolations merely hypothetical. Furthermore, the quantitative criteria are frequently questioned (Gutmann 1986:29). How many inhabitants per square mile does a site need in order to be labeled as a town? Comparing calculations that use different threshold levels can be hazardous. For instance Klep (1988:263–264; 1991:499–500; 1992:201–241), who in his research on the development of urban ratios in the Southern Low Countries during the Early Modern Period uses a threshold of a minimum 5,000 or even 10,000 inhabitants to give a settlement the status of "city," is fiercely challenged by Stabel (1997:19–21) who argues that such criteria ignore the existence of smaller cities, thus distorting historical reality. What is actually defined as a small city (rather than a village) is important, however, since calculations of the urban percentage differ according to the inclusion (or omission) of the population of smaller cities (de Vries 1990:45).

(b) Another option is to use economic criteria; i.e., to focus on the specialization of production (an indication of the division of labor) in a given area. According to Werner Sombart, every urban agglomeration depended on substances that originated from the immediate countryside, a point of view closely related to his underestimation of the role of capital in the medieval economy (Sapori 1970; Joris 1993:45). An interpretation as rigid as Sombart's, however, would exclude most medieval villages from consideration. But on the other hand, if one acknowledges the importance of trade and capital at the time, to what extent can a city be perceived as exclusively dependent on international commerce (e.g., Pirenne 1937, 1956, 1963], the real "motor" of economic progress? Nicholas, for instance, has accused Pirenne of having "conditioned generations of British and American students to think the medieval city as rigidly separated from the countryside. The city was [for him] a purely economic entity based on long-distance trade [and he] considered the cities to be islands of capitalism in a 'feudal' world" (1997a:xv).

If cities are defined by their capitalistic nature (consisting of advanced commercial aspects) and studied in order to better comprehend the importance of their economic expansion, one indirectly creates the view of a more stagnant, passive, "backward" countryside. Abu-Lughod—who underlines the "alliance between feudalism and urban capitalism" (1989:85) while focusing exclusively on the international trade patterns and intercity relations in order to explain the "making and breaking of entrepots" and regions (1989:98)—completely omits the crucial countryside relations from her discussion. The degree of professional differentiation as a criterion for defining a city (or for assessing the importance of a city in trade networks) is important, yet ambiguous. Sometimes there were early forms of specialized protoindustrialization in the countryside (Thoen 1992, 1993a) while a lot of small towns embodied rural characteristics, making the traditional town/countryside dichotomy difficult to establish (Stabel 1995a:15). Therefore, the traditional image of the city as an economic/political island surrounded by its antithesis, the feudal agrarian countryside, should be reconsidered (Rosener 1995:663).

(c) For those who are convinced that "urban life is more than a mere count of heads, or an account of the material and political base of activity, and that there is an urban culture distinct—not least in its demographic aspects—from that which prevails beyond the city walls" (Hohenberg 1990:353), perhaps the focus should be on the cultural attributes and civic symbols that differentiate the town from the countryside (Martines 1979; Muir 1981; Schilling 1992; Nijsten 1997:105–129). After all, strong cities were the loci where "Huldigungsfahrten" occurred with much pomp and circumstance (Populer 1994:30–31).

(d) Another possibility is to give analytical priority to purely legal aspects; i.e., whether a town had a charter and certain "liberties" and was legally able to call itself an urbs/city/communio. But to what extent can the creation of a legal system be an adequate indicator of the existence of a business community (which constituted the heart of a city) requiring laws and regulations, while the "traditional rural countryside anchored [itself] in customs" (Godding 1995:201)? Some rural areas, although definitely rural in outlook and character, were granted liberties similar to those of the cities (Stabel 1997:90; Wickham 1992:129–134). In such cases, it can be quite difficult to perceive a real and genuine dividing line between town and village (Mundy and Riesenberg 1958:9).

(e) One might also choose to examine the terminology used at the time; i.e., how citizens/burghers defined/considered themselves. As Erich Keyser stated: "Stadt ist, was sich selbst Stadt nennt" (Keyser in Joris 1993:44). But one problem with this criterion is that over time, the population of certain cities may decline to the point of rural villages (Sosson 1993:171–184). An additional problem is the extent to which the definitions/criteria for towns during the Early Middle Ages were still valid for the Late Middle Ages. And to what extent were these definitions/criteria valid all over Europe (or simply, Western Europe) (Joris 1993:40–45) as well as elsewhere, such as in Northern Africa? Furthermore, when analyzing an urban "system," should one define it as local, regional, intraregional, or international (Stabel 1995a)? And at what point in time? Finally, there may also be linguistic problems that further complicate any interpretation. Some languages have

had political and military power (Thiry 1995:461), but were unable to insti-
tutionalize their endeavors. Despite the fact that several Northern African
polities depended on trade more than their Western European counterparts
and the enormous caravan trade has been referred to as its "capitalist sector"
(Mojuetan 1995:19), no transition to capitalism occurred.

One should keep in mind that the *local* polarizations embedded in the
Western European town/countryside's core–periphery relationship, as well
as those found in the urban social struggles and the inter-city-state system's
laborer/merchant-entrepreneur relationships, were intimately linked with the
broader intraregional (Van Uytven 1983) as well as interregional (e.g., Ashtor
1983) export of textiles and metals.[52] This intra- and interregional long-distance
trade, promoted by urban merchant elites, was crucial to the economic and
political growth of the Western European inter-city-state system in the Late
Middle Ages.[53]

---

one principal word to describe an urban community, such as *ville* in French or *Stadt* in
German. English, by contrast has two: *city* and *town*. North American usage tends to favor
city except when the community is very small; British usage tends to favor *town* except
when the community is very large. But the distinction is never a precise one (Friedrichs
1995:x). Similar linguistic confusion occurs in Western Africa (*hilla; hagy; dem* in Arab or
galo-dougou and *badia-dougou* in Mali) (Coquery-Vidrovitch 1993:42). As noted earlier, I
use *town* and *city* interchangeably. It is my position that "exchange constitutes the raison
d'être of urban settlement, while imports of food, fuel, and (usually) people are essential
to the continuation of town life, to say nothing of urban growth" (Hohenberg 1990:360).
A city is therefore a densely populated area that constantly needs to import food from the
countryside in order for its citizens to survive. In exchange, these citizens will produce
many commodities and services not available in the countryside (Derville 2002:33). The
question is whether this exchange occurs through peaceful transactions (as in a neoclas-
sical economic model in which exchange and monetization are predominant) or whether
this is the result of "extraeconomic coercion." I would argue that it is the result of both
extraeconomic coercion in the countryside and exchange mechanisms operating in the
marketplace.

52. Similarly, intra- and interregional market fluctuations were intertwined with social struggles
in the (not so hidden) abodes of production, while the social conditions in the mining industry
(Piccini 1994:224–225) were a result of the European elites' cravings for imported materials from
the East (Bozorgnia 1998). The mines in Central and Eastern Europe provided crucial amounts
of bullion to sustain trade with the East from the Pax Mongolica onward, since "Die Edelmetalle
werden zum großen Teil für die Zahlungen im Orient- und Rußlandhandel verwendet" (Bauer
and Matis 1988:106; see Tadic 1973:70). On their own, however, these mines would have been
insufficient, hence the importance of Sudanese gold and North African trade (Blanchard 2005).
At the same time, textiles were exported to the East (Nahlik 1971; Ashtor 1976).

53. An example is the devastating impact of the disruption in the commodity chain between the
Flemish regional economy and the Northern Italian regional economy in the 1340s caused by the
outbreak of the Hundred Years' War, or the struggle between the city-states of Genoa and Venice for
the control of long-distance trade routes to the Middle East. For example, Ashtor (1978b:301–109)
discusses how cheap and bulky raw materials from Syria such as lume and cotton were imported
to the West, transformed into manufactured products with a higher added value (notably soap and
fustian textiles), and subsequently resold to the Middle East. Textiles in particular were dumped

Given that so much of the workforce was active in the textile industry, the high division of labor *within* the city necessitated a firm grip on the surrounding countryside in order to meet the former's food demands. As specialization in the textile industry increased over time, the immediate countryside was integrated into the production process (Kotelnikova 1976). Throughout most of the 13th and early 14th centuries, the division of labor within the cities and their countrysides continued to expand. Specialization within European guilds increased unabatedly, facilitated—unlike the Arab world—by their "autonomous corporate existence which expressed itself in mutual aid or strict rules about entry or apprenticeship" (Hourani 1991:135).[54] The decrease in protection and transaction costs (that resulted from the Pax Mongolica's appearance on the Eurasian landmass) led to an unprecedented expansion of the markets for Western European city-states, which in turn further increased the division of labor in most European urban industries. The export of Western textiles to Eastern Europe (Holbach 1993b:175),[55] the Middle East (Bratianu 1944:51; Ashtor 1978b; 1986:IV, VI:580–583; 1992:II:271), the Black Sea area (Nystazopoulou 1973:563), and to a lesser extent Northern Africa (Thiry 1995:492), was very important (Stearns, Adas, and Schwartz 1996:468).

By contrast, the political-economic reality in Northern Africa as well as in the Sudanic states was one of tribalization, at times called "organized anarchy" (Garcin et al. 2000a:117)—not quite conducive to state-building formation or capitalist development in the long run (Désiré-Vuillemin 1997:196, 201–203). This invokes not an image of Oriental despotism or absolutism, but quite the opposite: tribalism implies a relative *lack* of institutionalized power and a structurally fragile state (Mojuetan 1995:8), which leads to an inability to implement mercantilist policies, a conundrum that diverse polities in the Maghreb had to face together with the concurrent and continuing difficulty of creating larger and more enduring political entities (Kably 1986:98)—eventually called

---

in the Middle Eastern markets in ever-higher quantities from the late 14th century onward for mass consumption (Ashtor 1976:673; 1978b:305–306; 1986:IV:305). "Al-Makrizi lamented the changes in clothing among the Egyptians in the early 15th century: instead of wearing good Egyptian clothing one now wore all kinds of textiles made in Europe" (Ashtor 1992:VI:319). During the Egyptian economy's notable decline in the early 15th century, "even the very small Western merchants seized the opportunity to sell a whole variety of goods that Egypt used to produce itself earlier" (Verlinden 1981:85).

54. Hall is quite explicit in stating that during the same centuries that medieval Europe was recovering from its "dark age," commercial expansion was occuring in Asia, "an expansion which may, in part, have affected Europe's recovery" (1978:75).

55. It is illustrative to know that "Um 1300 klagte ein Dichter aus dem niederösterreichischen Waldviertel, daß sich die Bauern 'mit Tuch aus Gent' kleiden" (Tremel 1976:314). See Székely (1966).

"nation-states" (Claudot-Hawad 2006)—that become crucial power containers for the elites who construct them over time.[56]

As evidenced by the European example, mercantile power within city-states was crucial for the development of "commercial imperialism" (Picard 2000:118), embedded within capitalist dynamics.[57] The expansion of the great city of Herat in the early 15th century, by contrast, is due to its location at the center of a new "pastoralist" state (Garcin 1991:303), and to a certain extent one can see this same dynamic in Northern African polities as well (Le Tourneau 1969:107–108). In Europe, however, the political elites in charge of the city-state were more in control of the city's development and expansion (Chamberlain 1994:47–48). In addition, the significance of many European city-states' naval power and control over maritime trade, often closely intertwined with their foreign policy, should not be underestimated (Mauny 1970:241), as demonstrated by many Mediterranean city-states' attempts to control the seas. Although the Hafsid rulers in Ifriqiya waged war against the Christians throughout the 15th century and claimed a share of the profits that Muslim corsairs had obtained by seizing European vessels, they never gave these allies substantial support: "The corsairs operated independent of the state, which never developed a true navy" (Perkins 1986:51). Most of the time they were quite powerless against European naval aggression (Valérian 2000:134–135). This is a major difference from their European counterparts who did not underestimate the significance of supporting their merchants to establish or maintain control over maritime trade routes, but this fact should of course be interpreted

---

56. As a classic study by Weber (1979) points out, the "modern" nation-state also took a very long time to be constructed, even in industrialized, modern, and centralized 19th-century France. The point is, of course, that medieval and "early modern" *polities* in Western Europe gradually developed a more successful strategy to effectively accumulate power and capital in the long run, especially once they were increasingly controlled by their merchant elite. The transition from a city-state to a nation-state is therefore an important feature in this long-term process. As Flórez (2003:50) argued: "It is important to study thoroughly the legislation and institutions of the last centuries of the Middle Ages and especially the ones that concerned the economy in order to understand better the origins of the Modern State." A comparison with their counterparts in medieval Western Europe clearly shows that North African cities had limited power: "La ville y est d'avantage prise dans des réseaux tribaux ou religieux qui la débordent largement, et débordent encore plus largement l'état" (Garcin et al. 2000a:162). And within those cities, merchants had limited power despite their crucial role in the economy of Western Africa (Eisenstadt et al. 1983:1243). To quote Denoix (2000:285): "À la différence des villes occidentales à propos desquelles les historiens ont montré que la gestion se faisait par un gouvernement urbain, dans celles du monde arabo-musulman, dont nous traitons, il n'y a jamais eu émergence d'une classe de notables exerçant un contre-pouvoir institutionalisé face à celui de l'État central, jamais eu de gouvernement urbain à proprement parler du type de nos communes médiévales."

57. Of course the traditional Marxist interpretation (e.g., Wood 2002), given its obsession with examining the transformations within a specific nation-state's (e.g., England) agricultural realm, rejects this out of hand.

in the context of the limited resources available given the challenges that tribal
rebellions and nomadic incursions created for these polities and their respective rulers (Mansouri 1995:141–142). Even the most formidable polity, the
Almohad state, was unable to overcome the pressures of internal opposition
and external threats (Laroui 1977:185; Abun-Nasr 1987:101). Given that ships
were ideal for the transport of raw materials and heavy industrial commodities
and that they linked together dispersed markets (Heers 1965b:44–47), one
might actually wonder whether a capitalist economy could have ever occurred
without the necessary number of ships—ships built by merchants and states
alike. It is not surprising when Moseley states that even before the Industrial
Revolution, "there had already been a radical shift in the global balance of
power in favor of Europe, particularly by virtue of its control of the seaways of
world trade" (1992:538). Multiple European powers' obsession with shipping
and control of the maritime trade routes meant that in the long run, Europeans
could offer commodities in larger amounts and at cheaper prices than could the
local African economies (Miller 1988). Was it also not the power of European
shipping that ultimately destroyed the cowrie as a form of currency in Western
Africa, when the British refused to accept them as payment and dumped massive amounts of East African cowries on the West African shores (Sider 1997)?[58]
In Northern Africa, along with the merchants' relative lack of significant political power (Garcin et al. 2000a:273), these maritime reversals were crucial to
the weakening of the Muslim polities and their potential for similar economic
expansion (Kably 1986:166). In the case of the Italian city-states, the institutionalized "fusion" between military, political, and economic interests is clear,
but even the monarchies from the Iberian Peninsula, where merchants wielded
less power, found it expedient to give more "forceful support to their subjects
abroad" (Pryor 1997:207) than was the case in, for example, the Byzantine Empire or the Northern African polities (Yarrison 1982). From this perspective
then, the conquest of the Northern African enclave of Ceuta in A.D. 1415 was
not the pivotal event that gave way to the modern era, as is so often claimed (e.g.,
Abernethy 2000), or even the prelude to the colonization of Africa (Unali 2000).
It was just the beginning of a remarkable Iberian expansion (Diffie and Winius
1977:46), which in turn can only be understood with regard to the emergence of
capitalism within Western Europe. The increased presence of Portuguese ships
on the Western African coasts coincided with a gradual reorientation of Saharan trade routes, which initiated the long decline of cities such as Sijilmassa and
Northern African polities (Daoulatli 1976:83). Eventually, the Muslim states
on the North African coast could no longer function as intermediaries trading

---

58. Interestingly, Yang (2004:314) considers Yunnan, integrated in the Indian Ocean world economy, "the first victim" of the collapse of the cowrie system brought about by the expansion of the
capitalist world-system.

between Western Europe and the Sudan proper and as such obtained less and less gold (Lugan 2001:90–91) while considerable quantities of Berber slaves would come to dominate the plantation economies of sugarcane and vines on the Canary Islands, in the Azores and to a lesser degree, Madeira (Mojuetan 1995:56). Its subsequent decline in artisan activities and concurrent merchant splendor would ultimately lead to a Moroccan expedition, organized by Sultan Al-Mansour, into the Sudan at the close of the 16th century (Dramani-Issifou 1982). But by that time, the modern world-system had been created across the Atlantic and its capitalist dynamics would gradually but irrevocably impact the historical alternatives available to the Western African polities (Gallissot 1981:20; Mojuetan 1995:68).

CHAPTER FIVE

Conclusion: Was the Western-European City-State in the Middle Ages a European Miracle?

S O, WAS THE Western-European city-state in the Middle Ages a European Miracle? Some have said that Europe embarked upon a unique historical trajectory because of its investment in a "dynamic technological strategy" (Snooks 1996) or because its people were "inspired by a lively curiosity, insatiable greed, and a reckless spirit of adventure that contrasted sharply with the smug conservatism of Chinese, Moslem, and Hindu cultural leaders" (McNeill 1963:578). Some assert that in Western Europe "rationality was more valued" (Chirot 1994:68). Others have claimed that by the 15th century, "and perhaps long before then, the West had a greater proportion of individuals who understood wheels, levers, and gears than any other region on earth," thus enabling them to shift from a "rational perception to a quantificational perception" (Crosby 1997:49, 53). This in turn may have given the West technological superiority over the rest of the world (e.g., Cardwell 1994). But all of these presumptions are far from satisfactory.

Another position is that postulated by Holton: "Capitalism of a modern kind developed rather in the relatively decentralized West, where political structures were far from monolithic, allowing internal differentiation" (1986:134). But such a monocausal explanation of competition and dynamism is not warranted either. This oft-repeated claim makes the non-West appear unable or unwilling to foster or experience change or interstate competition (see Hymes 1997:347). It is equally Eurocentric to claim, as is done in Marxist theories (e.g., Brenner 1985; Wood 1999), that class struggle in Western Europe (Britain in particular) prepared the way for the "modern" (i.e., capitalist) world, as if "non-Europe had no important role in social evolution at any historical period" (Blaut 1993:

127–128, 149). It is important to avoid Eurocentric assumptions about Western "superiority" in the Middle Ages. This is especially true at a time when the European Union seeks to legitimate its political and socioeconomic integration by subsidizing research that emphasizes the long-term historical unity of Europe, as though the region had been an entity "an sich" and "für sich" for almost ten centuries (e.g. Blockmans 1997).

The truth is that the spirit to accumulate capital (e.g., Weber 1930) existed in other civilizations just as much as it did in Europe. As scholars like Joseph Needham have so aptly demonstrated, throughout the Middle Ages non-Europe actually had greater riches and military capacities than did Europe. When it came to technological, military, and socioeconomic matters, 13th- and 14th-century Europe clearly lagged behind the great Asian civilizations. Nevertheless, every scholar who studies the impact of long-term socioeconomic change is eventually confronted with the question of whether, in the period A.D. 1200 to 1500, a single important difference existed between Europe and the rest of the world, a difference that may have had long-term implications resulting in the subsequent "Rise of the West."

Without resorting to "unique exceptionalism" with a teleological streak, one might ask whether there was a significant "turning point" (Hourani 1980:145) in the European *political realm*. According to Udovitch, "merchants in the Mediterranean Islamic world did not achieve an articulated political identity or acquire political power in a manner comparable to their counterparts in Catholic Europe" (1993:792). Just as I have attempted to describe in the preceding chapters, this statement implies that European political structures were different from non-European ones. In the former, merchant communities and guilds struggled for power in their politically independent city-states (something of a precursor to the interstate system of the 16th century) (Arrighi 1994). Gaining this power was crucial to their success as the merchant elites were then able to use the state infrastructure to their advantage (Kedar 1976:58–80). After all, the key to successful capital accumulation in the long run is not only learning how to keep taxes down, but how to minimize transaction, transportation and security costs by using state resources, preferably taxes derived from the poor, to facilitate capital maximization. To a certain extent, this accumulation and implementation of power should downplay many of the ongoing debates about how "advanced" preindustrial Europe was when compared with the non-European world (e.g., Alam 2000).

Another exceptional variable that should be singled out in the context of the emergence of a merchant capitalist system in Western Europe in the Late Middle Ages is the notion of *citizenship* (both juridical and political) as a result of communal identity (Boone 2002b:627). Burghers, for instance, could not be tried outside their own city and were not to be imprisoned outside city walls, nor could any noncitizen testify against a citizen (van Uytven 1978:472). The bourgeoisie's identification of itself as citizens of a city-state can be symbolically compared with the adherence to a nation-state several centuries later, a *process*—if one does not want to call it a *project*—that has been under-researched (Genet 2005:572), due in part to the artificial intellectual separation of "medievalists" and "early modernists" on the one hand and "political scientists" and "sociologists" on the other.

In addition to notions of citizenship, in many European cities the "bourgeoisie fouraine" (*buitenpoorterij*) had specific juridical, political, and socio-economic powers over its countryside. This is not meant to imply that people from the countryside were passive and did not resist exploitation; in fact, numerous peasant rebellions occurred against taxation and arbitrary legislation that favored the city-states or the nobility. Many rural revolts,[1] however, were conducted in an ad-hoc and violent way and were brutally suppressed by local (urban) authorities. Thus, one of medieval Europe's exceptional features was its construction of a region in terms of an operating inter-city-state system with a politically powerful bourgeoisie.[2] This does not mean, however, that one should analyze the European city-state as nothing more than a "capitalist island" in a sea of feudalism (Alonso 1991:295). Within the European countryside, richer peasants who profited from the increasing commercialization were able to purchase their poorer neighbors' holdings and "invested surplus cash in purchasing rent-charges on the lands of others, and so increased their money income yet further."[3] The poorest peasants were forced into "the class of rural laborers" (Spufford 1988:246, 337). Those wealthy peasants who were able to purchase citizenship—either from a city-state or sometimes directly from a king—were advantaged in their pursuit to ceaselessly accumulate capital (Bruwier 1955).[4] The medieval European city-state, initially tolerated by the monarchy because of its revenue potential and counterweight against other

---

1. For example, the uprising in Western Flanders in the 1320s or that of the Jacquerie in France.

2. This is different from the cities and towns in the non-European arena, which, despite occasionally managing to free themselves from overlordship (Miura 1997:46), did not result in institutionalized power that allowed a merchant elite to pursue long-term military, economic, *and* political policies.

3. Similarly, the merchants' investments in real estate, both in and outside the city, were not an abandonment of "pure" mercantile activities or a "betrayal of the bourgeoisie," but rather a diversification of assets, a guarantee of credit worthiness, and during economic crises a safe refuge for capital (Leguay 1989).

4. Those who did not enjoy the privileges of citizenship, that is, people living in the subordinated countryside as well as those in the colonial periphery, were clearly at a disadvantage. By the 14th century, the wealthiest Byzantines attempted to obtain citizenship in the major Italian city-states. Such citizenship was associated with access to multiple privileges, benefits and status (Laiou 1992:VII:212). "Not every urban citizen was a citizen in the true sense of the word. In many towns, this status was not used for the clergy. . . . Neither were all laymen regarded as citizens. Only those inhabitants of a town were regarded as belonging to the bourgeoisie who had full rights according to municipal law, most of whom possessed a house and landed property" (Groten 1990:79).

noblemen (Blockmans 1973:10), was essentially a socioeconomic and juridical entity controlled by an oligarchy of intermarried merchants, wealthy craftsmen, and lesser noblemen (de Oliveira Marques 1981:41; Prevenier 1978:413; Uytven 1976b:100),[5] whose interests were intrinsically linked with the successful exploitation of those in the hinterlands (either the immediate rural countryside or a colony/province overseas) and the proletariat living within the city-state (Blockmans 1996:446).[6]

Unlike in East Asia, South Asia, or Northern Africa, the European city-state was also symbolically reproduced in the imagery of its population who identified with it. This occurred not only in the city-states of Renaissance Italy but also, albeit somewhat later, in the Low Countries (Prevenier 1996; Boone and Stabel 2000). This identification then led to the relatively easy outbreak of warfare between different city-states, which perceived their competitors as dangerous rivals (as do modern nation-states). The carving out of a territorial space with specific economic privileges (*hoofdvaartstructuuur*) or juridical privileges (*kasselrij/contado*)[7] had an impact on the social structures in the countryside in the long run. The idea that "town air makes a man free" and the increasing monetization of the countryside also affected the maintenance of the feudal system, which relied primarily on extraeconomic coercion for its continued existence. Although the major demographic downturn of the mid-14th century—brought about by the outbreak of the Black Death—contributed to

---

5. For a detailed analysis of how a city's elite managed to control a city's apparatus, see Boone (1994b). In his Marxist theoretical framework, Brenner (1985, 1986) fails to grasp the importance of the abovementioned coalition since he characterizes European feudalism as a mere class struggle between noblemen and peasants. In leaving merchants and cities out of his analysis, Brenner (1986:50) essentially believes that the nobility could only increase its wealth through intensifying extraeconomic compulsion on the peasants or by increasing its rural domain at the expense of fellow noblemen. It is precisely the institutionalized strength of the urban-based bourgeoisie in the period 1200–1450 (Rodrigues 1997:27; Gonzalez 1996:31) that enabled it to forge a coalition with the nobility, ultimately leading to a process of "social osmosis" (Boone and Dumolyn 1999:228) that was crucial to the European transition from feudalism to capitalism as well as for the genesis of early modern state formations (Blockmans 1978:209).

6. In general, citizens could be divided into "cives maiores, mediocres," and "minores" (Fasoli 1965:56; Dollinger 1955:387–395). It is important, however, to keep in mind that "the great majority of the townsfolk were poor: servants, laborers, beggars. A lot of these people had come from surrounding regions after running away from their masters" (Groten 1990:85; see Milis 1989:66). In 14th-century Spanish cities, for instance, the "ciutadans honrats" or honorable citizens constituted only 3 percent of the urban population, which implies that the overwhelming majority of the urban population "was completely excluded from governing circles" (MacKay 1977:108).

7. "Securing adequate [grain] supplies [for the city] was a primary motive behind expanding a city's jurisdictional boundaries into its surrounding district, and annonal laws were without exception weighed heavily in favor of urban interests. The 1415 laws in Florence, for example, promised rewards to producers who brought their grain to the city and imposed stiff penalties on those who exported it outside the district without special license" (Bullard 1982:286).

the crisis of feudalism (Gottfried 1983), it was certainly not the determinant, let alone the sole factor (Hilton 1985:131; Bois 2000).[8]

Another variable that was crucial to the "Rise of the West" from the 13th century onward was the growing strength of multiple city-states, which indirectly increased the bargaining power of tenants, employees, and peasants vis-à-vis the rural nobility (Bove 2004:588).[9] This does not imply that city-states completely liberated the peasants from extraeconomic coercion or that urban areas represented "embryonic" forms of democracy and "free trade," as is sometimes envisaged in Whiggish and Smithian historiography, which unequivocally idealizes the market's capacity to bring about "progressive" change (Arnade, Howell and Simons 2002:533). Most peasants were consistently squeezed by the economic demands of lay or ecclesiastical overlords; the fulfillment of obligations, such as rent or labor, in turn generated market activity as the overlords sold this acquired surplus on the market (Graus 1951:453; Deane 1973:381; Wolff 1982:499). Yet a major explanation for the 13th-century phenomenon of city-states' growing power—closely associated with the feudalism crisis in the long run (Bauer and Matis 1988:122)—was the increasing infiltration of city dwellers into the countryside and the concurrent increase in the amount of rural estates in the countryside; the urban residents subsequently demanded payment in cash and indirectly brought about the demise of the common fields (Cuadrada 1991:289–290). In the city-state's economic sphere in particular, often reflected in the size of its population, peasants were drawn into the expanding market economy (e.g., Kisch 1972:300–302).[10] Harsh living conditions

---

8. Many scholars have described the demographic variable as a major "endogenous" factor, capable of bringing about economic growth (North and Thomas 1973:8) or agricultural progress (Boserup 1965), or a "demise" of the feudal system (Gottfried 1983). However. it does not explain why, for example, the demographic increase and concurrent economic growth in China did not lead to a capitalist system. Seccombe (1992) argues that the transition from feudalism to capitalism cannot be separated from the unique Western European system of marriage, in turn leading to the appearance of the nuclear family. In Chapter 2, I express my reservations about the importance of the nuclear family as a factor in explaining this transition (see Goody 1990 for an in-depth criticism of the use of differential family structures as an explanation for the rise of the West). Yet one should not forget that in the preindustrialized world, demographic growth was closely related to economic growth (Halpérin 1950:25–31; Zientara 1981:196).

9. Interestingly, the existence of the bourgeoisie foraine was correctly perceived by the lower nobility as an encroachment upon its socioeconomic welfare and political power. Paradoxically, it was not only the city-state that fostered the expansion of its influence, but in some cases, it was aided by the higher nobility (the count or the king) who, in his desperate need for additional income to balance a budget, was eager to grant his own version of citizenship ("bourgeoisie royale"). In doing so, the power of the lesser nobility was undermined—which, from the monarch's or count's perspective, was not necessarily something to be deplored (Bruwier 1955).

10. It is not surprising that in those areas where the city-state structure was quite weak (e.g., Eastern Europe or to a certain extent, the Iberian Peninsula), the nobility and the monarchy worked to contain the breakdown of feudal structures. Sometimes feudal structures were even supported by the bourgeoisie (Alonso 1991). In Northwestern Europe and Italy, however, feudal structures

in the periphery motivated these poor migrants to move to the city as unskilled laborers, where they were subsequently employed in the urban industries for very low wages (Derville 2002:37, 63) and forced to inhabit the most-recently created slums that surrounded the city center (Derville 2002:50). Although living in the city enabled one to escape the extraeconomic coercion in the countryside, citizenship was not necessarily easy to obtain.[11] And once in the city, the unskilled worker faced market forces that were no less relentless as that worker became part of a major labor pool reserve (Geremek 1968b:569). The parallels with contemporary undocumented immigrants, who desperately look for menial labor in the core zones of the world-economy and who face hostility from unions and citizens alike, is no coincidence, but rather part of the long-term polarizing logic of the (now world) capitalist system (Mielants 2002). Unlike in India, China, or the Sudanese states, the nobility in Europe (i.e., the rural overlords) was forever cash strapped and faced increasing competition from a coalition of urban-based merchants and petty noblemen who were primarily interested in obtaining more capital—eventually at the expense of the old feudal order. The organizational structure in the city-states enabled them to do this (with varying degrees of success). The city-state, as an institutional form, made the constant renewal of capital accumulation possible, if not necessary. This institutional vehicle of exploitation is exceptional to Europe, indeed Western Europe, and explains its unique "path dependence."[12]

This does not mean, however, that once the Western European city-states became more powerful that capitalist development was an *inevitable* process. Clearly, all the relevant features necessary to ensure a gradual transition from feudalism to capitalism were available. Equally important, however, was the lack of other features, for example, the construction of a well-organized "world empire" or the recurring destructive raids of pastoral nomads on the emerging centers of capital accumulation. Indeed during the mid-13th century, the Mongols could have easily overrun Western Europe and destroyed its city-state structure, similar to the razing of various metropolises in Central Asia. The fact that the overwhelming military might of various nomadic forces did not penetrate Western Europe after the Magyar invasions was a crucial variable in

---

disappeared as the logic of capital accumulation via economic exploitation took precedence over extraeconomic coercion.

11. Depending on the city, citizenship could be obtained by birth within the city (*ius soli*), by marrying a male citizen, or provided that at least one parent was a citizen (*ius sanguinis*), but more importantly through *purchase*, effectively limiting citizenship to the most affluent immigrants who would not burden the *bonum commune*. As with most of today's nation-states, being granted citizenship in another city—crucial to obtaining the permission to enter certain professions there—automatically implied losing one's previous citizenship (De Nave 1973:87–94, 117).

12. For an overview of the use of the concept "path dependence" in historical sociology, cf. Mahoney (2000).

the gradual transition from feudalism to capitalism. The dynamic of recurring nomadic invasions, which only occasionally brought about the destruction of Empires (e.g., Sung China in the 13th century or the Sultanate of Delhi in the late 14th century), sapped enormous amounts of energy and resources out of the Asian state polities, which in the long run limited their resources for overseas expansion and to a certain extent, also limited their ability to effectively resist their future incorporation into the capitalist world-economy.

The relative lack of political power wielded by merchants in both India and China—despite their accumulation of incredible amounts of wealth—has been discussed in previous chapters. But in addition to their lack of power, it must be noted that wherever rural overlords (including nomadic ones) were capable of exercising great extraeconomic coercion, the successful and consistent implementation of mercantilist policies was lessened. In those cases where such policies were implemented, they were not consistently to the advantage of the merchant elite. But in those city-states in which merchants could deploy military and political force—most notably in Northern Africa and Western Europe—they had a clear comparative advantage over those who did not. As mentioned earlier, it was partially because European states used their power to support mercantilist policies overseas that European merchants were capable of eventually dominating the non-European world, incorporating it into the capitalist world-system. The existing ruling strata in South Asia, by contrast, were more preoccupied with imposing extraeconomic coercion on their agricultural producers than with formulating mercantilist policies. This had tremendous implications for the Western powers' success in Asia in the subsequent period (1500–1800). Contrary to Goldstone (2000:191), it can therefore be argued that the later "great divergence" is rooted in long-standing prior differences. Yet, by contrasting a lack of European prosperity with Asian wealth (e.g., Frank 1998), it has unfortunately become fashionable to dismiss European colonialism during this period as a mere accidental occurrence. But one should remember that Europe's aforementioned path dependence was different from that in other parts of the world due to the manner in which capital was accumulated.

Indeed, as was demonstrated in Chapters 2, 3, and 4, the accumulation of riches (even by merchants) was not peculiar across Asia, Africa, or Europe. But a systematic policy of capital accumulation derived from an ongoing process of colonization, exploitation, and domination of a subjugated periphery by a core area *was* a rather exceptional process, set in motion by European merchants. This process first occurred in the immediate countryside of European cities, the Mediterranean Basin, and Eastern Europe, and was subsequently copied (with certain modifications) in the non-European arena (e.g., the Atlantic Islands, Latin America) and much later in Asia and Northern Africa. Up to circa 1500, the European city-states were the "power containers" that made this process of underdevelopment possible; after 1500, the emerging nation-states performed this function in the non-European world. In China, India, and the Sudanese states, merchants as a "power elite" (see Blockmans and Genet 1996:17–18) were incapable of seizing and preserving structural and institutional power the way that European merchants could. Although profits derived from trade in the non-European world were substantial compared to those in Europe, enormous amounts of money collected by wealthy merchants did not lead to the creation of a *capitalist system*, nor did a merchant-turned-grand-vizier symbolize the long-term political power accumulated by the merchant class.

The European city-state, which was both an expression and guarantee of ongoing trade and continuous mercantile expansion, is therefore both an *explanandum* and an *explanans* (cf. Wrigley 1978); the former can be explained by the absence of pastoral nomadism and the exceptional weakness of the area's rural nobility (due to the decline of the feudal system), whereas the latter enables us to understand why the path dependence of European history was different from that of India, China, and the Sudanese states. The origins of modernity—capitalism and citizenship—can be properly located within the European city-states and the subsequent nation-states that were formed out of imperialism and warfare (Tilly 1992) within the dynamics of ceaseless capital accumulation, and not among the great civilizations of Northern Africa, India, or China. Though it is true that up to the late 18th century, living standards, degrees of commercialization, agricultural yields, and protoindustrialization were no more advanced in Western Europe than in many other parts of the world, and one therefore can speak to a certain extent of "multiple early modernities" (Goldstone 2002:330), military power gradually concentrated in the hands of European (mercantile) elites first enabled, and then subsequently guaranteed, increasing returns and market expansion both within Europe and ultimately in the non-European world. Modern forms of capital accumulation, based on military and technological power, degrees of illegal and legal monopolization, neocolonization, and the abuse of workers are rooted in the long-term processes of capitalist exploitation that were first generated in Western Europe. Such accumulation was most notable in the political appearance of the city-state in which the merchant class accumulated its power and established a juridical apparatus to preserve its power (the notion of citizenship), as well as in the economic strategies of the putting-out system, which concurred with colonization and peripheralization to benefit the same merchant class.

This historical reality has often been denied by numerous actors: Eurocentrists, for starters, have denied the impact and long lasting legacy of *centuries* of Western colonialism. Within modernization theory, the prevailing academic orthodoxies of laissez-faire, competition and functionalism as well as the erasure of historical specificity, in both economics and sociology alike, is no coincidence

(Hodgson 2001).[13] Indeed, Western academic discourse as such—hegemonic and continuously reproduced in contemporary "postcolonial" university settings and political outlets—is intrinsically "rooted in the rise of the West, in the history of capitalism, in modernity, and the globalization of Western state institutions, disciplines, cultures and mechanisms of exploitation" (Crush 1995:11). The creation of the social sciences in the Western world and how they, in their own fragmented ways, think about past, present, and future conditions, cannot be separated from how Western knowledge has been used to control, colonize and dominate the non-Western world both in reality, as well as epistemologically. It is no coincidence that protectionist doctrines are abandoned and laissez-faire policies embraced only when it is in the political and economic interests of specific elites in charge of particular nation-states. Most economic studies in the academic realm are good examples of this, similar to how Orthodox Marxist studies produced in the former Soviet Union were remarkable indicators of how past, present and future conditions across different times and areas of the world were molded to fit particular Eurocentric paradigms.

The historical discipline is of course not immune to the "condition" of being a byproduct of its own era: created to sanctify the bourgeois nation-state in the 19th century, the historical discipline, like other social sciences, has taken this unit of analysis for granted for far too long. Is it a coincidence that in a time when global disparities (in the context of ever widening and deepening capitalist forces) should be addressed with utmost urgency, that the field of economic history has decreased in favor of cultural studies and identity issues? Truly comparative and interdisciplinary social science is unfortunately still in its infancy, but is a most necessary endeavor if we are to rethink how we envision, interpret, and explain past, present, and future states of affairs. It is hoped that with this contribution, readers will take some steps in this direction.

---

13. There are of course exceptions, both within structural functionalist sociology and the subfield of institutional economics. In so far as they look to the past to explain the Rise of the West, this research usually limits itself to scrutinizing information flows, contractual problems and issues of trust (e.g., Greif 2006), thereby obliterating notions of exploitation and underdevelopment.

BIBLIOGRAPHY

Abernethy, David. *The Dynamics of Global Dominance.* Yale University Press, New Haven, 2000.

Abraham, Meera. "Two Medieval Merchant Guilds of South India." *South Asian Studies* 18. Manohar Publications, New Delhi, 1988.

Abraham-Thisse, Simonne. "Achats et consommation de draps de laine par l'Hôtel de Bourgogne, 1370–1380," in Philippe Contamine, Thierry Dutour, and B. Schnerb (eds.), *Commerce, Finances et Société (XI–XVIe siècles).* Cultures et Civilisations Médievales IX, Presses de l'Université de Sorbonne, Paris, 1993, p. 27–70.

———."Kostel Ypersch, gemeyn Ypersch," in Mark Dewilde et al., *Ypres and the Medieval Cloth Industry in Flanders.* Institute for the Archeological Heritage, Asse-Zellik, 1998, p. 125–145.

———. "Le commerce des draps de Flandre en Europe du Nord" in Marc Boone and Walter Prevenier (eds.), "Drapery Production in the Late Medieval Low Countries: Markets and Strategies for Survival (14th–16th Centuries)." Garant, Leuven, 1993b, p. 167–206.

———. "Le commerce des hanséates de la Baltique à Bourgneuf," in Michel Balard et al., *L'Europe et l'Océan au Moyen Âge.* Société des Historiens Médiévistes de l'Enseignement Supérieur et Cid éditions, Nantes, 1988, p. 131–180.

Abrams, Philip. "Towns and Economic Growth," in Philip Abrams and E. A. Wrigley (eds.), *Towns in Societies.* Cambridge University Press, 1978, p. 9–33.

Abulafia, David. "Asia, Africa and the Trade of Medieval Europe," in M. M. Postan and Edward Miller (eds.), *The Cambridge Economic History of Europe.* Cambridge University Press, 1987, 2:402–473.

———. "The Impact of the Orient," in Dionisius Agius and Ian Netton (eds.), *Across the Mediterranean Frontiers. Trade, Politics and Religion, 650–1450.* Turnhout, Brepols, 1997, p. 1–40.

———. "Industrial Products: The Middle Ages," in Simonetta Cavaciocchi (red.), "Prodotti e techniche d'oltremare nelle economie europee secc. XIII–XVIII." Atti della

'Ventinovesima Settimana di Studi,' Aprile 1997, Le Monnier, Istituto Internazionale di Storia Economica "F. Datini," Prato, 1998, p. 333–358.

———. "The Norman Kingdom of Africa and the Norman Expeditions to Majorca and the Muslim Mediterranean." *Anglo-Norman Studies* 7, 1985, p. 26–49.

———. "The Role of Trade in Muslim-Christian Contact during the Middle Ages," in Dionisius Agius and Richard Hitchcock (eds.), *The Arab Influence in Medieval Europe.* Ithaca Press, Reading, 1994, p. 1–24.

———. "Southern Italy, Sicily and Sardinia in the Medieval Mediterranean Economy," in David Abulafia, *Commerce and Conquest in the Mediterranean, 1100–1500.* Variorum Series, Norfolk, 1993.

———. *The Two Italies.* Cambridge University Press, 1977.

Abu-Lughod, Janet. *Before European Hegemony.* Oxford University Press, 1989.

———. "Discontinuities and Persistence," in A. Frank and B. Gills (eds.), *The World System: Five Hundred Years or Five Thousand?* Routledge, London, 1993.

Abun-Nasr, Jamil. *A History of the Maghrib in the Islamic Period.* Cambridge University Press, 1987.

Ackerman, Robert et al. (translation). *Chrétien de Troyes' Ywain.* Frederick Ungar Publishing, New York, 1977.

Adams, Paul et al. *Experiencing World History.* New York University Press, 2000.

Adams, Terence. "Aliens, Agriculturalists and Entrepreneurs," in Dorothy Clayton, Richard Davies, and Peter McNiven (eds.), *Trade, Devotion and Governance. Papers in Later Medieval History.* Alan Sutton, Dover, NH, 1994, p. 140–157.

Adshead, S.A.M. *Central Asia in World History.* St. Martin's Press, New York, 1993.

———. *China in World History* (3rd ed.). St. Martin's Press, New York, 2000.

Aerts, Erik, Willy Dupon, and Herman Van der Wee. *De Economische ontwikkeling van Europa.* Universitaire Pers Leuven, 1985.

Aerts, Erik, and R. Unger. "Brewing in the Low Countries," in E. Aerts, L. Cullen, and R. Wilson (eds.), "Production, Marketing and Consumption of Alcoholic Beverages since the Late Middle Ages." Proceedings 10th International Economic History Congress, Session B-14, Studies in Social and Economic History, Leuven University Press, 1990, p. 92–101.

Agius, D. "The Arab Salandi," in U. Vermeulen and J. Van Steenbergen (eds.), *Egypt and Syria in the Fatimid, Ayyubid and Mamluk Eras.* Uitgeverij Peeters, Leuven, 2001, 3:49–60.

Aigle, Denise. *Le Fars sous la domination mongole.* Cahiers Studia Iranica, Paris, 2005.

Akhmedov, B. "Central Asia under the Rule of Chinggis Khan's Successors," in M. S. Asimov and C. E. Bosworth (eds.), *History of Civilizations of Central Asia.* Multiple History Series, UNESCO Publishing, Paris, 1998, p. 261–268.

Alam, Shadid. "How Advanced Was Europe in 1760 After All?" *Review of Radical Political Economics* 32, no. 4, 2000, p. 610–630.

Alavi, Hamza. "India's Transition to Colonial Capitalism," in Hamza Alavi et al. *Capitalism and Colonial Production.* Croom Helm, London, 1982, p. 23–75.

Alberts, Jappe W., and H.P.H. Jansen. *Welvaart in wording.* Nijhoff, The Hague, 1964.

Alef, Gustave. "The Origin and Early Development of the Muscovite Postal Service." *Jahrbücher für Geschichte Osteuropas* 15, no. 1, 1967, p. 1–15.

Allsen, Thomas. *Commodity and Exchange in the Mongol Empire.* Cambridge University Press, 1997.

———. "Mongolian Princes and Their Merchants Partners." *Asia Major,* 3rd ser., 2, no. 2, 1989, p. 83–126.

———. "Spiritual Geography and Political Legitimacy in the Eastern Steppe," in Henri

Claessen and Jarich Oosten (eds.), *Ideology and the Formation of Early States*. Brill, Leiden, 1996, p. 116–135.

———. "The Yüan Dynasty and the Uighurs of Turfan in the 13th Century," in Rossabi Morris (ed.), *China Among Equals*. University of California Press, Berkeley, 1983, p. 243–280.

Alonso, Hilario. "Les habitants de Burgos et leurs propriétés rurales," in "Les sociétés urbaines en France méridionale et en péninsule Ibérique au Moyen Âge." Actes du Colloque de Pau, 21–23 septembre 1988, éditions du CNRS, Paris, 1991, p. 295–310.

———. "Villes et finances royales," in Denis Menjot and Jean-Luc Pinol (coords.), *Enjeux et expressions de la politique municipale (XIe–XXe siècles)*. L'Harmattan, Paris, 1997, p. 61–79.

Amin, Samir. "The Ancient World-Systems versus the Modern Capitalist World-System." *Review* 14, no. 3, Summer 1991, 349–385.

———. "The Ancient World-Systems versus the Modern Capitalist World-System," in A. G. Frank and B. Gills (eds.), *The World System: Five Hundred Years or Five Thousand?* Routledge, London, 1993.

———. "Modes of Production, History and Unequal Development." *Science and Society* 69, no. 2, Summer 1985, p. 194–207.

———. "Underdevelopment and Dependence in Black Africa." *Journal of Peace Research* 9, 1972, p. 103–120.

Amitai-Preiss, Reuven. "Mongol Imperial Ideology and the Ilkhanid War against the Mamluks," in Reuven Amitai-Press and David Morgan (eds.), *The Mongol Empire and Its Legacy*. Brill, Boston, 1999, p. 57–72.

———. *Mongols and Mamluks*. Cambridge University Press, 1995.

———. "Northern Syria between the Mongols and Mamluks," in Daniel Power and Naomi Standen (eds.), *Frontiers in Question*. St. Martin's Press, New York, 1999b, p. 128–152.

Ammann, Hektor. "Desarrollo desigual en los origines del capitalismo." Facultad de Filosofia y Letras de la Universidad de Buenos Aires, Tesis 11 Grupo Editor, Buenos Aires, 1992.

———. "Deutschland und die Tuchindustrie Nordwesteuropas im Mittelalter." *Hansische Geschichtblätter* 72e jg., 1954, p. 1–63.

———. "Wie gross war die mittelalterliche Stadt ?" *Studium Generale* t. IX, 1956.

Anderson, Perry. *Lineages of the Absolutist State*. New Left Books, London, 1974.

Anene, J. C. "The Central Sudan and North Africa," in Michel Mollat et al., "Les Grandes Voies maritimes dans le monde, XVe–XIXe siècles." VIIe Colloque de la Commission Internationale d'Histoire Maritime, Vienne, 29.8–5.9. 1965, SEVPEN, Paris, 1965, p. 191–207.

Andrade, Tonio. "The Company's Chinese Pirates." *Journal of World History* 15, no. 4, Dec. 2004, p. 415–444.

———. "The Rise and Fall of Dutch Taiwan." *Journal of World History* 17, no. 4, Dec. 2006, p. 429–450.

Angold, Michael. "The Shaping of the Medieval Byzantine 'City.' " *Byzantinische Forschungen* 10, 1985, p. 1–37.

Arasaratnam, Sinnappah. "European Port Settlements in the Coromandel Commercial System," in Frank Broeze (ed.), *Brides of the Sea*. University of Hawaii Press, Honolulu, 1989, p. 75–96.

———. "The Indigenous Ruling Class in Dutch Maritime Ceylon." *Indian Economic and Social History Review* 8, no. 1, March 1971, p. 57–71.

———. *Maritime Trade, Society and European Influence in South Asia, 1600–1800*. Variorum Press, Ashgate, Aldershot, 1995.

————. *Merchants, Companies and Commerce on the Coromandel Coast.* Oxford University Press, New Delhi, 1986.

————. "Review Symposium." *Indian Economic and Social History Review* 21, no. 1, 1984, p. 111–116.

————. "Some Notes on the Dutch in Malacca and the Indo-Malayan Trade 1641–1670." *Journal of Southeast Asian History* 10, no. 3, Dec. 1969, p. 480–490.

————. "Weavers, Merchants and Company." *Indian Economic and Social History Review* 17, no. 3, 1980, 257–281.

Arbel, Benjamin. *Cyprus, the Franks and Venice, 13th–16th Centuries.* Variorum Collected Studies, Ashgate, Aldershot, 2000.

Arenson, Sarah. "Navigation and Exploration in the Medieval World," in E. Rice (ed.), *The Sea and History.* Sutton Publishing, Phoenix Mill, 1996, p. 111–125.

Argenti, Philip. *The Occupation of Chios by the Genoese and Their Administration of the Island, 1346–1566.* Cambridge University Press, 1958.

Aricanli, Tosun, and Mara Thomas. "Sidestepping Capitalism." *Journal of Historical Sociology* 7, no. 1, March 1994, p. 25–48.

Arnade, Peter, Martha Howell, and Walter Simons. "The Productivity of Urban Space in Northern Europe." *Journal of Interdisciplinary History* 32, no. 4, Spring 2002, p. 515–548.

Arnoux, Mathieu. "Innovation technique et genèse de l'entreprise" *Histoire, économie et Société* 20e, no. 4, Dec. 2001, p. 447–454.

Arrighi, Giovanni. *The Long Twentieth Century.* Verso, New York, 1994.

Asdracha, Catherine, and Robert Mantran. "A Confrontation in the East," in Robert Fossier (ed.), *The Cambridge Illustrated History of the Middles Ages, III, 1250–1520.* Cambridge University Press, 1986, p. 306–355.

Asher, Catherine and Cynthia Talbot. *India Before Europe.* Cambridge University Press, 2006.

Ashrafyan, K. Z. "Central Asia under Timur from 1370 to the Early 15th Century," in M. S. Asimov and C. E. Bosworth (eds.), "History of Civilizations of Central Asia." Multiple History Series, UNESCO Publishing, Paris, 1998, p. 319–345.

Ashtor, Eliyahu. "The Diet of Salaried Classes in the Medieval Near East." *Journal of Asian History* 4 (1970), p. 1–24.

————. *East–West Trade in the Medieval Mediterranean.* Edited by Benjamin Kedar. Variorum Reprints, London, 1986.

————. "The Economic Decline of the Middle East during the Later Middle Ages." *Asian and African Studies* 15, no. 3, Nov. 1981, p. 253–286.

————. "Les lainages dans l'Orient médiéval," in Marco Spallanzani (ed.). "Produzione, commercio e consumo dei panni di lana nei sec. XII–XVIII." Atti della seconda settimana di studio, aprile 1970, Istituto Internazionale di storia economica "F. Datini," L Olschki Editore, Firenze, 1976, p. 657–686.

————. "Le Proche-Orient au Bas Moyen-Âge. Une région sous-développée," in A. Guarducci (red.), "Sviluppo e sottosviluppo in Europa e fuori d'Europa dal secolo XIII alla Revoluzione Industriale." Atti della Decima settimana di studio 7–12 aprile 1978, Instituto Internazionale di Storia Economica "F. Datini," Serie II, 10, Prato, 1983, p. 375–433.

————. "Recent Research on Levantine Trade." *Journal of European Economic History* 14, no. 2, May–August, 1985, p. 361–385.

————. "Républiques urbaines dans le Proche-Orient à l'époque des croisades?" *Cahiers de la civilisation médiévale* 18, no. 2, Juin 1975, p. 117–131.

————. *Studies on the Levantine Trade in the Middle Ages.* Variorum Reprints, London, 1978.

————. *Technology, Industry and Trade.* Variorum Series, Norfolk, 1992.

————. "Underdevelopment in the Pre-Industrial Era." *Journal of European Economic History* 7, nos. 2–3, Fall–Winter 1978b, p. 285–310.

Ashtor-Strauss, Eliyahu. "L'administration urbaine en Syrie médiévale." *Rivista degli Studi Orientali* [Roma] 31 (1956), p. 73–128.

Astuti, Guido. "L'organizzazione giuridica del sistema coloniale e della navigazione mercantile delle città italiane nel medioevo," in Manlio Cortelazzo (ed.), "Mediterraneo e Oceano Indiano." Atti del Sesto Colloquio Internazionale di Storia Marittima, Venezia, 20–29 settembre 1962, L Olschki Editore, Firenze, 1970, p. 57–89.

Attman, Arthur. "The Flow Of Precious Metals along the Trade Routes between Europe and Asia up to 1800," in Karl R. Haellquist (ed.), *Asian Trade Routes. Continental and Maritime.* Studies on Asian Topics 13. Scandinavian Institute of Asian Studies, Copenhagen, 1991, p. 7–20.

Atwell, William. "Time, Money and the Weather," *Journal of Asian Studies* 61, no. 1, Feb. 2002, p. 83–113.

Aubin, Jean. "Le royaume d'Ormuz au début du XVIe siècle." *Mare Luso-Indicum* 2, 1973, p. 77–179.

————. "Y a-t-il eu interruption du commerce par mer entre le Golfe Persique et l'Inde du XI au XIVe siècle?" in "Océan Indien et Méditerranée." Travaux du 6e Colloque International d'Histoire Maritime et du 2e Congrès de l'Association Historique Internationale de l'Océan Indien, SEVPEN, Paris, 1964, p. 165–171.

Austen, Ralph. *Africa in Economic History.* Heinemann Books, Portsmouth, 1987.

————. "The Mediterranean Islamic Slave Trade Out of Africa," in Elizabeth Savage (ed.), *The Human Commodity.* Frank Cass, London, 1992, p. 214–248.

————. "On Comparing Pre-Industrial African and European Economies." *African Economic History* 19, 1991, p. 21–24.

Aymard, Maurice. "Markets and Rural Economies in Mediterranean Europe," in Jaime Torras et al., *Els Espais del Mercat.* Disputacio de Valencia, 1993, p. 289–300.

Babel, Rainer, and Jean-Marie Moeglin, eds. *Identité régionale et conscience nationale en France et en Allemagne du Moyen Âge à l'époque moderne.* Jan Thorbecke Verlag, Sigmaringen, 1997.

Bacharach, Jere. "Monetary Movements in Medieval Egypt," in J. F. Richards (ed.), *Precious Metals in the Later Medieval and Early Modern Worlds.* Carolina Academic Press, Durham, 1983, p. 159–181.

Baechler, Jean. *Esquisse d'une histoire universelle.* Éditions Gallimard, Paris, 2002.

————. *Le capitalisme.* Vol. 1, *Les Origines.* Éditions Gallimard, Paris, 1995.

————. "The Origins of Modernity," in J. Baechler, J. Hall, and M. Mann (eds.), *Europe and the Rise of Capitalism.* Basil Blackwell, New York, 1988, p. 39–65.

Bairoch, Paul. "L'urbanisation des sociétés traditionnelles," in S. Cavaciochi (red.), "Metodi risultati e prospettive della storia economica secc. XIII–XVIII." Atti della 'Ventesima Settimana di Studi,' 19–23 aprile 1988, Instituto Internazionale di Storia Economica "F Datini," serie II, Prato, 1989, p. 193–233.

————. *Victoires et déboires.* Éditions Gallimard, Paris, 1997.

Balabanlilar, Lisa. "Lords of the Auspicious Conjunction." *Journal of World History* Vol. 18, no. 1, 2007, p. 1–39.

Balard, Michel. "L'activité commerciale en Chypre dans les années 1300," in Peter Edbury (ed.), *Crusade and Settlement.* University College Cardiff Press, 1985, p. 251–263.

————. "Byzance et les régions septentrionales de la mer Noire (XIIIe–XVe siècles)." *Revue Historique* 288/1, no. 583, July–Sept, 1992, p. 19–38.

————. dir. *État et colonisation au Moyen Âge.* La Manufacture, Lyon, 1989.

———. "État et colonisation au Moyen Âge. Bilan et perspectives," in Jean-Philippe Genet (ed.), "L'état Moderne." Éditions du CNRS, Paris, 1990, p. 65–73.

———. "Gênes et la mer Noire." *Revue Historique* 270/1, no. 547, July–Sept, 1983, p. 31–54.

———. "Les Génois dans l'Ouest de la mer Noire au XIVe siècle," in M. Berza and E. Stanescu (eds.), "Actes du XIVe congrès international des études Byzantines," Editura Academiei Republicii Socialiste Romania, Bucuresti, 1975, p. 21–32.

———. "Les Génois en Asie centrale et en Extrême-Orient au XIVe siècle," in *Économies et Sociétés au Moyen Âge*. Publications de la Sorbonne, Série "Études" Tome 5, Paris, 1973, p. 681–689.

———. "Il Mar Nero, Venezia e l'Occidente intorno al 1200," in Wolfgang von Stromer (ed.), *Venedig und die Weltwirtschaft um 1200*. Jan Thorbecke Verlag, Stuttgart, 1999, p. 191–202.

———. "L'impact des produits du Levant sur les économies européennes (XII–XVe siècles)," in Simonetta Cavaciocchi (red.), "Prodotti e techniche d'oltremare nelle economie europee secc. XIII–XVIII." Atti della 'Ventinovesima Settimana di Studi,' 14–19 aprile 1997, Le Monnier, Istituto Internazionale di Storia Economica "F. Datini," Prato, 1998, p. 31–57.

———. *La mer Noire et la Romanie génoise (XIIIe–XVe siècles)*. Variorum Reprints, London, 1989.

———. "La 'Révolution Nautique' à Gênes," in Christiane Villain-Gandossi, Salvino Busttil, and Paul Adam (eds.), *Medieval Ships and the Birth of Technological Societies*. Vol. 2, *The Mediterranean Area and European Integration*. Foundation for International Studies, University of Malta, 1991, p. 113–123.

———. *La Romanie génoise*. 2 vols. Atti della Società Ligure Storia Patria, Genoa, 1978.

Balard, Michel, and Alain Ducellier. "Conclusion," in Michel Balard and Alain Ducellier (dirs.), *Coloniser au Moyen Âge*. Armand Colin, Paris, 1995, p. 395–396.

———, dirs. *Le Partage du Monde. Échanges et colonisation dans la Méditerranée médiévale*. Publications de la Sorbonne, Paris, 1998.

Balazs, Étienne. *Chinese Civilization and Bureaucracy*. New Haven, Yale University Press, 1972.

———. "Urban Developments," in James Liu and Peter Golas (eds.), *Change in Sung China. Innovation or Renovation?* DC Heath and Co, Lexington, MA, 1969, p. 15–19.

Balletto, Laura. "Commercio di grano dal Mar Nero all'Occidente (1290–91)." *Critica storica* 14, 1977, p. 57–65.

———. *Genova, Mediterraneo, Mar Nero (secc. XII–XV)*. Civico Istituto Colombiano (Studi e testi, Serie Storica 1), Genova, 1976.

Banaji, Jairus. "Islam, the Mediterranean and the Rise of Capitalism." *Historical Materialism*, Vol. 15, no. 1, 2007, p. 47–74.

Bang, P. F. "Rome and the Comparative Study of Tributary Empires." *Medieval History Journal* 6, no. 2, Dec. 2003, p. 189–216.

Baradat, Leon. *Political Ideologies*. Prentice Hall, NJ, 1988.

Baratier, Édouard. "L'activité des Occidentaux en Orient au Moyen Âge," in Michel Mollat (dir.), *Sociétés et compagnies de commerce en Orient et dans l'océan Indien*. SEVPEN, Paris, 1970, p. 333–341.

Barendse, R. J. *The Arabian Seas*. M. E. Sharpe, Armonk, NY, 2002.

———. "Trade and State in the Arabian Seas." *Journal of World History* 11, no. 2, 2000, p. 173–225.

Barfield, T. J. *The Perilous Frontier, Nomadic Empires and China*. Oxford University Press, 1989.

Barfield, Thomas. "The Devil's Horsemen," in S. P. Reyna and R. E. Downs (eds.), *Studying War.* Gordon and Breach Science Publishers, Amsterdam, 1994, p. 157–184.

Barnett, Jo Ellen. *Time's Pendulum.* Plenum Trade: New York, 1998.

Bartlett, Robert. *The Making of Europe.* Princeton University Press, 1993.

Basa, Kishor. "Indian Writings on Early History and Archeology of Southeast Asia." *Journal of the Royal Asiatic Society* 8, no. 3, Nov. 1998, p. 395–410.

Baskin, Jonathan, and Paul Miranti. *A History of Corporate Finance.* Cambridge University Press, 1999.

Bauer, Leonhard, and Herbert Matis. *Geburt der Neuzeit.* Deutscher Taschenbuch Verlag, München, 1988.

Baumgartner, Tom, Walter Buckley, and Tom Burns. "Unequal Exchange and Uneven Development: The Structuring of Exchange Patterns." *Studies in Comparative International Development* 11, no. 2, Summer 1976, p. 51–72.

Bautier, Robert. "La circulation fluviale dans la France médiévale," in "Recherches sur l'économie de la France médiévale." Actes du 112e congrès national des sociétés savantes, Éditions CTHS, Paris, 1989, p. 7–36.

―――. *Commerce méditerranéen et banquiers italiens au Moyen Âge.* Variorum, Norfolk, 1992.

Bayly, C. A. "India and West Asia, c. 1700–1830." *Asian Affairs* 19, no. 1, Feb. 1988, p. 3–19.

―――. *Rulers, Townsmen and Bazaars.* Cambridge University Press, 1983.

―――. "South Asia and the Great Divergence." *Itinerario* 24, nos. 3/4, 2000, p. 89–103.

Beaujard, Philippe. "The Indian Ocean in Eurasian and African World-Systems before the Sixteenth Century." *Journal of World History* 16, no. 4, Dec. 2005, p. 411–465.

Bélénitsky, A. M. "Les Mongols et l'Asie Centrale." *Cahiers d'Histoire Mondiale* 5, no. 3, 1960, p. 606–620.

Belshaw, C. S. *Traditional Exchange and Modern Markets.* Prentice Hall, Englewood Cliffs, NJ, 1965.

Bendix, Reinhard. *Kings or People.* University of California Press, 1978.

Benevolo, Leonardo. *De Europese stad.* Agon, Amsterdam, 1993.

Bentley, Jerry. *Old World Encounters.* Oxford University Press, 1993.

Berg, Maxine. "In Pursuit of Luxury." *Past and Present* 182, Feb. 2004, p. 85–142.

Bergère, Marie-Claire. "On the Historical Origins of Chinese Underdevelopment." *Theory and Society* 13, no. 3, May 1984, p. 327–337.

Berkey, Jonathan. "The Muhtasibs of Cairo under the Mamluks," in Michael Winter and Amalia Levanoni (eds.), *The Mamluks in Egyptian and Syrian Politics and Society.* Brill, Boston, 2004, p. 245–276.

Bernard, Jacques. "Trade and Finance in the Middle Ages, 900–1500," Carlo Cipolla (ed.), *The Fontana Economic History of Europe.* Vol. 1, *The Middle Ages.* Barnes & Noble, New York, 1976, p. 274–338.

Berza, M. "La mer Noire à la fin du Moyen Âge." *Balcania* 4, 1941, p. 409–435.

Bing, Zhao. "L'importation de la céramique chinoise à Sharma (Hadramaout) au Yémen." *Annales Islamologiques* 38, no. 1, 2004, p. 255–284.

Black, Anthony. "Decolonization of Concepts." *Journal of Early Modern History* 1, no. 1, 1997, p. 55–69.

Blake, Steven. "The Patrimonial-Bureaucratic Empire of the Mughals." *Journal of Asian Studies* 39, no. 1, 1979, p. 77–94.

Blanchard, Ian. *Mining, Metallurgy and Minting in the Middle Ages Vol. 3.* Franz Steiner Verlag, Stuttgart, 2005.

―――. "African Gold and European Specie Markets," Paper presented at the Conference "Relazioni economiche tra Europa e mondo islamico", Fondazione Istituto Internazionale di Storia Economica "F. Datini" Prato, 1-5 maggio 2006.

Blanks, David. "Mountain Society: Village and Town in Medieval Foix," in Kathryn Reyerson and John Drendel (eds.), *Urban and Rural Communities in Medieval France. Provence and Languedoc, 1000–1500.* Brill, Boston, 1998, p. 163–192.

Blaut, J. M. *The Colonizer's Model of the World.* Guilford Press, New York, 1993.

Blickle, Peter. "The Rural World and the Communal Movement," in Eloy Ruano and Manuel Burgos (eds.), "Chronological Section I." 17th International Congress of Historical Sciences, Comité International des Sciences Historiques, Madrid, 1992, p. 95–99.

Bloch, Marc. *Feudal Society.* Chicago: University of Chicago Press, 1966.

Blockmans, Wim. "De Bourgondische Nederlanden." *Handelingen van de Koninklijke Kring voor Oudheidkunde, Letteren en Kunst van Mechelen* 77, no. 2, 1973, p. 7–26.

———. "The Economic Expansion of Holland and Zeeland in the 14th–16th Centuries," in Erik Aers, Brigitte Heneau, Paul Janssens, and Raymond van Uytven (eds.), *Studia Historica Oeconomica.* University Press Leuven, 1993, p. 41–58.

———. *A History of Power in Europe.* Fonds Mercator Paribas, Antwerp, 1997.

———. "The Impact of Cities on State Formation," in Peter Blickle (ed.), *Resistance, Representation, and Community.* Clarendon Press, Oxford, 1997b, p. 256–271.

———. "De ontwikkeling van een verstedelijkte samenleving," in Els Witte (red.), *Geschiedenis van Vlaanderen.* La Renaissance du Livre, Bruxelles, 1983, p. 43–103.

———. "A typology of representative institutions in late medieval Europe." *Journal of Medieval History,* 1978, 4:189–215.

———. "Beheersen en overtuigen." *Tijdschrift voor Sociale Geschiedenis,* jg. 16, 1, 1990, p. 18–30.

———. La manipulation du consensus," in Sergio Gensini (ed.), *Principi e città alla fine del medioevo.* Ministero per i beni culturali e ambientali, Pisa 1996, p. 433–447.

———. "De volksvertegenwoordiging in Vlaanderen in de overgang van middeleeuwen naar nieuwe tijden." Verhandelingen van de koninklijke academie voor wetenschappen, letteren en schone kunsten van Belgie, Klasse der Letteren 40, no. 90, Brussels, 1978.

Blockmans, Wim, and Jean-Philippe Genet. "Origins of the Modern State in Europe," in Wim Blockmans, Jorge Borges de Macedo, and Jean-Philippe Genet (eds.), *The Heritage of the Pre-Industrial European State.* Arquivos Nacionais/Torre do Tombo, Lisboa, 1996, p. 11–21.

Blockmans, Wim, and Walter Prevenier. "Poverty in Flanders and Brabant from the 14th to the Mid-16th Century," in *Acta Historiae Neerlandicae,* Vol 10. Boston, Nijhoff, 1978, p. 20–57.

Blomquist, Thomas. "Alien Coins and Foreign Exchange Banking in a Medieval Commune." *Journal of Medieval History* 20, Dec. 1994, p. 337–346.

———. "The Dawn of Banking in an Italian Commune," in *The Dawn of Modern Banking.* Yale University Press, New Haven, 1979, p. 53–75.

———. "The Drapers of Lucca and the Marketing of Cloth in the Mid-Thirteenth Century," in David Herlihy, Robert Lopez, and Vsevolod Slessarev (eds.), *Economy, Society and Government in Medieval Italy.* Kent State University Press, Ohio, 1969, p. 65–73.

Blum, Jerome. *Lord and Peasant in Russia from the 9th to the 19th Century.* Princeton University Press, 1972.

Bochaca, Michel. "L'aire d'influence et l'espace de relations économiques de Bordeaux vers 1475." in Noël Coulet and Olivier Guyotjeannin (dir.), *La Ville au Moyen Âge.* Éditions du Comité des travaux historiques et scientifiques, Paris, 1998, p. 279–292.

———. *La Banlieu de Bordeaux.* Éditions l'Harmattan, Paris, 1997.

Bogucka, Maria. "The Towns of East-Central Europe from the 14th to the 17th Century," in Antoni Maczak, Henryk Samsonowicz, and Peter Burke (eds.), *East-Central Europe in Transition.* Cambridge University Press, New York, 1985, p. 97–108.

Bois, Guy. "D'une économie des faits économiques à une histoire de l'économie médiévale." *Histoire and Sociétés Rurales* 3, 1995, p. 87–93.

———. "On the Crisis of the Late Middle Ages." *Medieval History Journal* 1, no. 2, Dec. 1998, p. 311–321.

———. *La grande dépression médiévale, XIVe et XVe siècles.* Presses Universitaires de France, Paris, 2000.

———. "Sur la crise du mode de production féodal," in Bernard Chavance (ed.), "Marx en perspective." Éditions de l'École des Hautes études en Sciences Sociales, Paris, 1985, p. 189–202.

Bonenfant, P., and G. Despy. "La noblesse en Brabant aux XIIe et XIIIe siècles." *Le Moyen Âge* 64, 1958, p. 27–66.

Bonney, Richard. "Introduction," in Richard Bonney, *Economic Systems and State Finance.* Oxford University Press, 1995, p. 1–18.

Boone, James, Emlen Myers, and Charles Redman. "Archaeological and Historical Approaches to Complex Societies." *American Anthropologist* 92, no. 3, 1990, p. 630–646.

Boone, Marc. "La construction d'un républicanisme urbain," in D. Menjot and J. L. Pinols (eds.), *Enjeux et expressions de la politique municipale (XIIe–XXe siècles).* L'Harmattan, Paris, 1997, p. 41–60.

———. "Droit de bourgeoisie et particularisme urbain dans la Flandre bourguignonne et habsbourgeoise." *Revue belge de philologie et d'histoire* 74, nos. 3–4, 1996, p. 707–725.

———. "Les ducs, les villes et l'argent des contribuables," in Ph. Contamine et al., *L'impôt au Moyen Âge.* Vol. 2, *Les espaces fiscaux.* Ministère de l'Économie, des Finances et de l'Industrie, Paris, 2002, p. 323–341.

———. "Les gens de métiers et l'usage de la violence dans la société urbaine flamande à la fin du Moyen Âge." *Revue du Nord* 87, no. 359, Mars 2005, p. 7–33.

———. "Gent en de Bourgondische hertogen ca. 1384–1453." Verhandelingen van de koninklijke academie voor Wetenschappen, Letteren en Schone kunsten van Belgie, KdL 52, no. 133, Brussels, 1990.

———. "Les métiers dans les villes flamandes au bas Moyen Âge (XIV–XVI siècles)," in P. Lambrechts and J. P. Sosson (eds.), *Les métiers au Moyen Âge. Aspects économiques et sociaux.* Université Catholique de Louvain-La-Neuve, 1994, p. 1–22.

———. "Openbare diensten en initiatieven te Gent tijdens de Late Middeleeuwen." Actes du 11e Colloque International, Spa, Sep. 1–4, 1982. Crédit Communal, Collection Histoire 8, no. 65, Bruxelles, 1984, p. 71–114.

———. "Städtische Selbstverwaltungsorgane vom 14. Bis 16. Jahrhundert," in Wilfried Ehrbrecht (ed.), *Verwaltung und Politik in Städten Mitteleuropas.* Böhlau Verlag, Köln, 1994b, p. 21–46.

———. "La terre, les hommes et les villes," in "Cities and the Transmission of Cultural Values in the Late Middle Ages and Early Modern Period." Crédit Communal, no. 96, Bruxelles, 1996b, p. 153–173.

———. "Triomferend privé-initiatief versus haperend overheidsoptreden?" *Tijdschrift voor Sociale Geschiedenis* 15, no. 2, May 1989, p. 113–138.

———. "Urban Space and Political Conflict in Late Medieval Flanders." *Journal of Interdisciplinary History* 32, no. 4, 2002b, p. 621–640.

Boone, Marc, and Hanno Brand. "Vollersoproeren en collectieve actie in Gent en Leiden in de 14e–15e eeuw." *Tijdschrift voor Sociale Geschiedenis* 19, no. 2, May 1993, p. 168–192.

Boone, Marc, and Jan Dumolyn. "Les officiers-créditeurs des ducs de Bourgogne dans l'ancien comté de Flandre," in "Rencontres d'Asti-Chambery," Sept. 24–27, 1998, Publication du Centre Européen d'études bourguignonnes (XIVe–XVIe siècles.) 39, 1999, p. 225–241.

Boone, Marc, and Maarten Prak. "Rulers, Patricians and Burghers," in Karel Davids and Jan Lucassen (eds.), *A Miracle Mirrored*. Cambridge University Press, 1995, p. 99–134.

Boone, Marc, and Peter Stabel. *Shaping Urban Identity in Late Medieval Europe*. Garant, Leuven, 2000.

Boone, Marc, and Walter Prevenier, eds. *Drapery Production in the Late Medieval Low Countries: Markets and Strategies for Survival (14th–16th Centuries)*. Garant, Leuven, 1993.

Boone, Marc, Hanno Brand, and Walter Prevenier. "Révendications salariales et conjuncture économique: les salaires de foulons à Gand et à Leyde au XVe siècle" in Erik Aers, Brigitte Heneau, Paul Janssens, and Raymond van Uytven (eds.), *Studia Historica Oeconomica. Liber amicorum Herman van der Wee*. University Press Leuven, 1993, p. 59–74.

Boris, Dieter. "Plus Ultra—bis ans Ende der Welt." *Peripherie* 11, nos. 43/44, 1991, p. 94–114.

Borlandi, Franco. "Futainers et futaines dans l'Italie du Moyen Âge," in *Éventail de l'histoire vivante. Hommage à Lucien Febvre*. Librairie Armand Colin, Paris, 1954, p. 133–140.

Borsa, Giorgio. "Recent Trends in Indian Ocean Historiography 1500–1800," in Giorgio Borsa (ed.), *Trade and Politics in the Indian Ocean. Historical and Contemporary Perspectives*. Manohar Publications, New Delhi, 1990, p. 3–14.

Boserup, E. *The Conditions of Agricultural Progress*. Aldine, Chicago, 1965.

Bouayed, Mahmoud-Agha. "Le port de Hunayn, trait d'union entre le Maghreb central et l'Espagne au Moyen Âge," in Mercedes García-Arenal and María Viguera (eds.), *Relaciones de la península ibérica con el Magreb siglos XIII–XVI*. Consejo Superior de Investigaciones Científicas, Madrid, 1988, p. 325–359.

Bouchon, Geneviève. *Inde découverte, Inde Retrouvée 1498–1630*. Centre Culturel Calouste Gulbenkian, Paris/Lisboa, 1999.

———. "Les musulmans du Kerala à l'époque de la découverte portugaise." *Mare Luso-Indicum* 2, 1973, p. 3–59.

Bouchon, Geneviève, and Denys Lombard. "The Indian Ocean in the Fifteenth Century," in Ashin Das Gupta and M. N. Pearson (eds.), *India and the Indian Ocean 1500–1800*. Oxford University Press, New Delhi, 1987, p. 46–70.

Boutillier, S., and D. Uzunidis. *La légende de l'entrepreneur*. La Découverte, Paris, 1999.

Bouvier, Jean, and Henry Germain-Martin. *Finances et financiers de l'Ancien Régime*. Presses Universitaires de France, Paris, 1964.

Bove, Boris. *Dominer la ville. Prévôts des marchands et échevins parisiens de 1260 à 1350*. Éditions du CTHS (Comité des travaux historiques et scientifiques), Paris, 2004.

Bovill, E. W. *The Golden Trade of the Moors*. Oxford University Press, London, 1968.

Bowles, Samuel. "Class versus World-Systems Analysis? Epitaph for a False Opposition." *Review* 11, no. 4, 1988, p. 433–451.

Bowsky, William. *The Finance of the Commune of Sienna 1287–1355*. Clarendon Press, Oxford, 1970.

Boxer, C. R. "A Note on Portuguese Relations to the Revival of the Red Sea Spice Trade and the Rise of Atjeh, 1540–1600." *Journal of Southeast Asian History* 10, no. 3, Dec. 1969, p. 415–428.

Boyle, John A. *The Mongol World Empire, 1206–1370*. Variorum Reprints, London, 1977.

Bozorgnia, S. M. *The Role of Precious Metals in European Economic Development*. Greenwood Press, Westport, CT, 1998.

Bradley, Helen. "The Datini Factors in London, 1380–1410," in Dorothy Clayton, Richard Davies, and Peter McNiven (eds.), *Trade, Devotion and Governance*. Alan Sutton, Dover, NH, 1994, p. 55–79.

Brady, Thomas. "The Rise of Merchant Empires, 1400–1700," in James Tracy (ed.), *The Political Economy of Merchant Empires*. Cambridge University Press, 1991, p. 117–160.

Brady Thomas, Jr. "Cities and State-Building in the South German-Swiss Zone of the 'Urban Belt,' " in Peter Blickle (ed.), *Resistance, Representation and Community*. Clarendon Press, Oxford, 1997, p. 236–250.

Brand, Hanno. *Over macht en overwicht. Stedelijke elites in Leiden (1420–1510)*. Garant, Leuven, 1996.

Brand, Hanno. "Urban Policy or Personal Government: The Involvement of the Urban Elite in the Economy of Leiden at the End of the Middle Ages," in Herman Diederiks, Paul Hohenberg, and M. Wagenaar (eds.), *Economic Policy in Europe since the Late Middle Ages*. Leicester University Press, 1992, p. 17–34.

Brand, Hanno, and Peter Stabel. "De ontwikkeling van vollerslonen in enkele laat–middeleeuwse textielcentra in de Nederlanden," in Jean Marie Duvosquel, and Erik Thoen (eds.), *Peasants and Townsmen in Medieval Europe*. Centre Belge d'Histoire Rurale, Gent, 1995, p. 203–222.

Bratianu, G. I. "La mer Noire, plaque tournante du trafic international à la fin du Moyen Âge." *Revue Historique du Sud-Est Européen* 21, 1944, p. 36–69.

Braudel, Fernand. *Afterthoughts on Material Civilization and Capitalism*. Johns Hopkins University Press, Baltimore, 1977.

———. *A History of Civilizations*. Penguin Books, NY, 1993.

———. *The Perspective of the World*. University of California Press, Berkeley, 1992b.

———. *The Wheels of Commerce*. University of California Press, Berkeley, 1992.

Braunstein, Philippe. "Les Forges champenoises de la comtesse de la Flandre (1372–1404)." *Annales ESC* 42, no. 4, July–August 1987, p. 747–777.

———. "Les métiers du métal. Travail et entreprise à la fin du moyen âge," in P. Lambrechts and J. P. Sosson (eds.), *Les métiers au Moyen Âge. Aspects économiques et sociaux*. Université Catholique de Louvain-La-Neuve, 1994, p. 23–34.

———, ed. *La sidérurgie alpine en Italie*. École Française de Rome, Rome, 2001.

Brenner, Robert. "Agrarian Class Structure and Economic Development in Pre-Agrarian Europe," in T. H. Aston and C.H.E. Philpin (eds.), *The Brenner Debate*. Cambridge University Press, [1976] 1985, p. 10–63.

———. "The Agrarian Roots of European Capitalism," in T. H. Aston and C.H.E. Philpin (eds.), *The Brenner Debate*. Cambridge University Press, [1976] 1985, p. 213–327.

———. "The Low Countries in the Transition to Capitalism," in Peter Hoppenbrouwers and Jan van Zanden (eds.), *Peasants into Farmers?* Brepols, Turnhout, 2001, p. 275–338.

———. "The Origins of Capitalist Development: A Critique of Neo-Smithian Marxism." *New Left Review* 104, July–August 1977, p. 25–92.

———. "The Social Basis of Economic Development," in John Roemer (ed.), *Analytical Marxism*. Cambridge University Press, 1986, p. 23–53.

Brenner, Robert, and Christopher Isett. "England's Divergence from China's Yangzi Delta." *Journal of Asian Studies* 61, no. 2, May 2002, p. 609–662.

Breton, Roland. "L'Inde, de l'empire Chola aux premiers Sultans de Delhi," in Georges Duby and Robert Mantran (dir.), *L'Eurasie XI–XIIIe siècles*. Presses Universitaires de France, Paris, 1982, p. 441–463.

Brett, Michael. "The Arab Conquest and the Rise of Islam in North Africa," in J. D. Fage (ed.), *The Cambridge History of Africa. Vol. 2, From c. 500 B.C. to A.D. 1050*. Cambridge University Press, 1978, p. 522–543.

———. "The Armies of Ifriqiya, 1052–1160." *Cahiers de Tunisie* 48, no. 170, 1995, p. 107–125.

————. "The City-State in Medieval Ifriqiya." *Cahiers de Tunisie* 34, 1986, p. 69–94.

————. "Ifriqiya as a Market for Saharan Trade from the Tenth to the Twelfth Century." *Journal of African History* 10, 1969, p. 347–364.

Brett, Michael, and Elizabeth Fentress. *The Berbers.* Blackwell, Oxford, 2002.

Bridbury, A. R. *England and the Salt Trade in the Later Middle Ages.* Greenwood Press, Westport, CT, 1973 edition.

Britnell, R. H. "Commerce and Capitalism in Late Medieval England," *Journal of Historical Sociology* 6, no. 4, Dec. 1993b, p. 359–376.

————. *The Commercialisation of English Society, 1000–1500.* Cambridge University Press, 1993a.

————. "Commercialisation and Economic Development in England, 1000–1300," in R. H. Britnell and B. M. S. Campbell (eds.), *A Commercialising Economy.* Manchester University Press, 1995.

————. "The English Economy and the Government, 1450–1550," in John L. Watts (ed.), *The End of the Middle Ages?* Sutton Publishing, Phoenix Mill, UK, 1998, p. 89–116.

————. "The Towns of England and Northern Italy in the Early 14th Century." *Economic History Review* 44, no. 1, February 1991, p. 21–35.

————. "Specialization of Work in England, 1100–1300," *Economic History Review* 54, no. 1, 2001, p. 1–16.

Britnell, R. H., and B. M. S. Campbell, eds. *A Commercialising Economy. England 1086 to circa 1300.* Manchester University Press, 1995.

Brooks, George. *Landlords and Strangers. Ecology, Society and Trade in Western Africa, 1000–1630.* Westview Press, Boulder, CO, 1993.

Brose, Michael. "Central Asians in Mongol China." *Medieval History Journal* 5, no. 2, Dec. 2002, p. 267–289.

Brucker, Gene. *Florence. The Golden Age 1138–1737.* University of California Press, Berkeley, 1998.

————. "The Florentine Popolo Minuto and its Political Role, 1340–1450," in Lauro Martines (ed.), *Violence and Civil Disorder in Italian Cities.* University of California Press, Berkeley, 1972, p. 155–183.

Brunschvig, Robert. *La berbérie orientale sous les Hafsides.* Vol. 2. Librairie d'Amérique et d'Orient, Paris, 1947.

Bruwier, Marinette. "La bourgeoisie fouraine en Hainaut au Moyen Âge." *Revue Belge de Philologie et d'Histoire* 2, no. 33, 1955, p. 900–920.

————. "Études sur le réseau urbain en Hainaut de 1350 à 1850." Actes du 15e Colloque International à Spa le 4–6 Sept. 1990, "Le Réseau urbain en Belgique dans une perspective historique (1350–1850)." Bruxelles, Crédit Communal, no. 86, 1992, p. 251–316.

Budak, Neven. "Elites cittadine in Dalmazia nel tre-e quattrocento," in Michele Ghezzo (red.), "Cittá e sistema Adriatico alla fine del medioevo." Atti e memorie della societá dalmata di storia patria 26, UNIPRESS, Padova, Dec. 1997, p. 161–180.

Buell, Paul. "Early Mongol Expansion in Western Siberia and Turkestan." *Central Asiatic Journal* 36, no. 1–2, 1992, p. 1–32.

Bugge, Henriette. "Silk to Japan." *Itinerario* 13, no. 2, 1989, p. 25–44.

Bullard, Melissa. "Grain Supply and Urban Unrest in Renaissance Rome" in P. Ramsey (ed.) *Rome in the Renaissance.* Center for Medieval and Early Renaissance Studies, Binghamton, New York, 1982, p. 279–292.

Bulliet, Richard. *The Patricians of Nishapur.* Cambridge, 1972.

Bulst, Neithard. "Les officiers royaux en France dans la deuxième moitié du XVe siècle" in Jean-Philippe Genet and Günther Lottes (eds.), *L'État moderne et les élites.* Publications de la Sorbonne, Paris, 1996, p. 111–121.

Burman, Edward. *The World before Columbus, 1100–1492.* W. H. Allen, London, 1989.

Burns, Ignatius R. "The Catalan Company and the European Powers, 1305–1311." *Speculum* 29, no. 4, Oct. 1954, p. 751–771.

Byres, T. J. *Capitalism from Above and Capitalism from Below.* St. Martin's Press, New York, 1996.

Byres, Terence. "Political Economy, the Agrarian Question and the Comparative Method." *Journal of Peasant Studies* 32, no. 4, July 1995, p. 561–580.

Cahen, Claude. "L'alun avant Phocée." *Revue d'Histoire Économique et Sociale* 41, 1963, p. 433–447.

———. "Economy, Society, Institutions," in P. M. Holt, Ann Lambton, and Bernard Lewis (eds.), *The Cambridge History of Islam.* Vol 2B, *Islamic Society and Civilization.* Cambridge University Press, 1980, p. 511–538.

———. *Les peoples musulmans dans l'histoire médiévale.* Institut Français de Damas, 1977.

———. *Orient et Occident au temps des Croisades.* Éditions Aubier Montaigne, Paris, 1983.

———. "Quelques Mots sur le Déclin Commercial du Monde Musulman à la Fin du Moyen Âge," in M. A. Cook, *Studies in the Economic History of the Middle East.* Oxford University Press, London, 1970, p. 31–36.

Caille, Jacqueline. "Urban Expansion in the Region of Languedoc from the 11th to the 14th Century," in Kathryn Reyerson and John Drendel (eds.), *Urban and Rural Communities in Medieval France.* Brill, Boston, 1998, p. 51–72.

Campbell, B. M. S. "Ecology versus Economics in Late Thirteenth- and Early Fourteenth-Century English Agriculture," in Del Sweeney (ed.), *Agriculture in the Middle Ages.* University of Pennsylvania Press, Philadelphia, 1995c, p. 76–108.

———. "Measuring the Commercialisation of Seigneurial Agriculture *circa* 1300," in R. H. Britnell and B.M.S. Campell (eds.), *A Commercialising Economy. England 1086 to circa 1300.* Manchester University Press, 1995, p. 132–193.

———. "Progressiveness and Backwardness in 13th and Early 14th Century English Agriculture," in J. M. Duvosquel and E. Thoen (eds.), *Peasants and Townsmen in Medieval Europe.* Snoeck-Ducaju, Gent, 1995b, p. 541–560.

Cancellieri, Jean. "Corses et Génois: éléments pour une phénoménologie de la colonisation dans la Méditerranée médiévale," in Michel Balard (dir.), *État et colonisation au Moyen Âge et à la Renaissance.* La Manufacture, Lyon, 1989, p. 35–53.

Cantor, N. F. *The Meaning of the Middle Ages.* Allyn and Bacon, Boston, 1973.

Cardon, Dominique. *La draperie au Moyen Âge. Essor d'une grande industrie européenne.* CNRS Éditions, Paris, 1999.

Cardwell, Donald. *The Fontana History of Technology.* Fontana Press, London, 1994.

Carpenter, Christine. "Town and Country: The Stratford Guild and Political Networks of 15th-Century Warwickshire," in Robert Bearman (ed.), *The History of an English Borough: Stratford-upon-Avon 1196–1996.* Sutton Publishing, Cornwall, 1997, p. 62–79.

Carrère, Claude. "La draperie en Catalogne et en Aragon au XVe siècle," in Marco Spallanzani (ed.), "Produzione, commercio e consumo dei panni di lana nei sec. XII-XVIII." Atti della seconda settimana di studio (10–16 aprile 1970). Istituto Internazionale di Storia Economica "F. Datini," L Olschki Editore, Firenze, 1976, p. 475–509.

Cartier, Michel. "L'Asie Orientale face à la conquête mongole," in Georges Duby and Robert Mantran (dirs.), *L'Eurasie XI–XIIIe siècles.* Presses Universitaires de France, Paris, 1982, p. 503–517.

Carus-Wilson, Eleonora. "The Industrial Revolution of the Thirteenth Century" *Economic History Review* 11, no. 1, 1941, p. 41–60.

————. "The Overseas Trade of Late Medieval Coventry," in *Économies et Sociétés au Moyen Âge*. Publications de la Sorbonne, Série "Études," Paris, 1973, 371–381.

————. "The Woollen Industy," in M. Postan and E. Rich, *The Cambridge Economic History of Europe*. Cambridge University Press, 1952, 2:355–428.

Cazel, Fred A. "Royal Taxation in 13th Century England," in 'L'Impôt dans le cadre de la ville et de l'état." Actes du Colloque International à Spa, Sept. 6–9, 1964. Pro Civitate Collection Histoire, No. 13, Bruxelles, 1966, p. 99–117.

Chakrabarty, Dipesh. *Provincializing Europe*. Princeton University Press, 2002.

Chakravarti, Ranabir. "Coastal Trade and Voyages in Konkan." *Indian Economic and Social History Review* 35, no. 2, 1998, p. 97–123.

————. "An Enchanting Seascape." *Studies in History* 20, no. 2, Dec. 2004, p. 305–315.

————. "Nakhudas and Nauvittakas: Ship-Owning Merchants in the West Coast of India (1000–1500)." *Journal of the Economic and Social History of the Orient* 43, no. 1, Feb. 2000, p. 34–64.

Chakravarti, Ranabir. "Overseas Transportation and Shipping of Horses in Medieval India," in K. S. Matkew (ed.), *Indian Ocean and Cultural Interaction (A.D. 1400–1800)*. Pondicherry University, 1996, p. 149–160.

Chamberlain, Michael. *Knowledge and Social Practice in Medieval Damascus*. Cambridge University Press, 1994.

Champakalakshmi, R. "State and Economy: South India *circa* A.D. 400–1300," in Thapar Romila (ed.), *Recent Perspectives of Early Indian History*. Popular Prakashan, Bombay, 1995, p. 266–308.

————. *Trade, Ideology and Urbanization. South India 300 B.C. to A.D. 1300*. Oxford University Press, 1996.

————. "Urbanization in South India." *Social Scientist*, Aug.–Sep. 1987.

Champakalakshmi, R. et al. *State and Society in pre-modern South India*. Cosmobooks, Thrissur, 2002.

Chan, Hok-Lam. "The Organization and Utilization of Labor Service under the Jurchen Ch'in Dynasty." *Harvard Journal of Asiatic Studies* 52, no. 2, 1992, p. 613–664.

Chandra, Satish. "Commercial Activities of the Mughal Emperors During the 17th Century," in Satish Chandra (ed.), *Essays in Medieval Indian Economic History*. Munshiram Manoharlal Publishers, New Delhi, 1987, p. 163–169.

————. *Medieval India*. Part I, *Delhi Sultanat: 1206–1526*. Har-Anand Publications, New Delhi, 1997.

Chang, Keui-Sheng. "The Maritime Scene in China at the Dawn of Great European Discoveries." *Journal of the American Oriental Society* 94, 1974, p. 347–359.

Chang, Pin-Tsun. "The First Chinese Diaspora in Southeast Asia in the Fifteenth Century," in Roderich Ptak and Dietmar Rothermund (eds.), *Emporia, Commodities, and Entrepreneurs in Asian Maritime Trade, c. 1400–1750*. Franz Steiner Verlag, Stuttgart, 1991b, p. 13–28.

————. "Smuggling as an Engine of Growth," in "The North Pacific to 1600." Proceedings of the Great Ocean Conferences. Oregon Historical Society, Portland, Oregon, 1991, 1:241–258.

————. "Work Ethics without Capitalism," in K. A. Sprengard and Roderich Ptak (eds.), *Maritime Asia. Profit Maximisation, Ethics and Trade Structure, c. 1300–1800*. Harrasowitz Verlag, Wiesbaden, 1994, p. 61–73.

Chapelot, Odette, and Jean Chapelot. "L'artisanat de la poterie et de la terre cuite architecturale," in M. Mousnier (ed.), *L'artisan au village dans l'Europe médiévale et moderne*. Presses Universitaires du Mirail, Toulouse, 2000, p. 87–147.

Chase-Dunn, Christopher, and Peter Grimes. "World-Systems Analysis." in *Annual Review of Sociology* 21, 1995, p. 387–417.

Chase-Dunn, Christopher, andThomas Hall, eds. *Rise and Demise: Comparing World-Systems*. Westview Press, 1997.

Chattopadhyay, Paresh. "Modernization of Economic Life in Underdeveloped Countries" in A.R. Desai (ed.), *Essays on Modernization of Underdeveloped Societies. Vol. 2* Humanities Press, New York, 1972, p. 184–213.

Chattopadhyaya, B. D. "Confronting Fundamentalisms: The Possibilities of Early Indian History." *Studies in History* 43, no. 1, June 2002, p. 103–120.

———. "Trade and Urban Centers in Early Medieval North India." *Indian Historical Review* 1–2, 1974, p. 203–219.

Chattopadhyaya, Brajadulal. *The Making of Early Medieval India*. Oxford University Press, New Delhi, 1994.

———. "Political Processes and the Structure of Polity in Early Medieval India," in Hermann Kulke (ed.), *The State in India, 1000–1700*. Oxford University Press, New Delhi, 1995, p. 195–232.

———. "State and Economy in North India: Fourth Century to Twelfth Century," in Thapar Romila (ed.), *Recent Perspectives of Early Indian History*. Popular Prakashan, Bombay, 1995b, p. 309–346.

Chaudhuri, K. N. *Asia before Europe*. Cambridge University Press, 1990.

———. "Proto-Industrialization: Structure of Industrial Production in Asia, European Export Trade, and Commodity Production," in René Leboutte (ed.), *Proto-Industrialization. Recent Research and New Perspectives—In Memory of Franklin Mendels*. Librairie Droz, Genève, 1996, p. 107–128.

———. *Trade and Civilization in the Indian Ocean*. Cambridge University Press, 1985.

———. "The World-System East of Longitude 20." *Review* 5, no. 2, Fall 1981, p. 219–245.

Chaunu, Pierre. *L'expansion européenne du XIIIe au XVe siècle*. Presses Universitaires de France, Paris, 1969.

Chédeville, A. *Le mouvement communal: milieu urbain et pouvoir en France du XI au XIIIe siècle*. XVII CISH, I, Section Chronologique, Madrid, 1992, pp. 108–123.

Chen, Xiyu. "The Treasure Ship and Cheng Ho's Expedition to Southeast Asia and the Indian Ocean in the Early Fifteenth Century," in "The North Pacific to 1600." Proceedings of the Great Ocean Conferences. Oregon Historical Society, Portland, Oregon, 1991, 1:215–230.

Cheng, Weiji et al. *History of Textile Technology of Ancient China*. Science Press, New York, 1992.

Cherubini, Giovanni. "The Market in Medieval Italy," in J. Torras et al. *Els Espais del Mercat*. Diputacio de Valencia, 1993, p. 277–288.

———. "The Peasant and Agriculture," in Jacques Le Goff (ed.), *The Medieval World*. Collins & Brown, London, 1990, p. 113–137.

———. "La proprieta fondiaria di un mercante toscano del Trecento," in *Signori, Contadini, Borghesi, Ricerche sulla societá italiana del basso medioevo*. La Nuova Italia, Firenze, 1974, p. 313–392.

Cheynet, Jean-Claude. *Pouvoir et contestations à Byzance (963–1204)*. Publications de la Sorbonne, Paris, 1996.

Cheyney, Edward. *The Dawn of a New Era, 1250–1453*. Harper, New York, 1962.

Chibber, Vivek. "Breaching the Nadu." *Journal of Peasant Studies* 26, no. 1, Oct. 1998, p. 1–42.

Childs, Wendy. *Anglo-Castilian Trade in the Later Middle Ages*. Manchester University Press, 1978.

Chirot, Daniel. *How Societies Change*. Pine Forge Press, London, 1994.

———. "The Rise of the West." *American Sociological Review* 50, no. 2, April 1985, p. 181–195.

Chittick, Neville. "East African Trade with the Orient," in D. S. Richards (ed.), *Islam and the Trade of Asia*. Bruno Cassirer Oxford/University of Pennsylvania Press, 1970, p. 97–104.

Chittolini, Giorgio. "La cité, le territoire, l'impôt" in Denis Menjot et al., *L'impôt dans les villes de l'Occident méditerrranéen XIIIe–XIVe siècle*. Ministère de l'Économie, des Finances et de l'Industrie, Paris, 2005, p. 305–329.

———. "Fiscalité d'état et prerogatives urbaines dans le duché de Milan," in Ph. Contamine et al., *L'impôt au Moyen Âge*. Vol. 1, *Le droit d'imposer*. Ministère de l'Économie, des Finances et de l'Industrie, Paris, 2002, p. 147–176.

Chorley, Patrick. "The Cloth Exports of Flanders and Northern France during the Thirteenth Century." *Economic History Review* 40, 1987, p. 349–379.

Chou, Chin-shêng. "An Economic History of China." Western Washington State College Program in East Asian Studies, Occasional Paper No. 7, Bellingham, Washington, 1974.

Christie, Jan Wisseman. "Javanese Markets and the Asia Sea Trade Boom." *Journal of the Economic and Social History of the Orient* 41, no. 3, 1998, p. 344–381.

———. "Negara, Mandala, and Despotic State," in David Marr and A. C. Milner (eds.), *Southeast Asia in the 9th to 14th Centuries*. Institute of Southeast Asian Studies, Singapore, 1986, p. 65–93.

Chun, Hae-Jong. "Sino-Korean Tributary Relations in the Ch'ing Period." in John K. Fairbank (ed.), *The Chinese World Order*. Harvard University Press, Cambridge, 1968, p. 90–111.

Church, Sally. "Zheng He: An Investigation into the Plausibility of 450-ft Treasure Ships." *Monumenta Serica* 53, 2005, p. 1–43.

Cipolla, Carlo M. *Before the Industrial Revolution*. 3rd ed. Norton, New York, 1994.

———. *Clocks and Culture*. Norton, New York, 1977.

Cissoko, S. M. "The Songhay from the 12th to the 16th Century," in D.T. Niane (ed.), *General History of Africa*. UNESCO, Berkeley, 1984, 4:187–210.

Cistozvonov, A. N. "Sulla questione dell'evoluzione economica e commerciale dell'Italia e dell'Olanda durante la depressione economica europea del XIV e XV secolo," in *Studia in Memoria di Federigo Melis*. Giannini Editore, Naples, 1978, 2:581–597.

Clark, Gregory. "The Cost of Capital and Medieval Agricultural Technique." *Explorations in Economic History* 25, no. 3, July 1988, p. 265–294.

———. "Labour Productivity in English Agriculture, 1300–1860," in Bruce M. Campbell and Mark Overton (eds.), *Land, Labour and Livestock: Historical Studies in European Agricultural Productivity*. Manchester University Press, 1991, p. 211–235.

Clark, Hugh. "Muslims and Hindus in the Culture and Morphology of Quanzhou from the Tenth to the Thirteenth Century." *Journal of World History* 6, no. 1, Spring 1995, p. 49–74.

Claudot-Hawad, Hélène. "Sahara et nomadisme." *Revue des Mondes Musulmans et de la Méditerranée* 2, nos. 111–112, Mars 2006, p. 221–244.

Coedès, George. "Some Problems in the Ancient History of the Hinduized States of South-East Asia." *Journal of Southeast Asian History* 5, no. 2, Sept. 1964, p. 1–14.

Cohen, Ronald. "Paradise Regained," in Henri Claessen and Pieter van de Velde (eds.), *Early State Economics*. Transaction Publishers, London, 1991, p. 109–129.

Cohn, Samuel. "Demography and the Politics of Fiscality," in William Connell and Andrea Zorzi (eds.), *Florentine Tuscany. Structures and Practices of Power*. Cambridge University Press, 2000, p. 183–206.

———. *Popular protest in late medieval Europe*. Palgrave, New York, 2004.

Coleman, D. C. "Proto-Industrialization: A Concept Too Many." *Economic History Review* 36, no. 3, 1981, p. 435–448.

Collins, James. "State Building in Early-Modern Europe." *Modern Asian Studies* 31, no. 3, 1997, p. 603–633.

Collins, Randall. "The Geopolitical and Economic World-Systems of Kinship-Based and Agrarian Coercive Societies." *Review* 15, no. 3, p. 373–388.

Colombijn, Freek. "The Volatile State in Southeast Asia." *Journal of Asian Studies* 62, no. 2, May 2003, p. 497–529.

Comninel, George. "English Feudalism and the Origins of Capitalism." *Journal of Peasant Studies* 27, no. 4, July 2000, p. 1–53.

Constable, G. "Was There a Medieval Middle Class?," in S. K. Cohn and S. A. Epstein (eds.), *Portraits of Medieval and Renaissance Living.* University of Michigan Press, 1996, p. 301–323.

Constable, O. A. *Trade and Traders in Muslim Spain.* Cambridge University Press, 1994.

Contamine, Philippe et al. *L'économie médiévale.* Arman Colin, Paris, 1993.

Cook, Michael. "Islam: A Comment," in J. Baechler, J. Hall, and M. Mann (eds.), *Europe and the Rise of Capitalism.* Basil Blackwell, New York, 1988, p. 131–135.

Coquery, Catherine. *La découverte de l'Afrique.* René Juliard, Mesnil-sur-l'Estrée, 1965.

Coquery-Vidrovitch, Catherine. "Analyse historique et concept de mode de production dans les sociétés pré-capitalistes," in René Gallissot (dir.), "Structures et cultures précapitalistes." éditions Anthropos, Paris, 1981, p. 473–483.

———. *Histoire des villes d'Afrique noire.* Albin Michel, Paris, 1993.

———. "Research on an African Mode of Production," in David Seddon (ed.), *Relations of Production.* Frank Cass, London, 1978, p. 261–288.

Cordier, Henri, ed. *Cathay and the Way Thither, Being a Collection of Medieval Notices of China.* Kraus Reprint [of Henry Yule's edition of the Hakluyt Society] Vol. 2, *Odoric of Poderone.* Nendeln, Liechtenstein, 1967.

Cowan, C. D. "Continuity and Change in the International History of Maritime South East Asia." *Journal of Southeast Asian History* 9, no. 1, March 1968, p. 1–11.

Craeybeckx, Jan. *Un grand commerce d'importation: les vins de France aux anciens Pays-Bas (XIII–XVIe siècles).* SEVPEN, Paris, 1958.

Crone, Patricia. *Pre-Industrial Societies.* Basil Blackwell, Oxford, 1989.

———. "Tribes and States in the Middle East." *Journal of the Royal Asiatic Society*, 3rd Series, 3, no. 3, Nov. 1993, p. 353–376.

Crosby, Alfred. *The Measure of Reality.* Cambridge University Press, 1997.

Crouzet-Pavan, Elisabeth. "Les Élites urbaines," in "Les Élites urbaines au Moyen Âge. XXIVe Congrès de la S.H.M.E.S (Rome, mai 1996)." Collection de l'école française de Rome, no. 238, Publications de la Sorbonne, Paris, 1997, p. 9–28.

Crush, Jonathan. "Imagining Development," in J. Crush (ed.) *Power of Development.* Routledge, NY, 1995, p. 1–23.

Cuadrada, Coral. "L'emprise de la cité de Barcelone sur les seigneuries féodales de sa contrée (XIIIe–XVe siècles)," in "Les sociétés urbaines en France méridionale et en péninsule Ibérique au Moyen Âge." Actes du Colloque de Pau, 21–23 septembre 1988. Éditions du CNRS, Paris, 1991, p. 279–294.

Cuoq, Joseph. *Histoire de l'islamisation de l'Afrique de l'ouest.* Librairie Orientaliste Paul Geuthner SA, Paris, 1984.

Curtin, Philip. *Cross-Cultural Trade in World History.* Cambridge University Press, 1984.

———. "The External Trade of West Africa to 1800," in J.F.A. Ajayi and Michael Crowder (eds.), *History of West Africa.* Longman, New York, 1985, 1:624–647.

Dahl, Gunnar. *Trade, Trust and Networks. Commercial Culture in Late Medieval Italy.* Nordic Academic Press, Lund, 1998.

Dale, Stephen. *Indian Merchants and Eurasian Trade, 1600–1750.* Cambridge University Press, 1994.

Daoulatli, Abdelaziz. *Tunis sous les Hafsides*. Institut National d'Archeologie et d'Art, Tunis, 1976.

Dardess, John. *Conquerors and Confucians*. Columbia University Press, NY, 1973.

Dars, Jacques. *La Marine Chinoise du Xe siécle au XIVe siécle*. Éditions Économica, Paris, 1992.

Das Gupta, Arun. "The Maritime Trade of Indonesia: 1500–1800," in Ashin Das Gupta and M. N. Pearson (eds.), *India and the Indian Ocean 1500–1800*. Oxford University Press, New Delhi, 1987, p. 240–316.

Dasgupta, Biplab. "Trade in Pre-Colonial Bengal." *Social Scientist* 28, no. 5–6, May–June 2000, p. 47–76.

Datta, Rajat. "Commercialisation, Tribute and the Transition from Late Mughal to Early Colonial in India." *Medieval History Journal* 6, no. 2, Dec. 2003, p. 259–291.

Dauvillier, Jean. "Byzantins d'Asie Centrale et d'Extrème-Orient au Moyen Âge." in *Revue des Études Byzantines* 11, 1953, p. 62–87.

Davidson, Basil. *West Africa before the Colonial Era*. Longman, London, 1998.

Davis, Richard. *Lives of Indian Images*. Princeton University Press, 1997.

———. *Wind against the Mountain*. Harvard University Press, Cambridge, 1996.

Dawson, Raymond. *Imperial China*. Hutchinson & Co, London, 1972.

Day, John. "Colonialisme monétaire en Méditerranée au Moyen Âge," in "Économies Méditerranéennes Équilibres et Intercommunications XIIIe–XIXe siècles." Actes du IIe Colloque International d'Histoire, Athènes, 18–25 septembre 1983. Centre de Recherches Néohelléniques de la Fondation Nationale de la Recherche Scientifique, Athènes, 1985, p. 305–319.

———. "The Great Bullion Famine of the Fifteenth Century." *Past and Present* 79, May 1978, p. 3–54.

———. *The Medieval Market Economy*. Basil Blackwell, Oxford, 1987.

———. *Money and Finance in the Age of Merchant Capitalism*. Blackwell, Oxford, 1999.

———. "Peuplement, cultures et régimes fonciers en Trexenta (Sardaigne)," in Annalisa Guarducci (ed.), "Agricoltura e trasformazione dell'ambiente, sec. XIII–XVIII" Atti della "undicesima settimana di studio" (25–30 aprile 1979), Instituto Internazionale di Storia Economica "F. Datini," Prato, Le Monnier, 1984, p. 683–708.

———. "Le Prétendu Renversement des Rapports Économiques entre l'Orient et l'Occident aux Derniers Siècles du Moyen Âge," in "L'histoire à Nice." Actes du Colloque International (6–9 Nov. 1980). Vol. 2: "Les relations économiques et culturelles entre l'Occident et l'Orient." Université de Nice/Musée d'Archéologie et d'Histoire d'Antibes, 1981, p. 35–46.

———. "Terres, marchés et monnaies en Italie et en Sardaigne du XIème au XVIIIème siècle." *Histoire, Économie et Société* 2, no. 2, 1983, p. 187–203.

Day, W.R. "The Population of Florence before the Black Death." *Journal of Medieval History* 28, no. 2, June 2002, p. 93–129.

De la Roncière, Charles. *Histoire de la découverte de la terre*. Libraire Larousse, Paris, 1938.

———. *Prix et Salaires à Florence au XIVe Siècle*. École française de Rome, Rome, 1982.

De Nave, Francine. "De oudste Antwerpse lijsten van nieuwe poorters." *Handelingen van de Koninklijke Commissie voor Geschiedenis* 139, 1973, p. 67–309.

de Oliveira, Marques A. H. "Late Medieval Lisbon," in Jürgen Schneider (ed.), *Wirtschaftskräfte und Wirtschaftswege V. Festschrift für Hermann Kellenbenz*. Beiträge zur Wirtschaftgeschichte, Band 8 in Kommission bei Klett-Cotta, Stuttgart, 1981, p. 33–45.

De Planhol, Xavier. "The Geographical Setting," in P. M. Holt, Ann Lambton, and Bernard

Lewis (eds.), *The Cambridge History of Islam*. Vol. 2B, *Islamic Society and Civilization*. Cambridge University Press, 1980, p. 443–468.

———. *L'Islam et la mer*. Librairie Académique Perrin, Paris, 2000.

de Roover, Raymond. "The Cambium Maritimum Contract According to the Genoese Notarial Records of the 12th and 13th Centuries," in David Herlihy, Robert Lopez and Vsevolod Slessarev (eds.), *Economy, Society and Government in Medieval Italy*. Kent State University Press, Ohio, 1969, p. 15–33.

———. "Early Banking before 1500 and the Development of Capitalism." *Revue Internationale d'Histoire de la Banque* 4, 1971, p. 1–16.

———. "Money, Banking and Credit in Medieval Bruges," in *The Mediaeval Academy of America* 51, Cambridge, 1948.

De Vliegher, Ruth. "Desertie bij Oostendse-Indiëvaarders in vergelijkend perspectief (18e eeuw)." Master's thesis, Dept. of History, University of Ghent, Belgium, 1999.

De Vries, Jan. "Problems in the Measurement, Description, and Analysis of Historical Urbanization," in A. van der Woude, A. Hayami, and J. De Vries (eds.), *Urbanization in History*. Clarendon Press, Oxford, 1990.

De Vries Jan, and A. van der Woude. *The First Modern Economy*. Cambridge University Press, 1997.

De Wachter, Astrid. "De Kempen in het Wereld-Systeem." Licentiaatsthesis, Dept. of Geography, State University of Ghent, 1996.

Deane, Phyllis. "The Timing of the Transition in Western Europe and its Settlements Overseas," in F. C. Lane (ed.), "Fourth International Conference of Economic History. Bloomington 1968." École Pratique des Hautes Études/Mouton, Paris, 1973, p. 377–386.

Delatouche, Raymond. *La chrétienté médiévale. Un modèle de développement*. Éditions Tequi, Paris, 1989.

Deloche, Jean. "Études sur les fortifications de l'Inde." *Bulletin de l'École Française d'Extrême Orient* 89, 2002, p. 39–106.

Delumeau, Jean-Pierre. "Communes, Consulats et la City-Republic," in C. Laurent, B. Merdrignac, and D. Pichot (red.), *Mondes de l'Ouest et villes du monde*. Presses Universitaires de Rennes, 1998, p. 491–509.

Demel, Walter. "Trade Aspirations and China's Policy of Isolation," in K. A. Sprengard and Roderich Ptak (eds.), *Maritime Asia. Profit Maximisation, Ethics and Trade Structure, c. 1300–1800*. Harrasowitz Verlag, Wiesbaden, 1994, p. 97–113.

Deng, Gang. *Chinese Maritime Activities and Socioeconomic Consequences, c. 2100 B.C.– A.D. 1900*. Greenwood, New York, 1997.

———. "A Critical Survey of Recent Research in Chinese Economic History." *Economic History Review* 53, no. 1, 2000, p. 1–28.

———. "The Foreign Staple Trade of China in the Pre-Modern Era." *International History Review* 19, no. 2, May 1997b, p. 253–285.

———. *The Premodern Chinese Economy. Structural Equilibrium and Capitalist Sterility*. Routledge, London, 1999.

Dennis, Giorgio. "Problemi storici concernenti I rapporti tra Venezia, I suoi domini diretti e le signorie feudali nelle isole Greche," in Agostino Pertusi (ed.), *Venezia e il Levante fino al secolo XV*. L. Olschki Editore, Firenze, 1973, 1:219–235.

Denoix, Sylvie. "Autorités urbaines et gestion de la ville," in Jean-Claude Garcin (dir.), *Grandes villes méditerranéens du monde musulman médiéval*. École Française de Rome, 2000, p. 285–295.

Derville, Alain. "Les draperies flamandes et artésiennes vers 1250–1350." *Revue du Nord* 215, 1972, p. 353–370.

————. "Douze études d'histoire rurale." *Revue Du Nord* Hors Serie, no. 11, Université Charles-de-Gaulle, Lille III, 1996.

————. *L'économie Française au Moyen Âge.* Ed. Ophrys, Paris, 1995.

————. "Les élites urbaines en Flandre et en Artois," in "Les Élites urbaines au Moyen Âge." Collection de l'école française de Rome, no. 238, Publications de la Sorbonne, Paris, 1997, p. 119–135.

————. "Le grenier des Pays Bas médiévaux." *Revue du Nord* 69, no. 273, avril–juin 1987, p. 267–280.

————. "L'héritage des draperies médiévales." *Revue du Nord* 69, no. 275, Oct.–Dec. 1987b, p. 715–724.

————. "Naissance du capitalisme," in F. Gasparri (red.), *Le XIIe siècle. Mutations et renouveau en France dans la première moitié du XIIe siècle.* Éd. Le Leopold d'Or, Paris, 1994, p. 33–60.

————. *Villes de Flandre et d'Artois (900–1500).* Presses Universitaires de Septentrion, Arras, 2002.

Desai, Sar, D. R. "The Portuguese Administration in Malacca, 1511–1641." *Journal of Southeast Asian History* 10, no. 3, Dec. 1969, p. 501–512.

Désire-Vuillemin, Geneviève. *Histoire de la Mauritanie.* Éditions Karthala, Paris, 1997.

Despy, G., and A. Verhulst, eds. "La fortune historiographique des thèses d'Henri Pirenne." *Archives et Bibliothèques de Belgique,* numéro spécial, 28, Bruxelles, 1986.

D'Eszlary, Charles. "Caractères et rôle de la bourgeoisie en Hongrie." *Revue d'Histoire Économique et Sociale* 41, 1963, p. 503–523.

Devisse, Jean. "Le Continent Africain," in Jean Favier (dir.) *XIVe et XVe siècles: crises et genèses.* Presses Universitaires de France, Paris, 1996, p. 859–903.

————. "Routes de commerce et échanges en Afrique occidentale en relations avec la Méditerranée." *Revue d'Histoire Économique et Sociale* 50, 1972, p. 42–73, 357–397.

————. "Trade and Trade Routes in West Africa," in M. El Fasi (ed.), *General History of Africa.* UNESCO/University of California Press, Berkeley, 1988, 3:367–435

————. "Une enquête à développer: le problème de la propriété des mines en Afrique de l'Ouest du VIIIe au XVIe siècle." *Bulletin de l'Institut Historique Belge de Rome* 44, 1974, p. 201–219.

Devisse, Jean, and Shuhi Labib. "Africa in Inter-continental Relations," in D. T. Niane (ed.), *General History of Africa.* UNESCO, Berkeley, 1984, 4:635–672.

Deyell, John. *Living without Silver.* Oxford University Press, 1990.

D'Haenens, Albert. "Manifestations d'une mutation," in Georges Duby and Robert Mantran (dirs.), *L'Eurasie XI–XIIIe siècles.* Presses Universitaires de France, Paris, 1982, p. 11–67.

Di Cosmo, Nicola. "Mongols and Merchants on the Black Sea Frontier in the 13th and 14th Centuries," in Amitai Reuven and Michael Baran (eds.), *Mongols, Turks and Others.* Brill, Boston, 2005.

————. "New Directions in Inner Asian History." *Journal of the Economic and Social History of the Orient* 42, no. 2, May 1992b, p. 247–263.

————. "State Formation and Periodization in Inner Asian History." *Journal of World History* 10, no. 1, 1999, p. 1–40.

————. *Ancient China and Its Enemies.* Cambridge University Press, 2002.

Di Meglio, Rita. "Arab Trade with Indonesia and the Malay Peninsula from the 8th to the 16th Century," in D. S. Richards (ed.), *Islam and the Trade of Asia.* Oxford/University of Pennsylvania Press, 1970, p. 105–135.

Diffie, Bailey, and George Winius. *Foundations of the Portuguese Empire, 1415–1580.* University of Minnesota Press, Minneapolis, 1977.

Digby, Simon. "Beyond the Ocean." *Studies in History* 15, no. 2, Dec. 1999, p. 247–259.

———. "The Maritime Trade of India," in Tapan Raychaudhuri and Irfan Habib (eds.), *The Cambridge Economic History of India*. Cambridge University Press, 1982, 1:125–159.

Diop, Brahim. "Le Noir et son pays dans l'imaginaire arabe médiéval." *Sociétés Africaines* [Paris] 11, Sept. 1998, p. 57–79.

Dixin, Xu, and Wu Chengming, eds. *Chinese Capitalism, 1522–1840*. St. Martin's Press, New York, 2000.

Dobb, Maurice. "A Reply," in Rodney H. Hilton (ed.), *The Transition from Feudalism to Capitalism*. NLB, London, 1976, p. 57–67.

———. *Studies in the Development of Capitalism*. International Publishers, New York, 1947.

Dohrn-van Rossum, Gerhard. *History of the Hour*. University of Chicago Press, 1996.

Dollinger, Philippe. "Les Villes Allemandes au Moyen Âge," in *La Ville*. Part 2, *Institutions Économiques et Sociales*. Recueils de la Société Jean Bodin pour l'Histoire Comparative des Institutions. Éditions de la Librairie Encyclopédique, Bruxelles, 1955, 7:371–401.

Doumerc, Bernard. *Venise et l'émirat hafside de Tunis (1231–1535)*. L'Harmattan, Paris, 1999.

Dowd, D. F. "The Economic Expansion of Lombardy 1300–1500." *Journal of Economic History*, 1961, p. 143–160.

Dramani-Issifou, Zakari. *L'Afrique Noire dans les relations internationales au XVIe siècle*. Ed. Karthala, Paris, 1982.

Drège, Jean-Pierre. "Des effets de l'imprimerie en Chine sous la dynastie des Song." *Journal Asiatique* 272, no. 2, 1994, p. 391–408.

Dreyer, Edward. *Early Ming China*. Stanford University Press, Stanford, 1982.

D' Souza, Rohan. "Crisis Before the Fall: Some Speculations on the Decline of the Ottomans, Safavids and Mughals." *Social Scientist* 30, nos. 9/10, Sept.–Oct. 2002, p. 3–30.

Du Boulay, F. R. *An Age of Ambition*. Nelson, London, 1970.

Ducatez, Guy. "Aden aux XIIe et XIIIe siècles selon Ibn Al-Mugawir." *Annales Islamologiques* 38, no. 1, 2004, p. 159–200.

Duchesne, Ricardo. "Asia First?" *Journal of the Historical Society* 6, no. 1, March 2006, p. 69–91.

———. "Barry Hindess and Paul Hirst: The Origins of Capitalism and the Origins of Post-Marxism." *Current Perspectives in Social Theory* 20, 2000, p. 153–186.

———. "Between Sinocentrim and Eurocentrism." *Science and Society* 65, no. 4, 2002, p. 428–463.

———. "On the Rise of the West." *Review of Radical Political Economics* 36, no. 1, Winter 2004, p. 52–81.

———. "Remarx—On the Origins of Capitalism." *Rethinking Marxism* 14, no. 3, Fall 2002b, p. 129–137.

———. "Reply to Goldstone and Wong." *Science and Society* 67, no. 2, Summer 2003, p. 195–205.

Dufourcq, Charles-Emmanuel. *L'espagne catalane et le Maghreb aux XIIIe et XIVe siècles*. Presses Universitaires de France, Paris, 1966.

———. *L'Ibérie chrétienne et le Maghreb XIIe–XVe siècles*. Variorum Press, Norfolk, 1990.

———. "Prix et niveaux de vie dans les pays catalans et maghrebins à la fin du XIIIe et au début du XIVe siècles." *Le Moyen Âge* 71, nos. 3/4, 1965, p. 475–520.

———. "La question de Ceuta au XIIIe siècle." *Hespéris* 42, 1955, p. 67–123.

Dumolyn, Jan. "Les conseillers flamands au XVe siècle," in Robert Stein (ed.), *Powerbrokers in the late Middle Ages*. Brepols, Turnhout, 2001, p. 67–85.

————. "The Legal Repression of Revolts in Late Medieval Flanders." *Legal History Review* 68, 2000, p. 479–521.

————. "Nobles, Paticians and Officers." *Journal of Social History* Vol. 40, no. 2, 2006, p. 431–452.

————. "Population et structures professionnelles à Bruges aux XIVe et XVe siècles." *Revue du Nord* 81, no. 329, Janvier–Mars 1999, p. 43–64.

Dumolyn, Jan, and Jelle Haemers. "Patterns of Urban Rebellion in Medieval Flanders." *Journal of Medieval History* 31, no. 4, Dec. 2005, p. 369–393.

Dumolyn, Jan, and Filip van Tricht. "Adel en nobiliteringsprocessen in het laatmiddeleeuwse Vlaanderen." *Bijdragen en Mededelingen betreffende de Geschiedenis der Nederlanden* 115, no. 2, 2000, p. 197–222.

Dumont, Louis. *Homo hierarchicus.* Paris, Gallimard, 1966.

Dunaway, Wilma. *The First American Frontier.* University of North Carolina Press, 1996b.

————. "Incorporation as an Interactive Process." *Sociological Inquiry* 66, no. 4, Nov. 1996, p. 455–470.

Duplessis, Robert. *Transitions to Capitalism in Early Modern Europe.* Cambridge University Press, 1997.

DuPlessis, Robert, and Martha Howell. "Reconsidering the Early Modern Urban Economy." *Past and Present* 94, Feb. 1982, p. 49–84.

Dyer, Christopher. "Medieval Stratford," in Robert Bearman (ed.), *The History of an English Borough.* Sutton Publishing, Cornwall, 1997, p. 43–61.

————. *Standards of Living in the Later Middle Ages. Social Change in England c. 1200–1520.* Cambridge University Press, 1989.

————. "Were There Any Capitalists in 15th Century England?" in Jennifer Kermode (ed.), *Enterprise and Individuals in 15th Century England.* Alan Sutton, Wolfeboro Falls, NH, 1991, p. 1–24.

Eberhard, Wolfram. *Conquerors and Rulers.* 2nd ed. Brill, Leiden, 1965.

————. *A History of China.* University of California Press, Berkeley, 1969.

Ebrey, Patricia. *The Cambridge Illustrated History of China.* Cambridge University Press, 1996.

Edwards, Richard, Michael Reich, and Thomas Weisskopf, eds. *The Capitalist System.* Prentice Hall, NJ, 1972.

Eisenstadt, S. N. "Breakdowns of Modernization." *Economic Development and Cultural Change* 12, no. 4, July 1964.

Eisenstadt, S. N., Michel Abitbol, and Noami Chazan. "Les origines de l'État." *Annales ESC* 38, no. 6, Dec. 1983, p. 1232–1255.

Elman, Benjamin. "Political, Social and Cultural Reproduction via Civil Service Examinations in Late Imperial China." *Journal of Asian Studies* 50, no. 1, Feb. 1991, p. 7–28.

Elvin, Mark. *Another History. Essays on China from a European Perspective.* University of Sydney East Asian Series, Vol. 10, Wild Peony Pty Ltd, Broadway, NSW, 1996.

————. "China as a Counterfactual," in J. Baechler, J. Hall, and M. Mann (eds.), *Europe and the Rise of Capitalism.* Basil Blackwell, New York, 1988, p. 101–112.

————. "Chinese Cities since the Sung Dynasty," in Ph. Abrams and E. Wrigley (eds.), *Towns in Societies.* Cambridge University Press, 1978, p. 79–89.

————. *The Pattern of the Chinese Past.* Stanford University Press, 1973.

————. "Why China Failed to Create an Endogenous Industrial Capitalism." *Theory and Society* 13, no. 3, May 1984, p. 379–391.

Endicott-West, Elizabeth. "Merchant Associations in Yüan China." *Asia Major*, 3rd series, 2, no. 2, 1989, p. 127–154.

————. "Review of Janet Abu-Lughod's before European Hegemony." *Modern Asian Studies* 49, no. 2, May 1990.

Engels, Friedrich. *The Origin of the Family, Private Property, and the State.* International Publishers, New York, 1972.

Ennahid, Said. "Political Economy and Settlement Systems of Medieval Northern Morocco: An Archaeological-Historical Approach." Master's thesis, Arizona State University, May 2001.

Epstein, S. R. "Cities, Regions and the Late Medieval Crisis." *Past and Present* 130, Feb. 1991b, p. 3–50.

———. "Craft guilds, Apprenticeships and Technological Change in Pre-industrial Europe." *Journal of Economic History* 58, no. 3, 1998, p. 684–713.

———. *Freedom and Growth.* Routledge, London, 2000b.

———. "Freedom and Growth" in Eileen Barker (ed.), *On Freedom.* London School of Economics Books, London, 1997, p. 165–181.

———. "Market Structures," in William Connell and Andrea Zorzi (eds.), *Florentine Tuscany.* Cambridge University Press, 2000, p. 90–121.

———. "The Textile Industry and the Foreign Cloth Trade in Late Medieval Sicily." *Journal of Medieval History* 15, 1989, p. 141–183.

———. "Town and Country: Economy and Institutions in Late Medieval Italy." *Economic History Review* 46, no. 3, Aug. 1993, p. 453–477.

———. *An Island for Itself.* Cambridge University Press, 1992.

Epstein, Steven A. "Labour in Thirteenth-Century Genoa," in I. Malkin and R. Hohlfelder (eds.), *Mediterranean Cities: Historical Perspectives.* Frank Cass, London, 1988b, p. 114–140.

———. "Business Cycles and the Sense of Time in Medieval Genoa." *Business History Review* 62, 1988, p. 238–260.

———. *Wage Labor and Guilds in Medieval Europe.* University of North Carolina Press, 1991.

Erner, Guillaume. "Christian economic morality" *International Social Science Journal*, vol. 57, no. 3, 2005, p. 469–479.

Espinas, Georges. *Les Origines du Capitalisme: Sire Jean Boinebroke, patricien et drapier douaisien.* Librairie Emile Raoust, Lille, 1933 (4 vols.).

Essid, Yassine. *A Critique of the Origins of Islamic Economic Thought.* Brill, Leiden, 1995.

Ewan, Elizabeth. *Townlife in Fourteenth-Century Scotland.* Edinburgh University Press, 1990.

Face, Richard. "Symon de Gualterio," in David Herlihy, Robert Lopez, and Vsevolod Slessarev (eds.), *Economy, Society and Government in Medieval Italy.* Kent State University Press, Ohio, 1969, p. 75–94.

Fairbank, John. *China: A New History.* Belknap, Cambridge, 1992.

———. "A Preliminary Framework," in John K. Fairbank (ed.), *The Chinese World Order.* Harvard University Press, Cambridge, 1968, p. 1–19.

———. *Trade and Diplomacy on the Chinese Coast.* Harvard University Press, 1953.

———. *The United States and China.* Harvard University Press, 1965.

Fairbank, John, and Edwin Craig Reischauer. *East Asia Tradition and Transformation.* Houghton Mifflin Company, Boston, 1973.

Fall, Yoro. *L'Afrique à la naissance de la cartographie moderne (14e–15e siècles).* Centre de Recherches Africaines and éditions Karthala, Paris, 1982.

Farmer, Edward et al. *Comparative History of Civilizations in Asia.* Addison-Wesley, London, 1977.

Farooqi, M. A. *The Economic Policy of the Sultans of Delhi.* Konark Publishers, New Delhi, 1991.

Farr, James. "On the Shop Floor: Guilds, Artisans and the European Market Economy, 1350–1750," *Journal of Early Modern History* 1, no. 1, 1997, p. 24–54.

Faruqui, Munis. "The Forgotten Prince." *Journal of Economic and Social History of the Orient* 48, no. 4, 2005, p. 487–523.

Fasoli, Gina. "Gouvernants et Gouvernés dans les Communes Italiennes du XIe au XIIIe Siècle," in *Gouvernés et Gouvernants*. Part 4, *Bas Moyen Âge et Temps Modernes (II)*. Recueils de la Société Jean Bodin pour l'Histoire Comparative des Institutions 25, Éditions de la Librairie Encyclopédique, Bruxelles, 1965, p. 47–86.

Favier, Jean. "Économies et Sociétés," in Jean Favier (dir.), *XIVe et XVe Siècles: Crises et Genèses*. Presses Universitaires de France, Série "peuple et civilisations," Paris, 1996, p. 127–274.

———. *Gold and Spices: The Rise of Commerce in the Middle Ages*. Holmes & Meier, New York, 1998.

Favreau, Robert. "Métiers du textile a Bressuire au Moyen Âge," in "Recherches sur l'économie de la France médiévale." Actes du 112e congrès national des sociétés savantes. Éditions CTHS, Paris, 1989, p. 157–177.

Fedalto, Giorgio. "La comunità greca a Venezia alla fine del medioevo," in Michele Ghezzo (red.), "Cittá e sistema Adriatico alla fine del medioevo." Atti e memorie della societá dalmata di storia patria 26, UNIPress, Padova, Dec. 1997, p. 201–219.

Ferguson, W. K. *Europe in Transition 1300–1520*. Houghton Mifflin, Boston, 1962.

Ferhat, Halima. "Fès," in Jean-Claude Garcin (dir.), *Grandes Villes Méditerranéens du Monde Musulman Médiéval*. École Francaise de Rome, 2000, p. 215–233.

Fernandes, Leonor. "The City of Cairo and its Food Supplies during the Mamluk Period," in Brigitte Marin and Catherine Virlouvet (eds.), *Nourrir les cités de Méditerranée: Antiquité–Temps Modernes*. Maisonneuve & Larose, Paris, 2003, p. 519–538.

Fernández-Armesto, Felipe. *Before Columbus*. University of Pennsylvania Press, Philadelphia, 1987.

Ferrand, Gabriel. *Relations de voyages et textes géographiques Arabes, Persans et Turcs relatifs à l'Extrême-Orient du VIIIe au XVIIIe siècles*. Ernest Leroux éditeur, Paris, 1913, 2 vols.

Feuerwerker, Albert. "Presidential Address." *Journal of Asian Studies* 51, no. 4, Nov. 1992, p. 757–769.

———. "The State and the Economy in Late Imperial China." *Theory and Society* 13, no. 3, May 1984, p. 297–326.

Filesi, Teobaldo. *China and Africa in the Middle Ages*. Frank Cass, London, 1972.

Findlay, Ronald. "The Roots of Divergence: Western Economic History in Comparative Perspective." *American Economic Review* 82, no. 2, May 1992, p. 158–161.

Finlay, Robert. "The Treasure-Ships of Zheng He." *Terrae Incognitae* 23, 1991, p. 1–12.

Fischel, W. J. "The Spice Trade in Mamluk Egypt." *Journal of the Economic and Social History of the Orient* 1, 1958, p. 157–174.

Fischer, David. *The Great Wave*. Oxford University Press, 1996.

Fisher, Humphrey J. "The Eastern Maghrib and the Central Sudan," in Roland Oliver (ed.), *The Cambridge History of Africa*. Vol. 3, *From c. 1050 to c. 1600*. Cambridge University Press, Cambridge, 1977, p. 232–330.

———. "He Swalloweth the Ground with Fierceness and Rage." *Journal of African History* 13, no. 3, 1972, p. 369–388.

Fitzpatrick, John. "The Middle Kingdom, the Middle Sea, and the Geographical Pivot of History." in *Review* 15, no. 3, p. 477–521.

Fletcher, Joseph. "The Mongols: Ecological and Social Perspectives." *Harvard Journal of Asiatic Studies* 46, no. 1, June 1986, p. 11–50.

Flores, Jorge. "Les Portugais et le Mer de Ceylan au début du XVIe siècle," in Jean Aubin et al., *Nouvelles Orientations de la recherche sur l'histoire de l'Asie portugaise*. Centre Culturel Calouste Gulbenkian, Paris, 1997, p. 31–43.

Flórez, Gloria. "Vicissitudes of Commercial Trading." *Medieval History Journal* 6, no. 1, June 2003, p. 33–53.

Folz, R. "Les Assemblées d'États dans les Principautés Allemandes (Fin XIIIe–Début XVIe Siècle)," in *Gouvernés et Gouvernants*. Part 4, *Bas Moyen Âge et Temps Modernes (II)*. Recueils de la Société Jean Bodin pour l'Histoire Comparative des Institutions 25, Éditions de la Librairie Encyclopédique, Bruxelles, 1965, p. 163–191.

Forbes Manz, Elisabeth. "The Ulus Chagatay before and after Temur's Rise to Power." *Central Asiatic Journal* 27, 1983, p. 79–100.

Fossier, Robert. *La Société Médiévale*. Ed. Armand Colin, Paris, 1991.

———. *Le Travail au Moyen Âge*. Hachette Littératures, 2000.

Fourquin, Guy. *Histoire économique de l'Occident médiéval*. Armand Colin, Paris, 1979.

Fox, R. G. *Kin, Clan, Raja and Rule*. University of California Press, Berkeley, 1971.

France, John. *Western Warfare in the Age of the Crusades*. Cornell University Press, Ithaca, NY, 1999.

Franceschi, Franco. *Oltre il "Tumulto": I lavoratori fiorentini dell'Arte della Lana fra Tre e Quattrocento*. Leo Olschki, Firenze, 1993.

François, Véronique. *Céramiques Médiévales à Alexandrie*. Institut Français d'Archéologie Orientale, Le Caire, 1999.

Frank, André Gunder. *L'accumulation mondiale (1500–1800)*. Calmann-Lévy, Paris, 1977.

———. "A Theoretical Introduction to Five Thousand Years of World System History." *Review* 13, no. 2, Spring 1990, p. 155–248.

———. "De quelles transitions et de quels modes de production s'agit-il dans le système mondial réel?" *Sociologie et Sociétés* 22, no. 2, Oct. 1990b, p. 207–219.

———. *ReOrient*. University of California Press, Berkeley, 1998.

———. "Reorient: From the Centrality of Central Asia to China's Middle Kingdom," in Ertürk Korkut (ed.), *Rethinking Central Asia*. Garnet Publishing, Reading, 1999, p. 11–38.

Frank, Andre Gunder, and Barry Gills. "5000 Years of World System History: The Cumulation of Accumulation," in Christopher Chase-Dunn and Thomas Hall (eds.), *Core/Periphery Relations in Precapitalist Worlds*. Boulder, CO, Westview Press, 1991, p. 67–112.

———. "The Five Thousand Year World System." *Humboldt Journal of Social Relations*, Arcata, 18, no. 1, Spring 1992a, p. 1–79.

———. "The Five Thousand Year World System in Theory and Practice," in Robert Denemark et al., *World System History*. Routledge, London, 2000, p. 3–23.

———. "World System Economic Cycles and Hegemonial Shift to Europe 100 B.C. to A.D. 1500." *Journal of European Economic History* 22, no. 1, Spring 1993a, p. 155–183.

———, eds. *The World System: Five Hundred Years or Five Thousand?* London, Routledge, 1993b.

Franke, Herbert. *China under Mongol Rule*. Variorum Press, Aldershot, 1994.

Friedrichs, Christopher. "Capitalism, Mobility and Class Formation in the Early Modern German City." *Past and Present* 69, nov. 1975, p. 24–49.

———. *The Early Modern City 1450–1750*. Longman, New York, 1995.

Fritze, Konrad. "Soziale Aspekte der Stadt-Land-Beziehungen im Bereich der Wendischen Hansestädte," in Hans Sculze (hrsg.), *Städtisches Um-und Hinterland in Vorindustrieller Zeit*. Böhlau Verlag, Köln, 1985, p. 21–32.

Fryde, E. B. "Italian Maritime Trade with Medieval England," in *Les Grandes Escales: Première Partie du 10e Colloque Internationale d'Histoire Maritime*. Recueils de la Société Jean Bodin pour l'Histoire Comparative des Institutions 32, Éditions de la Librairie Encyclopédique, Bruxelles, 1974, p. 291–337.

————. *Studies in Medieval Trade and Finance.* History Series, Vol. 13. Hambledon Press, London, 1983.

Fryde, N. "Consumption in the Thirteenth Century" in *Bijdragen tot de Geschiedenis*, 81, no. 1–3, 1998, p. 207–215.

Fu, Chu-fu, and Ching-neng Li. "Chungkuo fengchien shehui nei tzupenchuyi yinsu ti mengya" [The Sprouts of Capitalistic Factors within China's Feudal Society], Shangai, Jenmin ch'upanshe, 1956. Translated and republished in Chou Chin-shêng, "An Economic History of China," Western Washington State College Program in East Asian Studies, Occasional Paper No. 7, Bellingham, Washington, 1974, p. 233–245.

Furió, Antoni. "Impôt et dette publique," in Denis Menjot et al., *L'impôt dans les villes de l'Occident Méditerrranéen XIIIe–XIVe siècle.* Ministère de l'Économie, des Finances et de l'Industrie, Paris, 2005, p. 39–62.

Galland, Bruno. "Le pouvoir et la ville dans les États de la maison de Savoie (XIIe–XIVe siècles)," in Noël Coulet and Olivier Guyotjeannin (dirs.), *La Ville au Moyen Âge.* Vol. 2, *Société et pouvoirs dans la ville.* Éditions du Comité des Travaux Historiques et Scientifiques, Paris, 1998, p. 193–206.

Gallissot, René. "Vers un renversement de perspectives dans l'approche des modes de production et des sociétés précapitalistes," in René Gallissot (dir.), "Structures et cultures précapitalistes." Éditions Anthropos, Paris, 1981, p. 11–27.

Galloway, J. H. "The Mediterranean Sugar Industry." *Geographical Review* 67, no. 2, April 1977, p. 177–194.

Galvin, M. "Credit and Parochial Charity in Fifteenth Century Bruges." *Journal of Medieval History* 28, no. 2, June 2002, p. 131–154.

Gammer, Moshe. "Russia and the Eurasian Steppe Nomads," in Amitai Reuven and Michael Baran (eds.), *Mongols, Turks and Others.* Brill, Boston, 2005, p. 483–502.

Ganquan, Lin. "Tenency System and Autocratic Monarchy: Remarks on Some Characteristics of the Chinese Feudal System," in Eloy Ruano and Manuel Burgos (eds.), "Chronological Section I." 17th International Congress of Historical Sciences, Comité International des Sciences Historiques, Madrid, 1992, p. 78–83.

García-Arenal, Mercedes, and María Viguera, eds. *Relaciones de la península ibérica con el Magreb siglos XIII–XVI.* Consejo Superior de Investigaciones Científicas, Madrid, 1988.

Garcin, Jean-Claude. "Le Caire et l'évolution urbaine des pays musulmans à l'époque médiévale." *Annales Islamolog*iques 25, 1991, p. 289–304.

————. "Le système militaire Mamluk et le blocage de la société musulmane médiévale." *Annales Islamolog*iques 24, 1988, p. 93–110.

Garcin, Jean-Claude et al. *États, Sociétés et Cultures du Monde Musulman Médiéval.* Vol. 1. Presses Universitaires de France, 1995.

————. *États, Sociétés et Cultures du Monde Musulman Médiéval.* Vol. 2. Presses Universitaires de France, 2000a.

————. *États, Sociétés et Cultures du Monde Musulman Médiéval.* Vol. 3. Presses Universitaires de France, 2000b.

Gavitt, Philip. "Economy, Charity, and Community in Florence, 1350–1450," in Thomas Riis (ed.), *Aspects of Poverty in Early Modern Europe.* Sijthoff, Alphen aan den Rijn, 1981, p. 81–118.

Geertz, C. *Negara: The Theatre State in Nineteenth Century Bali.* Princeton University Press, 1980.

Geertz, Clifford. "Social Change and Modernization in Two Indonesian Towns," in G. Dalton (ed.), *Tribal and Peasant Economies.* Natural History Press, Garden City, NY, 1967, p. 366–394.

Genet, Jean-Philippe. "La genèse de l'état moderne." *Actes de la Recherche en Sciences Sociales* 118, Juin 1997, p. 3–18.

———. "Villes et fiscalité: et l'état?" in Denis Menjot, Albert Rigaudière, and Manuel S. Martínez (eds.), *L'impôt dans les villes de l'Occident Méditerranéen XIIIe–XVe siècle.* Ministère de l'Économie, des Finances et de l'Industrie, Paris, 2005, p. 571–577.

Geremek, Bronislaw. *Poverty: A History.* Blackwell, Oxford, 1994.

———. *Le salariat dans l'artisanat Parisien aux XIIIe–XVe siècles.* Mouton & Co, Paris, 1968.

———. "Les salariés et le salariat dans les villes au cours du moyen âge," in "Third International Conference of Economic History. Munich 1965" École Pratique des Hautes Études and Mouton, Paris, 1968b, p. 553–574.

Gernet, Jacques. *Daily Life in China on the Eve of the Mongol Invasion.* Stanford University Press, 1962.

———. *A History of Chinese Civilization.* Cambridge University Press, 1982.

———. "Note sur les villes chinoises au moment de l'apogée islamique," in A. H. Hourani and S. M. Stern (eds.), *The Islamic City.* University of Pennsylvania Press, Oxford, 1970, p. 77–85.

———. "Le pouvoir d'État en Chine." *Actes de la Recherche en Sciences Sociales* 118, Juin 1997, p. 19–27.

Gibb, H.A.R., trans. *The Travels of Ibn Battuta A.D. 1325–1354.* Vol. 4. The Hakluyt Society, London, 1994.

Giddens, Anthony. *A Contemporary Critique of Historical Materialism.* Vol. 1, *Power, Property and the State.* University of California Press, Berkeley, 1981.

Gieysztor, Aleksander. "Polish Villagers and their Contact with Local Markets in the Middle Ages," in *Studia in Memoria Federigo Melis.* Giannini Editore, Naples, 1978, 1:191–211.

Gillard, Alphonse. *L'industrie du fer dans les localités du comté de Namur et de l'entre-Sambre-et-Meuse de 1345 à 1600.* Pro Civitate Collection Histoire 29, Bruxelles, 1971.

Gille, Paul. "Les navires des deux routes des Indes," in Manlio Cortelazzo (ed.), "Mediterraneo e Oceano Indiano." Atti del Sesto Colloquio Internazionale di Storia Marittima, Venezia, 20–29 settembre 1962. L Olschki Editore, Firenze, 1970, p. 193–201.

Gimpel, Jean. *The Medieval Machine: The Industrial Revolution of the Middle Ages.* Penguin Books, New York, 1976.

Ginatempo, Maria. "Les transformations de la fiscalité dans l'Italie post-communale," in Denis Menjot (ed.), *L'impôt dans les villes de l'Occident Méditerrranéen XIIIe–XIVe siècle.* Ministère de l'Économie, des Finances et de l'Industrie, Paris, 2005, p. 193–215.

Giurescu, Constantin. "The Genoese and the Lower Danube in the XIIIth and XIVth Centuries," *Journal of European and Economic History* 5, no. 3, Winter 1976, p. 587–600.

Glete, Jan. *Warfare at Sea, 1500–1650.* Routledge, London, 2000.

Godding, Philippe. "Les ordonnances des autorites urbaines au Moyen Âge," in J. M. Duvosquel and E. Thoen (eds.), *Peasants and Townsmen in Medieval Europe. Studia in Honorem Adriaan Verhulst.* Belgisch Centrum voor Landelijke Geschiedenis no. 114, Snoeck-Ducaju, Gent, 1995, p. 185–201.

Godelier, Maurice. "Ordres, Classes, État chez Marx," in Wim Blockmans and Jean-Philippe Genet (eds.), *Visions sur le Développement des États Européens.* École Française de Rome, Palais Farnèse, Rome, 1993, p. 117–135.

Goitein, S. D. "From the Mediterreanean to India." *Speculum* 29, no. 2, Part 1, April 1954, p. 181–197.

———. *Letters of Medieval Jewish Traders.* Princeton University Press, Prinecton, 1973.

Golas, Peter. "Rural China in the Song." *Journal of Asian Studies* 39, no. 2, Feb. 1980, p. 291–332.

Golden, Peter. *An Introduction to the History of the Turkic peoples.* Harrassowitz Verlag, Wiesbaden, 1992.

―――. *Nomads and Sedentary Societies in Medieval Eurasia.* American Historical Association, Washington DC, 1998.

Goldstone, Jack. "Efflorescences and Economic Growth in World History." *Journal of World History* 13, no. 2, 2002, p. 323–389.

―――. "The Problem of the Early Modern World." *Journal of the Economic and Social History of the Orient* 41, no. 3, August 1998, p. 249–284.

―――. "The Rise of the West—Or Not?" *Sociological Theory* 18, no. 2, July 2000, p. 175–194.

Goldthwaite, Richard. "Urban Values and the Entrepreneur," in "L'Impresa Industria Commercio Banca Secc. XIII–XVIII." Atti della Ventiduesima Settimana di Studi 30 aprile–4 maggio 1990. Instituto Internazionale di Storia Economica "F. Datini," Serie II, 22, Prato, 1991, p. 641–662.

Golvin, L. *Le Maghrib Central a l'Epoque des Zirides.* Arts et Métiers Graphiques, Paris, 1957.

Gommans, Jos. "Mughal India and Central Asia in the 18th Century." *Itinerario* 15, no. 1, 1991, p. 51–70.

―――. "The Silent Frontier of South Asia." *The Journal of World History* Vol. 9, no. 1, 1998, p. 1-23.

Gonthier, N. "Dans le Lyon Médiéval: Vie et Mort d'un Pauvre." *Cahiers d'Histoire*, 23, no. 3, 1978, p. 335–347.

Goodrich, Carrington L., and Fêng Chia-Shêng. "The Early Development of Firearms in China." *ISIS* 36(2): 104, Jan. 1946, p. 114–123.

Goody, Jack. *Capitalism and Modernity.* Cambridge, Polity Press, 2004.

―――. *The East in the West.* Cambridge University Press, 1996.

―――. *The Oriental, the Ancient and the Primitive.* Cambridge Univerity Press, 1990.

―――. *Tradition, Technology and the State in Africa.* Cambridge University Press, 1971.

Gopal, Lallanji. *The Economic Life of Northern India, c. A.D. 700–1200.* Motilal Banarsidass, New Delhi, 1965.

Gottfried, R. S. *The Black Death.* The Free Press, New York, 1983.

Gottlieb, Roger. "Feudalism and Historical Materialism." *Science and Society* 48, no. 1, Spring 1984, p. 1–37.

Gough, Kathleen. "Modes of Production in Southern India." *Economic and Political Weekly*, XI, Feb. 1981, p. 337–364.

Gould, Richard. *Archeology and the Social History of Ships.* Cambridge University Press, 2000.

Gourdin, Philippe. "Les États Européens du Nord de la Méditerranée Occidentale et le Maghreb au XIIIe Siècle" in Mohammed Tahar Mansouri (dir.), *Le Maghreb et la Mer à Travers l'Histoire.* Éds Hêrodotos–Mésogeios, Paris, 2000, p. 113–125.

―――. "Les fortifications du Maghreb d'après les sources écrites," in Rika Gyselen (ed.), *Res Orientales.* Vol. 8, *Sites et Monuments disparus d'après les témoignages de voyageurs.* Peeters Press, Louvain, 1996, p. 25–32.

Grassby, Richard. *The Idea of Capitalism before the Industrial Revolution.* Rowan & Littlefield, Oxford, 1999.

Graus, F. "La crise monétaire du 14e siècle." *Revue Belge de Philologie et d'Histoire* 29, no. 1, 1951, p. 445–454.

Graves, Michael. *The Parliaments of Early Modern Europe.* Pearson, London, 2001.

Greif, Avner. *Institutions and the Path to the Modern Economy*. Cambridge University Press, 2006.

Greilsammer, M. "Pour blanchir son argent et son âme." *Revue Belge de Philologie et d'Histoire* 72, 1994, p. 793–833.

Grekov, Boris, and A. Iakoubovski. *La Horde d'Or.* Payot, Paris, 1939.

Grewal, J. S. (ed.) *The State and Society in Medieval India*. Oxford University Press, New Delhi, 2005.

Groten, Manfred. "Forms of Economic Life in the High Middle Ages," in Rolf Toman (ed.), *The High Middle Ages in Germany.* B Taschen Verlag, Koln, 1990, p. 66–85.

Grzybowski, Stanislaw. "Découverte et Diplomatie." *Revue d'Histoire Économique et Sociale* 47, 1969, p. 215–236.

Guarducci, Annalisa (ed.). "Sviluppo e sottosviluppo in Europa e fuori d'Europa dal secolo XIII alla Revoluzione Industriale." Atti della Decima settimana di studio 7–12 aprile 1978. *Instituto Interazionale di Storia Economica* "f. Datini," Serie II, 10, Prato, 1983.

Gueret-Laferte, Michèle. *Sur les Routes de l'Empire Mongol.* Éd. Honoré Champion, Paris, 1994.

Guérreau, Alain. *Le féodalisme: Un horizon théorique.* Le Sycomore, Paris, 1980.

———. "Quelques caractères spécifiques de l'espace féodal Européen," in Neithard Bulst, Robert Descimon, and Alain Guérreau (eds.), *L'État ou le roi.* Éditions de la Maison des Sciences de l'Homme, Paris, 1996, p. 85–101.

Gunawardana, R. A. L. H. "Changing Patterns of Navigation in the Indian Ocean and Their Impact on Pre-colonial Sri Lanka," in Satish Chandra (ed.), *The Indian Ocean Explorations in History, Commerce and Politics.* Sage, London, 1987, p. 54–89.

Gunst, Péter. "Agrarian Systems of Central and Eastern Europe," in Daniel Chirot (ed.), *The Origins of Backwardness in Eastern Europe.* University of California Press, Berkeley, 1989, p. 53–91.

Guo, Li. *Commerce, Culture and Community in a Red Sea Port in the 13th Century.* Brill, Boston, 2004.

Gurevitch, Aron. "The Merchant," in Jacques Le Goff (ed.), *The Medieval World.* Collins & Brown, London, 1990, p. 243–283.

Gutmann, Myron P. "The Dynamics of Urban Decline in the Late Middle Ages and Early Modern Times." 9th International Economic History Congress, Bern, 1986. Verlach der Fachvereine, Zürich, 1986, p. 23–56.

———. *Toward the Modern Economy.* Temple University Press, Philadelphia, 1988.

Gutnova, Evgenia. "The Influence of Economic Evolution on Changes in the Social Hierarchy in Rural England (14th–15th Centuries)," in "Gerarchie Economiche e Gerarchie Sociali Secoli XII–XVIII." Atti della Dodicesima Settimana di Studi 18–23 Aprile 1980. Instituto Internazionale di Storia Economica "F. Datini," Serie II, 22, Le Monnier, Prato, 1990, p. 91–124.

Guy, John. "Tamil Merchant Guilds and the Quanzhou Trade," in Angela Schottenhammer (ed.), *The Emporium of the World.* Brill, Boston, 2001, p. 283–308.

Habib, Irfan. "Capitalism in History." *Social Scientist* 23, no. 268, July–Sept. 1995b, p. 15–31.

———. "Changes in Technology in Medieval India." *Studies in History* 2, no. 1, 1980, p. 15–39.

———. "Classifying Pre-Colonial India," in T. J. Byres and Harbans Mukhia (eds.), *Feudalism and Non-European Societies.* Frank Cass, London, 1985, p. 44–53.

———. "Economic History of the Delhi Sultanate." *Indian Historical Review* 4, no. 2, 1978, p. 287–303.

————. "Non-Agricultural Production and Urban Economy," in Tapan Raychaudhuri and Irfan Habib (eds.), *The Cambridge Economic History of India.* Cambridge University Press, 1982, 1:76–93.

————. "Usury in Medieval India." *Comparative Studies in Society and History* 6, no. 4, July 1964, p. 393–419.

————. "Was There Feudalism in Indian History?" in Hermann Kulke (ed.), *The State in India, 1000–1700.* Oxford University Press, 1995, p. 86–133.

Habib, Mohammad. *Politics and Society during the Early Medieval Period.* People's Publishing House, New Delhi, 1974.

Hagesteijn, Renée. *Circles of Kings: Political Dynamics in Early Continental Southeast Asia.* Foris Publications [KIVTLV No. 138], Dordrecht, 1989.

Halaga, Ondrej. "A Mercantilist Initiative to Compete with Venice." *Journal of European Economic History* 12, no. 2, Fall 1983, p. 407–435.

Haldon, John. *Byzantium: A History.* Tempus Publishing Ltd, Charleston, SC, 2000.

Hall, John. *Powers and Liberties.* Basil Blackwell, Oxford, 1985b.

————. "States and Economic Development," in John Hall (ed.), *States in History.* Basil Blackwell, New York, 1987, p. 154–176.

————. "States and Societies: The Miracle in Comparative Perspective," in J. Baechler, J. Hall, and M. Mann (eds.), *Europe and the Rise of Capitalism.* Basil Blackwell, New York, 1988, p. 20–38.

Hall, Kenneth. "Coinage, Trade and Economy in Early South India and Its Southeast Asian Neighbours." *Indian Economic and Social History Review* 36, no. 4, Oct.–Dec. 1999, p. 431–459.

————. "Economic History of Early Southeast Asia," in Nicholas Tarling (ed.), *The Cambridge History of Southeast Asia.* Cambridge University Press, 1992, p. 1:183–275.

————. "International Trade and Foreign Diplomacy in Early Medieval South India." *Journal of the Economic and Social History of the Orient* 21, no. 1, 1978, p. 75–98.

————. *Maritime Trade and State Development in Early Southeast Asia.* University of Hawaii Press, Honolulu, 1985.

————. "Price-Making and Market Hierarchy in Early Medieval South India." *Indian Economic and Social History Review* 14, no. 2, April–June 1977, 207–230.

————. *Trade and Statecraft in the Age of the Cholas.* Abhinav Publications, New Delhi, 1980.

————. "Upstream and Downstream Unification in Southeast Asia's First Islamic Polity." *Journal of the Economic and Social History of the Orient* 44, no. 2, May 2001, p. 198–229.

Hall, Kenneth, and George Spencer. "The Economy of Kancipuram." *Journal of Urban History* 6, no. 2, Feb. 1980, p. 127–151.

Hall, Thomas. "The World System Perspective." *Sociological Inquiry* 66, no. 4, Fall 1996, p. 440–454.

Hallam, H. E. "The Medieval Social Picture," in Eugene Kamenka and R.S. Neale (eds.), *Feudalism, Capitalism and Beyond.* St. Martin's Press, New York, 1976, p. 28–49.

Halperin, Charles. *The Tatar Yoke.* Slavica Publishers, Inc., Colombus, OH, 1986.

Halpérin, Jean. "Les Tranformations Économiques aux XII et XIIIe Siècles." *Revue d'Histoire Économique et Sociale* 28, 1950, p. 21–34, 129–147.

Halpern, Jan. "Traditional Economy in West Africa." *Africana Bulletin* 7, 1967, p. 91–112.

Hamdani, Abbas. "The Rasa'il Ikhwan al-Safa' and the Controversy about the Origin of Craft Guilds in Early Medieval Islam," in Hanna Nelly (ed.), *Money, Land and Trade.* I. B. Tauris, New York, 2002, p. 157–173.

Hanawalt, Barbara. "Peasant Resistance to Royal and Seignorial Impositions," in F. X. Newman (ed.), *Social Unrest in the Late Middle Ages.* Center for Medieval and Early Renaissance Studies, Binghamton, 1986, p. 23–47.

Hangloo, Rattan Lal. *The State in Medieval Kashmir.* Manohar, New Delhi, 2000.

Haquette, Bertrand. "Des Lices et des Joncs." *Revue du Nord* 79, no. 322, Oct.–Dec. 1997, p. 859–882.

Hardach, Karl. "Some Remarks on German Economic Historiography." *Journal of European Economic History* 1, no. 1, Spring 1972, p. 37–99.

Hardy, Peter. "The authority of Muslim kings in Medieval India" in Marc Gaborieau (ed.) *Islam et Société en Asie du Sud.* EHESS, Paris, 1986, p. 37–55.

Hardy-Guilbert, Claire. "Al-Sihr, Porte du Hadramawt sur L'Océan Indien." *Annales Islamologiques* 38, no. 1, 2004, p. 95–157.

Harriss, G. L. "Parliamentary Taxation and the Origins of Appropriation of Supply in England, 1207–1340," in *Gouvernés et Gouvernants.* Part 3, *Moyen Âge et Temps Modernes.* Recueils de la Société Jean Bodin pour l'Histoire Comparative des Institutions 24, Éditions de la Librarie Encyclopédique, Bruxelles, 1966, p. 165–179.

Hartwell, Robert. "A Cycle of Economic Change in Imperial China." *Journal of the Economic and Social History of the Orient*, 10, 1967, p. 102–159.

———. "A Revolution in the Chinese Iron and Coal Industries during the Northern Sung, A.D. 960–1126." *Journal of Asian Studies* 21, 1962, p. 153–162.

———. "Markets, Technology, and the Structure of Enterprise in the Development of the 11th century Chinese Iron and Steel Industry" in *Journal of Economic History*, vol. 26, 1966, pp. 29–58.

———. "A Cycle of Economic Change in Imperial China: Coal and Iron in Northeast China, 750–1350" in *Journal of the Economic and Social History of the Orient*, 10, 1967, pp. 102–159.

———. "Demographic, Political, and Social Transformations of China, 750–1550" in *Harvard Journal of Asiatic Studies*, vol. 42, nr. 2, 1982, pp. 365–442.

Harvey, B. F. "Introduction: The Crisis of the Early Fourteenth Century," in B. M. S. Campbell (ed.), *Before the Black Death.* Manchester University Press, 1991, p. 1–24.

Harvey, David. *The Urbanization of Capital.* Johns Hopkins University Press, Baltimore, 1985.

Hatcher, John. "A Diversified Economy: Later Medieval Cornwall." *Economic History Review* (2nd Series) 22, no. 2, August 1969, p. 208–227.

Hatcher, John, and Mark Bailey. *Modelling the Middle Ages: The History and Theory of England's Economic Development.* Oxford University Press, 2001.

Haverkamp, Alfred, (ed.) *Information, Kommunimation und Selbstdarstellung in mittelalterlichen Gemeinden.* Oldenbourg Verlag, München, 1998.

Hay, Day, and John Law. *Italy in the Age of the Renaissance.* Longman, London, 1989.

Heaton, Herbert. *Economic History of Europe.* Harper, New York, 1948.

Heers, Jacques. *Esclaves et Domestiques au Moyen Âge dans le Monde Méditerranéen.* Fayard, Paris, 1981.

———. "The 'Feudal' Economy and Capitalism." *Journal of European Economic History* 3, no. 4, Winter 1974, p. 609–653.

———. "La Mode et les Marchés des Draps de Laine," in Marco Spallanzani (ed.), "Produzione, commercio e consumo dei panni di lana nei sec. XII–XVIII." Atti della seconda settimana di studio, 10–16 aprile 1970. Istituto Internazionale di storia economica "F. Datini," L Olschki Editore, Firenze, 1976, p. 199–220.

———. *Le Moyen Âge, une Imposture.* Ed. Perrin, Paris, 1992.

———. *L'Occident aux XIVe et XVe Siècles: Aspects Économiques et Sociaux.* Presses Universitaires de France, Paris, 1963.

———. *Précis d'Histoire du Moyen Âge.* Presses Universitaires de France, Paris, 1973.

———. "Le Prix de l'Assurance Maritime à la Fin du Moyen Âge." *Revue d'Histoire Économique et Sociale* 37, 1959, p. 1–19.

―――. "Rivalité ou Collaboration de la Terre et de l'Eau?," in Michel Mollat et al., "Les Grandes Voies Maritimes dans le Monde, XVe–XIXe Siècles." VIIe Colloque de la Commission Internationale d'Histoire Maritime. SEVPEN, Paris, 1965b, p. 13–63.

―――. *Société et Économie à Gênes (XIVe–XVe Siècles)*. Variorum Reprints, London, 1979.

―――. *Le Travail au Moyen Âge*. Presses Universitaires de France, Paris, 1965.

―――. "Types de Navire et Spécialisation des Traffics en Méditerranée à la Fin du Moyen Âge," in Michel Mollat (ed.), *Le Navire et l' Économie Maritime du Moyen Âge au XVIIIe Siècle Principalement en Méditerranée*. SEVPEN, 1958, p. 107–118.

Heesterman, J. C. "Littoral et Intérieur de l'Inde," in L. Blussé, H. Wesseling, and G. Winius (eds.), *History and Underdevelopment*. Éditions de la Maison des Sciences de l'Homme, Paris, 1980, p. 87–92.

―――. "Warriors and Merchants." *Itinerario* 15, no. 1, 1991, p. 37–49.

Heilbroner, Robert. *The Nature and Logic of Capitalism*. Norton, New York, 1985.

Heitzman, James. *Gifts of Power*. Oxford University Press, 1997.

―――. "State Formation in South India, 850–1280," in Hermann Kulke (ed.), *The State in India, 1000–1700*. Oxford University Press, New Delhi, 1995, p. 162–194.

Herbert, Eugenia. "The West African Copper Trade in the 14th and 16th Centuries," in Herman Kellenbenz (ed.), *Precious Metals in the Age of Expansion*. Klett-Cotta, Stuttgart, 1981, p. 119–130.

Herlihy, David. "Direct and Indirect Taxation in Tuscan Urban Finance c. 1200–1400," in "Finances et Comptabilité Urbaines du XIIIe au XVIe Siècle." Actes du Colloque International à Blankenberge, Sept. 6–9, 1962. Pro Civitate Collection Histoire No. 7, Bruxelles, 1964, p. 385–405.

―――. "Distribution of Wealth in a Renaissance Community," in P. Abrams and E. A. Wrigley (eds.), *Towns in Societies*. Cambridge University Press, 1978, p. 131–157.

Hess, Andrew. "The Evolution of the Ottoman Seaborne Empire in the Age of the Oceanic Discoveries, 1453–1525." *American Historical Review* 75, no. 7, Dec. 1970, p. 1892–1919.

―――. *The Forgotten Frontier*. University of Chicago Press, 1978.

Hesse, Philippe-Jean. "Artistes, Artisans ou Prolétaires?," in Xavier Barral I Altet (ed.), "Artistes, Artisans et Production Artistique au Moyen Âge." Colloque International Université de Rennes II, 2–6 Mai 1983. Picard, Paris, 1986, p. 431–473.

Heyd, W. *Histoire du Commerce du Levant au Moyen Âge*. Edited by Adolf Hakkert. Amsterdam, [1885], Hakkert, 1959 ed.

Hicks, John. *A Theory of Economic History*. Oxford University Press, 1969.

Hickson, Charles, and Earl Thompson. "A New Theory of Guilds and European Economic Development." *Explorations in Economic History* 28, no. 2, April 1991, p. 127–168.

Hilton, Rodney. *Class Conflict and the Crisis of Feudalism*. 2nd edition. Verso, New York, 1990.

―――. "A Crisis of Feudalism," in T. H. Aston and C.H.E. Philpin (eds.), *The Brenner Debate*. Cambridge University Press, 1985, p. 119–137.

―――. "Medieval Peasants: Any Lessons?" *Journal of Peasant Studies* 1, no. 2, January 1974, p. 207–219.

―――. "Resistance to Taxation and to Other State Impositions in Medieval England," in J. Ph. Genet and M. Le Mené (eds.), *Genèse de l'État Moderne: Prélèvement et Redistribution*. Éditions du CNRS, Paris, 1987, p. 169–177.

Hindess, Barry, and Paul Hirst. *Precaptalist Modes of Production*. Routledge, London, 1975.

Ho, Ping-Ti. *The Ladder of Success in Imperial China.* Columbia University Press, New York, 1962.

Hobsbawm, Eric. *Economic History of Britain.* Vol. 3, *Industry and Empire: From 1750 to the Present Day.* Penguin Books, New York, 1969.

Hobson, John. *The Eastern Origins of Western Civilisation.* Cambridge University Press, 2004.

Hocquet, Jean-Claude. "À Chioggia au XVe Siècle," in Jean Kerhervé and Albert Riguadière (dirs.), *Finances, Pouvoirs et Mémoire.* Fayard, Paris, 1999, p. 497–512.

———. "Fiscalité et Pouvoir Colonial.," in Michel Balard (dir.), *État et Colonisation au Moyen Âge et à la Renaissance.* La Manufacture, Lyon, 1989, p. 277–316.

———. "Productivity Gains and Technological Change." *Journal of European Economic History* 24, no. 3, Winter 1995, p. 537–556.

———, ed. *Le Roi, le Marchand et le Sel.* Presses Universitaires de Lille, 1987.

———. *Le Sel et la Fortune de Venise: Production et Monopole.* Presses Universitaires de Lille, 1979.

———. *Le Sel et la Fortune de Venise: Voiliers et Commerce en Méditerranée.* Presses Universitaires de Lille, 1979b.

———. *Le Sel et le Pouvoir.* Éd. Albin Michel, Paris, 1985.

———. "À Venise, Dette Publique et Spéculations Privées," in Denis Menjot et al., *L'Impôt dans les Villes de l'Occident Méditerrranéen XIIIe–XIVe Siècle.* Ministère de l'Économie, des Finances et de l'Industrie, Paris, 2005, p. 15–37.

Hodgett, Gerald. *A Social and Economic History of Medieval Europe.* Harper & Row, New York, 1972.

Hodgson, Geoffrey. *How Economics Forgot History.* Routledge, NY, 2001.

Hodgson, Marshall. "The Interrelations of Societies in History." *Comparative Studies in Society and History* 5, 1963, p. 227–250.

Hofstede, Geert. *Cultures and Organizations.* McGraw Hill, NY, 1997.

Hogendorn, J. S., and H. A. Gemery. "Continuity in West African Monetary History?" *African Economic History* 17, 1988, p. 127–146.

Hohenberg, P. "The City, Agent or Product of Urbanization," in A. van der Woude, A. Hayami, and J. de Vries (eds.). *Urbanization in History.* Clarendon Press, Oxford, 1990.

Holbach, Rudolf. "Formen des Verlags im Hanseraum vom 13. bis 16. Jahrhundert." *Hansische Geschichtsblätter* 103, 1985, p. 41–73.

———. "Frühformen von Verlag und Grossbetrieb in der gewerblichen Produktion." *Vierteljahrschrift für Sozial- und Wirtschaftgeschichte* 110, 1994, p. 51–78.

———. "Some Remarks on the Role of 'Putting-Out' in Flemish and Northwest European Cloth Production," in Marc Boone and Walter Prevenier (eds.), *Drapery Production in the Late Medieval Low Countries: Markets and Strategies for Survival (14th–16th Centuries).* Garant, Leuven, 1993, p. 207–250.

———. "Zur Handelsbedeutung vom Wolltuchen aus dem Hanseraum," in Stuart Jenks and Michael North (eds.), *Der Hansische Sonderweg?* Böhlau Verlag, Köln, 1993, p. 135–190.

Holsinger, Bruce, and Ethan Knapp. "The Marxist Premodern" *Journal of Medieval and Early Modern Studies*, Vol. 34, no. 3, 2004, p. 463–471.

Holt, Richard, and Gervase Rosser. "Introduction," in Richard Holt and Gervase Rosser (eds.), *The English Medieval Town.* Longman, London, 1990, p. 1–18.

Holton, R. J. "Cities, Capitalism and Civilization," in T. Bottomore and M. Mulkay (eds.) *Controversies in Sociology.* Vol. 20. Allen & Unwin, London, 1986.

———. *The Transition from Feudalism to Capitalism.* Macmillan, London, 1985.

Hopkins, A. G. *An Economic History of West Africa.* Columbia University Press, New York, 1973.

————. "The Western Sudan in the Middle Ages." *Past and Present* 37, July 1967, p. 149–156.

Hoppenbrouwers, Peter. "Agricultural Production and Technology in the Netherlands c. 1000–1500," in Grenville Astill and John Langdon (eds.), *Medieval Farming and Technology*. Brill, New York, 1997, p. 89–114.

————. "Mapping an Unexplored Field: The Brenner Debate and the Case of Holland," in Peter Hoppenbrouwers and Jan van Zanden (eds.), *Peasants into Farmers?* Brepols, Turnhout, 2001, p. 41–66.

Hoppenbrouwers, Peter, and Jan van Zanden, eds. *Peasants into Farmers?* Brepols, Turnhout, 2001.

Horden, Peregrine, and Nicholas Purcell. *The Corrupting Sea*. Blackwell, Oxford, 2000.

Horlings, Edwin. "Pre-industrial Economic Growth and the Transition to an Industrial Economy," in Maarten Prak (ed.), *Early Modern Capitalism*. Routledge, London, 2001, p. 88–104.

Horton, Mark, and John Middleton. *The Swahili*. Blackwell, Oxford, 2000.

Hourani, Albert. *A History of the Arab Peoples*. Faber & Faber, London, 1991.

Hourani, George. "Disputation," in Khalil Semaan (ed.), *Islam and the Medieval West*. State University of New York Press, Albany, 1980, p. 134–161.

Howell, Martha. "Woman's Work in the New and Light Draperies of the Low Countries," in N. B. Harte (ed.), *The New Draperies in the Low Countries and England, 1300–1800*. Oxford University Press, 1997, p. 197–216.

Howell, Martha. *Women, Production, and Patriarchy in the Late Medieval Cities*. University of Chicago Press, Chicago, 1986.

Howell, Martha, and Marc Boone. "Becoming Early Modern in the Late Medieval Low Countries." *Urban History* 23, no. 3, Dec. 1996, p. 300–324.

Hrbek, Ivan. "The Disintegration of Political Unity in the Maghrib," in D. T. Niane (ed.), *General History of Africa*. UNESCO, Berkeley, 1984, 4:78–101.

————. "Egypt, Nubia and the Eastern Deserts," in Roland Oliver (ed.), *The Cambridge History of Africa*. Vol. 3, *From 1050 to 1600*. Cambridge University Press, 1977, p. 10–97.

Hsü, I-T'ang. "Social Relief during the Sung Dynasty," in Zen Sun E-Tu and John De Francis, *Chinese Social History*. Octagon Books, New York, 1972, p. 207–215.

Huang, Ray. "Fiscal Administration during the Ming Dynasty," in Charles Hucker (ed.), *Chinese Government in Ming Times*. Columbia University Press, New York, 1969, p. 73–128.

Hubert, Étienne. "La Construction de la Ville." *Annales HSS* 59, no. 1, Jan–Fev 2004, p. 109–139.

Hudson, G. F. "China and the World," in Raymond Dawson (ed.), *The Legacy of China*. Clarendon Press, Oxford, 1964, p. 340–363.

Hudson, Geoffrey. "The Medieval Trade of China," in D. S. Richards (ed.), *Islam and the Trade of Asia*. Bruno Cassirer Oxford/University of Pennsylvania Press, 1970, p. 159–167.

Hui, Po-Keung. "Overseas Chinese Business Networks: East Asian Economic Development in Historical Perspective." Unpublished Ph.D. diss., Sociology Dept., SUNY-Binghamton, 1995.

Humphrey, Caroline, and Altanhuu Hurelbaatar. "Regret as a Political Intervention." *Past and Present* 186, Feb. 2005, p. 3–45.

Humphreys, Stephen. "Egypt in the World System of the Later Middle Ages," in Carl Petry (ed.), *The Cambridge History of Egypt*. Vol. 1, *640–1517*. Cambridge University Press, 1998, p. 445–461.

Hung, Ho-fung. "Imperial China and Capitalist Europe in the 18th Century Global Economy." *Review* 24, no. 4, 2001, p. 473–513.

Hunt, Edwin S. *The Medieval Super-Companies.* Cambridge University Press, 1994.

Hunt, Edwin, and James Murray. *A History of Business in Medieval Europe. 1200–1550.* Cambridge University Press, 1999.

Hymes, Robert. "Song China, 960–1279," in Ainslie Embree and Carol Gluck (eds.), *Asia in Western and World History.* Sharpe, Armonk, NY, 1997, p. 336–351.

Ibn, Khaldun. *The Muqaddimah.* Routledge & Kegan Paul, London, 1958.

Idris, R. "Society in the Maghrib after the Disappearance of the Almohads," in D. T. Niane (ed.), *General History of Africa.* UNESCO, Berkeley, 1984, 4:102–116.

Imsen,Steinar, and Günther Vogler. "Communal Autonomy and Peasant Resistance in Northern and Central Europe," in Peter Blickle (ed.), *Resistance, Representation, and Community.* Clarendon Press, Oxford, 1997, p. 5–43.

Inden, Ronald. *Imagining India.* Basil Blackwell, Oxford, 1990.

Indrapala, K. "South Indian Mercantile Communities in Ceylon, *circa* 950–1250." *Ceylon Journal of Historical and Social Studies* 1, no. 2, July–Dec. 1971, p. 101–113.

Iniesta, Ferran. "Mansaya, Califat et Fanga: Un Aperçu sur l'Évolution de la Royauté au Soudan Occidental du Xe au XVIIe Siècle," in Odile Redon and Bernard Rosenberger (eds.), *Les Assises du Pouvoir.* Presses Universitaires de Vincennes, Saint-Denis, 1994, p. 111–128.

Inikori, Joseph. *Africans and the Industrial Revolution in England.* Cambridge University Press, 2002.

Iorga, N. "La Politique Vénitienne dans les Eaux de la Mer Noire." *Bulletin de la Section Historique* [Bucarest] 2, 1914, p. 289–370.

Irwin, Robert. "Gunpowder and Firearms in the Mamluk Sultanate Reconsidered," in Michael Winter and Amalia Levanoni (eds.), *The Mamluks in Egyptian and Syrian Politics and Society.* Brill, Leiden, 2004, p. 117–139.

Isaacs, Ann, and Maarten Prak. "Cities, Bourgeoisies and States," in Wolfgang Reinhard (ed.), *Power Elites and State Building.* Clarendon Press, Oxford, 1996, p. 207–234.

Isichei, Elizabeth. *A History of African Societies to 1870.* Cambridge University Press, 1997.

Islam, Zafarul. "Origin and Development of Fatawa Compilation in Medieval India." *Studies in History* 12, no. 2, Dec. 1996, p. 223–241.

Issawi, Charles. "The Decline of Middle Eastern Trade," in D. S. Richards (ed.), *Islam and the Trade of Asia.* Bruno Cassirer Oxford/University of Pennsylvania Press, 1970, p. 245–266.

Jackson, P. "Delhi", in R. E. Frykenberg (ed.), Delhi through the ages. Oxford University Press, New Delhi, 1986, p. 18–33.

———. "The Dissolution of the Mongol Empire." *Central Asiatic Journal* 22, nos. 3/4, 1978, p. 186–244.

Jackson, Peter. *The Delhi Sultanate.* Cambridge University Press, 1999.

———. "From Ulus to Khanate," in Reuven Amitai-Press and David Morgan (eds.), *The Mongol Empire and Its Legacy.* Brill, Boston, 1999, p. 12–38.

———. "The Mongols and the Delhi Sultanate in the Reign of Muhammad Tughluq." *Central Asiatic Journal* 19, 1975, p. 118–157.

Jacoby, David. "Cretan Cheese: A Neglected Aspect of Venetian Medieval Trade," in E. Kittell and T. Madden (eds.), *Medieval and Renaissance Venice.* University of Illinois Press, Chicago, 1999, p. 49–68.

———. "The Migration of Merchants and Craftsmen," in "Le Migrazioni in Europa secc. XIII–XVIII." Atti della Settimane di studio 3–8 maggio 1993. Instituto Internazionale di Storia Economica "F. Datini," Serie II, 25, Prato, 1994, p. 533–560.

————. *Recherches sur la Méditerranée Orientale du XIIe au XVe siècle.* Variorum Reprints, London, 1979.

————. *Studies on the Crusader States and on Venetian Expansion.* Variorum Reprints, Northampton, 1989a.

————. *Trade, Commodities and Shipping in the Medieval Mediterranean.* Variorum Collected Studies, Ashgate/Aldershot, 1997.

Jacotey, Marie-Louise. *Juges, Consuls et Marchands des Origines à Nos Jours.* Vol. 1. Presses de Dominique Guéniot, Langres, 1998.

Jacq-Hergoualc'h, M. et al., "Une Étape de la Route Maritime de la Soie." *Journal Asiatique* 286, no. 1, 1998, p. 235–320.

Jacques-Meunié, D. *Le Maroc Saharien des Origines au XVIe Siècle.* Vol. 1. Librairie Klincksieck, Paris, 1982.

Jain, Vardhman K. *Trade and Traders in Western India (A.D. 1000–1300).* Munshiram Manoharlal Publishers, New Delhi, 1990.

James, Margery. "The Fluctuations of the Anglo-Gascon Wine Trade during the Fourteenth Century." *Economic History Review* [2nd Series] 4, no. 1, 1951, p. 170–196.

Jansen, H.P.H. "Handel en nijverheid 1000–1300," in *Algemene Geschiedenis der Nederlanden.* Fibula-Van Dishoeck, Haarlem, 1982, p. 148–186.

————. *Geschiedenis van de Middeleeuwen.* Aula, Utrecht, 1989.

Jehel, Georges. "Gênes et Tunis au Moyen Âge." *Cahiers de Tunisie* 48, no. 170, p. 89–104.

————. *Les Génois en Méditerrannée Occidentale (Fin XIème–Début XIVème Siècle): Ébauche d'une Stratégie pour un Empire.* Centre d'Histoire des Sociétés, Université de Picardie, 1993.

Jha, D. N., ed. *The Feudal Order.* Manohar, New Delhi, 2000.

Johnson, Marion. "The Cowrie Currencies of West Africa." *Journal of African History* 11, no. 1, 1970, p. 17–49, 331–353.

Jones, E. L. *The European Miracle.* Cambridge University Press, 1981.

————. *Growth Recurring.* Clarendon Press, Oxford, 1988.

Jones, Ph. *The Italian City-State.* Clarendon Press, Oxford, 1997.

Jorda, Henri. *Le Moyen Âge des Marchands.* L'Harmattan, Paris, 2002.

Jordan, William C. *The Great Famine.* Princeton University Press, 1998.

Joris, André. *Villes, Affaires, Mentalités Autour du Pays Mosan.* De Boeck-Université, 1993.

Ju-kang, T'ien. "Cheng Ho's Voyages and the Distribution of Pepper in China." *Journal of the Royal Asiatic Society of Great Britain and Ireland* 2, 1981, p. 186–197.

Julien, C. A. *Études maghrébines.* Presses Universitaires de France, Paris, 1964.

Kably, Mohamed. *Société, Pouvoir et Religion au Maroc à la Fin du "Moyen-Âge" (XIVe–XVe Siècle).* Éditions Maisonneuve et Larose, Paris, 1986.

Kahan, Arcadius. "Notes on Serfdom in Western and Eastern Europe." *Journal of Economic History* 33, no. 1, March 1973, p. 86–99.

Kai, Zhang. "The Social Reasons for the Expansion of Chinese Overseas Trade during the Song and Yuan Dynasties," in "The North Pacific to 1600." Proceedings of the Great Ocean Conferences. Oregon Historical Society, Portland, Oregon, 1991, 1:231–239.

Kaké, Ibrahima, and Elikia M'Bokolo. *Histoire Générale de l'Afrique.* Vol. 2, *L'Ere des Grands Empires.* Casterman, Tournai, 1978.

Kanaka Durga, P. S. "Identity and Symbols of Sustenance." *Journal of the Economic and Social History of the Orient* 44, no. 2, May 2001, p. 141–174.

Kaptein, Herman. *De Hollandse textielnijverheid 1350–1600.* Verloren, Hilversum, 1998.

Kapur, Nandini. *State Formation in Rajasthan.* Manohar, New Delhi, 2002.

Karashima, Noburu. *Towards a new formation*. Oxford University Press, New Delhi, 1992.
———. (ed.) *Ancient and Medieval Commercial Activities in the Indian Ocean: Testimony of Inscriptions and Ceramic-Sherds*. Taisho University, Tokyo, 2002.
———. "The Family of Mallappa Nayaka," *Medieval History Journal* 4, no. 1, June 2001, p. 35–42.
———. (ed.). *In search of Chinese ceramic-sherds in South India and Sri Lanka*. Taisho University Press, Tokyo, 2004.
———. *South Indian History and Society: Studies from Inscriptions A.D. 850–1800*. Oxford University Press, New Delhi, 1984.
Karpinski, Rafal. "Considérations sur les Échanges de Caractère Local et Extérieur de la Sénégambie." *Africana Bulletin* 8, 1968, p. 65–83.
Karpov, S. P. "The Grain Trade in the Southern Black Sea Region: The Thirteenth to Fifteenth Century." *Mediterranean Historical Review* 8, no. 1, June 1993, p. 55–71.
Kathirithamby-Wells, J. "Introduction," in J. Kathirithamby-Wells and John Villiers (eds.), *The Southeast Asian Port and Polity*. Singapore University Press, 1990, p. 1–16.
Katz, Claudio. *From Feudalism to Capitalism: Marxian Theories of Class Struggle and Social Change*. Greenwood Press, New York, 1989.
Kaviraj, Sudipta. "An Outline of a Revisionist Theory of Modernity." *European Journal of Sociology* 46, no. 3, 2005, p. 497–526.
Kea, Ray. "Expansions and Contractions." *Journal of World-Systems Research*, X, 3, 2004, p. 723–816.
Keay, John. *India: A History*. Atlantic Monthly Press, New York, 2000.
Kedar, Benjamin. *Merchants in Crisis*. Yale University Press, New Haven, 1976.
Kellenbenz, Hermann. "Marchands Capitalistes et Classes Sociales," in F. C. Lane (ed.), "Fourth International Conference of Economic History." Bloomington, 1968. École Pratique des Hautes Études, Paris, 1973, p. 19–51.
Kennedy, Paul. *The Rise and Fall of the Great Powers*. Fontana Press, London, 1989.
Kervan, Monique. "Le Port Multiple des Bouches de L'Indus," in Rika Gyselen (ed.), *Res Orientales*. Vol. 8, *Sites et Monuments Disparus d'après les Témoignages de Voyageurs*. Groupe pour l'Étude de la Civilisation du Moyen-Orient/Peeters Press, Louvain, 1996, p. 45–92.
Keswani, D. G. "Western Commercial Entrepreneurs in the East," in Michel Mollat (dir.), *Sociétés et Compagnies de Commerce en Orient et dans l'Océan Indien*. SEVPEN, Paris, 1970, p. 543–573.
Keyao, Ma. "A Comparative Study of Chinese and West-European Feudal Institutions," in Eloy Ruano and Manuel Burgos (eds.), "Chronological Section I." 17th International Congress of Historical Sciences, Comité International des Sciences Historiques, Madrid, 1992, p. 57–69.
Khan, Iqtidar Alam. "The State in Mughal India." *Social Scientist* 30, nos. 1/2, Jan.–Feb. 2001, p. 16–45.
Khazanov, Anatoly. *Nomads and the Outside World*. 2nd ed. University of Wisconsin Press, Madison, 1984.
———. "The Spread of World Religions in Medieval Nomadic Societies of the Eurasian Steppes," in Michael Gervers and Wayne Schlepp (eds.), *Nomadic Diplomacy, Destruction and Religion from the Pacific to the Adriatic*. Joint Centre for Asia Pacific Studies, Toronto, 1994, p. 11–33.
Kieniewicz, Jan. "Asian Merchants and European Expansion," in Karl Haellquist (ed.), *Asian Trade Routes*. Scandinavian Institute of Asian Studies, Copenhagen, 1991, 13:78–86.
———. "L'Asie et l'Europe Pendant les XVIe–XIXe Siècles," in "L'histoire à Nice." Actes du Colloque International, 6–9 Nov, 1980. Vol. 2, *Les Relations Économiques et Culturelles*

entre l'Occident et l'Orient. Université de Nice/Musée d'Archéologie et d'Histoire d'Antibes, 1981, p. 217–229.

Kirby, Stuart. *Introduction to the Economic History of China.* George Allen & Unwin, London, 1954.

Kisch, Herbert. "From Monopoly to Laissez-faire." *Journal of European Economic History* 1, no. 2, Fall 1972, p. 298–407.

Klep, P. M. "Long-Term Developments in the Urban Sector of the Netherlands," in "Het stedelijk in Belgie in historisch perspectief (1350–1850)." Handelingen van het 15e Internationaal Colloquium, Sp. 4–6 september 1990, Gemeentekrediet van Belgie, 86, Brussel, 1992, p. 201–242.

———. "Population Estimates of Belgium by Province (1375–1831)," in *Histoires et Population.* Liber Amicorum Etienne Helin, Louvain-la-Neuve, 1991.

———. "Urban Decline in Brabant," in H. Van der Wee (ed.), *The Rise and Decline of Urban Industries in Italy and the Low Countries (Late Middle Ages–Early Modern Times).* Leuven University Press, 1988.

Kloczowksi, Jerzy, "L'essor de l'Europe du centre-est et les transformations en Europe Byzantino-Slave de l'est," in Jean Favier (dir.), *XIVe et XVe Siècles: Crises et Genèses.* Presses Universitaires de France, Paris, 1996, p. 423–540.

Koenigsberger, Hans G. *Medieval Europe, 400–1500.* Longman, Hong Kong, 1987.

Koran, Jan, and Vanecek Vaclav. "Czech Mining and Mining Laws." *Cahiers d'Histoire Mondiale* 7, no. 1, 1962, p. 27–45.

Kotelnikova, Liubov. "La produzione dei panni di lana della campagna Toscana nei secoli XIII–XIV e la politica della città e della artie della lana," in Marco Spallanzani (ed.), "Produzione, commercio e consumo dei panni di lana nei sec. XII–XVIII." Atti della seconda settimana di studio (10–16 aprile 1970). Istituto Internazionale di Storia Economica "F. Datini," L Olschki Editore, Firenze, 1976, p. 221–229.

Kowaleski, Maryanne. *Local Markets and Regional Trade in Medieval Exeter.* Cambridge University Press, 1995.

Kracke, E. A. "Change within Tradition," in James Liu and Peter Golas (eds.), *Change in Sung China: Innovation or Renovation?* DC Heath, Lexington, MA, 1969, p. 9–15.

Kracke, E. A., Jr. "Sung K'ai-feng: Pragmatic Metropolis and Formalistic Capital," in John Haeger (ed.), *Crisis and Prosperity in Sung China.* The University of Arizona Press, Tuscon, AZ, 1975, p. 49–77.

———. "Sung Society." *Far Eastern Quarterly* 14, no. 4, Aug. 1955, p. 479–488.

Krader, Lawrence. "The Centrality of Central Asia." *Studies in History* 8, no. 1, Jan–June 1992, p. 113–118.

Krishna, Brajesh. *Foreign Trade in Early Medieval India.* Harman Publishing, New Delhi, 2000.

Krueger, Hilmar. "Genoese Trade with Northwest Africa in the 12th Century." *Speculum* 8, no. 3, 1933, p. 377–395.

———. "The Wares of Exchange in the Genoese-African Traffic of the 12th Century." *Speculum* 12, no. 1, 1937, p. 57–71.

Krueger, Hilmar C. "Economic Aspects of Expanding Europe," in Marhsall Clagett, Gaines Post, and Robert Reynolds (eds.), *Twelfth-Century Europe and the Foundations of Modern Society.* University of Wisconsin Press, Madison, 1961, p. 59–76.

———. "The Genoese Exportation of Northern Cloths to Mediterranean Ports." *Revue Belge de Philologie et d'Histoire* 65, no. 4, 1987, p. 722–750.

Kuchenbuch, Ludolf. "Marxens Werkentwicklung und die Mittelalterforschung," in Alf Lüdtke (ed.), *Was bleibt von marxistischen Perspektiven in der Geschichtsforschung?* Wallstein Verlag, Gottingen, 1997, p. 33–66.

Kuhn, Dieter. "Silk Technology during the Sung Period." *T'oung Pao* 67, 1981, p. 48–90.

Kulke, Hermann. "The Early and the Imperial Kingdom in Southeast Asian History," in David Marr and A. C. Milner (eds.), *Southeast Asia in the 9th to 14th Centuries.* Institute of Southeast Asian Studies, Singapore, 1986, p. 1–22.

———. "Introduction," in Hermann Kulke (ed.), *The State in India, 1000–1700.* Oxford University Press, New Delhi, 1995, p. 1–47.

———. and Dietmar Rothermund. *History of India.* Routledge, London, 1998.

Kumar, Dharma. "Private Property in Asia?" *Comparative Studies in Society and History* 27, no. 2, April 1985, p. 340–366.

Kumar, Sunil. "La communauté musulmane et les relations hindous-musulmans dans l'Inde du Nord au début du XIIIe siècle." *Annales* 60, no. 2, Mars–Avril 2005, p. 239–264.

Kuran, Timur. "The Islamic Commercial Crisis." *The Journal of Economic History*, 63, no. 2, 2003, p. 414–446.

———. "Why the Middle East is Economically Underdeveloped." *Journal of Economic Perspectives,* 18, no. 3, 2004, p. 71–90.

Kwanten, Luc. *Imperial Nomads.* University of Pennsylvania Press, 1979.

Labal, Paul. *Histoire: Le Moyen Âge.* Hachette, Paris, 1962.

Labh, Vijay Lakshmi. *Contributions to the Economy of Early Medieval India.* Radha Publications, New Delhi, 1996.

Labib, S. "Les Marchands Karimis en Orient et sur l'Océan Indien," in Michel Mollat (dir.), *Sociétés et Compagnies de Commerce en Orient et dans l'Océan Indien.* SEVPEN, Paris, 1970, p. 209–214.

———. "Medieval Islamic Maritime Policy in the Indian Ocean Area," in *Les Grandes Escales: Première Partie du 10e Colloque Internationale d'Histoire Maritime.* Recueils de la Société Jean Bodin pour l'Histoire Comparative des Institutions 32, Éditions de la Librairie Encyclopédique, Bruxelles, 1974, p. 225–241.

Lachaud, Frédérique. "L'Assiette de l'Impôt sur les Biens Meublés en Angleterre (1188–1332)," in Ph. Contamine et al., *L'Impôt au Moyen Âge.* Vol. 1, *Le Droit d'Imposer.* Comité pour l'Histoire Économique et Financière de la France, Ministère de l'Économie, des Finances et de l'Industrie, Paris, 2002, p. 289–311.

Lachmann, Richard. *Capitalists in Spite of Themselves.* Oxford University Press, 2000.

———. *From Manor to Market.* University of Wisconsin Press, Madison, 1987.

Lacoste, Yves. "General Characteristics and Fundamental Structures of Mediaeval North African Society." *Economy and Society* 3, 1974, p. 1–17.

———. *Ibn Khaldun: The Birth of History and The Past of the Third World.* Verso, London, 1984.

Laiou, Angeliki. *Gender, Society and Economic Life in Byzantium.* Variorum Press, Ashgate, VT, 1992.

———. "Venice as a Centre of Trade and of Artistic Production in the 13th Century," in Hans Belting (ed.), *Il Medio Oriente e l'Occidente nell'arte dell XIII secolo.* Editrice CLUEB, Bologna, 1982, p. 11–26.

Lal, Deepak. "Globalization: What Does It Mean for Developing and Developed Countries?" in Siebert Horst (ed.), *Globalization and Labor.* Institut für Weltwirtschaft an der Universität Kiel, Mohr Siebeck, Tübingen, 1999, p. 211–221.

———. *Unintended Consequenses.* MIT Press, Cambridge, MA, 1998.

Lal, K. S. *Muslim Slave System in Medieval India.* Aditya Prakashan, New Delhi, 1994.

Lalik, Tadeusz. "Les Fonctions des Petites Villes en Pologne au bas Moyen Âge." *Acta Poloniae Historica* 37, 1978, p. 5–28.

Lambton, Ann. *Continuity and Change in Medieval Persia.* SUNY Press, NY, 1988.

Lamouroux, Christian. "Commerce et bureaucratie dans la Chine des Song." *Études Rurales*, no. 162, 2002, p. 183–213.

————. *Fiscalité, Comptes Publics et Politiques Financières dans la Chine des Song*. Collège de France—Instititut des Hautes Études Chinoises, Paris, 2003.

Landes, David. *Revolution in Time*. Harvard University Press, 1983.

————. *The Wealth and Poverty of Nations*. Norton, NY, 1998.

Lane, Frederic. "Economic Consequences of Organized Violence." *Journal of Economic History* 18, no. 4, Dec. 1958, p. 401–417.

Lane, Frederic C. "Double Entry Bookkeeping and Resident Merchants." *Journal of European Economic History* 6, 1977, p. 177–191.

————. *Profits from Power*. State University of New York Press, Albany, 1979.

Langdon, John. "Was England a Technological Backwater in the Middle Ages?" in Grenville Astill and John Langdon (eds.), *Medieval Farming and Technology: The Impact of Agricultural Change in Northwest Europe*. Brill, 1997, p. 275–291.

Lange, Dierk. "La Region du la Tchad d'après la Géographie d'Ibn Sa'id." *Annales Islamologiques* 16, 1980, p. 149–181.

Lapidus, Ira. *Muslim Cities in the Later Middle Ages*. Cambridge University Press 1984.

Laroui, Abdallah. *The History of the Maghrib*. Princeton University Press 1977.

Laurent, Henri. *Un Grand Commerce d'Exportation au Moyen Âge: La Draperie des Pays-Bas en France et dans les Pays Méditerranéens XIIe–XVe Siècle*. Droz, Paris, 1935.

Lawless, Richard. "Tlemcen, Capitale du Maghreb Central. Analyse des Fonctions d'une Ville Islamique Médiévale." *Revue de l'Occident Musulman et de la Méditerranée* 20, no. 2, 1975, p. 49–66.

Le Goff, Jacques. "L'Apogée de la France Urbaine Médiévale," in J. Le Goff (red.), *La Ville en France au Moyen Âge*. Seuil, Paris, 1998, p. 185–394.

————. "Introduction," in J. Le Goff (red.), *La Ville en France au Moyen Âge*. Seuil, Paris, 1998, p. 7–25.

————. "Introduction: Trois Regards sur le Moyen Âge," in Jacques Le Goff and Guy Lobrichon (dirs.), *Le Moyen Âge Aujourd'hui*. Le Léopard D'Or, Paris, 1998b, p. 5–15.

————. *Marchands et Banquiers du Moyen Âge*. Presses Universitaires de France, Paris, 1962.

————. *Pour un Autre Moyen Âge*. Gallimard, Paris, 1991

————. "Travail," in Jacques Le Goff and Jean-Claude Schmitt (eds.), *Dictionnaire Raisonné de l'Occident Médiéval*. Fayard, Paris, 1999, p. 1137–1149.

————. "The Usurer and Purgatory," in Center for Medieval and Renaissance Studies, UCLA, *The Dawn of Modern Banking*. Yale University Press, New Haven, 1979, p. 25–52.

————. *Your Money or Your Life: Economy and Religion in the Middle Ages*. Zone Books, New York, 1988.

Le Mené, Michel. *L'Économie Médiévale*. Presses Universitaires de France, Vendôme, 1977.

Le Tourneau, Roger. *The Almohad Movement in North Africa in the Twelfth and Thirteenth Centuries*. Princeton University Press, 1969.

Leenders, Kathleen A.H.W. "Verdwenen Venen," in *Gemeentekrediet Historische Uitgaven*, no. 78, Gemeentekrediet, Brussels, 1989.

Leguai, André. "Les Troubles Urbains dans le Nord de la France." *Revue d'Histoire Économique et Sociale* 54, no. 3, 1976, p. 281–303.

Leguay, Jean-Pierre. "La Propriété et le Marché de l'Immobilier à la Fin du Moyen Âge," in Jean-Claude Maire Vigueur (ed.), *D'Une Ville à l'Autre: Structures Matérielles et Organisation de l'Espace dans les Villes Européennes (XIIIe–XVIe Siècle)*. École Française de Rome, Palais Farnèse, 1989, p. 135–199.

Lenhoff, Gail, and Janet Martin, "The Commercial and Cultural Context of Afanasij Nikitin's Journey Beyond Three Seas." *Jahrbücher für Geschichte Osteuropas* 37, no. 3, 1989, p. 321–344.

Leone, Alfonso. "Maritime Insurance as a Source for the History of International Credit in the Middle Ages." *Journal of European Economic History* 12, no. 2, Fall 1983, p. 363–369.

Lestocquoy, Jean. *Aux Origines de la Bourgeoisie.* Presses Universitaires de France, Paris, 1952.

Leuilliot, Paul. "Influence du Commerce Oriental sur l'Économie Occidentale," in Michel Mollat (dir.), *Sociétés et Compagnies de Commerce en Orient et dans l'Océan Indien.* SEVPEN, Paris, 1970, p. 611–629.

Levathes, Louise. *When China Ruled the Seas.* Simon & Schuster, New York, 1994.

Levi, Scott. "Hindus Beyond the Hindu Kush: Indians in the Central Asian Slave Trade," *Journal of the Royal Asiatic Society* 12, no. 3, Nov. 2002, p. 277–288.

Levtzion, Nehemia. *Ancient Ghana and Mali.* Methuen, London, 1973.

———. "The Early States of the Western Sudan to 1500," in J.F.A. Ajayi and Michael Crowder (eds.), *History of West Africa.* Vol 1. Longman, New York, 1985 ed., p. 129–166.

———. *Islam in West Africa: Religion, Society and Politics to 1800.* Variorum Press/Ashgate, Brookfield, VT, 1994.

———. "The Western Maghrib and Sudan," in Roland Oliver (ed.), *The Cambridge History of Africa.* Vol. 3, *From c. 1050 to c. 1600.* Cambridge University Press, 1977, p. 331–462.

Levztion, Nehemia, and J.F.P. Hopkins, eds. *Corpus of Early Arabic Sources for West African History.* Cambridge University Press, 1981.

Lewis, Archibald. "Les Marchands dans l'Océan Indien." *Revue d'Histoire Economique et Sociale* 54, no. 4, 1976, p. 441–475.

———. *Medieval Society in Southern France and Catalonia.* Variorum Reprints, London, 1984.

Lewis, Archibald. *The Sea and Medieval Civilizations.* Variorum Reprints, London, 1978.

Lewis, Archibald, ánd Timothy Runyan. *European Naval and Maritime History, 300–1500.* Indiana University Press, Bloomington, 1985.

Lieber, Alfred. "Eastern Business Practices and Medieval European Commerce." *Économic History Review* 21, no. 2, Aug. 1968, p. 230–243.

Lieberman, Victor. "Transcending East-West Dichotomies." *Modern Asian Studies* 31, no. 6, 1997, p. 463–546.

———. "Wallerstein's System and the International Context of Early Modern History." *Journal of Asian History* 24, no. 1, 1990, p. 70–90.

Linck, Gudula. "Visions of the Border in Chinese Frontier Poetry," in Sabine Dabringhaus and Roderich Ptak (eds.), *China and Her Neighbours: Borders, Visions of the Other, Foreign Policy 10th to 19th Century.* Harrasowitz Verlag, Wiesbaden, 1997, p. 99–117.

Ling, Wang. "On the Invention and Use of Gunpowder and Firearms in China." *ISIS* 37, pts. 1–2, nos. 107–108, May 1947, p. 160–178.

Lipman, Jonathan. *Familiar Strangers: A History of Muslims in Northwest China.* University of Washington Press, Seattle, 1997.

Lippit, Victor. *The Economic Development of China.* Sharpe, Armonk, NY, 1987.

Lis, Catharina, and Hugo Soly. "Ambachtsleden in vergelijkend perspectief," in C. Lis and H. Soly (eds.), *Werelden van verschil.* VUB Press, Brussels, 1997b, p. 11–42.

———. "Corporatisme, Onderaanneming en Loonarbeid." *Tijdschrift voor Sociale Geschiedenis* 20, no. 4, November 1994, p. 365–390.

———. "Different Paths of Development." *Review* 20, no. 2, Spring 1997, p. 211–242.

———. "Economische en Sociale Geschiedenis van de Nieuwe Tijd," in Erik Aerts, Brigitte Heneau, Paul Janssens, and Raymond van Uytven (eds.), *Studia Historica Oeconomica: Liber Amicorum Herman van der Wee.* Leuven University Press, 1993, p. 183–197.

———. *Poverty and Capitalism in Pre-Industrial Europe.* Humanities Press, NJ, 1979.

Little, Lester. *Religious Poverty and the Profit Economy in Medieval Europe.* Cornell University Press, Ithaca, 1978.

Lloyd, T. H. *Alien Merchants in England in the High Middle Ages.* St. Martin's Press, New York, 1982.

———. *England and the German Hanse.* Cambridge University Press, 1991.

———. *The English Wool Trade in the Middle Ages.* Cambridge University Press, 1977.

Lo, Jung-Pang. "Chinese Shipping and East-West Trade from the Tenth to the Fourteenth Century," in Michel Mollat (dir.) *Sociétés et Compagnies de Commerce en Orient et dans l'Océan Indien.* SEVPEN, Paris, 1970, p. 167–176.

———. "The Decline of the Early Ming Navy." *Oriens Extremus* 5, December 1958, p. 149–168.

———. "The Emergence of China as a Sea Power during the Late Sung and Early Yuan Periods." *Far Eastern Quarterly* 14, no. 4, August 1955, p. 489–503.

———. "Maritime Commerce and its Relation to the Sung Navy." *Journal of the Economic and Social History of the Orient* 12, 1969c, p. 57–101.

———. "Policy Formulation and Decision Making on Issues Respecting Peace and War," in Charles Hucker (ed.), *Chinese Government in Ming Times.* Columbia University Press, 1969b, p. 41–72.

———. "The Rise of China as a Sea Power," in James Liu and Peter Golas (eds.), *Change in Sung China* DC Heath, Lexington, MA, 1969, p. 20–26.

Loewe von, Karl. "Commerce and Agriculture in Lithuania, 1400–1600." *Economic History Review* [2nd series] 26, no. 1, 1973, p. 23–37.

Lombard, Denys. "Y a-t-il une Continuité de Réseaux Marchands Asiatiques?" in Denys Lombard and Jean Aubin (eds.), *Marchands et Hommes d'Affaires Asiatiques dans l'Ocean Indien et la Mer de Chine 13e–20e Siècles.* Éditions de l'École des Hautes Études en Sciences Sociales, Paris, 1988, p. 11–18.

Lopez, R. S. "Economic Depression of the Renaissance?" *Economic History Review* 16, no. 3, April 1964, p. 525–527.

———. "Foreigners in Byzantium." *Bulletin de l'Institut Historique Belge de Rome*, fasc. 44, Bruxelles, 1974, p. 341–352.

———. "Les Influences Orientales et l'Éveil Économique de l'Occident." *Cahiers d'Histoire Mondiale* 1, no. 3, Paris, Jan. 1954, p. 594–622.

———. *Su e giù per la storia di Genova.* Bozzi, Genoa, 1975.

Lopez, Robert. "China Silk in Europe in the Yuan Period." *Journal of the American Oriental Society* 72, 1952, p. 72–76.

———. "European Merchants in the Medieval Indies." *Journal of Economic History* 3, no. 2, 1943, p. 164–184.

———. "The Trade of Medieval Europe: The South," in M. Postan and E. Rich (eds.), *The Cambridge Economic History of Europe.* Cambridge University Press, 1952, 2:257–354.

Lopez, Robert S. *The Commercial Revolution of the Middle Ages 950–1350.* Cambridge University Press, 1976.

———. "Les Méthodes Commerciales des Marchands Occidentaux en Asie du XIe au XIVe Siècle," in Michel Mollat (dir.), *Sociétés et Compagnies de Commerce en Orient et dans l'Océan Indien.* SEVPEN, Paris, 1970, p. 343–351.

————. "Nouveaux Documents sur les Marchands Italiens en Chine à l'Époque Mongole." *Académie des Inscriptions and Belles-Lettres* [Paris] comptes rendus, Avril–Juin, 1977, p. 445–458.

————. "Il problema della bilancia dei pagamenti nel commercio di Levante," in Agostino Pertusi (ed.), *Venezia e il Levante fino al secolo XV.* L Olschki Editore, Firenze, 1973, 1:431–452.

Lopez, Robert S., and Harry A. Miskimin. "The Economic Depression of the Renaissance." *Economic History Review* [2nd Series] 14, no. 3, April 1962, p. 408–426.

Lopez, Robert, Harry Miskimin, and Abraham Udovitch. "England to Egypt, 1350–1500," in M. A. Cook, *Studies in the Economic History of the Middle East.* Oxford University Press, London, 1970, p. 93–128.

Lorcin, M. T. *La France au XIIIe Siècle.* Éditions F. Nathan, Millau, 1975.

Louca-Bloch, Claire. "Mamluk Silks (13th–15th Century)," in Simonetta Cavaciocchi (red.), "Prodotti e techniche d'oltremare nelle economie europee secc. XIII–XVIII." Atti della 'Ventinovesima Settimana di Studi, 14–19 aprile 1997. Le Monnier, Istituto Internazionale di Storia Economica "F. Datini," Prato, 1998, p. 507–514.

Ludden, David. *An Agrarian History of South Asia: The New Cambridge History of India.* Vol. 4. Cambridge University Press, 1999.

————. *Peasant History in South India.* Princeton University Press, 1985.

————. "Spectres of agrarian territory in southern India." *The Indian Economic and Social History Review*, Vol. 39, no. 3, 2002, p. 233–257.

Lugan, Bernard. *Atlas Historique de l'Afrique des Origins à Nos Jours.* Éditions du Rocher, Lonrai, 2001.

Luzzatto, Gino. *Studi di Storia Economica Veneziana.* Cedam, Padova, 1954.

Lyon, Bryce. *Studies of West European Medieval Institutions.* Variorum Reprints, London, 1978.

Ma, Debin. "The Great Silk Exchange," in D. Flynn, L. Frost, and A. Latham (eds.), *Pacific Centuries.* Routledge, New York, 1999, p. 38–69.

Ma, Laurence. *Commercial Development and Urban Change in Sung China (960–1279).* Dept. Of Geography, Michigan Geographical Publication No. 6, University of Michigan, Ann Arbor, 1971.

Macfarlane, Alan. "The Cradle of Capitalism," in Jean Baechler, John Hall, and Michael Mann (eds.), *Europe and the Rise of Capitalism.* Basil Blackwell, New York, 1988, p. 185–203.

MacKay, Angus. *Spain in the Middle Ages.* Macmillan, London, 1977.

Mackenney, Richard. *Tradesmen and Traders: The World of the Guilds in Venice and Europe.* Croom Helm, London, 1987.

Madan, G. R. *Western Sociologists on Indian Society.* Routledge & Kegan Paul, London, 1979.

Madan, T. N. "The Comparison of Civilizations." *International Sociology* 16, no. 3, 2001, p. 474–487.

Maddicott, J. R. "The English Peasantry and the Demands of the Crown 1294–1341." *Past and Present* [Supplement 1], Oxford, 1975.

Maddison, Angus. *Chinese Economic Performance in the Long Run.* OECD Development Centre Studies, Paris, 1998.

Magelhaes-Godinho, Vitorino. *L'Économie de l'Empire Portugais aux XV et XVIe Siècles.* SEVPEN, Paris, 1969.

Maguin, Martine. *La Vigne et le Vin en Lorraine, XIVe–XVe Siècle.* Presses Universitaires de Nancy, 1982.

Mahajan, Vidya Dhar. *The Sultanate of Delhi.* S. Chand & Co, New Delhi, 1963.

Mahapatra, Pinaki. "Position of the Local Merchants of Orissa, 1550–1757," in Chandra Satish (ed.), *Essays in Medieval Indian Economic History*. Munshiram Manoharlal Publishers, New Delhi, 1987, p. 258–261.

Mahoney, James. "Path Dependence in Historical Sociology." *Theory and Society* 29, 2000, p. 507–548.

Maire Vigueur, Jean-Claude. "Guerres, Conquête du Contado et Transformations de l'Habitat en Italie Centrale au XIIIe Siècle," in André Bazzana (ed.), *Castrum 3. Guerre, Fortification et Habitat dans le Monde Méditerranéen au Moyen Âge*. Collections de l'École Française de Rome, 1988, p. 271–277.

———. *Cavaliers et Citoyens*. Éditions de l'École des Hautes Études en Sciences Sociales, Paris, 2003.

Majumdar, R. C. *India and South-East Asia*. B. R. Publishing Company, Delhi, 1979.

Makkai, László. "Neo-Serfdom: Its Origin and Nature in East Central Europe." *Slavic Review* 34, no. 2, June 1975, p. 225–238.

Malanima, Paolo. "La formazione di una regione economica: La Toscana nei secoli XIII–XV." *Società e storia* 20, 1983, p. 229–269.

———. "Politica ed economia nella formazione dello Stato regionale: Il caso toscano." *Studi veneziani* 11, 1986, p. 61–72.

———. "Pisa and the Trade Routes to the Near East in the Late Middle Ages." *Journal of European Economic History* 16, no. 2, Fall 1987, p. 335–356.

Malefakis, Edward. "The Rise and Fall of Western Empire in Asia," in Ainslie Embree and Carol Gluck (eds.), *Asia in Western and World History*. M. E. Sharpe, Armonk, NY, 1997, p. 172–189.

Malowist, Marian. "Les Aspects Sociaux de la Première Phase de l'Expansion Coloniale." *Africana Bulletin* 1, 1964, p. 11–33.

———. "Le Commerce d'Or et d'Esclaves au Soudan Occidental." *Africana Bulletin* 4, 1966b, p. 49–72.

———. *Croissance et Régression en Europe: XIVe–XVIIe Siècles*. Librairie Armand Colin, Paris, 1972.

———. "L'Évolution Industrielle en Pologne du XIVe au XVII Siècle," in *Studi in Onore di Armando Sapori*. Instituto Editoriale Cisaplino, Milano, 1957, p. 571–603.

———. "Problems of the Growth of the National Economy of Central-Eastern Europe in the Late Middle Ages." *Journal of European Economic History* 3, no. 2, Fall 1974, p. 319–357.

———. "The Social and Economic Stability of the Western Sudan in the Middle Ages." *Past and Present* 33, no. 3, 1966, p. 3–15.

Mancall, Mark. "The Ch'ing Tribute System," in John K. Fairbank (ed.), *The Chinese World Order*. Harvard University Press, Cambridge, 1968, p. 63–89.

Mandalios, John, "Historical Sociology," in Bryan S. Turner (ed.), *The Blackwell Companion to Social Theory*. Blackwell, Oxford, 1996, p. 278–302.

Mandel, Ernest. *Traité d'Économie Marxiste*. Vol. 1. René Juliard, Paris, 1962.

Manguin, Pierre-Yves. "Les Cités-États de l'Asie du Sud-Est Côtière." *Bulletin de l'École Française d'Extrême Orient* 87, no. 1, 2000, p. 151–182.

Mann, Michael. "The Autonomous Power of the State," in John Hall (ed.), *States in History*. Basil Blackwell, New York, 1987, p. 109–136.

———. "European Development," in J. Baechler, J. Hall, and Michael Mann (eds.), *Europe and the Rise of Capitalism*. Basil Blackwell, New York, 1988, p. 6–19.

———. *The Sources of Social Power*. Vol. 1. Cambridge University Press, 1986.

———. "State and Society, 1130–1815," in *Political Power and Social Theory*. 1980, 1:165–208.

Manolescu, Radu. "Les Villes Portuaires Roumaines au Moyen Âge (Milieu du XIVe–milieu du XVIe Siècles)," in Jürgen Schneider (ed.), *Wirtschaftskräfte und Wirtschaftswege V. Festschrift für Hermann Kellenbenz*. Beiträge zur Wirtschaftgeschichte, Band 8 in Kommission bei Klett-Cotta, Stuttgart, 1981, p. 47–63.

Mansfield, Peter. *The Arabs*. 3rd ed. Penguin Books, New York, 1992.

Mansouri, Mohamed Tahar. "Le Maghreb Médiéval Face aux Expéditions Occidentals." *Cahiers de Tunisie* 48, no. 170, 1995, p. 139–147.

Mantran, Robert, and Charles de la Roncière. "Africa Opens Up to the Old Worlds," in Robert Fossier (ed.), *The Cambridge Illustrated History of the Middle Ages. Vol. 3, 1250–1530*. Cambridge University Press, 1986, p. 356–395.

Maréchal, Griet. "Het openbaar initiatief van de gemeenten in het vlak van de openbare onderstand,'" Actes du 11e Colloque International, Spa Sep. 1–4, 1982. Crédit Communal, no. 65, Bruxelles, 1984, p. 497–539.

Markovits, Claude. "L' État Colonial vu par les Historiens," in J. Pouchepadass and H. Stern (eds.), *From Kingship to State*. Éditions de l'École des Hautes Études en Sciences Sociales—Collection Purusartha 13, Paris, 1992, p. 193–206.

Marks, Robert. *Tigers, Rice, Silk, and Silt*. Cambridge University Press, 1997.

Marongiu, Antonio. *Medieval Parliaments: A Comparative Study*. Eyre & Spottiswoode, London, 1968.

Marshall, Robert. *Storm from the East*. University of California Press, 1993.

Martel-Thoumian, M. "Les Élites Urbaines sous les Mamlouks Circassiens," in U. Vermeulen and J. Van Steenbergen (eds.), *Egypt and Syria in the Fatimid, Ayyubid and Mamluk Eras*. Peeters, Leuven, 2001, 3:271–308.

Martin, Hervé. *Mentalités Médievales (XIe–XVe Siècles)*. Presses Universitaires de France, Paris, 1996.

Martin, Janet. "The Land of Darkness and the Golden Horde." *Cahiers du Monde Russe et Soviétique* 19, no. 4, Oct.–Dec. 1978, p. 401–421.

———. *Treasure of the Land of Darkness*. Cambridge University Press, 1986.

Martines, L. *Power and Imagination: City-States in Renaissance Italy*. New York, Random House, 1979.

Marx, Karl. *Capital*. Vol. 1. Vintage Books, New York, 1977.

Masschaele, James. *Peasants, Merchants and Markets*. Macmillan, Basingstoke, 1997.

Matthee, Rudolph. *The Politics of Trade in Safavid Iran*. Cambridge University Press, 1999.

Mattoso, José. "Les Ancêtres des Navigateurs," in Michel Balard et al., *L'Europe et l'Océan au Moyen Âge*. Société des Historiens Médiévistes de l'Enseignement Supérieur & Cid Éditions, Nantes, 1988, p. 95–110.

Mauny, Raymond. "Le Déblocage d'un Continent par les Voies Maritimes," in Michel Mollat et al., "Les Grandes Voies Maritimes dans le Monde, XVe–XIXe Siècles." VIIe Colloque de la Commission Internationale d'Histoire Maritime. SEVPEN, Paris, 1965, p. 175–190.

———. *Les Siècles Obscurs de l'Afrique Noire*. Librairie Fayard, Paris, 1970.

———. "Tableau Géographique de l'Ouest Africain au Moyen Âge d'après les Sources Écrites, la Tradition et l'Archéologie." *IFAN* 61, Dakar, 1961.

Mauro, Frédéric. "Les Ports Comme Entreprise Économique," in "I Porti Come Impresa Economica I." Atti della Diciannovesima Settimane di studi 2–6 maggio 1987. Instituto Internazionale di Storia Economica "F. Datini," Serie II, 19, Prato, 1988, p. 751–777.

May, Timothy. "The Training of an Inner Asian Nomad Army." *Journal of Military History* 70, no. 3, 2006, p. 617–36.

Mazzaoui, Maureen. *The Italian Cotton Industry in the Late Middle Ages*. Cambridge University Press, New York, 1981.

McDougall, E. A. "The Sahara Reconsidered." *African Economic History* 12, 1983, p. 263–286.

McDougall, E. A. "The View from Awdaghust." *Journal of African History* 26, no. 1, 1985, p. 1–31.

McKnight, Brian. *Village and Bureaucracy in Southern Sung China.* University of Chicago Press, 1971.

McNeill, William. *The Global Condition.* Princeton University Press, NJ, 1992.

——. *The Rise of the West.* University of Chicago Press, 1963.

——. "World History and the Rise and Fall of the West." *Journal of World History* 9, no. 2, Fall 1998, p. 215–236.

McPherson, Kenneth. *The Indian Ocean: A History of People and The Sea.* Oxford University Press, 1993.

Meilink-Roelofsz, M.A.P. "Arab Trade with Indonesia and the Malay Peninsula from the 8th to the 16th Century," in D. S. Richards (ed.), *Islam and the Trade of Asia.* Oxford/University of Pennsylvania Press, 1970, p. 105–157.

——. "The Dutch East India Company's Ports of Call," in *Les Grandes Escales.* Part 2, *Les Temps Modernes.* Recueils de la Société Jean Bodin pour l'Histoire Comparative des Institutions 33, Éditions de la Librairie Encyclopédique, Bruxelles, 1972, p. 171–196.

——. "European Influence in Southeast Asia, 1500–1630." *Journal of Southeast Asian History* 5, no. 2, Sept. 1964, p.184–197.

Meillassoux, Claude. *L'Esclavage en Afrique Pré-Coloniale.* Éditions Maspero, Paris, 1975.

——. "The Role of Slavery in the Economic and Social History of Sahelo-Sudanic Africa," in J. E. Inikori (ed.), *Forced Migration.* Hutchinson University Library, London, 1982, p. 74–99.

Melis, Federigo. "La Participacion Toscana en la Navegacion Atlantica," in "Les Routes de l'Atlantique." Travaux du 9e Colloque International d'Histoire Maritime, Séville, 24–30 septembre 1967. SEVPEN, Paris, 1969, p. 281–293.

Meloy, John. "Imperial Strategy and Political Exigence." *Journal of American Orientalist Society* 123, no. 1, March 2003, p. 1–19.

Menant, François. *Campagnes Lombardes du Moyen Âge.* École Française de Rome, Palais Farnèse, Roma, 1993.

——. "Pour une Histoire Médiévale de l'Entreprise Minière en Lombardie." *Annales ESC* 42, no. 4, Juillet–Août 1987, p. 779–796.

Menard, Russell R. "Transport Costs and Long-Range Trade, 1300–1800," in James D. Tracy (ed.), *The Political Economy of Merchant Empires.* Cambridge University Press, 1997, p. 228–275.

Menjot, Denis, and Manuel Sánchez Martinez, eds. *La Fiscalité des Villes au Moyen Âge.* Vol. 2, *Les Systèmes Fiscaux.* éd Privat, Lavour (Tarn), 1999.

Mercer, John. *The Canary Islanders: Their Prehistory, Conquest and Survival.* Collings, London, 1980.

Merrington, John. "Town and Countryside in the Transition to Capitalism," in Rodney H. Hilton (ed.), *The Transition from Feudalism to Capitalism.* NLB, London, 1976, p. 170–185.

Messier, Ronald, and Abdallah Fili. "La Ville Caravanniére de Sijilmasa," in Antonio Silva and Virgilio Enamorado (dir.), *La Cuidad en Al-Andalus y el Magreb. II Congreso Internacional.* Junta de Andalucia, Granada, 2002, p. 501–510.

Meyer, Jean. *Les Capitalismes.* Presses Universitaires de France, Paris, 1981.

——. "La France et l'Asie: Essai de Statistiques," in *Histoire, Économie et Société,* 2e trimestre, 1982, p. 297–312.

Mickwitz, G. *Die Kartellfunktionen der Zunfte und ihre Bedeutung bei der Entstehung der Zunftwesens. Eine Studie in spätantiker und mittelalterlicher Wirtschaftgeschichte.* Helsinki/Leipzig, Societas Scientarium Fennica, 1936.

Mielants, Eric. "Mass Migration in the World System" in Ramon Grosfoguel and Ana Margarita Rodriguez (eds.), *The Modern Colonial Capitalist World-System in the 20th Century.* Greenwood Press, Westport, CT, 2002, p. 79–102.

Milis, Ludo. "The Medieval City," in Johan Decavele (ed.), *Ghent: In Defence of a Rebellious City.* Mercatorfonds, Antwerp, 1989, p. 61–79.

Miller, Edward. "English Town Patricians, c. 1200–1350," in Annalisa Guarducci (ed.), "Gerarchie Economiche e Gerarchie Sociali Secoli XII–XVIII." Atti della Dodicesima Settimana di Studi 18–23 Aprile 1980. Instituto Internazionale di Storia Economica "F. Datini," Serie II, 22, Le Monnier, Prato, 1990, p. 217–240.

———. "Government Economic Policies and Public Finance 1000–1500," in Carlo M. Cipola, *The Fontana Economic History of Europe.* Vol. 1, *The Middle Ages.* Barnes & Noble, New York, 1976, p. 339–373.

Miller, Edward, and John Hatcher. *Medieval England: Rural Society and Economic Change 1086–1348.* Longman, London, 1978.

———. *Medieval England: Towns, Commerce and Crafts 1086–1348.* Longman, London, 1995.

Miller, Joseph. *Way of Death.* Univ. of Wisconsin Press, Madison, 1988.

Miskimin, Harry. *The Economic of Early Renaissance Europe.* Cambridge University Press, 1975.

Miura, Toru. "The City as a Frame of Reference," in Mohamed Naciri and André Raymond (dirs.), *Sciences Sociales et Phénomènes Urbains dans le Monde Arabe.* Fondation du Roi Abdul-Aziz Al Saoud pour les Études Islamiques et les Sciences Humaines, Casablanca, 1997, p. 43–57.

Modelski, George, and William Thompson. *Leading Sectors and World Powers.* University of South Carolina Press, 1996.

Mojuetan, Benson. *History and Underdevelopment in Morocco.* International African Institute & LIT Verlag, Munster, 1995.

Mokyr, Joel. *The Lever of Riches.* Oxford University Press, 1990.

Molenda, Danuta. "Investments in Ore Mining in Poland from the 13th to the 17th Centuries." *Journal of European Economic History* 5, no. 1, Spring 1976, p. 151–169.

———. "Investissements Industriels et Investissements Culturels dans les Villes Minières de l'Europe Centrale aux XIIIe–XVIIe Siècles," in "Investimenti e Civiltà Urbana Secoli XIII–XVIII." Atti della Nona Settimana di Studi 22–28 Aprile 1977. Instituto Internazionale di Storia Economica "F. Datini," Serie II, 9, Prato, 1989, p. 911–926.

Mollat, Michel. *Études sur l'Économie et la Société de l'Occident Médiéval XIIe–XVe Siècles.* Variorum Press, London, 1977.

———. "L'Europe et l'Océan au Moyen Âge," in Michel Balard et al., *L'Europe et l'Océan au Moyen Âge.* Société des Historiens Médiévistes de l'Enseignement Supérieur/Cid Éditions, Nantes, 1988b, p. 9–18.

———. *Europe and the Sea.* Blackwell, Oxford, 1993.

———. *Jacques Coeur ou l'Esprit d'Entreprise au XV Siècle.* Aubier, Paris, 1988.

———. "Passages Français dans l'Océan Indien au Temps de François I," in "Océan Indien et Méditerranée." Travaux du 6e Colloque International d'Histoire Maritime et du 2e Congrès de l'Association Historique Internationale de l'Océan Indien. Session de Lourenço Marques:13–18 aoÛt 1962. SEVPEN [Paris], 1964, p. 239–250.

———. *The Poor in the Middle Ages.* Yale University Press, New Haven, 1986.

————, ed. *Le Rôle du Sel dans l'Histoire.* Presses Universitaires de France, Paris, 1968.

Mollat, Michel, and Philippe Wolff. *The Popular Revolutions of the Late Middle Ages.* Allen & Unwin, London, 1973.

Moore, Barrington Jr. *Social Origins of Dictatorship and Democracy.* Beacon, Boston, 1966.

Moosvi, Shireen. "The Pre-Colonial State." *Social Scientist* 33, nos. 3–4, March–April 2005, p. 40–53.

Morgan, David. *Medieval Persia, 1040–1797.* Longman, New York, 1988.

————. *The Mongols.* Basil Blackwell, Oxford, 1986.

————. "The Mongols and the Eastern Mediterranean," in Benjamin Arbel, Bernard Hamilton, and David Jacoby (eds.), *Latins and Greeks in the Eastern Mediterranean after 1204.* Frank Cass, London, 1989, p. 198–211.

————. "The Mongols in Syria, 1260–1300," in Peter Edbury (ed.), *Crusade and Settlement.* University College Cardiff Press, 1985, p. 231–235.

Morimoto, Yoshiki. "Villes et Campagnes au Moyen Âge" in Adriaan Verhulst and Yoshiki Morimoto (eds.), *Landwirtschaft und Stadwirtschaft im Mittelalter.* Kyushu University Press, Fukuoka, 1994, p. 11–22.

Morley, J.A.E. "The Arabs and the Eastern Trade." *Journal of the Malayan Branch of the Royal Asiatic Society* 22, no. 1, 1949, p. 143–176.

Morris, David Morris. "Values as an Obstacle to Economic Growth in South Asia." *Journal of Economic History* 27, no. 4, Dec. 1967, p. 588–607.

Morton, W. Scott. *China: Its History and Culture.* McGraw-Hill Inc., New York, 1995.

Moseley, K. P. "Caravel and Caravan." *Review* 15, no. 3, Summer 1992, p. 523–555.

Mote, F. W. *Imperial China, 900–1800.* Harvard University Press, 1999.

Mote, Frederick. "Chinese Society under Mongol Rule," in Herbert Franke and Denis Twitchett (eds.), *The Cambridge History of China.* Cambridge University Press, 1994, 6:616–664.

————. "The Rise of the Ming Dynasty," in F. Mote and D. Twitchett (eds.), *The Cambridge History of China.* Vol. 7, Part I. Cambridge University Press, 1988, p. 11–57.

————. "Yuan and Ming," in K. C. Chang (ed.), *Food in Chinese Culture.* Yale University Press, New Haven, 1977, p. 195–257.

Mousnier, Mireille. *La Gascogne Toulousaine aux XIIe–XIIIe Siècles: Une Dynamique Sociale et Spatiale.* Presses Universitaires de Mirail, Toulouse, 1997.

Muir, E. *Civic Ritual in Renaissance Venice.* Princeton Univ. Press, Princeton, 1981.

Mukerji, Chandra. *From Graven Images.* Cambridge University Press, 1983.

Mukhia, Harbans, ed. *The Feudalism Debate.* Manohar, New Delhi, 2000.

————. *Perspectives on Medieval History.* Vikas Publishing House, New Delhi, 1993.

Mukund, Kanakalatha. *The Trading World of the Tamil Merchants.* Orient Longman, Chennai, 1999.

Mundy, J. H., and P. Riesenberg. *The Medieval Town.* Van Nostrand, Princeton, NJ, 1958.

Mundy, John H. *Europe in the High Middle Ages 1150–1309.* 3rd ed. Longman, London, 2000.

————. *Society and Government at Toulouse in the Age of the Cathars.* Pontifical Institute of Mediaeval Studies, Toronto, 1997.

Munro, John H. "English Backwardness and Financial Innovations in Commerce with the Low Countries," in Peter Stabel, Bruno Blondé, and Anke Greve (eds.), *International Trade in the Low Countries (14th–16th enturies).* Garant, Leuven, 2000, p. 105–167.

————. "Industrial Entrepreneurship in the Late-Medieval Low Countries," in Paul Klep and Eddy Van Cauwenberghe (eds.), *Entrepreneurship and the Transformation of the*

Economy: Essays in Honor of Herman Van der Wee. Leuven University Press, 1994b, p. 377–388.

———. "Industrial Protectionism in Medieval Flanders" in Harry Miskimin, David Herlihy, and A. L. Udovitch (eds.), *The Medieval City.* Yale University Press, New Haven, 1977, p. 229–267.

———. "Industrial Transformations in the North-West European Textile Trades, c. 1290–c. 1340" in B. M. S. Campbell (ed.), *Before the Black Death.* Manchester University Press, 1991, p. 110–148.

———. "Monetary Contraction and Industrial Change in the Late Medieval Low Countries, 1335–1500," in N. J. Mayhew (ed.), *Coinage in the Low Countries (880–1500).* Bar International Series 54, Oxford, 1979, p. 95–161.

———. "The Origins of the English 'New Draperies' " in N. B. Harte (ed.), *The New Draperies in the Low Countries and England, 1300–1800.* Oxford University Press, 1997, p. 35–127.

———. "Textile Technology in the Middle Ages," in Joseph Strayer et al. (eds.), *The Dictionary of the Middle Ages.* New York, 1988.

———. "Textiles as Articles of Consumption in Flemish Towns, 1330–1575." *Bijdragen tot de Geschiedenis,* 81, nos. 1–3, 1998, p. 275–288.

———. *Textiles, Towns and Trade.* Variorum Press, Norfolk, 1994.

———. "Urban Regulation and Monopolistic Competition in the Textile Industries of the Late-Medieval Low Countries," in Erik Aerts (ed.), Proceedings Tenth International Economic History Congress, Leuven, Session B-15. Leuven University Press, 1990, p. 41–52.

———. "Wage Stickiness, Monetary Changes, and Real Incomes in Late Medieval England and the Low Countries, 1300–1500." *Research in Economic History* 21, 2003, p. 185–297.

Murphey, Rhoads. "Colombo and the Re-making of Ceylon," in Frank Broeze (ed.), *Gateways of Asia: Port Cities of Asia in the 13th–20th Centuries.* Kegan Paul International, London, 1996, p. 191–210.

Murray, Alexander. *Reason and Society in the Middle Ages.* Clarendon Press, Oxford, 1978.

Murray, James. *Bruges, Cradle of Capitalism.* Cambridge University Press, 2005.

———. "Cloth, Banking and Finance in Medieval Bruges," in E. Aerts and J. Munro (eds.), "Textiles of the Low Countries in European Economic History." Proceedings 10th International Economic History Congress, Session B 15, Studies in Social and Economic History 19, Leuven University Press, 1990, p. 24–31.

Nag, Prithvish. "The Indian Ocean, India and Africa: Historical and Geographical Perspectives," in Satish Chandra (ed.), *The Indian Ocean Explorations in History, Commerce and Politics.* Sage, London, 1987, p. 151–173.

Nahlik, Adam. "Les Techniques de l'Industrie Textile en Europe Orientale, du Xe au XVe Siècle." *Annales ESC* 26, no. 6, Nov.–Dec. 1971, p. 1279–1290.

Nandi, R. N. "Agrarian Growth and Social Conflicts in Early India," in D. N. Jha (ed.), *Feudal Social Formation in Early India.* Chanakya Publications, New Delhi, 1987, p. 239–284.

Nazet, Jacques. "Les Bourgeois dans les Villes du Hainaut au XIIIe Siècle." *Revue de l'Université de Bruxelles* 4, 1978, p. 437–450.

Needham, Joseph. "Abstract of Material Presented to the International Maritime History Commission at Beirut," in Michel Mollat (dir.), *Sociétés et Compagnies de Commerce en Orient et dans l'Océan Indien.* SEVPEN, Paris, 1970, p. 139–165.

———. "China, Europe and the Seas Between," in Felipe Fernandez-Armesto (ed.), *The Global Opportunity.* Variorum Press, Brookfield, VT, 1995, p. 1–31.

———. *Clerks and Craftsmen in China and the West.* Cambridge University Press, 1970c.

―――. "Discussion," in Michel Mollat (dir.), *Sociétés et Compagnies de Commerce en Orient et dans l'Océan Indien*. SEVPEN, Paris, 1970b, p. 214.

―――. *The Grand Titration*. Allen & Unwin, London, 1969.

―――. "Science and China's Influence on the World," in Raymond Dawson (ed.), *The Legacy of China*. Clarendon Press, Oxford, 1964, p. 234–308.

―――. *Science and Civilization in China*. Vol. 1, *Introductory Orientations*. Cambridge University Press, 1954.

Newitt, M. D. "East Africa and Indian Ocean Trade: 1500–1800," in Ashin Das Gupta and M. N. Pearson (eds.), *India and the Indian Ocean 1500–1800*. Oxford University Press, New Delhi, 1987, p. 201–223.

Ng, Chin-keong. "Maritime Frontiers, Territorial Expansion and Hai-fang during the Late Ming and High Ch'ing," in Sabine Dabringhaus and Roderich Ptak (eds.), *China and Her Neighbours: Borders, Visions of the Other, Foreign Policy 10th to 19th Century*. Harrasowitz Verlag, Wiesbaden, 1997, p. 211–257.

Niane, D. T. "Mali and the Second Mandingo Expansion," in D. T. Niane (ed.), *General History of Africa*. UNESCO, Berkeley, 1984a, 4:117–171.

―――. "Relationships and Exchanges among the Different Regions," in D. T. Niane (ed.), *General History of Africa*. UNESCO, Berkeley, 1984b, 4:614–634.

―――. *Le Soudan Occidental au Temps des Grands Empires*. Présence Africaine, Paris, 1975.

Nicholas, David. "Economic Reorientation and Social Change in Fourteenth Century Flanders." *Past and Present* 70, Feb. 1976, p. 3–29.

―――. *The Growth of the Medieval City*. Longman, New York, 1997a.

―――. *The Later Medieval City*. Longman, New York, 1997b.

―――. *Urban Europe, 1100–1700*. Palgrave, New York, 2003.

―――. *Town and Countryside: Social, Economic and Political Tensions in Fourteenth-Century Flanders*. De Tempel, Brugge, 1971.

Nicolle, D. "The Manufacture and Importation of Military Equipment in the Islamic Eastern Mediterranean (10th–14th Centuries)," in U. Vermeulen and J. Van Steenbergen (eds.), *Egypt and Syria in the Fatimid, Ayyubid and Mamluk Eras*. Peeters, Leuven, 2001, 3:139–162.

Nightingale, Pamela. "Knights and Merchants." *Past and Present* 169, nov. 2000, p. 36–62.

Nijsten, G. "Toneel in de stad," in W. Prevenier (a.o.), "Core and Periphery in Late Medieval Urban Society." Leuven, Garant, 1997, p. 105–129.

Nizami, Khaliq. *Religion and Politics in India during the Thirteenth Century*. Oxford University Press, 2002.

―――. *State and Culture in Medieval India*. Adam Publishers, New Delhi, 1985.

North, Douglass. "A Framework for Analyzing the State in Economic History." *Explorations in Economic History* 16, no. 3, July 1979, p. 249–259.

―――. "Institutions, Transaction costs, and the Rise of Merchant Empires," in James Tracy (ed.), *The Political Economy of Merchant Empires*. Cambridge University Press, 1991, p. 22–40.

North, Douglass, and Robert Thomas. *The Rise of the Western World*. Cambridge University Press, 1973.

Nystazopoulou, Marie. "Venise et la Mer Noire du XIe au XVe Siècle," in Pertusi Agostino (ed.), *Venezia e il Levante fino al secolo XV*. Parte Seconda. Leo S. Olschki Editore, Firenze, 1973, p. 541–582.

O'Brien, Patrick. "European Industrialization: From the Voyages of Discovery to the Industrial Revolution," in Hans Pohl (ed.), *The European Discovery of the World and its Economic Effects on Pre-Industrial Society, 1500–1800*. F. Steiner Verlag, Stuttgart, 1990, p. 154–177.

————. "The Foundations of European Industrialization." *Journal of Historical Sociology* 4, no. 3, Sep. 1991, p. 288–316.

————. "The Foundations of European Industrialization," in José Pardo (ed.), *Economic Effects of the European Expansion, 1492–1824.* Franz Steiner Verlag, Stuttgart, 1992, p. 463–502.

Oikonomidès, Nicolas. *Hommes d'Affaires Grecs et Latins à Constantinople (XIIIe–XVe Siècles).* Institut d'Études Médiévales Albert-Le-Grand, Montréal, 1979.

Ojha, Dhirendra. *Aristocracy in Medieval India.* Orient Publications, New Delhi, 1993.

O'Leary, Brendan. *The Asiatic Mode of Production.* Oxford, Basil Blackwell, 1989.

Omvedt, Gail. "Modernization Theories: The Ideology of Empire?" in A.R. Desai (ed.), *Essays on Modernization of Underdeveloped Societies. Vol. 1* Humanities Press, New York, 1972, p. 119–137.

Ould, Cheikh Abdel Wedoud. *Éléments d'Histoire de la Mauritanie.* Institut Mauritanien de Recherche Scientifique/Centre Culturel Français, Nouakchott, 1991.

Pacey, Arnold. *The Maze of Ingenuity.* MIT Press, Cambridge, 1978.

Padfield, Peter. *Tide of Empires: Decisive Naval Campaigns in the Rise of the West.* Vol. 1, Routledge & Kegan Paul, London, 1979.

Pal Pách, Zsigmond. *Hungary and the European Economy in Early Modern Times.* Variorum Press, Hampshire, 1994.

Palat, Ravi. "From World-Empire to World-Economy: Southeastern India and the Emergence of the Indian Ocean World Economy, 1350–1650" Unpublished Ph.D. diss., SUNY-Binghamton, Sociology Dept., 1988.

————. "Historical Transformations in Agrarian Systems Based on Wet-Rice Cultivation," in Philip McMichael (ed.), *Food and Agrarian Orders in the World Economy.* Praeger, Westport, CT, 1995, p. 55–77.

————. "Popular Revolts and the State in Medieval South India," in *Bijdragen tot de Taal-, Land- en Volkenkunde* 112, 1986, p. 128–144.

————. "Symbiotic Sisters: Bay of Bengal Ports in the Indian Ocean World-Economy," in R. Kasaba (ed.), *Cities in the World-System.* Greenwood Press, Westport, CT, 1991, p. 17–40.

Palat, Ravi, et al. "The Incorporation and Peripheralization of South Asia." *Review* 10, no. 1, Summer 1986, p. 171–208.

Palat, Ravi, and Immanuel Wallerstein. "Of What World-System Was Pre-1500 'India' a Part?" in Sushil Chaudhury and Michel Morineau (eds.), *Merchants, Companies and Trade.* Cambridge University Press, 1999, p. 21–41.

Pamuk, Sevket. *A Monetary History of the Ottoman Empire.* Cambridge University Press, 2000.

Papacostea, Serban. "Venise et les Pays Roumains au Moyen Âge," in Pertusi Agostino (ed.), *Venezia e il Levante fino al secolo XV.* Part II. Leo S. Olschki Editore, Firenze, 1973, p. 599–624.

Park, Young-Heiu. "A Study of the Transition from Feudalism to Capitalism." Unpublished Ph.D. diss., Dept. of Economics, Salt Lake City, Utah University, August 1995.

Parsons, Talcott. *The Social System.* Free Press, Glencoe, IL, 1952.

Parthasarathi, Prasannan. "Merchants and the Rise of Colonialism," in Burton Stein and Sanjay Subrahmanyam (eds.), *Institutions and Economic Change in South Asia.* Oxford University Press, New Delhi, 1996, p. 85–104.

————. "Rethinking Wages and Competitiveness in the 18th Century." *Past and Present* 158, Feb. 1998, p. 79–109.

————. The Transition to a Colonial Economy. Cambridge University Press, 2001.

Paul, Jurgen. "Perspectives Nomades." *Annales HSS* 59, nos. 5–6, Sept.–Dec. 2004, p. 1069–1093.

Paulme, Denise. "L'Afrique Noire Jusqu'au XIVe Siècle." *Cahiers d'Histoire Mondiale* 3, no. 3, 1957, p. 561–582.

Pauly, M. "La Consommation Urbaine de Vin au Bas Moyen Âge." *Bijdragen tot de Geschiedenis* 81, nos. 1–3, 1998, p. 289–303.

Paviot, Jacques. "England and the Mongols (1260–1330)." *Journal of the Royal Asiatic Society* 10, no. 3, Nov. 2000, p. 305–318.

Pavlov, Vladimir. "Premises for the Genesis of Capitalism in Lagged Non-European Regions," in Annalisa Guarducci (red.), "Sviluppo e sottosviluppo in Europa e fuori d'Europa dal secolo XIII alla Revoluzione Industriale." Atti della Decima settimana di studio 7–12 aprile 1978. Instituto Internazionale di Storia Economica "F. Datini," Serie II, 10, Prato, 1983, p. 589–625.

Pearson, M. N. *Before Colonialism: Theories on Asian-European Relations 1500–1750.* Oxford University Press, 1988.

———. "India and the Indian Ocean in the Sixteenth Century," in Ashin Das Gupta and M. N. Pearson (eds.), *India and the Indian Ocean 1500–1800.* Oxford University Press, New Delhi, 1987b, p. 71–93.

———. "The Indian Ocean and the Red Sea," in Nehemia Levtzion and Randall Pouwels (eds.), *The History of Islam in Africa.* Ohio University Press, Athens, 2000, p. 37–59.

———. "Introduction I: The Subject," in Ashin Das Gupta and M. N. Pearson (eds.), *India and the Indian Ocean 1500–1800.* Oxford University Press, New Delhi, 1987, p. 1–24.

———. *Merchants and Rulers in Gujarat.* University of California Press, Berkeley, 1976.

———. "Merchants and States," in James Tracy (ed.), *The Political Economy of Merchant Empires.* Cambridge University Press, 1991, p. 41–116.

———. "Political Participation in Mughal India." *Indian Economic and Social History Review* 9, no. 2, 1972, p. 113–131.

———. *Port Cities and Intruders.* Johns Hopkins University Press, Baltimore, 1998.

———. *The Portuguese in India.* Cambridge University Press, 1987c.

Pelizzon, Sheila. "But Can She Spin? The Decline in the Social Standing of Women in the Transition from Feudalism to Capitalism." Unpublished Ph.D. diss., Sociology Dept., SUNY-Binghamton, 1999.

Perkins, Kenneth. *Tunisia: Crossroads of the Islamic and European Worlds.* Westview Press, Boulder, CO, 1986.

Perlin, Frank. *The Invisible City.* Variorum Press/Ashgate, Aldershot/ /Brookfield, VT, 1993.

———. "Precolonial South Asia and Western Penetration in the 17th to 19th Centuries." *Review* 4, no. 2, Fall 1980, p. 267–306.

———. "Proto-industrialization and Pre-Colonial South Asia." *Past and Present* 98, Feb. 1983, p. 30–95.

———. "State Formation Reconsidered. Part Two." *Modern Asian Studies* 19, no. 3, 1985, p. 415–480.

Pernoud, Régine. *De Middeleeuwen: Een herwaardering.* Ambo, Baarn, 1992. [Translated from the 1977 edition, *Pour en Finir avec le Moyen Âge.* Ed. du Seuil, Paris.]

Pernoud, Régine, Jean Gimpel, and Robert Delatouche. *Le Moyen Âge pour Quoi Faire?* Ed. Stock, Paris, 1986.

Perrot, Jean-Claude. "Développement et Sous-Développement Régionales," in A. Guarducci (red.), "Sviluppo e sottosviluppo in Europa e fuori d'Europa dal secolo XIII alla Revoluzione Industriale." Atti della Decima settimana di studio 7–12 aprile 1978. Instituto Internazionale di Storia Economica "F. Datini," Serie II, 10, Prato, 1983, p. 91–102.

Perroy, Edouard. "Wage Labour in France in the Later Middle Ages," in Sylvia Thrupp (ed.), *Change in Medieval Society*. Appleton-Century-Crofts, New York, 1964, p. 237–246.

Persson, Karl Gunnar. *Pre-Industrial Economic Growth*. Basil Blackwell, Oxford, 1988.

Pescatello, Ann. "The African Presence in Portuguese India." *Journal of Asian History* 11, no. 1, 1977, p. 26–48.

Petech, Luciano. "Les Marchands Italiens dans l'Empire Mongol." *Journal Asiatique* 250, 1962, p. 549–574.

Peterson, Mark. "Innovation, Investment and the Development of Commercial Beer Brewing within the Wendish Towns of Late Medieval Germany." Ph.D. diss., University of Wisconsin, Madison, 2000.

Pfeiffer, Friedrich. "Politiques et Pratiques Douanières sur le Rhin aux XIVe et XVe Siècles," in Ph. Contamine et al., *L'Impôt au Moyen Âge*. Vol. 2, *Les Techniques*. Ministère de l'Économie, des Finances et de l'Industrie, Paris, 2002, p. 741–762.

Phillips, J. R. S. *The Medieval Expansion of Europe*. 2nd ed. Clarendon Press, Oxford, 1998.

Phillips, William. *Slavery from Roman Times to the Early Transatlantic Trade*. University of Minnesota Press, Minneapolis, 1985.

Picard, Christophe. *Le Monde Musulman du XIe au XVe Siècle*. SEDES, Paris, 2000.

———. *L'Océan Atlantique Musulman*. Éd Maisonneuve & Larose, UNESCO, Paris, 1997.

Piccinni, Gabriella. "Economy and Society in Southern Tuscany in the Late Middle Ages," in Thomas Blomquist and Maureen Mazzaoui (eds.), *The Other Tuscany*. Kalamazoo, Medieval Institute Publications, Western Michigan University, 1994, p. 215–233.

Piergiovanni, Paola M. "Technological Typologies and Economic Organisation of Silk Workers in Italy, from the XIVth to the XVIIIth Centuries." *Journal of European Economic History* 22, no. 3, Winter 1993, p. 543–564.

Pirenne, Henri. *Early Democracies in the Low Countries*. Harper & Row, New York, 1963.

———. *Economic and Social History of Medieval Europe*. Harcourt, Brace & Co, New York, 1937.

———. *Histoire de Belgique*. M. Lamertin, Bruxelles, 1947.

———. *Medieval Cities: Their Origins and the Revival of Trade*. Doubleday, New York, 1956.

———. *Les Villes et les Institutions Urbaines*. 2 vols. Nouvelle Societé d'Éditions, Bruxelles, 1939.

Pistarino, Geo. *Genovesi d'Oriente*. Civico Istituto Colombiano, Genova, 1990.

Poisson, Jean-Michel "Élites Urbaines Coloniales et Autochtones dans la Sardaigne Pisane (XIIe–XIIIe Siècle)," in "Les Élites Urbaines au Moyen Âge." XXIVe Congrès de la S.H.M.E.S (Rome, mai 1996). Collection de l'Ecole Française de Rome 238, École Française de Rome, Publications de la Sorbonne, Paris, 1997, p. 165–181.

———. "Formes Urbaines de la Colonisation Pisane en Sardaigne (XIII–XIVe Siècle)," in Michel Balard and Alain Ducellier (dirs.), *Coloniser au Moyen Âge*. Armand Colin, Paris, 1995, p. 39–49.

Pollard, Sidney. *Marginal Europe*. Clarendon Press, Oxford, 1997.

Pollock, Sheldon. "India in the Vernacular Millennium." *Daedalus* 127, no. 3, Summer 1998, p. 41–74.

Pomeranz, Kenneth. "Beyond the East-West Binary." *Journal of Asian Studies* 61, no. 2, May 2002, p. 539–590.

———. *The Great Divergence*. Princeton University Press, 2000.

Ponting, Clive. *A Green History of the World*. New York, Penguin, 1993.

Populer, Michèle. "Les Entrées Inaugurales des Princes dans les Villes." *Revue du Nord* 76, no. 304, Jan.–Mars 1994, p. 25–52.

Postan, M. M., ed. *Cambridge Economic History of Europe*. Vol. 1. 2nd ed., Cambridge University Press, 1966.

————. Essays on Medieval Agriculture and General Problems of the Medieval Economy. Cambridge University Press, 1973.

Postan, M. M., and J. Hatcher. "Population and Class Relations in Feudal Society," in T. H. Aston and C.H.E. Philpin (eds.), *The Brenner Debate*. Cambridge University Press, 1985, p. 64–78.

Pouchepadass, Jacques. "L'Inde," in Jean Favier (dir.), *XIVe et XVe Siècles: Crises et Genèses*. Presses Universitaires de France, Série "Peuple et Civilisations," Paris, 1996, p. 687–727.

Pounds, N.J.G. *An Economic History of Medieval Europe*. Longman, London, 1994 ed.

Powers, James. "Townsmen and Soldiers." *Speculum* 46, no. 4, Oct. 1971, p. 641–655.

Prak, Maarten, ed. *Early Modern Capitalism*. Routledge, London, 2001.

————. "Het verdeelde Europa." *Amsterdams Sociologisch Tijdschrift* 19, no. 1, May 1992, p. 118–139.

Prakash, Buddha. "A Debated Question: The Genesis and Character of Landed Aristocracy in Ancient India." *Journal of the Economic and Social History of the Orient* 14, 1971, p. 196–220.

Prakash, Om. "Asian Trade and European Impact," in Blair Kling and M. N. Pearson (eds.), *The Age of Partnership: Europeans in Asia before Dominion*. University Press of Hawaii, Honolulu, 1979, p. 43–70.

————. "The Dutch East India Company in Bengal." *Indian Economic and Social History Review* 9, no. 3, 1972, p. 258–287.

————. *European Commercial Enterprise in Pre-Colonial India*. Cambridge University Press, 1998.

Prawer, Joshua. *The Latin Kingdom of Jerusalem*. Weidenfeld & Nicolson, London, 1972.

Prevenier, Walter. "Bevolkingscijfers en professionele strukturen der Bevolking van Gent en Brugge in de 14de eeuw," in *Album Charles Verlinden*. Universa, Gent, 1975, p. 269–303.

————. "Bij wijze van besluit," in Myriam Carlier, Anke Greve, Walter Prevenier, and Peter Stabel (eds.), "Core and Periphery in Late Medieval Urban Society." Garant, Leuven, 1997, p. 193–199.

————. "La Bourgeoisie en Flandre au XIIIe Siècle." *Revue de l'Université de Bruxelles* 4, 1978, p. 407–427.

————. "Conscience et Perception de la Condition Sociale chez les gens du Commun dans les Anciens Pays-Bas des XIIIe et XIVe Siècles," in Pierre Boglioni, Robert Delort, and Claude Gauvard (eds.), *Le Petit Peuple dans l'Occident Médiéval*. Publications de la Sorbonne, Paris, 2002, p. 175–189.

————. "Court and City Culture in the Low Countries from 1100 to 1530," in Erik Kooper (ed.), *Medieval Dutch Literature in Its European Context*. Cambridge University Press, 1994, p. 11–29.

————. "Culture et Groupes Sociaux dans les Villes des Anciens Pays-Bas au Moyen Âge," in J. M. Duvosquel, J. Nazet, and A. Vanrie (red.), *Les Pays-Bas Bourguignons: Histoire et Institutions*. Archives et Bibliothèques de Belgique, Bruxelles, 1996, p. 349–359.

————. "La Démographie des Villes du Comté de Flandre aux XIIIe et XIVe Siècles." *Revue du Nord* 65, no. 257, Avril–Juin 1983, p. 255–275.

————. "Élites, Classes Moyennes et Ouvriers," in Walter Prevenier (dir.), *Le Prince et le Peuple*. Mercator Fonds, Anvers, 1998, p. 73–92.

————. "Inzicht van kritische tijdgenoten in de sociale facetten der fiscaliteit en in sociaal-politiek onrecht in Vlaanderen (13e–15e eeuw)," in Guido Peeters and Magda de Moor (red.), *Arbeid in veelvoud*. VUB Press, Brussel, 1988, p. 51–60.

————. "Les Perturbations dans les Relations Commerciales Anglo-Flamandes entre 1379 et 1407," in *Économies et Sociétés au Moyen Âge*. Publications de la Sorbonne, Paris, 1973, p. 477–497.

Prevenier, Walter, and Marc Boone. "The 'City-State' Dream," in Johan Decavele (ed.), *Ghent: In Defence of a Rebellious City*. Mercatorfonds, Antwerp, 1989, p. 81–105.

Prevenier, Walter, Jean-Pierre Sosson, and Marc Boone. "Le Réseau Urbain en Flandre (XIIIe–XIXe Siècle)," in "Le Réseau Urbain en Belgique dans une Perspective Historique." Bruxelles, Crédit Communal, Collection Histoire, no. 86, 1992, p. 157–200.

Pryor, Frederic. "The Asian Mode of Production as an Economic System." *Journal of Comparative Economics* 4, 1980, p. 420–442.

Pryor, John. *Geography, Technology and War*. Cambridge University Press, 1988.

————. "The Problem of Byzantium and the Mediterranean World," in Benjamin Kedar, Jonathan Riley-Smith, and Rudolf Hiestand (eds.), *Montjoie: Studies in Crusade History in Honour of Hans Eberhard Meyer*. Asghate/Variorum, Aldershot, 1997, p. 199–211.

Ptak Roderich. "China and the Trade in Tortoise-shell (Sung to Ming Periods)" in Ptak Roderich and Rothermund Dietmar (eds.) "Emporia, Commodities, and entrepreneurs in Asian Maritime Trade", c. 1400–1750" Franz Steiner Verlag, Stuttgart, 1991, p. 195-229

————. "Quanzhou: at the Northern Edge," in Angela Schottenhammer (ed.), *The Emporium of the World*. Brill, Boston, 2001, p. 395–427.

————. "China and the Trade in Cloves, *circa* 960–1435." *Journal of the American Oriental Society* 113, no. 1, 1993, p. 1–13.

————. *China's Seaborne Trade with South and Southeast Asia (1200–1750)*. Variorum Reprints, Ashgate, Aldershot, 1999.

————. *China, the Portuguese and the Nanyang*. Variorum Reprints, Ashgate, Aldershot, 2004.

————. "From Quanzhou to the Sulu Zone and Beyond." *Journal of Southeast Asian Studies* 29, no. 2 , September 1998, p. 269–294.

————. ed. *Hsing-Ch'a Sheng-Lan: The Overall Survey of the Star Raft by Fei Hsin*. Vol. 4 of *South China and Maritime Asia*. Trans. by J. Mills. Harrassowitz Verlag, Wiesbaden, 1996.

————. "Merchants and Maximization: Notes on Chinese and Portuguese Entrepreneurship in Maritime Asia, c. 1350–1600," in K. A. Sprengard and Roderich Ptak (eds.), *Maritime Asia: Profit Maximisation, Ethics and Trade Structure, c. 1300–1800*. Harrasowitz Verlag, Wiesbaden, 1994, p. 29–59.

Putseys, Johan. "De militaire organisatie in de steden van het graafschap Vlaanderen in de late middeleeuwen." Unpublished Master's thesis, Dept. of History, University of Ghent, 1994.

Qaisar, Ahsan. *The Indian Response to European Technology and Culture*. Oxford University Press, New Delhi, 1982.

Raban, Sandra. *England under Edward I and Edward II*. Blackwell, Oxford, 2000.

Racine, Pierre. "Marchands Placentins à L'Aias à la Fin du XIIIe Siècle." *Byzantinische Forschungen* 4, 1972, p. 195–205.

Raftis, J. A. *Peasant Economic Development within the English Manorial System*. McGill-Queen's University Press, 1996.

Ragheb, Youssef. "Les Marchands Itinérants du Monde Musulman," in *Voyages et Voyageurs au Moyen Âge*. Publications de la Sorbonne, Paris, 1996, p. 177–215.

Ramaswamy, Vijaya. "Artisans in Vijayanagar Society." *Indian Economic and Social History Review* 22, no. 4, Oct.–Dec. 1985a, p. 417–444.

————. "Peasant State and Society in Medieval South India." *Studies in History* 4, no. 2, 1982, p. 307–319.

————. *Textile Weavers in Medieval South India.* Oxford University Press, 1985b.

————. "Interactions and Encounters," in A. Rahman (ed.), *India's Interaction with China, Central and West Asia.* Oxford University Press, New Delhi, 2002, p. 428–444.

Ramsay, George. "The Merchants of the Staple and the Downfall of the English Wool Export Traffic," in Marco Spallanzani (ed.), "La Lana come Materia Prima." Atti della Prima Settimana di Studio 18–24 aprile 1969. Instituto Internazionale di Storia Economica "F. Datini," Prato, L Olschki, Firenze, 1974, p. 45–63.

Rawski, Evelyn. *Agricultural Change and the Peasant Economy of South China.* Harvard University Press, 1972.

Ray, Haraprasad. "Bengal's Textile Products Involved in Ming Trade during Cheng Ho's Voyages to the Indian Ocean," in Roderich Ptak and Dietmar Rothermund (eds.), *Emporia, Commodities, and Entrepreneurs in Asian Maritime Trade, c. 1400–1750.* Franz Steiner Verlag, Stuttgart, 1991, p. 81–93.

————. "China and the 'Western Ocean' in the Fifteenth Century," in Satish Chandra (ed.), *The Indian Ocean Explorations in History, Commerce, and Politics.* Sage, London, 1987, p. 109–124.

————. "Indian Settlements in China: An Exploration of the Phenomenon of Indian Diaspora from A.D. 1015 to 1487," in K. S. Matkew (ed.), *Indian Ocean and Cultural Interaction.* Pondicherry University, 1996, p. 52–81.

————. *Trade and Diplomacy in India-China Relations: A Study of Bengal in the 15th Century.* Radiant Publishers, New Delhi, 1993.

Ray, Indrajit. "Imperial policy and the decline of the Bengal salt-industry under colonial rule." *Indian Economic and Social History Review* 38, no. 2, 2001, p. 181–205.

Raymond, André. "L'Impact de la Pénétration Européenne sur l'Économie de L'Égypte au XVIIIe Siècle." *Annales Islamologiques* 18, 1982, p. 217–235.

————. "Islamic City, Arab City: Orientalist Myths and Recent Views." *British Journal of Middle Eastern Studies* 21, 1994, p. 3–18.

Redon, Odile. *L'Espace d'une Cité: Sienne et le Pays Siennois (XIIIe–XIVe Siècles).* École Française de Rome, Palais Farnèse, 1994.

Reichert, Folker. *Begegnungen mit China: Die Entdeckung Ostasiens in Mittelalter.* Jan Thorbecke Verlag, Sigmaringen, 1992.

Reid, Anthony. *Charting the Shape of Early Modern Southeast Asia.* Silkworm Books, Bangkok, 1999.

————. "Some Effects on Asian Economies of the European Maritime Discoveries," in José Pardo (ed.), *Economic Effects of the European Expansion, 1492–1824.* Franz Steiner Verlag, Stuttgart, 1992, p. 435–462.

————. *Southeast Asia in the Age of Commerce, 1450–1680.* Vol. 2. Yale University Press, New Haven, 1993.

Rénouard, Yves. *Études d'Histoire Médiévale.* École Pratique des Hautes Études, Paris, 1968.

————. *Hommes d'Affaires Italiens du Moyen Âge.* Armand Colin, Paris, 1949.

Reuter, Timothy. "Medieval: Anothers Tyrannous Construct?" *Medieval History Journal* 1, no. 1, June 1998, p. 25–45.

Reyerson, Kathryn. "Urban/Rural Exchange: Reflections on the Economic Relations of Town and Country in the Region of Montpellier before 1350," in Kathryn Reyerson and John Drendel (eds.), *Urban and Rural Communities in Medieval France: Provence and Languedoc, 1000–1500.* Brill, Boston, 1998, p. 253–273.

Reynolds, Clark. *Command of the Sea.* William Morrow & Co, New York, 1974.

Reynolds, Robert. *Europe Emerges*. The University of Wisconsin Press, Madison, 1961.
———. "The Markets for Northern Textiles in Genoa, 1179–1200." *Revue Belge de Philologie et d'Histoire* 8, 1929, p. 831–851.
Richard, Jean. "An Account of the Battle of Hattin." *Speculum* 27, 1952, p. 168–177.
———. *Croisés, Missionnaires et Voyageurs*. Variorum Reprints, London, 1983.
———. *Francs et Orientaux dans le Monde des Croisades*. Variorum Reprints/Ashgate, Aldershot, 2003.
———. "La Laine de Bourgogne: Production et Commerce (XIIIe–XVe Siècles)," in Marco Spallanzani (ed.), "La Lana come Materia Prima." Atti della Prima Settimana di Studio 18–24 aprile 1969. Instituto Internazionale di Storia Economica "F. Datini," Prato, L Olschki, Firenze, 1974, p. 325–340.
———. "Les Navigations des Occidentaux sur l'Océan Indien et la Mer Caspienne (XIIe–XVe Siècles)," in Michel Mollat (dir.), *Sociétés et Compagnies de Commerce en Orient et dans l'Océan Indien*. SEVPEN, Paris, 1970, p. 353–363.
———. *Orient et Occident au Moyen Âge: Contacts et Relations (XIIe–XVe Siècles.)*. Variorum Reprints, London, 1976.
———. *Les Relations entre l'Orient et l'Occident au Moyen Âge*. Variorum Reprints, London, 1977.
Richard, John F. *The Mughal Empire*. Cambridge University Press, 1993.
———. (ed.). *Precious Metals in the Later Medieval and Early Modern Worlds*. Carolina Academic Press, Durham, NC, 1983.
Rigby, Stephen. "Historical Materialism: Social Structure and Social Change in the Middle Ages" *Journal of Medieval and Early Modern Studies*, Vol. 34, no. 3, 2004, p. 473–522.
Risso, Patricia. *Merchants and Faith: Muslim Commerce and Culture in the Indian Ocean*. Westview Press, Boulder, CO, 1995.
Robert, Louise. "A Venetian Naval Expedition of 1224." *Explorations in Economic History* 7, nos. 1–2, 1970, p. 141–151.
Roberts, J .A. G. *A History of China*. Vol. 1. St. Martin's Press, New York, 1996.
Roberts, J. M. *The Pelican History of the World*. Penguin Books, New York, 1980.
Roberts, Richard. *Warriors, Merchants and Slaves*. Stanford University Press, 1987.
Rodinson, Maxime. *Islam and Capitalism*. University of Texas Press, Austin, 1978.
———. "Le Marchand Musulman," in D. S. Richards (ed.), *Islam and the Trade of Asia*. Bruno Cassirer Oxford/University of Pennsylvania Press, 1970, p. 21–35.
Rodney, Walter. *How Europe Underdeveloped Africa*. Howard University Press, Washington, DC, 1982 ed.
Rodrigues, Ana Maria. "La Lutte pour la Prise et la Conservation du Pouvoir dans les Villes Portugaises à la Fin du Moyen Âge," in Denis Menjot and Jean-Luc Pinol (coords.), *Enjeux et Expressions de la Politique Municipale (XIe–XXe Siècles)*. L'Harmattan, Paris, 1997, p. 21–40.
Rodzinski, Wittold. *A History of China*. Vol. 1. Pergamon Press, Oxford, 1979.
Rodzinski, Wittold. *The Walled Kingdom*. London, 1984.
Romano, Ruggiero. "A Propos du Commerce du Blé dans la Méditerranée des XIVe et XVe Siècles," in *Éventail de l'Histoire Vivante: Hommage à Lucien Febvre*. Librairie Armand Colin, Paris, 1954, p. 149–161.
Romano, Ruggiero, Alberto Tenenti, and Ugo Tucci. "Venise et la Route du Cap. 1499–1517," in Manlio Cortelazzo (ed.), "Mediterraneo e Oceano Indiano." Atti del Sesto Colloquio Internazionale di Storia Marittima, Venezia, 20–29 settembre 1962. L Olschki Editore, Firenze, 1970, p. 110–139.
Rösch, Gerhard. "Reichsitalien als Wirtschaftsraum im Zeitalter der Staufer," in Wolfgang

von Stromer (ed.), *Venedig und die Weltwirtschaft um 1200.* Jan Thorbecke Verlag, Stuttgart, 1999, p. 93–116.

Rosenberg, Nathan, and L. E. Birdzell. *How the West Grew Rich.* Basic Books, New York, 1986.

Rosenberger, Bernard. "La Croisade Africaine et le Pouvoir Royal au Portugal au XVe Siècle," in Henri Bresc et al., *Genèse de l'Etat Moderne en Méditerranée.* École Française de Rome, Palais Farnèse, 1993, p. 329–348.

———. "Les Vieilles Exploitations Minières et les Anciens Centres Métallurgiques du Maroc." *Revue de Géographie du Maroc* 17, 1970, p. 71–108.

Rösener, Werner. "Aspekte der Stadt-Land-Beziehungen Im Spatmittelalterlichen Deutschland," in J. M. Duvosquel and E. Thoen (eds.), *Peasants and Townsmen in Medieval Europe.* Belgisch Centrum voor Landelijke Geschiedenis 114, Snoeck-Ducaju & Zoon, Gent, 1995, p. 663–680.

———. *The Peasantry of Europe.* Blackwell, Oxford, 1994.

Rossabi, Morris, ed. *China among Equals: The Middle Kingdom and Its Neighbors.* University of California Press, Berkeley, 1983.

———. "The 'Decline' of the Central Asian Caravan Trade," in James Tracy (ed.), *The Rise of Merchant Empires.* Cambridge University Press, 1990, p. 351–370.

———. "Ming Foreign Policy" in Sabine Dabringhaus and Roderich Ptak (eds.), *China and Her Neighbours: Borders, Visions of the Other, Foreign Policy 10th to 19th Century.* Harrasowitz Verlag, Wiesbaden, 1997, p. 79–97.

———. "The Mongols and the West," in Ainslie Embree and Carol Gluck (eds.), *Asia in Western and World History.* Sharpe, Armonk, NY, 1997, p. 55–62.

———. "The Reign of Khubilai Khan," in Herbert Franke and Denis Twitchett (eds.), *The Cambridge History of China.* Cambridge University Press, 1994b, 6:414–489.

Rosser, Gervase. "Crafts, Guilds and the Negotiation of Work in the Medieval Town." *Past and Present* 154, Feb. 1997, p. 3–31.

Rossiaud, Jacques. "The City-Dweller and Life in Cities and Towns," in Jacques Le Goff (ed.), *The Medieval World.* Collins & Brown, London, 1990, p. 139–179.

———. "Crises et Consolidations: 1330–1530," in J. Le Goff (red.), *La Ville en France au Moyen Âge.* Seuil, Paris, 1998, p. 403–587.

Rothermund, Dietmar. "Asian Emporia and European Bridgeheads," in Roderich Ptak and Dietmar Rothermund (eds.), *Emporia, Commodities, and Entrepreneurs in Asian Maritime Trade, c. 1400–1750.* Franz Steiner Verlag, Stuttgart, 1991, p. 3–8.

Rotz, Rhiman. "Investigating Urban Uprisings with Examples from Hanseatic Tows, 1374–1416," in William Jordan, Bruce McNab, and Teofilo Ruiz (eds.), *Order and Innovation in the Middle Ages.* Princeton University Press, 1976, p. 215–233.

Rougeulle, Axelle. "Le Yémen entre Orient et Afrique." *Annales Islamologiques* 38, no. 1, 2004, p. 201–253.

Roux, Simone. *Le Monde des Villes au Moyen Âge.* Hachette Livre, Paris, 1994.

Rowan, Steven. "Urban Communities: The Rulers and the Ruled," in Thomas Brady, Heiko Oberman, and James Tracy (eds.), *Handbook of European History 1400–1600: Late Middle Ages, Renaissance and Reformation.* Brill, Leiden, 1994, 1:197–229.

Rudra, Ashok. "Pre-Capitalist Modes of Production in Non-European Societies." *Journal of Peasant Studies* 15, no. 3, April 1988, p. 373–394.

Ryan, James. "Preaching Christianity along the Silk Route" *Journal of Early Modern History* 2, no. 4, 1998, p. 350–373.

Saad, Elias. *Social History of Timbuktu.* Cambridge University Press, 1983.

Saberwal, Satish. *Wages of Segmentation: Comparative Historical Studies on Europe and India.* Orient Longman, New Delhi, 1995.

Sabra, Adam. *Poverty and Charity in Medieval Islam: Mamluk Egypt. 1250–1517.* Cambridge University Press, 2000.

Saey, Pieter. "Wereld-Systeem Analyse en het probleem van territoriale integratie." *Vlaams Marxistisch Tijdschrift* 28, no. 4, Dec. 1994, p. 63–78.

Saey, Pieter, and A. Verhoeve. "The Southern Netherlands: Part of the Core or Reduced to a Semi-Peripheral Status?" in H. J. Nitz (ed.), *The Early Modern World-System in Geographical Perspective.* Erdkundliches Wissen 110, Fr. Steiner Verlag, Stuttgart, 1993, p. 93–114.

Saletore, R. N. *Indian Pirates.* Concept Publishing Company, New Delhi, 1978.

Samsonowicz, Henryk. "Changes in the Baltic Zone in the XIII–XVI Centuries." *Journal of European Economic History* 4, no. 3, Winter 1975, p. 655–672.

———. "Grain Consumption in Gdansk in the Mid-15th Century." *Bijdragen tot de Geschiedenis* 81, nos. 1–3, 1998, p. 305–308.

———. "Remarque sur la Comptabilité Commerciale dans les Villes Hanséatiques au XVe Siècle," in "Finances et Comptabilité Urbaines du XIIIe au XVIe Siècle." Actes du Colloque International à Blankenberge, Sept. 6–9, 1962. Pro Civitate Collection Histoire, No. 7, Bruxelles, 1964, p. 207–221.

———. "La Stratégie et la Technique des Affaires Commerciales en Pologne du XIIIe au XVI Siècle," in Sara Mariotti (ed.), "Produttività e tecnologie nei secoli XII–XVII." Atti della Terza Settimana di Studio, 23–29 aprile 1971. Instituto Internazionale di Storia Economica "F. Datini," Serie II, 3, Prato, Le Monnier, 1981, p. 471–481.

———. "Les Villes d'Europe Centrale à la Fin du Moyen Âge." *Annales ESC* 43, no. 1, 1988, p. 173–184.

———. "Les Villes en Europe Centre-Orientale," in Sergio Gensini (red.), "Principi e città alla fine del medioevo." Centro Studi sulla Civiltà del Tardo Medioevo, Collana di Studi e Ricerche 6, Pacini Editori Pisa, Comune San Miniato, 1996, p. 41–52.

Samsonowicz, Henryk, and Antoni Maczak. "Feudalism and Capitalism," in Antoni Maczak, Henryk Samsonowicz, and Peter Burke (eds.), *East-Central Europe in Transition.* Cambridge University Press, New York, 1985, p. 6–23.

Sanderson, Stephen. *Social Transformations: A General Theory of Historical Development.* Blackwell, Oxford, 1995.

———. "The Transition from Feudalism to Capitalism: The Theoretical Significance of the Japanese Case." *Review* 17, no. 1, Winter 1994, p. 15–55.

Sanderson, Stephen K. "The Colonizer's Model of the World." *Sociological Inquiry* 66, no. 4, Fall 1996.

Sapori, Armando. *The Italian Merchant in the Middle Ages.* Norton, New York, 1970.

Sarkar, Jagadish Narayan. *Glimpses of the Medieval Bihar Economy.* Ratna Prakashan, Calcutta, 1978.

Sastri Nilakanta, K. A. *The Colas.* 2nd ed. University of Madras, 1975.

———. K. A., ed. *Foreign Notices of South India: From Megasthenes to Ma Huan.* University of Madras, 1972 ed.

———. *A History of South India from Prehistoric Times to the Fall of Vijayanagar.* 3rd ed. Oxford University Press, 1966.

Saunders, J. J. *Muslims and Mongols: Essays on Medieval Asia.* University of Canterbury & Whitcoulls Ltd., Christchurch, NZ, 1977.

Sayous, André-E. "Le Rôle du Capital dans la Vie Locale et le Commerce Extérieur de Venise entre 1050 et 1150." *Revue Belge de Philologie et d'Histoire* 13, 1934, p. 657–696.

Scammell, G. V. *Ships, Oceans and Empire.* Variorum, Aldershot, 1995.

———. *The World Encompassed.* Berkeley, University of California Press, 1981.

Scanlon, George. "Egypt and China: Trade and Imitation," in D. S. Richards (ed.), *Islam and the Trade of Asia.* Oxford/University of Pennsylvania Press, 1970, p. 81–95.

Schildhauer, Johannes. *The Hansa.* Edition Leipzig, Leipzig, 1985.

Schilling, H. "Civic Republicanism in Late Medieval and Early Modern German Cities," in H. Schilling, *Religion, Political Culture and Emergence of Early Modern Society.* Brill, Leiden, 1992.

Schneider, Jane. "Was There a Precapitalist World-System?" in Christopher Chase-Dunn and Thomas Hall (eds.), *Core/Periphery Relations in Precapitalist Worlds.* Westview Press, 1991, p. 45–66.

Schneider, Jean. "Les Villes Allemandes au Moyen Âge," in *La Ville.* Part 2, *Institutions Économiques et Sociales.* Recueils de la Société Jean Bodin pour l'Histoire Comparative des Institutions 7, Éditions de la Librairie Encyclopédique, Bruxelles, 1955, p. 403–482.

Schumann, Reinhold. *Italy in the Last Fifteen Hundred Years.* University Press of America, 1986.

Schurmann, H. F. "Traditional Property in China." *Far Eastern Quarterly* 15, no. 4, Aug. 1956, p. 507–516.

Schurmann, Herbert. *Economic Structure of the Yüan Dynasty.* Harvard University Press, Cambridge, 1967.

Seccombe, Wally. *A Millennium of Family Change: Feudalism to Capitalism in Northwestern Europe.* Verso, New York, 1992.

Sée, Henri. *Modern Capitalism: Its Origin and Evolution.* Adelphi Co, New York, 1928.

Seifert, Dieter. *Kompagnons unde Konkurrenten: Holland und die Hanse im späten Mittelalter.* Böhau Verlag, Köln, 1997.

Sen, S. P. "The Role of Indian Textiles in Southeast Asian Trade in the 17th Century." *Journal of Southeast Asian History* 3, 1962, p. 92–110.

Serjeant, R. B. *Islamic Textiles.* Librarie du Liban, Beirut, 1972.

Serruys, Henry. "The Dearth of Textiles in Traditional Mongolia." *Journal of Asian History* 16, no. 2, 1982, p. 125–140.

———. "Sino-Mongol Trade during the Ming." *Journal of Asian History* 9, no. 1, 1975, p. 34–56.

Shanin, Teodor. "The Nature and Logic of the Peasant Economy." *Journal of Peasant Studies* 1, no. 1, October 1973, p. 63–80.

Shanmugam, P. *The Revenue System of the Cholas, 850–1279.* New Era Publications, Madras, 1987.

Sharma, Ram Sharan. *Early Medieval Indian Society.* Orient Longman, Kolkata, 2001.

———. "How Feudal Was Indian Feudalism?" in Hermann Kulke (ed.), *The State in India, 1000–1700.* Oxford University Press, New Delhi, 1995, p. 48–85.

———. *Indian Feudalism—c. 300–1200.* University of Calcutta, 1965.

Sharma, Yogesh. "A Life of Many Parts." *Medieval History Journal* 1, no. 2, Dec. 1998, p. 261–290.

Shatzmiller, Maya. *The Berbers and the Islamic State.* Markus Wiener Publishers, Princeton, 2000.

———. *Labour in the Medieval Islamic World.* Brill, Leiden, 1994.

———. "Women and Wage Labor in the Medieval Islamic West." *Journal of the Economic and Social History of the Orient* 40, no. 2, May 1997, p. 174–206.

Shiba, Yoshinobu. *Commerce and Society in Sung China.* Center for Chinese Studies, University of Michigan, 1970.

———. "Sung Foreign Trade," in Morris Rossabi (ed.), *China among Equals.* University of California Press, Berkeley, 1983, p. 89–115.

———. "Urbanization and the Developments of Markets in the Lower Yangtze Valley," in

John Haeger (ed.), *Crisis and Prosperity in Sung China*. University of Arizona Press, Tuscon, 1975, p. 13–48.

Shihab, Hassan Saleh. "Aden in Pre-Turkish Times (1232–1538)," in Frank Broeze (ed.), *Gateways of Asia: Port Cities of Asia in the 13th–20th Centuries*. Kegan Paul International, New York, 1996, p. 17–32.

Shokoohy, Mehrdad, and Natalie Shokoohy. "A History of Bayana, Part I." *Medieval History Journal* 7, no. 2, Dec. 2004, p. 279–324.

———. "A History of Bayana, Part II." *Medieval History Journal* 8, no. 2, Dec. 2005, p. 323–400.

Sider, Gerald. "The Making of Peculiar Local Cultures," in Alf Lüdtke (ed.), *Was bleibt von marxistischen Perspektiven in der Geschichtsforschung?* Wallstein Verlag, Gottingen, 1997, p. 99–148.

Singh, Chetan. "Conformity and Conflict: Tribes and the Agrarian System of Mughal India." *IESHR* 23, no. 3, 1988, p. 319–340.

Singh, Hira. "Classifying Non-European, Pre-Colonial Formations." *Journal of Peasant Studies* 20, no. 2, Jan. 1993, p. 317–347.

Sinha, N. K., and Nisith Ray. *A History of India*. 2nd ed. Orient Longman, Calcutta, 1986.

Sinopoli, Carla. "From the Lion Throne: Political and Social Dynamics of the Vijayanagara Empire." *Journal of the Economic and Social History of the Orient* 43, no. 3, August 2000, p. 364–398.

———. "The Organization of Craft Production at Vijayanagara" *American Anthrolopologist*, no. 90, 1988, p. 580–597.

———. "Political Choices and Economic Strategies in the Vijayanagara Empire," in Elizabeth Brumfiel (ed.), *The Economic Anthropology of the State*. University Press of America, Lanham, MD, 1994, p. 223–242.

———. *The Political Economy of Craft Production*. Cambridge University Press, 2003.

Sinopoli, Carla, and Kathleen Morrison. "Dimensions of Imperial Control." *American Anthropologist* 97, no. 1, March 1995, p. 83–96.

Sinor, Denis. "Horse and Pasture in Inner Asian History." *Oriens Extremus* 19, Dec. 1972, p. 171–183.

———. "Les Mongols et l'Europe." *Cahiers d'Histoire Mondiale* 3, no. 1, 1956, p. 39–62.

———. "The Mongols and the West." *Journal of Asian History* 33, no. 1, 1999, p. 1–44.

———. *Studies in Medieval Inner Asia*. Variorum Press, Ashgate, 1997.

Sivéry, Gérard. *Les Comtes de Hainaut et le Commerce du Vin au XIVe et au Début du XVe Siècle*. Lille, 1969.

Slicher van Bath, B. H. *The Agrarian History of Western Europe A.D. 500–1850*. Edward Arnold Ltd., London, 1963.

Small, Carola. "The Builders of Artois in the Early 14th Century." *French Historical Studies* 16, no. 2, 1989.

Smith, Adam. *An Inquiry into the Nature and Causes of the Wealth of Nations*. Clarendon Press, Oxford, 1976 ed.

Smith, Alan K. *Creating a World Economy*. Westview Press, Boulder, CO, 1991.

Smith, John M. "Ayn Jalut." *Harvard Journal of Asiatic Studies* 44, no. 2, December 1984, p. 307–345.

———. "Nomads on Ponies versus Slaves on Horses." *Journal of the American Oriental Society* 118, no. 1, January–March 1998, p. 54–62.

Smith, Paul J. "Family, Landsman, and Status-Group Affinity in Refugee Mobility Strategies." *Harvard Journal of Asiatic Studies* 52, no. 2, 1992, p. 665–708.

———. "Fear of Gynarchy in an Age of Chaos." *Journal of the Economic and Social History of the Orient* 41, no. 1, Feb. 1998, p. 1–95.

————. *Taxing Heaven's Storehouse.* Harvard University Press, Cambridge, 1991.

Smith, Rex. *Studies in the Medieval History of the Yemen and South Arabia.* Variorum/Ashgate, Aldershot, 1997.

Smith, Robert. "The Canoe in West African History." *Journal of African History* 11, 1970, p. 515–533.

Snellnow, Irmgard. "Ways of State Formation in Africa," in Henri Claessen and Peter Skalnik (eds.), *The Study of the State.* Mouton, The Hague, 1981, p. 303–316.

Snooks, Graeme. "The Dynamic Role of the Market in the Anglo-Norman Economy and Beyond, 1086–1300," in R. H. Britnell and B. M. S. Campbell (eds.), *A Commercialising Economy: England 1086 to circa 1300.* Manchester University Press, 1995, p. 27–54.

————. *The Dynamic Society.* Routledge, London, 1996.

————. *Was the Industrial Revolution Necessary?* Routledge, NY, 1994.

Solow, Barbara. "Capitalism and Slavery in the Exceedingly Long Run," in Barbara Solow and Stanley Engerman (eds.), *British Capitalism and Caribbean Slavery.* Cambridge University Press, 1987, p. 51–77.

Soly, Hugo. "Economische ontwikkeling en sociale politiek in Europa tijdens de overgang van de middeleeuwen naar de nieuwe tijden." *Tijdschrift voor Geschiedenis* 88, 1975, p. 584–597.

Sosson, J. P. "Les Petites Villes du Zwin (XIVe–XVIe Siècles)," in Ph. Contamine (ed.), *Commerce, Finances et Société (XIe–XVIe Siècles).* Presses de l'Université de Sorbonne, Paris 1993.

Sosson, Jean-Pierre. "Corporation et Paupérisme au XIVe et XVe Siècles." *Tijdschrift voor Geschiedenis* 92, 1979, p. 557–575.

————. "L'Entrepreneur Médiéval," in "L'Impresa Industria Commercio Banca Secc. XIII–XVIII." Atti della Ventiduesima Settimana di Studi 30 aprile–4 maggio 1990. Instituto Internazionale di Storia Economica "F. Datini," Serie II, 22, Prato, 1991, p. 275–293.

————. "Les Métiers: Norme et Réalité," in Jacqueline Hamesse and Colette Muraille-Samaran (eds.), *Le Travail au Moyen Âge.* Université Catholique del Louvain-la-Neuve, Louvain-la-Neuve, 1990, p. 339–348.

————. *Les Travaux Publics de la Ville de Bruges XIVe–XVe Siècles.* Credit Communal de Belgique, Bruxelles, 1977.

Soucek, Svat. *A History of Central Asia.* Cambridge University Press, 2000.

Soullière, Ellen. "Reflections on Chinese Despotism and the Power of the Inner Court." *Asian Profile* 12, no. 2, April 1984, p. 129–145.

Southall, A. W. *Alur Society.* Cambridge University Press, 1956.

Southall, Aidan. *The City in Time and Space.* Cambridge University Press, 1998.

Spencer, George. *The Politics of Expansion.* New Era Publications, Madras, 1983.

————. "The Politics of Plunder: The Cholas in 11th Century Ceylon." *Journal of Asian Studies* 35, no. 3, May 1976, p. 405–419.

Spencer, George, and Kenneth Hall. "Towards an Analysis of Dynastic Hinterlands." *Asian Profile* 2, no. 1, Feb. 1974, p. 51–62.

Spodek, Howard. "Rulers, Merchants and Other Groups in the City-States of Saurashtra, India, around 1800." *Comparative Studies in Society and History* 16, no. 4, Sep. 1974, p. 448–470.

Sprandel, Rolf. *Das Eisengewerbe im Mittelalter.* A. Hiersemann, Stuttgart, 1968.

Sprengard, Karl Anton. "Free Entrepreneurship, Rational Business Philosophy and Overseas Trade with Asia" in K. A. Sprengard and Roderich Ptak (eds.), *Maritime Asia: Profit Maximisation, Ethics and Trade Structure, c. 1300–1800.* Harrasowitz Verlag, Wiesbaden, 1994, p. 3–26.

Spruyt, Hendrik. *The Sovereign States and Its Competitors.* Princeton University Press, 1994.

Spufford, Peter. "Interventi," in Vera Barbagli Bagnoli (ed.), "La Moneta Nell' Economia Europa Secoli XIII–XVIII." Atti della Settimane di studio 11–17 aprile 1975. Instituto Internazionale di Storia Economica "F. Datini," Serie II, 7, Prato, 1981, p. 619–624.

———. *Money and Its Use in Medieval Europe.* Cambridge University Press, 1988.

———. *Power and Profit.* Thames & Hudson, New York, 2003.

Srinivas, M. N. *Collected Essays.* Oxford University Press, New Delhi, 2002.

Stabel, Peter. *Dwarfs Among Giants: The Flemish Urban Network in the Late Middle Ages.* Garant, Leuven, 1997.

———. "Guilds in Late Medieval Flanders." *Journal of Medieval History* 30, no. 2, 2004, p. 187–212.

———. "De kleine stad in Vlaanderen." *Verhandelingen van de Koninklijke Academie voor Wetenschappen, Letteren en Schone Kunsten van Belgie, Klasse der Letteren* 57, no. 156, Brussel, 1995.

———. "Markt en hinterland," in "Le Réseau Urbain en Belgique dans une Perspective Historique (1350–1850)."Actes du 15e Colloque International à Spa le 4–6 Sept. 1990, Bruxelles, Crédit Communal, Collection Histoire, série in-8, no. 86, 1992, p. 341–363.

———. "Women at the Market," in Wim Blockmans, Marc Boone, and Thérèse de Hemtinne (eds.), *Secretum Scriptorum.* Garant, Leuven, 1999, p. 259–276.

Stargardt, Janice. "Burma's Economic and Diplomatic Relations with India and China from Early Medieval Sources." *Journal of the Economic and Social History of the Orient* 14, no. 1, 1971, p. 38–62.

Stark, Rodney. *The Victory of Reason.* Random House, New York, 2005.

Stark, Walter. "über Techniken und Organisationsformen des Hansischen Handels im Spätmittelalter," in Stuart Jenks and Michael North (eds.), *Der Hansische Sonderweg? Beiträge zur Sozial- und Wirtschaftsgeschichte der Hanse.* Böhlau Verlag, Köln, 1993b, p. 191–201.

Stavrianos, L. S. *A Global History.* Prentice Hall, NJ, 1999.

Stearns, Peter, Michael Adas, and Stuart Schwartz. *World Civilizations.* 2nd ed. HarperCollins, New York, 1996.

Steensgaard, Niels. *The Asian Trade Revolution of the Seventeenth Century.* University of Chicago Press, 1974.

———. "Emporia: Some Reflections," in Roderich Ptak and Dietmar Rothermund (eds.), *Emporia, Commodities, and Entrepreneurs in Asian Maritime Trade, c. 1400–1750.* Franz Steiner Verlag, Stuttgart, 1991, p. 9–12.

———. "The Indian Ocean Network and the Emerging World Economy, c. 1500–1750," in Satish Chandra (ed.), *The Indian Ocean Explorations in History, Commerce and Politics.* Sage, London, 1987, p. 125–150.

———. "Violence and the Rise of Capitalism." *Review* 5, no. 2, Fall 1981, p. 247–273.

Stein, Burton. "Coromandel Trade in Medieval India," in John Parker (ed.), *Merchants and Scholars: Essays in the History of Exploration and Trade.* University of Minnesota Press, Minneapolis, 1965, p. 47–62.

———. *Peasant State and Society in Medieval South India.* Oxford University Press, 1980.

———. "The Segmentary State," in Hermann Kulke (ed.), *The State in India, 1000–1700.* Oxford University Press, New Delhi, 1995, p. 134–161.

———. "South India: Some General Considerations," in Raychaudhuri Tapan and Habib Irfan (eds.), *The Cambridge Economic History of India.* Cambridge University Press, 1982, 1:14–42.

———. "State Formation and Economy Considered." *Modern Asian Studies* 19, no. 3, 1985, p. 102–124.

————. "Vijayanagara c. 1350–1564," in Raychaudhuri Tapan and Habib Irfan (eds.), *The Cambridge Economic History of India*. Cambridge University Press, 1982, 1:387–413.

Stella, Alessandro. "La Bogetta E I Lavoranti." *Annales ESC* 44, no. 3, May–June 1989, p. 529–551.

————. "Un Conflit du Travail dans les Vignes d'Auxerre aux XIVe et XVe Siècles." *Histoire et Sociétés Rurales*, no. 5, 1r Semestre, 1996, p. 221–251.

————. *La Révolte des Ciompi.* Éditions de l'École des Hautes Études en Sciences Sociales, Paris, 1993.

Stern, S. M. "The Constitution of the Islamic City," A. H. Hourani and S. M. Stern (eds.), *The Islamic City.* University of Pennsylvania Press, Oxford, 1970, p. 25–50.

Stigler, G. *The Economist as Preacher and Other Essays.* Chicago University Press, 1982.

Stouff, Louis. "Nobles et Bourgeois dans l'Arles du Bas Moyen Age" in Charles De la Ronciére et al., *Histoire et Société: Mélanges Offerts à Georges Duby.* Publications de l'Université de Provence, Aix-en-Provence, 1992, 2:181–193.

Strayer, Joseph. "The Costs and Profits of War," in Harry Miskimin, David Herlihy, and A. L. Udovitch (eds.), *The Medieval City.* Yale University Press, New Haven, 1977, p. 269–291.

Subbarayalu, Y. "The Cola State." *Studies in History* 4, no. 2, 1982, p. 265–306.

Subrahmanyam, Sanjay. "Aspects of State Formation in South India and Southeast Asia." *Indian Economic and Social History Review* 23, 1986, p. 358–377.

————. "Hearing Voices: Vignettes of Early Modernity in South Asia," in Shmuel Eisenstadt et al., *Public Spheres and Collective Identities.* Transaction Publishers, London, 2001, p. 75–104.

————. "Institutions, Agency and Economic Change in South Asia," in Burton Stein and Sanjay Subrahmanyam (eds.), Institutions and Economic Change in South Asia. Oxford University Press, Delhi, 1996, p. 14–47.

————. "Introduction," in Sanjay Subrahmanyam (ed.), *Money and the Market in India 1100–1700.* Oxford University Press, Delhi, 1994a, p. 1–56.

————. "Of Imarat and Tijarat." *Comparative Studies in Society and History* 37, no. 4, Oct. 1995, p. 750–780.

————. "Making Sense of Indian Historiography." *Indian Economic and Social History Review* 39, no. 3, 2002, p. 121–130.

————. "Notes on Circulation and Asymmetry in Two Mediterraneans, c. 1400–1800," in Claude Guillot, Denys Lombard, and Roderich Ptak (eds.), *From the Mediterreanean to the China Sea.* Harrassowitz Verlag, Wiesbaden, 1998, p. 21–43.

————. The Political Economy of Commerce. Cambridge University Press, 1990.

————. *The Portuguese Empire in Asia, 1500–1700.* Longman, London, 1993.

————. "The Tail Wags the Dog." *Moyen Orient et Océan Indien* 5, 1988, p. 131–160.

————. "World-Economies and South Asia, 1600–1750." *Review* 12, no. 1, Winter 1989, p. 141–148.

————. "Writing History Backwards." *Studies in History* 10, no. 1, June 1994b, p. 131–145.

Subrahmanyam, Sanjay, and C. A. Bayly. "Portfolio Capitalists and the Political Economy of Early Modern India." *Indian Economic and Social History Review* 25, 4, 1988, p. 401–424.

Sun, Laichen. "Ming–Southeast Asian Overland Interactions, 1368–1644." Unpublished Ph.D. diss., University of Michigan, 2000.

Sun, Lung-kee. "Interpretative Essay," in Frank Thackeray and John Findling (eds.), *Events That Changed the World Through the Sixteenth Century.* Greenwood Press, Wesport, CT, 2001, p. 69–84.

Sweezy, Paul. "A Critique," in Rodney Hilton (ed.), *The Transition from Feudalism to Capitalism*. NLB, London, 1976, p. 33–56.

Szeftel, Marc. "La Participation des Assemblées Populaires dans le Gouvernement Central de la Russie Depuis l'Époque Kiévienne Jusqu'à la Fin du XVIIIe Siècle," in *Gouvernés et Gouvernants*. Part 4, *Bas Moyen Âge et Temps Modernes (II)*. Recueils de la Société Jean Bodin pour l'Histoire Comparative des Institutions 25, Éds de la Librairie Encyclopédique, Bruxelles, 1965, p. 339–365.

Székely, György. "Niederländische und Englische Tucharten im Mitteleuropa des 13–17. Jahrhunderts." *Annales Universitatis Scientiarum Budapestinensis de Rolando Eötvös Nominatae* 8, 1966, p. 11–42.

Szúcs, Jenó. *Les Trois Europes*. Domaines Danubiens. L'Harmattan, Paris, 1985.

Tadic, Jorjo. "Les Premiers Éléments du Capitalisme dans les Balkans du 14e au 17e Siècle," in F. C. Lane (ed.), Fourth International Conference of Economic History, Bloomington, 1968. École Pratique des Hautes Études and Mouton, Paris, 1973, p. 69–77.

Takahashi, K. "A Contribution to the Debate" in R. H. Hilton (ed.), *The Transition from Feudalism to Capitalism*. London, 1976, p. 68–97.

Taleqani, Seyyed. *Islam and Ownership*. Mazdá Publishers, Lexington, KY, 1983.

Tampoe, Moira. *Maritime Trade between China and the West*. BAR International Series 555, Oxford, 1989.

Tangheroni, Marco. "Pise en Sardaigne." in Michel Balard and Alain Ducellier (dirs.), *Coloniser au Moyen Âge*. Armand Colin, Paris, 1995, p. 35–39.

Tarvel, Enn. "The Stability of Social Hierarchies in the Economic Development of the Baltic Region in the Period of Feudalism," in "Gerarchie Economiche e Gerarchie Sociali Secoli XII–XVIII." Atti della Dodicesima Settimana di Studi 18–23 Aprile 1980, Instituto Internazionale di Storia Economica "F. Datini," Serie II, 22, Le Monnier, Prato, 1990, p. 53–71.

Tawney, Richard H. *Religion and the Rise of Capitalism*. Harcourt, NY, 1926.

Tebrake, W. H. *Medieval Frontier*. Texas A&M University Press, 1985.

Terlouw, C. P. *The Regional Geography of the World-System*. State University of Utrecht, 1992.

Terlouw, Kees. "A General Perspective on the Regional Development of Europe from 1300 to 1850." *Journal of Historical Geography* 22, no. 2, 1996, p. 129–146.

Terrasse, Henri. "Citadins et Grands Nomades dans l'Histoire de l'Islam." *Studia Islamica* 29, 1969, p. 5–15.

Thakur, Vijay Kumar. *Historiography of Indian Feudalism: Towards a Model of Early Medieval Indian Economy*. Commonwealth Publishers, New Delhi, 1989.

Thapar, Romila. *History and Beyond*. Oxford University Press, 2000.

———. *A History of India*. Vol. 1. Penguin Books, Baltimore, 1966.

———. "Social Mobility in Ancient India with Special Reference to Elite Groups," in R. S. Sharma (ed.), *Indian Society: Historical Probings in Memory of D. D. Kosambi*. People's Publishing House, New Delhi, 1974, p. 95–123.

Thiriet, Freddy. *Études sur la Romanie Greco-Vénitienne (Xe–XVe Siècles)*. Variorum Reprints, London, 1977.

Thiry, Jacques. "L'Egypte et le Déclin de l'Afrique du Nord," in U. Vermeulen and D. De Smet (eds.), *Egypt and Syria in the Fatimid, Ayyubid and Mamluk Eras*. Peeters, Leuven, 1998, 2:237-248.

———. *Le Sahara Libyen dans L'Afrique du Nord Médiévale*. Peeters, Leuven, 1995.

Thoen, Erik. "The Count, the Countryside and the Economic Development of Towns in Flanders from the Eleventh to the Thirteenth Century," in Erik Aerts, Brigitte Heneau, Paul Janssens, and Raymond van Uytven (eds.), *Liber Amicorum Herman Van der Wee*. Leuven University Press, 1993, p. 259–278.

―――. "Immigration to Bruges during the late Middle Ages," in "Le Migrazioni in Europa Secc. XIII–XVIII." Atti della Venticinqesima Settimana di Studi 3–8 maggio 1993, Instituto Internazionale di Storia Economica "F Datini," serie II, 25, Prato, 1994, p. 335–353.

―――. *Landbouweconomie en bevolking in Vlaanderen gedurende de late Middeleeuwen en het begin van de Moderne Tijden.* 2 vols., Universiteit Gent, 1988b.

―――. "Rechten en plichten van plattelanders als instrumenten van machtspolitieke strijd tussen adel, stedelijke burgerij en grafelijk gezag in het laat-middeleeuwse Vlaanderen," in "Les Structures du Pouvoir dans les Communautés Rurales en Belgique et dans les Pays Limitrophes (XIIe–XIXe Siècle)." Actes du 13e Colloque International, Crédit Communal, no. 77, Bruxelles, 1988a, p. 469–490.

―――. "Technique Agricole, Cultures Nouvelles et Économie Rurale en Flandre au Bas Moyen Âge." Actes de Colloque Flaran 12 (1990), Centre Belge d'Histoire Rurale 107. Gand, 1992.

Thoen, Erik, and Adriaan Verhulst. "Le Réseau Urbain et les Campagnes dans l'Ancien Comté de Flandre (ca. 1350–1800)." *Storia della Citta* 36, Milano, 1986, p. 53–60.

Thomaz, Luis. "Malaka et Ses Communautés Marchandes au Tournant du 16e Siècle," in Denys Lombard and Jean Aubin (eds.), *Marchands et Hommes d'Affaires Asiatiques dans l'Océan Indien et la Mer de Chine 13e–20e Siècles.* Éditions de l'EHESS, Paris, 1988, p. 31–48.

Thompson, E. P. *Customs in Common.* The New Press, New York, 1993.

Thomson, J.K.J. *Decline in History: The European Experience.* Polity Press, Cambridge, 1998.

Thornton, John. *Africa and Africans in the Making of the Atlantic World, 1400–1800.* Cambridge University Press, 1998 ed.

Tibbetts, G. R. "Early Muslim Traders in South-East Asia." *Journal of the Malayan Branch of the Royal Asiatic Society* 30, pt. 1, 1957, p. 1–45.

T'ien, Ju-kang. "Chêng Ho's Voyages and the Distribution of Pepper in China." *Journal of the Royal Asiatic Society* 2, 1981, p. 186–197.

Tilly, Ch. *Coercion, Capital and European States A.D. 990–1992.* Cambridge University Press, 1992.

Titow, J. Z. "Some Evidence of the Thirteenth Century Population Increase." *Economic History Review* 14 [2nd ser.], no. 2, December 1961, p. 218–224.

Tits-Dieuaide, Marie-Jeanne. *La Formation des Prix Céréales en Brabant et en Flandre au XVe Siècle.* Éditions de l'Université de Bruxelles, Bruxelles, 1975.

Toch, Michael. "Lords and Peasants." *Journal of European Economic History* 15, no. 1, Spring 1986, p. 163–182.

Togan, Ahmet Zeki. "Economic Conditions in Anatolia in the Mongol Period." *Annales Islamologiques* 25, 1991, p. 203–240.

Tomich, Dale. "World Market and American Slavery," in Jaimé Torras et al., *Els Espais del Mercat.* Diputacio de Valencia, Valencia, 1993, p. 213–240.

Torras, Jaimé. "The Building of a Market," in Jaimé Torras et al., *Els Espais del Mercat.* Diputacio de Valencia, 1993, p. 197–212.

―――. "Class Struggle in Catalonia. A Note on Brenner." *Review* 4, no. 2, Fall 1980, p. 253–265.

Toussaint, Auguste. *History of the Indian Ocean.* Routledge, London, 1966.

―――. "Les Routes de l'Océan Indien au XVIIe et XVIIIe Siècles," in "Océan Indien et Méditerranée." Travaux du 6e Colloque International d'Histoire Maritime et du 2e Congrès de l'Association Historique Internationale de l'Océan Indien. Session de Lourenço Marques, 13–18 08 1962. SEVPEN, Paris, 1964, p. 303–313.

Tracy, J. A. *Financial Revolution in the Habsburg Netherlands*. University of California Press, Berkeley, 1985.

Tremel, Ferdinand. "Tucherzeugung und Tuchhandel im Ostalpenraum vom 13. Bis zum 16.Jahrhundert," in Marco Spallanzani (ed.), "Produzione, commercio e consumo dei panni di lana nei sec. XII–XVIII." Atti della seconda settimana di studio (10–16 aprile 1970), Istituto Internazionale di storia economica "F. Datini," L Olschki Editore, Firenze, 1976, p. 311–323.

Triaud, Jean-Louis. *Islam et Sociétés Soudanaises au Moyen-Âge*. Recherches Voltaiques 16, CNRS-CVRS, Paris, 1973.

Trimingham, Spencer. *A History of Islam in West Africa*. Oxford University Press, 1962.

T'Serstevens, A. *Les Précurseurs de Marco Polo*. Ed. B. Arthaud, Paris, 1959.

Tucci, Ugo. "Entre Orient et Occident," in "L'Histoire à Nice." Actes du Colloque International (6–9 Nov. 1980). Vol. 2, "Les Relations Économiques et Culturelles entre l'Occident et l'Orient." Université de Nice/Musée d'Archéologie et d'Histoire d'Antibes, 1981, p. 117–127.

Tuma, Elias. *European Economic History*. Pacific Book Publishers, Palo Alto, CA, 1979.

Turnock, David. *The Making of Eastern Europe*. Routledge, London, 1988.

Tymowski, Michal. "The Early State and After in Precolonial West Sudan," in Henri Claessen and Pieter van de Velde (eds.), *Early State Dynamics*. Brill, Leiden, 1987, p. 54–69.

———. "Early State and Mature State in the History of East-Central Europe and the Western Sudan." *Africana Bulletin* 42, 1994, p. 21–38.

———. "Le Niger, Voie de Communication des Grands États du Soudan." *Africana Bulletin* 6, 1967, p. 73–95.

———. "Wolof Economy and Political Organization" in Henri Claessen and Pieter van de Velde "Early State Economics" Transaction Publishers, London, 1991, p. 131–142

Udovitch, Abraham. "Commercial Techniques in Early Medieval Islamic Trade," in D. S. Richards (ed.), *Islam and the Trade of Asia*. Oxford/University of Pennsylvania Press, 1970, p. 37–62.

———. "Merchants and Amirs." *Asian and African Studies* 22, nos. 1–3, Nov. 1988, p. 53–72.

———. "Market and Society in the Medieval Islamic World," in *Mercati e mercanti nell'alto medioevo l'area Euroasiatica e l'area Mediterranea: Settimane di Studio del centro Italiano di studi sull'alto medioeve XL*. Presso La Sede del Centro, Spoleto, 1993, p. 767–798.

Unali, Anna. *Ceuta 1415: alle origini dell'espansione europea in Africa*. Bulzoni, Roma, 2000.

Unger, Richard W. "Beer, Wine and Land Use in the Late Medieval Low Countries," in *Bijdragen tot de Geschiedenis*, 81, nos. 1–3, 1998, p. 329–337.

———. "Grain, Beer and Shipping in the North and Baltic Seas," in Christiane Villain-Gandossi, Salvino Busuttil, and Paul Adam (eds.), *Medieval Ships and the Birth of Technological Societies*. Vol. 1, *Northern Europe*. Foundation for International Studies, Malta, 1989, p. 121–135.

———. *The Ship in the Medieval Economy, 600–1600*. McGill-Queen's University Press, Montreal, 1980.

Unger, Roberto. *Plasticity into Power*. Cambridge University Press, 1987.

Valérian, Dominique. "Contribution à l'Etude de la Guerre dans le Maghreb Médiéval," in Mohammed Tahar Mansouri (dir.), *Le Maghreb et la Mer à Travers l'Histoire*. Éditions Hêrodotos–Mésogeios, Paris, 2000, p. 126–142.

Van Caenegem, Raoul C. "La Peine dans les Anciens Pays-Bas (12e–17e S.)," in "Punishment." Transactions of the Jean Bodin Society for Comparative Institutional History 56, Part 2, De Boeck Université, Bruxelles, 1991, p. 117–141.

Van der Wee, Herman. "Consumptie van textiel en industriële ontwikkeling in de steden van de Nederlanden tijdens de late Middeleeuwen en de Nieuwe Tijd." *Bijdragen tot de Geschiedenis* 81, nos. 1–3, 1998, p. 339–350.

————. "Industrial Dynamics and the Process of Urbanization and De-Urbanization in the Low Countries from the Late Middle Ages to the Eighteenth Century." in Herman Van der Wee (ed.), *The Rise and Decline of Urban Industries in Italy and the Low Countries.* Leuven University Press, 1988, p. 307–381.

————. *The Low Countries in the Early Modern World.* Cambridge University Press, Variorum, 1993.

————. "Productivité, Progrès Technique et Croissance Économique du XIIe au XVIIIe Siècle," in Sara Mariotti (ed.), "Produttività e tecnologie nei secoli XII–XVII." Atti della Terza Settimana di Studio 23–29 aprile 1971. Instituto Internazionale di Storia Economica "F. Datini," Serie II, 3, Prato, Le Monnier, 1981, p. 9–16.

————. "Structural Changes and Specialization in the Industry of the Southern Netherlands, 1100–1600." *Economic History Review* [2nd Series] 28, no. 2, May 1975, p. 203–221.

Van der Wee, Herman, and Eddy Van Cauwenberghe (eds.), Productivity of Land and Agricultural Innovation in the Low Countries (1250–1800). Leuven University Press, 1978.

Van der Woude, A. M. "Large Estates and Small Holdings, Lords and Peasants in the Netherlands during the Late Middle Ages and Early Modern Times," in Péter Gunst and Tamás Hoffmann (eds.), *Large Estates and Small holdings in Europe in the Middle Ages and Modern Times.* Akadémiai Kiadó, Budapest, 1982, p. 193–207.

Van Dyke, Paul. "How and Why the Dutch East India Company Became Competitive in the Intra-Asian Trade in East Asia in the 1630s." *Itinerario* 21, no. 3, 1997, p. 41–56.

Van Gerven, Jan. "War, Violence and an Urban Society," in Wim Blockmans, Marc Boone, and Thérèse de Hemtinne (eds.), *Secretum Scriptorum.* Garant, Leuven, 1999, p. 183–211.

Van Houtte, Jan A. "Production et Circulation de la Laine Comme Matière Première du XIIIe au XVIIe Siècle," in Marco Spallanzani (ed.), "La Lana come Materia Prima." Atti della Prima Settimana di Studio 18–24 aprile 1969. Instituto Internazionale di Storia Economica "F. Datini," Prato, L Olschki, Firenze, 1974, p. 381–395.

Van Klaveren, Jacob. *General Economic History, 100–1760[FU27].* Gerhard Kieckens, München, 1969.

Van Leur, J.C. *Indonesian Trade and Society.* Van Hoever, The Hague, 1955.

Van Nierop, Henk. "Popular Participation in Politics in the Dutch Republic," in Peter Blickle (ed.), *Resistance, Representation, and Community.* Clarendon Press, Oxford, 1997, p. 272–290.

Van Santen, H. W. "Trade between Mughal India and the Middle East, and Mughal Monetary Policy," in Karl R. Haellquist (ed.), *Asian Trade Routes: Continental and Maritime.* Scandinavian Institute of Asian Studies, Copenhagen, 1991, p. 87–95.

van Uytven, Raymond. "L'Approvisionnement des Villes des Anciens Pays-Bas au Moyen Âge," in "L'Approvisionnement des Villes de l'Europe Occidentale au Moyen Âge et aux Temps Modernes." Centre Culturel de l'Abbaye de Flaran, Cinquièmes Journées Internationales d'Histoire, Auch, 1985, p. 75–116.

————. "Les Bourgeois dans les Villes Brabançonnes au XIIIe Siècle." *Revue de l'Université de Bruxelles* 4, 1978, p. 468–482.

————. "Cloth in Medieval Literature of Western Europe," in N. B. Harte and K. G. Ponting (eds.), *Cloth and Clothing in Medieval Europe.* Heinemann Educational Books, London, 1983, p. 151–183.

————. "La Conjuncture Commerciale et Industrielle aux Pays-Bas Bourguignons: Une Récapitulation," in J. M. Duvosquel, J. Nazet, and A. Vanrie (red.), *Les Pays-Bas Bourguignons. Histoire et Institutions.* Archives et Bibliothèques de Belgique, Bruxelles, 1996b, p. 435–468.

————. "La Draperie Brabanconne et Malinoise du XIIe au XVIIe Siècle," in Marco Spallanzani (ed.), "Produzione, commercio e consumo dei panni di lana nei sec. XII–XVIII." Atti della seconda settimana di studio (10–16 aprile 1970). Istituto Internazionale di Storia Economica "F. Datini," L Olschki Editore, Firenze, 1976, p. 85–97.

————. "Economische groei in het Hertogdom Brabant tijdens de twaalfde eeuw," in Raoul Bauer et al., *Brabant in de twaalfde eeuw: een renaissance?* Centrum Brabantse Geschiedenis, UFSAL, Brussel, 1987, p. 113–129.

————. "The Fulling Mill," in *Acta Historiae Neerlandicae* 7, Martinus Nijhoff, The Hague, 1971, p. 1–14.

————. "De macht van het geld," in Dick de Boer and E. Cordfunke and Herbert Sartafij (eds.), *WI Florens . . . De Hollandse graaf Floris V in de samenleving van de dertiende eeuw.* Uitg. Matrijs, Utrecht, 1996, p. 212–223.

————. "Les Pays-Bas du XIVe au XVIe Siècle," in Annalisa Guarducci (dir.), "Prodotto Lordo e finanza pubblica secoli XIII–XIX." Atti della Ottava Settimana di Studi 3–9 maggio 1976. Instituto Internazionale di Storia Economica "F. Datini," Serie II, 22, Prato, Le Monnier, 1988, p. 533–554.

————. "Stadsgeschiedenis in de Noorden en het Zuiden," in *Algemene Geschiedenis der Nederlanden.* Fibula-Van Dishoeck, Haarlem, 1982, p. 188–253.

————. "Technique, Productivité et Production au Moyen Âge," in Sara Mariotti (ed.), "Produttività e tecnologie nei secoli XII–XVII." Atti della Terza Settimana di Studio 23–29 aprile 1971. Instituto Internazionale di Storia Economica "F. Datini," Serie II, 3, Le Monnier, Prato, 1981, p. 283–293.

————. "Vorst, adel en steden." *Bijdragen tot de geschiedenis* 59, 1976b, p. 93–122.

————. "What Is New Socially and Economically in the Sixteenth-Century Netherlands?" in *Acta Historiae Neerlandicae* 7. Martinus Nijhoff, The Hague, 1974, p. 18–53.

Van Werveke, Hans. "Industrial Growth in the Middle Ages." *Economic History Review* 6, no. 3, 1954, p. 237–245.

Vanacker, Claudette. "Géographie Économique de l'Afrique du Nord Selon les Auteurs Arabes, du IXe Siècle au Milieu du XIIe Siècle." *Annales ESC* 28, no. 3, Mai–Juin, 1973, p. 659–680.

Vanaja, R. "Kenneth Hall's Trade and Statecraft in the Age of the Colas." *Studies in History* 4, no. 2, 1982, p. 321–333.

Vanina, E. "Urban Industries of Medieval India." *Studies in History* 5, no. 2, Dec. 1989, p. 271–286.

Varadarajan, Lotika. "Commodity Structure and Indian Participation in the Trade of the Southern Seas, *circa* 9th to 13th Centuries," in Satish Chandra (ed.). *The Indian Ocean Explorations in History, Commerce and Politics.* Sage, London, 1987, p. 90–108.

Veluthat, Kesavan. *The Political Structure of Early Medieval South India.* Orient Longman, New Delhi, 1993.

Verhulst, Adriaan. "Agrarian Revolutions: Myth or Reality?" *Sartoniana* 2, 1989b, p. 71–95.

————. "The 'Agricultural Revolution' of the Middle Ages Reconsidered," in S. Bachrach and David Nicholas (eds.), *Law, Custom and the Social Fabric in Medieval Europe.* Kalamazoo: Medieval Institute Publications, 1990, p. 17–28.

————. "L'Économie Rurale de la Flandre et la Dépression Économique du bas Moyen Âge." *Études Rurales* [École Pratique des Hautes Études, 6e Section] 10, juillet–sept. 1963, p. 68–80.

————. *Précis d'Histoire Rurale de la Belgique.* Éditions de l'Université de Bruxelles, 1990b.

————. "The State of Research. Medieval Socioeconomic Historiography in Western Europe." *Journal of Medieval History* 23, no. 1, 1997, p. 89–101.

————. "Towns and Trade, 400–1500," in Robin Butlin and Robert Dodgshon (eds.), *An Historical Geography of Europe.* Clarendon Press, Oxford, 1998, p. 100–114.

Verlinden, Charles. "Aspects de la Production, du Commerce et de la Consommation des Draps Flamands au Moyen Âge," in Marco Spallanzani (ed.), "Produzione, commercio e consumo dei panni di lana nei sec. XII–XVIII." Atti della seconda settimana di studio (10–16 aprile 1970). Istituto Internazionale di Storia Economica F. Datini, L Olschki Editore, Firenze, 1976, p. 99–112.

———. *The Beginnings of Modern Colonization.* Cornell University Press, Ithaca, NY, 1970.

———. "De la Colonisation Médiévale Italienne au Levant à l'Expansion Ibérique en Afrique Continentale et Insulaire" *Bulletin de l'Institut Historique Belge de Rome* Fasc. 53–54, Rome, 1984, p. 99–121.

———. *L'Esclavage dans l'Europe Médiévale.* 2 vols. Rijksuniversiteit Gent, 1977.

———. "From the Mediterranean to the Atlantic." *Journal of European Economic History* 1, no. 3, Winter 1972, p. 625–646.

———. "Les Italiens et l'Ouverture des Routes Atlantiques," in "Les Routes de l'Atlantique." Travaux du 9e Colloque International d'Histoire Maritime. SEVPEN, Paris, 1969, p. 259–279.

———. "Marchands Chrétiens et Juifs dans l'État Mamelouk au Début du XVe Siècle." *Bulletin de l'Institut Historique Belge de Rome,* Fasc. 51, 1981, p. 19–86.

———. "Le Traffic et la Consommation des Vins Français," in Michel Mollat (dir.), "Les Sources de l'Histoire Maritime." Actes du 4e Colloque International d'Histoire Maritime. SEVPEN, Paris, 1962, p. 345–364.

Vikor, Knut. "The Desert-Side Salt Trade of Kawar." *African Economic History*, no. 11, 1982, p. 115–144.

Vink, Markus. "From Port City to World-System" *Itinerario* 28, no. 2, 2004, p. 45–116.

Von Glahn, Richard. *Fountain of Fortune.* University of California Press, Berkeley, 1996.

Von Sivers, Peter. "Pays Riches, Pays Pauvres," in Henri Bresc et al., *Genèse de l'Etat Moderne en Méditerranée.* École Française de Rome, Palais Farnèse, 1993, p. 169–181.

Von Stromer, Wolfgang. "Une Clé du Succès des Maisons de Commerce d'Allemagne du Sud." *Revue Historique* 285/1, no. 577, Janvier–Mars 1991, p. 29–49.

———. "Mittelalterliche Städte als quasi-merkantilistische Gewerbe-Gründer und Unternehmer," in "Investimenti e civiltà urbana secoli XIII–XVIII." Atti della Nona Settimana di Studi 22–28 Aprile 1977. Instituto Internazionale di Storia Economica "F. Datini," Serie II, 22, Le Monnier, Prato, 1989, p. 873–882.

———. "Die Struktur von Produktion und Verteilung von Bunt- und Edelmetallen an der Wende vom Mittelalter zur Neuzeit," in Herman Kellenbenz (ed.), *Precious Metals in the Age of Expansion.* Klett-Cotta, Stuttgart, 1981, p. 13–26.

Von Wartburg, Marie-Louise. "Production de Sucre de Canne à Chypre," in Michel Balard and Alain Ducellier (dirs.), *Coloniser au Moyen Âge.* Armand Colin, Paris, 1995, p. 126–131.

Vries, Peer. "Governing Growth: A Comparative Analysis of the Role of the State in the Rise of the West." *Journal of World History* 13, no. 1, 2002, 67–138.

———. *Via Peking Back to Manchester.* Leiden, CNWS Publications, 2003.

Wade, Geoff. "Some Topoi in Southern Border Historiography During the Ming," in Sabine Dabringhaus and Roderich Ptak (eds.), *China and Her Neighbours: Borders, Visions of the Other, Foreign Policy 10th to 19th Century.* Harrasowitz Verlag, Wiesbaden, 1997, p. 135–158.

Waldron, Arthur. "Introduction," in Bertold Spuler, *The Mongol Period: History of the Muslim World.* Markus Wiener, Princeton, 1994, p. 7–33.

Walker, Thomas. "The Italian Gold Revolution of 1252," in J. F. Richards (ed.), *Precious Metals in the Later Medieval and Early Modern Worlds.* Carolina Academic Press, Durham, NC, 1983, p. 29–52.

Wallerstein, Immanuel. "The Construction of a European World-Economy, 1450–1750." Unpublished paper, 1993b.

———. "European Economic Development." *Economic History Review* 36, no. 4, 1983, p. 580–583.

———. "From Feudalism to Capitalism: Transition or Transitions?" in *The Capitalist World-Economy*. Cambridge University Press, 1979, p. 138–151.

———. "The Incorporation of the Indian Subcontinent into the Capitalist World-Economy," in Satish Chandra (ed.), *The Indian Ocean Explorations in History, Commerce and Politics*. Sage, London, 1987, p. 222–253.

———. *The Modern World System*. New York, Academic Press, 1974.

———. *The Modern World-System*. Vol. 2. New York, Academic Press, 1980.

———. *The Modern World-System*. Vol. 3. Academic Press, San Diego, CA, 1989.

———. *The Politics of the World-Economy*. Cambridge University Press, 1984.

———. "Système Mondial Contre Système-Monde." *Sociologie et Sociétés* 22, no. 2, Oct. 1990, p. 219–222.

———. "The West, Capitalism and the Modern World-System," in Timothy Brook and Gregory Blue (eds.), *China and Historical Capitalism*. Cambridge University Press, 1999, p. 10–56.

———. "World Systems versus World-Systems. A Critique," in Andre Gunder Frank and Barry Gills (eds.), *The World System: Five Hundred Years or Five Thousand?* London, 1993, p. 292–296.

Wang, Gungwu. "China and South-East Asia, 1402–1424," in Jerome Ch'en and Nicholas Tarling (eds.), *Studies in the Social History of China and South-East Asia*. Cambridge University Press, 1970b.

———. *China and the Chinese Overseas*. Times Academic Press, Singapore, 1991.

———. "Merchants without Empire," in James Tracy (ed.), *The Rise of Merchant Empires*. Cambridge University Press, 1990, p. 400–421.

———. "Public and Private Overseas Trade in Chinese History," in Michel Mollat (dir.), *Sociétés et Compagnies de Commerce en Orient et dans l'Océan Indien*. SEVPEN, Paris, 1970, p. 215–226.

Wang, Jianping. *Concord and Conflict*. Lund Studies in African and Asian Religions 11, Lund, 1996.

Washbrook, David. "From Comparative Sociology to Global History." *Journal of the Economic and Social History of the Orient* 40, no. 4, Nov. 1997, p. 410–443.

———. "Progress and Problems: South Asian Economic and Social History." *Modern Asian Studies* 22, no. 1, Feb. 1988, p. 57–96.

———. "South Asia, the World System and World Capitalism." *Journal of Asian Studies* 49, no. 3, August 1990, p. 479–508.

Watson, Andrew. *Agricultural Innovation in the Early Islamic World*. Cambridge University Press, 1983.

———. "Back to Gold—and Silver." *Economic History Review* [2nd Series] 20, no. 1, April 1967, p. 1–34.

Watt, Montgomery. *The Influence of Islam on Medieval Europe*. Edinburgh University Press, 1972.

Weber, Eugen. *Peasants into Frenchmen*. Stanford University Press, 1979.

Weber, Max. *The City*. New York, Free Press, 1958.

———. *The Protestant Ethic and the Spirit of Capitalism*. Roxbury Publishing Co, LA, 1996 [1930].

———. *The Religion of India: The Sociology of Hinduism and Buddhism*. Free Press, Glencoe, IL, 1958b.

Weczerka, Hugo. "Les Routes Terrestres de la Hanse," in *L'Homme et la Route en Europe Occidentale au Moyen Âge et aux Temps Modernes.* Centre Culturel de l'Abbaye de Flaran, Auch, 1982, p. 85–105.

Weede, Erich. "Ideas, Institutions and Political Culture in Western Development." *Journal of Theoretical Politics* 2, no. 4, Oct. 1990, p. 369–386.

Wendelken, Rebecca. "The Falling Dominoes," in Andrew Bell-Fialkoff (ed.), *The Role of Migration in the History of the Eurasian Steppe.* St. Martin's Press, New York, 2000, p. 229–249.

Werner, Karl. "Political and Social Structures of the West, 300–1300," in Jean Baechler, John Hall, and Michael Mann (eds.), *Europe and the Rise of Capitalism.* Basil Blackwell, New York, 1988, p. 169–184.

Wertheim, Wim. *Comparative Essays on Asia and the West.* Comparative Asian Studies 12. VU University Press for Centre of Asian Studies, Amsterdam, 1993.

Weulersse, Delphine. "La Chine des Yuan et des Ming," in Jean Favier (dir.), *XIVe et XVe siècles: crises et genèses.* Presses Universitaires de France, Paris, 1996, p. 757–804.

Wheatley, Paul. "Analecta Sino-Africana Recensa," in Neville Chittick and Robert Rotberg (eds.), *East Africa and the Orient: Cultural Syntheses in Pre-Colonial Times.* Africana Publishing Co, London, 1975, p. 76–114.

———. "Geographical Notes on some Commodities involved in Sung Maritime Trade." *Journal of the Malayan Branch of the Royal Asiatic Society* 32, pt. 2, no. 186, 1959, p. 1–140.

White, L. *Medieval Religion and Technology.* University of California Press, 1978.

———. *Medieval Technology and Social Change.* Oxford University Press, 1962.

Whitmore, John. *Vietnam, Hô Quý Ly and the Ming (1371–1421).* The Lac-Viet Series 2. Yale Center for International and Area Studies/Council on Southeast Asia Studies, New Haven, CT, 1985.

Whitrow, G. J. *Time in History.* Oxford University Press, 1988.

Whittle, Jane. *The development of agrarian capitalism.* Oxford University Press, NY, 2000.

Wickham, Chris. "The Uniqueness of the East," in T. J. Byres and Harbans Mukhia (eds.), *Feudalism and non-European societies.* Frank Cass, London, 1985, p. 166–196.

Wicks, Robert. *Money, Markets and Trade in Early Southeast Asia.* Southeast Asia Program, Cornell University, Ithaca, NY, 1992.

Wijetunga, W.M.K. "South Indian Corporate Commercial Organizations in South and South-East Asia." Proceedings of the 1st International Conference-Seminar of Tamil Studies, University of Malaya, 1968, p. 494–508.

Willetts, William. "The Maritime Adventures of Grand Eunuch Ho." *Journal of Southeast Asian History* 5, no. 2, Sept. 1964, p. 25–42.

Williamson, Edwin. *The Penguin History of Latin America.* Penguin Books, New York, 1992.

Willmott, W. E. "History and Sociology of the Chinese in Cambodia Prior to the French Protectorate." *Journal of Southeast Asian History* 7, no. 1, March 1966, p. 15–38.

Wills, John Jr. "Maritime Asia, 1500–1800: The Interactive Emergence of European Domination." *American Historical Review* 98, no. 1, Feb. 1993, p. 83–105.

Wink, André. "Al-Hind. India and Indonesia in the Islamic World-Economy." *Itinerario* 12, no. 1, 1988, p. 33–72.

———. *Al-Hind: The Making of the Indo-Islamic World.* Vol 1. Brill, Leiden, 1990.

———. *Al-Hind: The Making of the Indo-Islamic World.* Vol 2. Brill, Leiden, 1997.

———. "Sovereignty and universal dominion in South Asia." *Indian Economic and Social History Review* 21, no. 3, 1984, p. 265–292.

Wittfogel, Karl. *Oriental Despotism*. Yale University Press, New Haven, 1957.

Wolf, Eric. *Europe and the People without History*. University of California Press, Berkeley, 1982.

Wolff, Jacques. *Histoire Économique de l'Europe, 1000–2000*. Éd. Économica, Paris, 1995.

Wolff, Philippe. *Automne du Moyen Âge ou printemps des temps nouveaux?* Aubier, Paris, 1986.

———. "Un grand commerce médiéval: les céréales dans le bassin de la Méditerranée occidentale," in VI Congreso de Historia de la Corona de Aragon, Madrid, 1959, p. 147–164.

———. "Monnaie et développement Économique dans l'Éurope médiévale." *Histoire, Économie et Société*, 4e trimestre, 1982, p. 491–510.

———. "Pouvoirs et investissements urbains en Europe occidentale et centrale du XIIIe au XVIIe siècle," in "Investimenti e civiltà urbana secoli XIII–XVIII." Atti della Nona Settimana di Studi 22–28 Aprile 1977. Instituto Internazionale di Storia Economica "F. Datini," Serie II, 22, Le Monnier, Prato, 1989, p. 31–71.

Wolff, Philippe, and Frédéric Mauro. *Histoire générale du travail*. Nouvelle Librairie de France, Paris, 1965.

Wolpert, Stanley. *A New History of India*. 6th ed., Oxford University Press, Oxford, 2000.

Wong, R. Bin. *China Transformed: Historical Change and the Limits of European Experience*. Cornell University Press, 1997.

———. "Les émeutes de subsistances en Chine et en Europe Occidentale." *Annales ESC* 38, no. 2, Mars–Avril 1983, p. 234–258.

———. "The Political Economy of agrarian empire and its modern legacy," in Timothy Brook and Gregory Blue (eds.), *China and Historical Capitalism*. Cambridge University Press, 1999, p. 210–245.

———. "The Search for European Differences and Domination in the Early Modern World." *American Historical Review* 107, no. 2, April 2002, p. 447–469.

Wood, Ellen. *The Origin of Capitalism*. Monthly Review Press, New York, 1999.

———. "The Question of Market Dependence." *Journal of Agrarian Change*, 2, no. 1, 2002, p. 50–87.

Woodward, David. "The Means of Payment and Hours of Work in Early Modern England," in Carol Leonard and B. N. Mironov (eds.), "Hours of Work and Means of Payment." 11th International Economic History Congress Proceedings B3b. Universita Bocconi, Milano, 1994, p. 11–21.

Wright, John. *The trans-Saharan slave trade*. Routledge, NY, 2007.

Wrigley, E. A. *Continuity, chance and change*. Cambridge University Press, 1988.

———. *Poverty, Progress, and Population*. Cambridge University Press, 2004.

———. "The Town in a Pre-industrial Economy," in Ph. Abrams and E. Wrigley (eds.), *Towns in Societies*. Cambridge University Press, 1978, p. 295–309.

Wunder, Heide. "Serfdom in Later Medieval and Early Modern Germany," in T.H. Aston, P. Cross, Chr. Dyer, and Joan Thirsk (eds.), *Social Relations and Ideas*. Cambridge University Press, 1983, p. 249–272.

Wyffels, Carlos. "De oorsprong der ambachten in Vlaanderen en Brabant" Verhandelingen van de Koninklijke Academie voor Wetenschappen, Letteren en Schone Kunsten van Belgie (jg . 13, no. 3), Brussel, 1951.

———. "L'usure en Flandre au XIIIe siècle." *Revue Belge de Philologie et d'Histoire*, 1991, p. 853–871.

Wyrozumski, Jerzy. "Le problème de l'évolution technique dans la tissanderie en Pologne aux XI–XVe siècles," in Sara Mariotti (ed.), "Produttività e tecnologie nei secoli XII–XVII." Atti della Terza Settimana di Studio 23–29 aprile 1971. Instituto Internazionale di Storia Economica "F. Datini," Serie II, 3, Prato, Le Monnier, 1981, p. 295–301.

————. "La société urbaine en Pologne au bas Moyen Âge." *Revue du Nord* 60, no. 236, Jan.–Mars 1978, p. 31–41.

Xiaonan, Deng, and Christian Lamouroux. "Les règles familiales des ancêtres." *Annales HSS* 59, no. 3, Mai–Juin 2004, p. 491–518.

Yadav, B. N. S. "Problem of the Interaction between Socioeconomic Classes in the Early Medieval Complex." *Indian Historical Review* 3, no. 1, 1976, p. 43–58.

————. *Society and Culture in North India in the Twelfth Century.* Allahabad, 1973.

Yang, Bin. "Horses, Silver and Cowries: Yunnan in Global Perspective." *Journal of World History* 15, no. 3, Sep. 2004, p. 281–322.

Yante, Jean-Marie. "L'emploi: concept contemporain et réalités médiévales," in Jacqueline Hamesse and Colette Muraille-Samaran (eds.), *Le travail au Moyen Âge: Une Approche interdisciplinaire.* Université Catholique de Louvain-la-Neuve, Louvain-la-Neuve, 1990, p. 349–378.

————. "Le rôle des autorités communales dans l'organisation, la réglementation,et la police des transactions commerciales." Actes du 11e Colloque International, Spa, 1–4 Sept. 1982. Crédit Communal, no. 65, Bruxelles, 1984, p. 425–436.

Yarrison, J. L. "Force as an instrument of policy." Unpublished Ph.D. Thesis. Princeton, 1982.

Young, Stephen. "The Law of Property and elite prerogatives during Vietnam's Lê dynasty." *Journal of Asian History* 10, no. 1, 1976, p. 1–48.

Yun, Bartolomé. "Economic Cycles and Structural Changes," in Thomas Brady, Heiko Oberman, and James Tracy (eds.), *Handbook of European History 1400–1600: Late Middle Ages, Renaissance and Reformation.* Vol. 1. Brill, Leiden, 1994, p. 113–145.

Yver, Georges. *Le commerce des marchands dans l'Italie méridionale au XIIIe and au XIVe siècle.* Burt Franklin, NY, 1968 ed.

Yvon-Tran, Florence. "Marchés ruraux, commerce et fiscalité dans Viet-Nam ancien." *Histoire et Sociétés Rurales* 17, 1er Semestre 2002, p. 11–35.

Zientara, Benedykt. "L'Occidentalisation de la Pologne au XIIIe siècle," in *L'histoire à Nice.* Vol. 2, *Les relations Économiques et culturelles entre l'Occident et l'Orient.* Actes du Colloque International (6–9 Nov. 1980). Université de Nice/Musée d'Archéologie et d'Histoire d'Antibes, 1981, p. 193–201.

Zolberg, Aristide. "Origins of the modern world system." *World Politics* 33, no. 2, 1981, p. 253–281.

Zubaida, Sami. "The city and its 'other' in Islamic political ideas and movements." *Economy and Society* 14, no. 3, August 1985, p. 313–330.

Zurndorfer, Harriet. "A Guide to the 'New' Chinese History." *International Review of Social History* 33, 1988, p. 148–201.

————. "Violence and Political Protest in Ming and Qing China." *International Review of Social History* 28, pt. 3, 1983, p. 304–319.

Zylbergeld, Léon. "L'initiative communale dans l'organisation défensive et les institutions militaires des villes en Brabant au Moyen Âge." Actes du 11e Colloque International, Spa, 1–4 Sept. 1982. Crédit Communal, no. 65, Bruxelles, 1984, p. 287–376.

INDEX

Abu-Lughod, Janet, 30, 31, 37, 45, 56, 60, 69, 77, 107, 122, 125, 148
Aden, 87, 108
Afghanistan, 13, 114, 116, 118
Aghmât, 127, 134
Agricultural Revolution, 3, 9
Ala-ud-Din, Sultan, 114–15
Alexandria, 137, 140
Algiers, 139
Al-Mansour, Sultan, 153
Almohads, 127, 128, 133, 137, 138, 140, 152
Almoravids, 126–28, 133
Amsterdam, 89, 109
Anfa, 140
Arabia, 49, 51, 87, 88, 103, 108
Aragon, 79, 138, 139
Artois, 144
Asiatic Mode of Production, 1, 12, 93, 95
Aurangzeb, Emperor, 118
Awdaghost, 126, 132
Azores, 29, 153

Baghdad, 82, 143, 145
Balkans, 41
Balkh, 55, 105
Baltic Sea, 16, 17, 62, 144
Banlieu, 154
Barcelona, 139
Bay of Bengal, 87
Beijing, 143
Bengal, 87, 89, 96, 107, 121

Black Death, 37, 157
Black Sea, 14, 16, 17, 27, 82, 144, 150
Bologna, 40
Bookkeeping, 23
Bourgeoisie, 9, 17, 25, 39, 41, 43, 65, 70, 71, 72, 77–80, 97, 101, 105, 111, 120, 132, 133, 134, 143, 155, 156, 157, 158
Brask, 138
Braudel, Fernand, viii, 23, 24, 25, 26, 73, 76, 77, 95
Brechk, 139
Brenner, Robert, v, 2–7, 9, 11, 18, 30, 33, 71, 99, 146, 154, 157
Brennerism, v, 1, 2, 4, 45
Bruges, 19, 25, 27, 38, 80, 104, 105
Brussels, 38
Bukhara, 72
Bulk goods, 14, 16, 48, 49, 92
Bullion, 23, 51, 81, 82, 91, 113, 122, 123, 126, 128, 130, 137, 138, 149
Bureaucrats, 64, 71, 73, 76, 89
Burghers, 27, 78, 79, 97, 104, 148, 155
Byzantine Empire, 28, 29, 57, 62, 91, 106, 137, 152

Cairo, 131, 138, 141, 145
Calicut, 88, 103
Calukyas, 118
Cambay, 89
Canary Islands, 29, 153
Canton, 49

Capitalism: in South Asia, vi, ix, x, 51, 62, 86–125, 129, 145, 157, 160; in Europe, 1–46; in the Sudan, vi, 125–36, 143, 149, 150, 153, 159, 161; in East Asia, 57, 62, 69, 74, 81–84, 88, 90, 91, 100, 103, 123, 157
Cartaz system, 109
Caste, 94, 95
Catalonia, 2, 25, 110, 139
Central Asia, 51, 57, 58, 72, 88, 89, 91, 92, 105, 114, 118, 122, 159
Ceuta, 139, 140, 147, 152
Ceylon, 96, 106
Chagatai Khanate, 63
Champa, 51, 115
Charles V, 70, 80
Chinese Empire, 48, 60, 64, 70, 71, 73–75, 84, 105, 113, 131
Ch'ing dynasty, 74
Ciompi, 37, 40, 145
Citizenship, 39, 65, 72, 73, 78, 79, 103, 148, 155, 156, 159, 161
City-states, 7, 16–18, 27–30, 33–35, 37, 39, 41–43, 45, 54, 57, 61–64, 68–75, 79–81, 83, 91, 97, 101–5, 111, 113, 120, 133–34, 139, 142, 144–46, 149–52, 155–61
Class struggle, 1–4, 31, 44, 154, 157
Clergy, 3, 37, 104, 156
Clocks, 20
Cola Empire, 88–89, 91, 94, 96–97, 99–100, 105, 111–12, 115, 118, 121
Colonies, 10, 28–30, 62, 63, 71, 76, 147
Constantinople, 29, 73
Contado, 28, 39, 144, 147, 157
Core, ix, 10–12, 14, 24, 30, 34, 39, 40, 44, 45, 71, 83, 101, 107, 111, 121, 146, 147, 149, 159, 160
Corsica, 27, 137
Cowrie trade, 129, 152
Credit, 6, 8, 20, 23, 24, 47, 53, 70, 77, 79, 84, 88, 100, 156
Crete, 27, 29, 136
Cyprus, 29, 136, 139

Dalmatia, 27
Daybul, 86
Deccan, 98, 115
Delhi, Sultanate of, 97, 98, 105, 110, 111, 114–19, 131, 160
Division of labor, 2, 7, 11, 13, 16–18, 21, 24, 25, 28, 30, 31, 34–36, 39, 41, 42, 44, 45, 50, 51, 53, 69, 71, 77, 81, 89, 101, 107, 124, 127, 141, 144, 146, 148, 150
Djenne, 127, 132, 134

Djerba, 138
Djidjelli, 138
Douai, 40
Dubrovnik, 72
Dutch power in the Indian Ocean, 61, 69, 106

Eastern Africa, 87
Eastern Europe, 11, 16–18, 34, 57, 121, 149, 150, 158, 160
Economic growth, 4, 7, 10, 19, 40, 44, 48, 68, 69, 72, 76, 86, 111, 120, 121, 126, 130, 158
Edward III of England, 70
Egypt, 51, 57, 85, 87, 89, 121, 125, 127, 128, 134, 136–38, 143, 150
Eilat, 108
England, 2–6, 8, 10, 14, 16, 30, 33, 34, 36–38, 40, 44, 45, 60, 69, 70, 81, 97, 100, 104, 110, 151
Eurocentrism, 1, 21, 31, 43, 48, 54, 60, 81, 94, 105, 111, 121–23, 125, 154–55, 161–62

Fatimids, 137, 138
Feudalism, 2, 4, 6, 7, 9, 12, 13, 15, 18, 19, 22, 23, 30, 32, 76, 83, 95, 119, 148, 156–60
Firuz Shah, 115
Firuz Tughluq, 98
Fitna, 119
Flanders, 5, 24, 26, 27, 34, 36, 37, 40, 41, 156
Florence/Firenze, 24–26, 37, 40, 104, 145, 147, 157
Formentera, 62
Food, 17, 28, 29, 36, 75, 110, 128, 132, 138, 149, 150
France, 3–5, 14, 25, 30, 33, 34, 37, 38, 44, 70, 82, 97, 114, 151
Fukien, 51, 54, 65
Funduq, 139

Gabes, 138
Gao, 127, 128, 132
Ghaznavids, 105, 114
Genoa, 16, 23, 27, 29, 30, 37, 40, 54, 68, 89, 110, 140, 149
Gentry, 37, 70, 71, 76, 78, 79, 83, 97
Germany, 7, 15, 28, 44, 114
Ghana, 126, 127
Ghent, viii, 25, 37–39, 80, 144
Ghurids, 114
Granada, 137
Gujarat, 87, 89, 110, 115, 121
Guilds, 7–9, 26, 34, 35, 38, 64, 72, 73, 81, 86, 100, 104, 111, 141, 150, 155
Gulf of Aqaba, 108
Gunder Frank, Andre, 107

Hafsids, 137
Hajj, 137
Hanseatic League (cities), 54, 62, 104
Harat, 55
Henry VII of England, 60
Hindu Kush, 114
Holland, 27, 34, 36
Hormuz, 87, 103
Hunayn, 139
Hungary, 17, 120
Huns, 75

Ibiza, 62
Ibn Battuta, 47, 73, 127
Ibn Khaldoun, 137
ibn Tughluq, Mohammed (Sultan), 115, 117, 118
Idjil, 131
Idrisids, 127
Ifriqiya, 126, 138, 140, 151
Il-Khans, 57
Indian Ocean, 33, 48–50, 61, 68, 69, 75, 85, 86, 88, 90–93, 99, 101–3, 106–10, 112, 113, 120–22, 152
Industrial Revolution, 2, 3, 8–11, 15, 83, 106, 107, 120, 121, 152
Insurance, 23, 24
Iqta, 98
Italy, 7, 9, 15, 16, 19, 23, 26, 27, 40, 44, 79, 82, 114, 141, 157, 158

Jagir, 98, 99
Jahangir, Emperor, 90
Jaunpur, 115, 116
Japan, 31, 50, 58, 63, 77
Java, 58, 63, 65, 88
Jurchen, 51, 75

K'aifeng, 73
Kanem Bornou, 129
Karimi merchants, 51, 85, 143
Kawar, 129
Kerkenna Islands, 138
Khanate of the Golden Horde, 58, 83
Khurasan, 55, 89
Kilwa, 87
Kitans, 75
Ksatriyas, 101
Kwantung, 51, 54, 65

Lahore, 89, 114, 118
Laissez-faire, 9, 112, 162
Latin Kingdom, 108

Levant, 14, 27, 57, 62, 90, 138, 140
Lisbon, 89
Lodi dynasty, 116
London, 37, 89
Low Countries, 6, 7, 15–17, 19, 23, 25–27, 34, 35, 37, 38, 40, 41, 44, 79, 81, 97, 144, 147, 157
Lucca, 104
Luxuries, 3, 14, 15, 48, 52, 54, 83, 86, 93, 135

Madeira Islands, 29
Maghreb, 50, 125–27, 131, 133, 134, 136, 138–40, 150
Magyars, 114, 119
Mahdiya, 138
Malabar coast, 87
Malacca, see Melaka
Mali, Empire, of 127, 130–35, 137, 139, 149
Malwa, 115
Mamluks, 83, 85, 143
Mansabdar, 98, 99
Marinids, 127, 137, 138
Marrakech, 127
Marseilles, 140
Marx, Karl, x, 2, 12, 19, 143
Maximilian, Emperor, 97
Mazagran, 139
Mediterranean, vi, 2, 16, 22, 24, 27–29, 54, 57, 62, 69, 70, 85, 89, 101, 108, 125–27, 129, 135–42, 151, 155, 160
Melaka (also Malacca), 63, 84, 87, 89, 102, 112
Mentalities and capitalism, 19
Mercantilism, 74, 92, 112, 138
Merchant capitalism, v, 1–46, 83, 90, 121
Merchant entrepreneur, 15, 24, 33, 35, 70, 71, 78, 102, 144, 145, 149
Mesopotamia: Mongol occupation of, 55, 57
Milan, 27, 147
Ming Dynasty, 59–61, 63, 64, 66, 67, 72, 74, 75, 79
Modernization Theory, v, x, 1, 3, 7–11, 45, 77, 80, 161
Mongols, v, 54–59, 63, 64, 67, 73, 75, 81, 82, 114–16, 159
Monsoon winds, 106
Montpellier, 16, 79
Morocco, 126–28, 137, 141
Mostaganem, 139
Mughal empire, 90, 98, 109, 110, 112, 114, 119
Muhtasib, 142
Multan, 89

Nadir Shah Afshar, 117
Nadu, 97, 103, 118

Nanjing, 74
Nation-states, 33, 42, 43, 61, 64, 68, 69, 74, 75, 103, 111, 151, 157, 159–62
Nattar, 97, 118
Naval power, 51, 54, 59, 61, 91, 93, 109, 136–38, 140, 151
Nayakas, 96, 119
Niger river, 126, 127, 129, 134, 135
Nishapur, 55
Nobility, 3, 6, 17, 25, 33, 34, 42, 63, 71, 75, 78–81, 97, 98, 102, 104, 105, 109, 112, 118–20, 141, 146, 156–59, 161
Nomadism, 113, 116, 161
Novgorod, 57
Nuclear family, 80

Omayyad Spain, 128
Oriental Despotism, 67, 80, 93, 96, 150
Ottomans, 57, 70, 113

Palestine, 137
Palma, 139
Pax Mongolica, 45, 50, 56, 57, 59, 75, 81, 83, 91, 122, 125, 149, 150
Peace of Stralsund, 104
Pearson, M.N., 31, 67, 69, 73, 83–85, 87, 90, 101–3, 106, 107, 109, 110, 122
Periphery, ix, 9–12, 14, 18, 24, 28–30, 32, 34, 39, 40, 51, 61, 71, 83, 84, 103, 108, 111, 120, 121, 131, 146, 149, 156, 159, 160
Peripheralization, 17, 96, 107, 112, 120, 126, 161
Persia, 48, 49, 55, 57, 83, 87, 103, 104, 109, 110, 117
Persian Gulf, 48, 87, 103
Peter II of Aragon, 79
Philip the Good, Duke of Burgundy, 105
Pisa, 140
Poland, 17, 26, 120
Polygamy, 133
Pomeranz, Kenneth, 100, 106, 107, 123
Population growth, 8, 26, 52, 89
Portugal, 113
Portuguese in Indian Ocean, 61, 69, 85, 88, 90
Primitive accumulation, 5, 78, 81
Proselytism, 126
Punjab, 116
Putting-out system, 7, 19, 26, 35, 101, 123, 141, 161

Qarakhanids, 105
Quanzhou, 50

Rajput, 118, 119
Raw materials, 10, 11, 16, 17, 24, 28, 29, 35, 36, 40, 45, 53, 127, 139, 146, 149, 152
Refeudalization, 146
Revolts, 26, 34, 41, 70, 143, 156
Richard I of England, 47
Roger II of Sicily's, 138
Ryu Kyu Islands, 87
Russia, 55, 57

Safavid Empire, 108, 110, 114
Sahara, 125–128, 130–32, 134–36, 139, 152
Sahel, 131, 135
Sale, 139
Samarkand, 72, 116
Saracens, 119, 139
Sardinia, 27, 137
Scotland, 36, 104
Segmentary state, 95, 96
Semiperiphery, 24
Senegal River, 126, 135, 140
Seville, 21, 89
Sicily, 14, 27, 44, 125, 137–39
Sijilmasa, 126, 127, 133, 134, 139, 152
Slave labor, 117, 130, 131, 139
Slave trade, 29, 87, 117, 128, 129
Smithian growth, 76, 77, 120
Smithian perspective, 8, 11, 12, 72, 75, 77, 158
Sofala, 87
Songhai, 127
South Asia, vi, ix, x, 51, 62, 86–124, 125, 129, 145, 157, 160
Southeast Asia, 49, 51, 53, 57, 58, 69, 84, 86, 90, 92, 95, 96, 98, 102, 103, 109–12, 115, 119, 121
Spain, 27, 36, 40, 41, 44, 125, 128, 136, 138
Spice trade, 24, 81, 90, 138
Sudanic states, vi, 125, 126, 131, 133, 150
Sudras, 101
Sumatra, 49, 59
Sung Dynasty, v, 48–50, 52, 54–56, 64, 68, 71, 74
Syria, 57, 149

Taghaza, 131
Takedda, 129, 131
Taiwan, 109
T'ang dynasty, 48, 49
Tanguts, 75
Tanistry, 118
Taoudeni, 131
Taxation, 5, 47, 50, 68, 70, 73, 74, 76, 79, 99, 110, 129, 130, 146, 147, 156
Timbuktu, 127, 132–34

Timur/Tamerlane, 59, 115–17, 119
Tlemcen, 127, 139
Transition from feudalism to capitalism, 2, 6, 12, 13, 15, 19, 22, 30, 83, 157–60
Tributary trade, 60, 61, 66
Tripoli, 128, 138–40
Tunis, 14, 137, 139

Uighurs, 75
Unequal exchange, 11, 21, 32, 45, 83, 103, 107
Usury, 19, 20, 126

Van der Wee, Herman, 10, 19, 25, 38, 42, 144
Vaisyas, 101
Venice, 16, 27, 29, 30, 34, 54, 62, 63, 68, 89, 90, 110, 120, 144, 149
Vereenigde Oostindische Compagnie (VOC), 90, 101, 113
Vietnam, 58, 64, 77
Vijayanagar Empire, 94, 111
Vikings, 119

Wages, 8, 11, 14, 16, 26, 35, 37–39, 117, 137, 146, 159
Walata, 127, 132
Waldemar IV, 104

Wallerstein, Immanuel, vii, 9, 11–18, 22–24, 30, 39, 41, 63, 73, 79, 82, 93, 106, 107, 110, 120–22, 126
Weber, Max, ix, 7, 22, 48, 94, 95, 118, 151, 155
Western Europe, vi, x, 1, 5–7, 10, 14, 16–18, 20, 21, 23, 26, 28, 30, 31, 33, 41–45, 48, 53, 58, 59, 62, 70–72, 74–78, 80–83, 85, 89, 91, 92, 94, 96, 97, 99, 101–4, 107, 111, 112, 114, 117, 119–21, 123, 124, 125–53, 154, 155, 158–61
Wood, Ellen, 4, 7, 18, 71, 151, 154
World-System, vii, x, 11–15, 17, 18, 24, 27, 30, 31, 44, 56, 92, 106, 107, 122, 152, 153, 160
World Systems Analysis, 1, 11, 12, 24, 30, 32, 43, 45, 125

Ypres, 25, 27, 38–40, 144
Yuan Dynasty, 55, 58, 59, 63, 78, 116
Yung-lo, Emperor, 60, 61, 63
Yunnan, 67, 152

Zheng He, Admiral, 54, 59–61, 63, 64, 69
Ziyanids, 137